Reconsidering Eusebius

Supplements

to

Vigiliae Christianae

Texts and Studies of
Early Christian Life and Language

Editors

J. den Boeft—B.D. Ehrman—J. van Oort –
D.T. Runia—C. Scholten—J.C.M. van Winden

VOLUME 107

Reconsidering Eusebius

Collected Papers on Literary, Historical, and Theological Issues

Edited by

Sabrina Inowlocki and Claudio Zamagni

BRILL

LEIDEN • BOSTON

2011

This book is printed on acid-free paper.

Library of Congress Cataloging-in-Publication Data

Reconsidering Eusebius : collected papers on literary, historical, and theological issues / edited by Sabrina Inowlocki and Claudio Zamagni.
    p. cm. — (Supplements to Vigiliae Christianae, ISSN 0920-623X ; v. 107)
    Includes bibliographical references and index.
    ISBN 978-90-04-20385-3 (hardback : alk. paper)
    1. Eusebius, of Caesarea, Bishop of Caesarea, ca. 260-ca. 340—Congresses.
I. Inowlocki, S. II. Zamagni, Claudio. III. Title. IV. Series.

    BR65.E76R43 201
    270.1092—dc22

                                   2011010562

BR
65
·E76
R43
2011

ISSN 0920-623x
ISBN 9789004203853

Copyright 2011 by Koninklijke Brill NV, Leiden, The Netherlands.
Koninklijke Brill NV incorporates the imprints Brill, Global Oriental, Hotei Publishing, IDC Publishers, Martinus Nijhoff Publishers and VSP.

PRINTED BY DRUKKERIJ WILCO B.V. - AMERSFOORT, THE NETHERLANDS

CONTENTS

PREFACE

Eusebius of Caesarea is undeniably one of the most important Church Fathers of late antiquity. Works such as the *Historia ecclesiastica*, the *Praeparatio evangelica*, his commentaries on Isaiah and on Psalms, the *Evangelical Canons*, his Constantinian speeches, his *Chronicon* and many other writings make him a key figure of late antiquity. Had he written only one of these works, he would still be an essential author for the understanding of Christian history, theology, and literature.

The reception of his writings as well as his perception as an author and as an historical figure by later writers and by modern scholars have been deeply ambiguous: on the one hand, 'the father of Church History' has most often been—and occasionally still is—considered as an almost sacred authority for the early history of the Church, a post-Gospel of sorts.[1] On the other hand, Eusebius and his writings have often been tainted with contempt and suspicion: already in the ninth century, Photius claims: "But as regards his [Eusebius'] diction, it is by no means either pleasing or brilliant. The man is indeed very learned, although as regards shrewdness of mind and firmness of character, as well as accuracy in doctrine, he is deficient."[2]

In modern times, the elders' doctrinal defiance towards Eusebius seems to have turned into scholarly contempt for his skills as an author. On many occasions, Eusebius has been described as an unreliable historiographer, a mediocre thinker and writer, a dishonest apologist, and a servile caesaropapist.[3]

Both viewpoints have been detrimental to the understanding of Eusebius as a literary, historical, and religious figure and of his work: the lack of critical judgement on his texts has contributed to erect

---

[1] A good example of a recent work which dangerously presents Eusebius as a sort of sacred authority, devoid of a critical approach to the the Church History is P.L. Maier, Eusebius. *The* Church History. *Translation and Commentary by P.L. Maier* (Grand Rapids: Kregel, 2007[2]). See the review by S. Inowlocki in *Review of Biblical Literature* (2008), http://www.bookreviews.org/pdf/5993_6380.pdf.

[2] Photius, *Bibliotheca*, cod. 13.

[3] See, e.g., Fr. Young, *Nicaea to Chalcedon* (London: SCM, 1983) 17–23; J.N.D. Kelly, Early Christian Doctrine (London: A.C. Black, 1977) 225; C.R.B. Shapland, The Letters of Saint Athanasius Concerning the Holy Spirit (New York: Philosophical Library, 1951) 20–21;

Eusebius as one of the most prominent figures of Christian imperial-
ism; as for his works, the *Historia ecclesiastica* in particular considered
as his most emblematic and significant writing, became the master
narrative of the triumph of early Christianity over "Judaism", "heresy", and "paganism".[4] Such an approach concealed the way in which
Eusebius' huge influence, from antiquity to modern times, was often
exerted to the detriment of other Christian narratives and forms of
Christianity other than 'orthodox'.

Yet the mere rejection of his work on the grounds of his lack of
"objectivity"—whatever this shady term may signify then or now—
is also greatly problematic. It led to restrict Eusebius to a reservoir
of citations. He was seen as a crucial source, but hardly as a crucial
author. As a result, some of his works (e.g., the *Historia ecclesiastica*,
the *Chronicon*, the *Praeparatio evangelica*) have been copiously used
by modern scholars but only as sources of information and quotations, while numerous others have largely been ignored. Therefore,
a new approach to the subject was greatly needed. The more critical
approach to the Eusebian model of the writing of early Christian history that emerged in the course of the last century[5] undeniably led
to a healthy reconsideration of the historical value of his testimony.
Emblematic of this renewal is, for instance, the seminal work of T.D.
Barnes on Constantine and Eusebius.[6]

Over the last decade, Eusebius has become the focus of scholarly
attention. New light has been shed both on his writings and on his
personality[7], which has led to a welcome re-assessment of his signifi-

---

[4] On this point, see the critique by E. Clark, *History, Theory, Text: Historians and
the Linguistic Turn* (Cambridge, Mass.: Harvard University Press, 2004) 169.

[5] In particular since W. Bauer, *Rechtgläubigkeit und Ketzerei im ältesten Christentum* (Tübingen: Mohr, 1934) who dealt with the Eusebian construction of orthodoxy
and heresy.

[6] T.D. Barnes, *Constantine and Eusebius* (Cambridge Mass.: Harvard University
Press, 1981). See also, A.J. Droge, "The Apologetic Dimension of the *Ecclesiastical
History*", in *Eusebius, Christianity, and Judaism*, ed. H.W. Attridge – G. Hata (StPB
42; Leiden – New York – Köln: Brill, 1992), 492–509.

[7] See, e.g., A. Cameron and S.G. Hall, *Eusebius: Life of Constantine* (Oxford:
Clarendon Press, 1999); E. Carotenuto, *Tradizione e innovazione nella Historia ecclesiastica di Eusebio di Cesarea* (Bologna: Il Mulino, 2001); A. Carriker, *The Library
of Eusebius of Caesarea* (SVigChr 67; Leiden – Boston: Brill, 2003); M.J. Hollerich,
*Eusebius of Caesarea's Commentary on Isaiah: Christian Exegesis in the Age of Con-
stantine* (Oxford: Oxford University Press, 1999); A. Kofsky, *Eusebius of Caesarea
Against Paganism* (Leiden: Brill, 2000); A.P. Johnson, *Ethnicity and the Argumentation
in Eusebius' Praeparatio evangelica* (Oxford: Oxford University Press, 2006; reprint,

cance. The influence of post-modern studies has contributed to see Eusebius as an active participant in the construction of late antique history, theology, and literature.

However, it seemed to us that more work needed to be done in different directions and this is why an international group of scholars was gathered for a workshop at the Université libre de Bruxelles on March 3, 2008, in the Centre Interdisciplianaire d'Etude des Religions et de la Laïcité (CIERL).

This workshop aimed to continue the re-evaluation of Eusebius' life and writings initiated by earlier scholars as well as to provide new insights in this field of investigation. The underlying principle of the workshop and of these papers was to analyze Eusebius as an author *à part entière*: this means that instead of seeing him as a mere broker or slavish compiler, we have tried to focus on his own specific way to construct literature, history, politics, and theology, taking into account his late antique Christian Mediterranean context and heritage.

Yet the purpose of the volume was neither to glorify the figure nor his writings. We have been particularly careful to approach his life and work critically, with a full awareness of his rhetoric of dominance. In order to do this, we have made the deliberate methodological choice not to treat the *Church History*. Indeed, albeit a major work of Eusebius, we have thought that the numerous—and much needed—debates that it has raised have overshadowed his other works and other relevant questions. Indeed, many other works of Eusebius do not receive the attention they deserve because scholars' attention is, so to speak, monopolized by this work. In many cases, his other works are analyzed only to justify a certain reading of the *Church History*.

In distinction to this, we wished to reflect on Eusebius "without" the *Church History*, to explore in more depth "the other Eusebius", the Eusebius of other significant writings. To put it differently, we sought to shift the focus from 'the father of Church History' to Eusebius as a fourth century author by avoiding centripetal and even centrifugal

---

2009); S. Inowlocki, *Eusebius and the Jewish Authors: His Citation Technique in an Apologetic Context* (AJEC 64; Leiden: Brill, 2006); A. Grafton and M. Williams, *Christianity and the Tranformation of the Book: Origen, Eusebius, and the Library of Caesarea* (Cambridge, Mass.: The Belknap Press of Harvard University Press, 2006), 192–193; M. Willing; *Eusebius von Cäsarea als Häresograph* (PTS, 63; Berlin-New York, 2008); S. Morlet, La *Démonstration Évangélique* d'Eusebe de Césarée. Étude sur l'apologetique chretiénne à l'époque de Constantin (EAug, Série Antiquité, 187); Paris; Études Augustiniennes, 2009).

movements to and from the *Church History*. We thought this may be a fruitful way to avoid methodological pitfalls if we wanted to provide a fresh look at this major figure. However, it would have been a great mistake to exclude this work because of its significance. Therefore, most papers in this volume refer to and/or discuss the *Church History*.

The fact that the *Church History* is not the main focus in this book does not mean that we have tried to avoid the ideological stakes: each paper attempts in its own way to identify Eusebius' claims for dominance in regards to the "Jews", the "Pagans", or the "Heretics", as well as his justifications of specific institutions, beliefs, or teachings.

The approach taken in this book is clearly interdisciplinary: coming from different fields (theology, history, philology, and archaeology), this volume seeks to break with a trend in previous scholarship which tended to see Eusebius solely as an historian, a biblical scholar, or an apologist. A more fruitful approach, we believe, is to consider him as a multi-faceted author who is at once a historian, a theologian, a scholar, and an apologist.

The first paper of the collection provides the context for Eusebius' life, career, and writings. Joseph Patrich's contribution presents Eusebius' Caesarea through the lens of the archaeological data. He surveys the archaeological and literary evidence on Caesarea as an urban center at the time of Eusebius, shedding light on the multi-ethnic and multi-religious environment in which he lived.

Oded Irshai's article reviews Eusebius' political career, providing fresh insight into the rivalry between the sees of Jerusalem and Caesarea. He suggests that this rivalry did not erupt on political grounds but on theological grounds: the divide between Arian and orthodox and the council of Nicea provide the background against which to analyze this conflict as well as some of Eusebius' political moves.

The council of Nicea is also at the center of Mark DelCogliano's paper, although he does not focus on the Arian controversy but on a less studied aspect of the council, the Paschal controversy. He offers the first English translation of the entirety of a fragment from Eusebius' *On the Feast of Pascha* as well as a new analysis of this text. This analysis provides a better understanding not only of the paschal controversy, but also of Eusebius' and Constantine's agenda in relation to Nicea; in addition, it sheds light on the bishop's attitude towards Jews and Judaism, from both an exegetical and a theological point of view.

The question of the status of the Jews also appears in Eduard Iricinschi's article on the new apologetic map created by Eusebius in order to inscribe the Christians as an *ethnos* in the Roman Empire. Analyzing his use of the ethnic categories "Hebrews", "Jews", "Greeks", "Christians", Iricinschi shows the manner in which Eusebius not only subverts the traditional opposition between, on the one hand, Greeks and Barbarians, and on the other, Jews and Greeks, but also legitimates the new Christian identity.

Elizabeth Penland's paper on the *Martyrs of Palestine* deals with the concept of the "Caesarean school" as a philosophical one. She calls into question the modern assessments of the so-called "school", which mostly cast doubt on the existence of such an institution starting with Origen and continuing in the time of Eusebius. Reading Caesarea as a philosophical school with Eusebius, she helps us to better understand his philosophical and apologetic project.

In the same vein, Aaron Johnson concentrates on Eusebius' pedagogical endeavor in the *General Elementary Introduction*, a work too often overlooked in Eusebian research. Investigating Eusebius' pedagogical and literary methods, Johnson shows how Eusebius interwove textual and doctrinal approaches in a way similar to Porphyry, his legendary rival.

Porphyry is also the focus of Sébastien Morlet, who calls into question the widespread assumption that the *Praeparatio* and the *Demonstratio* constitute a systematic refutation of Porphyry. He demonstrates that Celsus' arguments, as they are reflected in Origen, are very likely to have constituted the background of Eusebius' answer.

Along the same line, Origen's influence on Eusebius is discussed by Cl. Zamagni, but from an exegetical point of view. Focusing on the *Questions to Stephanos*, his analysis of the issue of the genealogy of Mary enables him to contribute to the question of the evolution of Eusebius' exegesis. In his opinion, the view that it diachronically evolved from Alexandrian allegory to Antiochian literalism is an erroneous simplification.

Two papers, those of Sabrina Inowlocki and Jeremy Schott, dealing with two different texts, have a similar, albeit converse, focus: the textualization of space and the spatialization of texts. J. Schott's article on Eusebius' panegyric on the building of Churches investigates the complex relationship between spatial and textual practices. He sheds light on the manner in which Eusebius' description of the Church at

Tyre intersects with his allegorical exegesis of the scriptures. He also demonstrates the convergence of past and present, as well as ecclesiological, theological, and political concerns in the textual space of his discourse.

Sabrina Inowlocki's reading of the *Praeparatio* as a library and a 'performance of erudition' aims to clarify the manner in which Eusebius' appropriated Greek—and more specifically Alexandrian—erudition in order to subordinate it to the Christian culture he attempted to construct. The paper also aims to analyze how Eusebius' apologetic and cultural projects are intertwined in the *Praeparatio*.

Finally, William Adler's paper focuses on an important source of Eusebius, namely Alexander Polyhistor. Polyhistor's literary endeavor and the judgments passed on him show striking similarities with Eusebius' own project and reputation: belittled as mere compilers, they are nevertheless some of the best representatives of Greek erudition in the Roman Empire. In Eusebius' *Praeparatio*, numerous Jewish authors are quoted through Polyhistor, but in Eusebius' view, Alexander remains the ultimate source of authority.

As a final point, we are pleased to thank those persons and institutions that have made this project possible. First and foremost, we wish to express our appreciation to the Belgian Fonds National de la Recherche Scientifique (FNRS) for their generous financial contribution to the workshop, which ultimately led to this publication. We also wish to extend our gratitude to the Université libre de Bruxelles (ULB) and particularly to the Centre Interdisciplinaire d'Etude des Religions et de la Laïcité (CIERL) and its president, Professor Jean-Philippe Schreiber, for their active support in the organization of the workshop. Finally, we would like to thank the Brill team and editorial board of the Vigiliae Christianae Supplements Series for making this book possible. In particular, Professor Jan den Boeft's editorial work and support, as well as Mattie Kuiper's and Wilma de Weert's efficiency and reliability throughout, have been invaluable for the project.

Sabrina Inowlocki
Claudio Zamagni

Academic Journals and collections of books are abridged according to Siegfrid M. Schwertner, *Internationales Abkürzungsverzeichnis für Theologie und Grenzgebiete*, 2. überarbeitete und erweiterte Auflage (Berlin – New York: De Gruyter, 1992).

CAESAREA IN THE TIME OF EUSEBIUS

Joseph Patrich

Caesarea, the capital of *Syria Palaestina*,[1] was the seat of the Roman governor and of the financial procurator of that province. Under Severus Alexander (222–235 CE) it acquired the title of *Metropolis Palaestinae*, reflecting its superior administrative status in the province.[2] According to Flavius Josephus Herod the Great, who had founded the city, built there a vast harbor, a temple dedicated to Rome and Augustus, a theater and an amphitheater, a royal palace, market places, dwellings, and an underground sewer system. Soon after its foundation Caesarea became a prosperous maritime city, of a heterogeneous ethnicity and a cosmopolitan flavor, as is reflected by the archaeological record: the city coins, statuary, and inscriptions, attesting to its pantheon, and the imported ware and numismatic finds, attesting to its international commerce (Fig. 1).

How did the city look like in the time of Eusebius, after more than three centuries since its foundation? after the crisis of the third century, and the reforms of Diocletian and Constantine, when the Latinate element in the provincial and municipal administration everywhere in the East gave way to Greek speaking *officiales*. According to Eusebius on April 2, 306 a severe earthquake struck the city, making the entire city to tremble, so that people had supposed that the whole place, together with its inhabitants, was about to be destroyed on that day. Neither casualties, nor damages are mentioned by him.[3] So far this

---

[1] *Caput provinciae*, according to Tacitus, *Hist.*, II.78.

[2] L. Kadman, *The Coins of Caesarea Maritima* (Corpus Nummorum Palaestinensium 2; Tel Aviv – Jerusalem: Schocken 1957); J. Ringel, *Césarée de Palestine: Étude Historique et Archéologique* (Paris: Ophrys, 1975), 151–162; M. Rosenberger, *City-Coins of Palestine* (The Rosenberger Israel Collection; Jerusalem: [Rosenberger], 1975), 1–28.

[3] Eusèbe de Césarée, *Histoire Ecclésiastique, Livres VIII–X et Les Martyrs en Palestine* (hereafter *MP* Gr.), par G. Bardy (SC 55; Paris: Cerf, 1967), 135–136 (IV.15); Eusebius, *History of The Martyrs in Palestine* (hereafter *MP* Syr.), by W. Cureton (London – Paris: Williams and Norgate – Borrani, 1861, 17, § 18. This earthquake of 306 at Caesarea is not mentioned neither by K.W. Russell, "The Earthquake Chronology of Palestine and Northwest Arabia from the 2nd through the Mid-8th Century A.D." *BASOR* 260 (1985), 37–59, nor by E. Guidoboni, A. Comastri, and G. Traina,

earthquake had not been recognized in the archaeological record at
the site. Hence, it seems that it was not as devastating for Caesarea. A
late third century Rabbinic source denotes it and its territory (together
with Tyre and its territory), as a city of plenty, where everything is
cheap.[4] A 4th c. literary source praises Caesarea as "wealthy in all good
things", excelling in its purple cloth, olive oil, wine, and grains.[5] The
period that followed the Diocletianic persecutions and the "Peace of
the Church" marks the beginning of a new age for the Roman Empire,
but the end of paganism and the takeover of Christianization in the
urban space were gradual; their pace in Caesarea is not reported by
any ancient source. Seemingly, like in other cities, such as Gaza, or
Alexandria, it took about a century until the pagan temples were
abandoned.

Although Latin was still a living language among the more educated people of Caesarea,[6] the epigraphic habit had changed. All the
inscriptions of the new era in Caesarea are in Greek or in the local
Semitic scripts and languages (Aramaic, Hebrew and Samaritan).[7] The
Greek, that returned to be the language of administration in the entire

---

Catalogue of Ancient Earthquakes in the Mediterranean Area up to the 10th Century,
tr. from the Italian by B. Phillips (Roma: Istituto nazionale di geofisica, 1994). In his
Chronicon (éd. Migne, PG 27.664), Eusebius, mentions a terrible earthquake which
destroyed many buildings in Tyre and Sidon and crushed innumerable people. In
a marginal note in Migne's edition the date 306 CE is suggested for this event, but
Caesarea is not mentioned in the *Chronicon*. Russell (*ibid.*, p. 42) suggested a date of
ca. 303 for the earthquake that had struck Tyre and Sidon.

[4] *Talmud Yerushalmi, Kilaim* 9.5.32b; *Ketuvot* 12.3.35b; *Genesis Rabba* 74.1,
p. 857.

[5] *"Abundans omnibus"*: *Expositio totius mundi et gentium*, XXVI; XXXI (éd. Rougé,
SC 124, p. 60 and 164). For agricultural products in Caesarea mentioned in the Rabbinic sources, such as citrons, wheat, grapes, figs, dates, rice and cumin see I.L. Levine,
Caesarea Under Roman Rule (Leiden: Brill, 1975), 51–52. Dyed linen textiles and silk
were manufactured there, and clay and glass vessels were produced there as well (*ibid.*,
pp. 53–56).

[6] J. Geiger, "Latin in Roman Palestine," *Cathedra* 74 (1994), 3–21 (Hebrew); *Id.*,
"How Much Latin in Roman Palestine?" in H. Rosén (ed.), *Aspects of Latin: Papers
from the Seventh International Colloquium on Latin Linguistics, Jerusalem, April 1993*
(Innsbrucker Beiträge zur Sprachwissenschaft 86; Innsbruck: Institut für Sprachwissenschaft der Universität Innsbruck, 1996), 39–57.

[7] A. Hamburger, "A Greco-Samaritan Amulet from Caesarea," *IEJ* 9 (1959), 43–45
and Pl. 4 A, B); I. Ben Zvi, "A Lamp with a Samaritan Inscription," *IEJ* 11 (1961),
139–42. On the use of the old Hebrew script by the Samaritans see: Babylonian Talmud, *Sanhedrin* 21b; Jerome, *Comm. In Ezech.*, 3.9.4. (CCSL 75, p. 106). According
to A.D. Crown, "The Byzantine and Moslem Period," in *Id.* (ed.), *The Samaritans*
(Tübingen: Mohr, 1989), p. 59, the Samaritans at Caesarea comprised about one third
of the population.

east, was spoken by all religious groups: pagans, Christians, Jews and Samaritans.

Under Roman rule Caesarea became a center of Greek wisdom—philosophy, grammar and rhetoric—and a school of Roman law.[8] Its Hellenistic culture was praised already in the 1st c. CE by the famous philosopher Apollonius of Tyana in his letter to the city council.[9] Shortly after it became a Roman colony a Latin rhetor of the city, named Flavius Agrippa was honored by the city council.[10] In the first half of the 3rd c. Theodore of Neocaesarea in Pontus, the future bishop of the city better known as Gregorius *Thaumatourgos* came and studied Latin in the city, planning to move and study law in Berytus. His encounter in Caesarea with Origen brought a change in the course of his life. In his youth, Eusebius attended classes in the holy scripture with the priest Dorotheus of Antioch, who was well acquainted with the Hebrew Bible, and Greek learning.[11] Apphianus of Lycia, the future martyr of the city, and his brother Aedesius went to study law in Berytus and then reached Caesarea, joining the company of Pamphilus. Similarly in the early 4th c. Gregorius of Nazianzus, the future Cappadocian father, first acquired his learning in Caesarea. His teacher there was Thespasius, who was active in the city in the 340's.[12] According to Libanius due to its wealth Caesarea could compete with Antioch in attracting the best teachers. In ca. 361–365 was active there the rhetor Acacius (a contemporaneous of the bishop of that name, who had succeeded Eusebius on the See of Caesarea). He was an epical poet, and an author of drama,[13] as well as a correspondent of Libanius, friend

---

[8] J. Geiger, "'Voices Reciting the Shma' in Greek': Jews, Gentiles and Greek Wisdom in Caesarea," *Cathedra* 99 (2001), 27–36 (Hebrew). See also Levine, *Caesarea Under Roman Rule*, cit., 57–60.

[9] Philostratus, *The life of Apollonius of Tyana*, edited and translated by C.P. Jones (LCL 458; Cambridge, Mass.: Harvard University Press, 2005–2006), 16–19 (*Ep. 11*); R.J. Penella, *The letters of Apollonius of Tyana: a critical text with prolegomena, translation and commentary* (Mn.S 56; Leiden: Brill, 1979), 38–41.97–98. The authenticity of the letter is discussed there on pp. 23–29.

[10] C.M. Lehman and K.G. Holum, *The Greek and Latin Inscriptions of Caesarea Maritima* (The Joint Expedition to Caesarea Maritima. Excavation Reports 5; Boston: American Schools of Oriental Research, 2000), 36–37, inscr. n. 3.

[11] Eusebius, *Hist. eccl..*, VII.32.2–4.

[12] He is also mentioned as a *rhetor* by Hieronymus. For references about him and about other persons and notices mentioned in the short survey on Greek wisdom in Caesarea given below see Geiger, *supra*, n. 6.

[13] According to Geiger, *ibid.*, the *Okypous* (the "fast feet"—an adjective of horses in Homer)—a drama full of humor, generally attributed to Lucianus, should be attributed to Acacius.

and adversary. His sons and son-in-law were sent by him to study with Libanius in Antioch. His nephew was the Latin historian Eutropius, the author of *Breviarium ab urbe condita*—an abridged history of Rome, in ten books. It was dedicated to emperor Valens in 369. Paenius, another Caesarean, translated shortly thereafter (in ca. 380) this composition into Greek, and Hieronymus used it. This translation is still extant almost in its entirety. Another Palestinian *rhetor* mentioned by Libanius, seemingly a Caesarean as well, was Helpidius, who was teaching later in Athens and finally settled in Constantinople. Two other Palestinian sophists, seemingly Caesareans, were the late 4th c. sophists Pangyrius and Priskion (Fig. 2).[14]

During the third and fourth centuries Caesarea was the seat of a Jewish academy, led by Rabbi Oshayah (first half of the 3rd c.) and Rabbi Abbahu (d. 309 CE),[15] and of a Christian academy, founded by Origen (d. ca. 254), and headed by Pamphilus and then by Eusebius. The Christian community suffered martyrdom in the persecutions under Decius, Valerian, and Diocletian.

Pamphilus (martyred in 309 CE in Caesarea) collected and copied the writings of Origen. He established a school in Caesarea, which was open to pagans and Christian alike, and provided elementary education for both. The library he established comprised of 30.000 scrolls.[16] It included many secular books on Greek science, philosophy, history, drama, poetry, rhetoric etc., and compositions of Jewish Greek

---

[14] In the 5th c. we hear of two pro-Hermogenean Caesarean rhetors—Paul, and his disciple John. The Hermogenean school of rhetorics stood at odds with the Antiochean school. See Geiger, *supra*, n. 6, p. 33.

[15] I.L. Levine, "R. Abbahu of Caesarea," in J. Neusner (ed.), *Christianity, Judaism, and Other Greco-Roman Cults: Studies for Morton Smith at Sixty* (Leiden: Brill, 1975), 56–76; *Id.*, *Caesarea Under Roman Law* (Leiden: Brill, 1975), 61–106; *Id.*, "The Jewish Community at Caesarea in Late Antiquity", in R.L. Vann (ed.), *Caesarea Papers: Straton's Tower, Herod's Harbour, and Roman and Byzantine Caesarea...*(Journal of Roman Archaeology. Supplementary Series 5; Ann Arbor, MI: Journal of Roman Archaeology, 1992), 268–273; S. Lieberman, "How Much Greek in Jewish Palestine?" in A. Altmann (ed.), *Biblical and other Studies* (Cambridge, Mass.: Harvard University Press, 1963), 123–141 (S. Lieberman, *Texts and Studies* (New York: New York Ktav Pub. House, 1974), 216–234). See also: S.J. Zuri, *Rabbi Yose bar Hanina of Caesarea* (Jerusalem: Sifriyyā biyyôgrāfît-talmûdît, 686 [1925/26]) (Hebrew).

[16] *Hist. eccl.*, VII.32.25. On his activity in Caesarea see: A. Kofsky, "Pamphilus and the Christian Library of Caesarea," *Cathedra* 122 (2006), 53–64 (Hebrew), with farther references; Geiger, *supra*, n. 6, pp. 30–31.

authors, residues of which were preserved in the writings of Eusebius.[17] Pamphilus and Eusebius took upon themselves to catalogue this collection.[18] He and his successors on the See of Caesarea—Acacius and Euzoius took care to copy the papyri scrolls to codices of parchment.[19] Scribal work at Caesarea started already in the time of Origen, with the financial assistance of his wealthy companion Ambrose.[20] Later its *scriptorium* was famous by its attentive work in producing copies of scriptures for the free use of scholars, disciples and pious women. In ca. 325 CE, at the request of Constantine, fifty copies of scripture, in codices of parchment, were dispatched by Eusebius to Constantinople.[21]

The Samaritans were another vital component in the Caesarean society, representing the lucrative peasantry of the fertile agricultural hinterland of the city—the Sharon plain and the hilly country of Samaria. According to a Rabbinic source the staff (*taxis*) of the Byzantine governor of the province in the city (as opposed to that of the *dux*) was composed mainly of Samaritans. There were also separate Samaritan troops in the Roman army.[22]

THE URBAN SPACE[23]

All the Herodian structures were built of the local *kurkar* sandstone. In the later Roman period some were gradually replaced by marble structures. This is evident in the Severan *skenefrons* of the theater, as

---

[17] D.T. Runia, "Caesarea Maritima and the Survival of Hellenistic-Jewish Literature," in A. Raban and K.G. Holum (eds.), *Caesarea maritima. A Retrospective after two Millenia* (Leiden – Boston: Brill, 1996), 476–495.

[18] *Hist. eccl.*, VI.32. On the library see: A. Carriker, *The Library of Eusebius of Caesarea* (SVigChr 67; Leiden – Boston: Brill, 2003).

[19] Jerome, *Ep.*, 34.

[20] *Hist. eccl.*, VI.23, 1–2.

[21] Eusebius, *Vit. Const.* IV.36; G.A. Robins, "Fifty Copies of the Sacred Writings" (V.C. 4.36): Entire Bible or Gospel Books?", in *StPatr* 19, Leuven 1987, 93–98; Kofsky, "Pamphilus and the Christian Library of Caesarea," *cit.*, 55.

[22] *Jerusalem Talmud, Avodah Zarah* 1.2—39c; S. Lieberman, "The Martyrs of Caesarea," *AIPh* 7 (1939–44), 405–406. The period alluded to in this text is the time of the Diocletianic persecutions. See also Levine, *Caesarea Under Roman Rule, cit.*, 107–112.

[23] For literary allusions to the urban space in the period under discussion see: J. Patrich, "*The Martyrs of Caesarea*: the urban context," *LASBF* 52 (2002), 321–346; for more details on the archaeological finds see: *Id.* "Urban Space in Late Antique Caesarea Maritima, Israel," in J.W. Eadie and T. Burns (eds.), *Urban Centers and Rural Contexts* (East Lansing: Michigan State University Press, 2001), 77–110.

well as in the main temple. Marble was applied for column shafts, capitals and bases, entablature, statuary, pavement and wall revetment.

GATES WITHOUT A WALL

Already in the late first-early second centuries CE the city expanded beyond its Herodian walls. Under Hadrian the wall was hardly recognized on the east as a significant landmark in the urban space.[24] At that time a Roman circus was constructed on the outskirts of the expanded city, on the south-east. In the 2nd or in the 3rd c. an oval amphitheater was added in a similar location on the north-east. But since no excavations were carried out in this zone, other than those in the circus, we have no information about its exact process of inhabitation during the 2nd to the 4th c. However, the addition of the lower level aqueduct in the 3rd c. (see below), may indicate that by then a significant increase of population was already attained. By the mid-4th century the Herodian fortification line was abandoned also on the north and on the south. The expanded Roman city had no outer wall for more than three centuries. It acquired a new city wall, encompassing the extra-mural quarters only in the fifth century. The total area was about three time larger than in the Herodian period, reflecting perhaps a similar increase in population.

The road system emerging from the city suggests the existence of four gates. These were free standing gates, with no wall associated with them. Like in the case of Gerasa, Jerusalem, Scythopolis, Gadara (and Athens), the limits of the city were indicated by a monumental arch long before a city wall was actually constructed. Police guards and tax collectors were stationed there. A Greek inscription on a monumental arch referring to the city as *metropolis*, was uncovered near the conjectured location of the east gate of Caesarea.[25] The north gate disappeared, being eroded by the sea. Here as well, like in the east, a gate

---

[24] J. Patrich, "The Wall Street, the Eastern Stoa, the Location of the Tetrapylon, and the Halakhic Status of Caesarea Maritima (interpreting Tosefta, Ahilot, 18:13)", in L. Di Segni, Y. Hirschfeld, J. Patrich and R. Talgam (eds.), *Man Near a Roman Arch. Archaeological Studies Presented to Prof. Yoram Tsafrir* (Jerusalem: Israel Exploration Society, 2009), 142*–168*.

[25] F.M. Abel and A. Barrois, "Fragment de Césarée la metropole," *RB* 40 (1931) 294–295; Lehman – Holum, *The Greek and Latin Inscriptions of Caesarea Maritima*, cit., 84–86, inscr. nos. 60–61.

without a wall might have marked the outskirt of the extended city, although the Herodian/Early Roman north gate might still have been in use. The location of one or two other gates are unknown.

THE CITY STREETS

The orthogonal city-plan within the Herodian wall was maintained throughout antiquity with only minor modifications. Under Hadrian this wall seemingly gave way to a curvilinear colonnaded street that replaced an earlier simple wall-street.[26] It seems that beyond this line the east-west streets attained a somewhat radial orientation (Fig. 1), which is still quite evident in aerial photographs of the south-eastern zone. Such layout was extraordinary relative to the more common orthogonal layout of many Roman cities. Hence this urban layout of Caesarea was praised by a 4th c. source.[27] Colonnaded streets (πλατεῖαι), public stoas and market places (ἀγοραί) are mentioned in the literary sources.[28]

The line of the *cardo maximus* seems to be preserved in the line of the Crusader eastern city wall, along which several columns were uncovered in recent excavations. The *decumanus maximus* ran seemingly parallel to the present asphalt road. Its intersection with Cardo 2E was uncovered recently ca. 200m to the east of the eastern Crusaders Gate. In later periods the streets were stripped off their columns, being incorporated in the Muslim and Crusader city walls and in the north quay of the Crusader harbor. But most of the streets were not colonnaded (Fig. 3). The underlying sewage system was maintained and restored. The new religion was manifested, *inter alia*, by capitals decorated with crosses.

Caesarea had an exceptional *tetrapylon*, praised as "famous everywhere because it presents a special and extraordinary look" (trans. Leah

---

[26] Patrich, "The Wall Street, the Eastern Stoa, the Location of the Tetrapylon, and the Halakhic Status of Caesarea Maritima", *cit.*

[27] *Supra*, n. 4, XXVI, p. 160. For a different opinion see: K.G. Holum, "*Et dispositione civitatis in multa eminens*: Comprehending the Urban Plan of Fourth-Century Caesarea," in L. Di Segni, et al. (eds.), *Man Near a Roman Arch, cit.*, 169*–189*.

[28] *MP* Syr. 34, p. 31 (*shwqa*); 35, pp. 33–34; *MP* Gr. IX.2, p. 148 (ἀγοραί); IX.12, p. 151. Similarly the pillars of Caesarea are mentioned in the Rabbinic sources: BT *Moed Katan* 25b; PT, *Abodah Zarah* III.1, 42c. Colonnaded streets (*platea* and *stoai*) in Caesarea are also mentioned in other Rabbinic sources: PT, *Nazir* VII.1.56a; Tosefta, *Oholot* XVIII.13.

Di Segni).[29] Seemingly it replaced the eastern gate of the Herodian wall. Another *tetrapylon*, seemingly of a *tetrakionion* type, apparently stood on the site of the eastern gate of the Crusaders wall, where two of its pedestals can still be seen.

The Herodian Harbor was a huge enterprise, compared by Josephus to Piraeus, with many quays, landing places and secondary anchorage.[30] The moles and quays were constructed of huge stones, and of *pozzolana* (volcanic ashes imported from Puteoli, Italy) cement that was cast into huge floating wooden forms, more than 6m high. These wooden barges were first dragged to their planned location, and then let sink by pouring in the cement and a fill of stone aggregates. After being dragged in sea, each barge was let sink next to the other, thus forming a long mole. The most advanced Roman harbor technology was applied.[31] The outer mole and breakwater, on the S and W, penetrated ca. 400m into the sea, enclosing an outer and an intermediate basins. The inner basin was rock-cut in-land, incorporating the closed harbor (*limen kleistos*) of Hellenistic Straton's Tower; it encompassed an area 250m long (NS) by 120m broad (EW). The entrance to the outer harbor, flanked by three colossal statues on either side, was from north, at the west end of the north mole.

Several inscribed lead ingots of a wreck cargo found over the north-west end of the western mole[32] suggest that this section of the pier

---

[29] *Expositio totius mundi et gentium*, XXVI (éd. Rougé, SC 124, p. 160): *Tetrapylon enim eius nominatur ubique, quod unum et nouum aliquod spectaculum*. A dome like structure along a *platea*, seemingly a *tetrapylon* of a *quadrifrons* type, is mentioned in the Rabbinic sources. This might have been the same as the previous one, unless there were altogether three *tertrapyla* in Caesarea. See references and discussion in Patrich, "The Wall Street, the Eastern Stoa, the Location of the Tetrapylon, and the Halakhic Status of Caesarea Maritima", *cit.*, p. 151*–154*.

[30] *Bell.*, 1.410; *Ant.*, 15.332.

[31] R.L. Vann, "Herod's Harbor Construction Recovered Underwater," *BARe* 9.3 (May/June 1983), 10–14; A. Raban, "Sebastos, the Herodian Harbor of Caesarea: How It Was Built and Operated," *University of Haifa Center for Maritime Studies News, Report no. 19* (1992); J.P. Oleson and G. Branton, "The technology of King Herod's harbour," in Vann, *Caesarea Papers*, *cit.*, 49–67; Ch. Brandon, "Cements, Concrete, and Settling Barges at Sebastos: Comparisons with Other Roman Harbor Examples and the Descriptions of Vitruvius," in Raban – Holum, *Caesarea maritima*, *cit.*, 25–40; R.L. Hohlfelder, "Caesarea's Master Harbor Builders: Lessons Learned, Lessons Applied?" *ibid.*, 77–101; E.G. Reinhardt and A. Raban, "Site formation and stratigraphic development of Caesarea's ancient harbor," in K.G. Holum, J.A. Stabler and E.G. Reinhardt (eds.), *Caesarea Reports and Studies* [BAR International Series 1784; Oxford: Archaeopress, 2008), 155–182.

[32] A. Raban, "The Lead Ingots from the Wreck Site (Area K8)," in: K.G. Holum, A. Raban and J. Patrich (eds.), *Caesarea papers, 2: Herod's temple, the provincial*

was submerged already at the end of the first century CE due to tectonic slumping, causing a rapid silting of parts of the inner harbor. But municipal bronze coin struck under Trajan Decius (249–243), carrying the inscription *Portus Augusti*, suggests a certain restoration of the outer breakwater. Another restoration occurred in the 4th c. by the addition of rubble to the crest and outer faces of the breakwaters, enabling renewal of trade to the 6th c.[33] As for the inner harbor, by the end of the 4th c. its southern part was already a lagoon of still water, and much of the northern part was already silted (Fig. 4). Only small boats could sail in and download merchandise from ships that dropped their anchors farther away.[34]

Warehouses were uncovered on the northern side of the middle harbor (in area LL of the Combined Caesarea Expeditions).[35] In ca. 300 CE twelve vaults built below the temple platform (see below), to the east of the partially silted inner harbor seems to have served as warehouses as well. A complex of six warehouses of local commodities—mainly oil, wine and grains, was attached to the palatial mansion located to the south of the *praetorium procuratoris* (see below).[36]

Religious Buildings

Temples: Of the many temples suggested by the deities depicted on the city coins (Tyche, Isis, Serapis, Demeter, Apollo),[37] and inscriptions (Jupiter Dolichenus),[38] only three temples yielded architectural remains. As for the evidence of the statuary of deities (Tyche, Isis

---

governor's Praetorium and granaries...(Journal of Roman Archaeology. Supplementary Series 35; Portsmouth, RI: Journal of Roman Archaeology, 1999), 179–88.

[33] P.J. Oleson, "Artifactual Evidence for the History of the Harbors of Caesarea," in Raban – Holum, *Caesarea maritima, cit.,* 367.

[34] A. Raban, "The Inner Harbor Basin of Caesarea: Archaeological Evidence for its Gradual Demise," in Raban – Holum, *Caesarea maritima, cit.,* 628–666, p. 653, Fig. 27.

[35] See J. Stabler, K.G. Holum, F.H. Stanley, Jr., M. Risser, A. Iamim, "The warehouse quarter (area LL) and the Temple Platform (area TP), 1996–2000 and 2002 seasons," in Holum et al., *Caesarea Reports and Studies, cit.,* 1–7.

[36] J. Patrich, "Warehouses and Granaries in Caesarea Maritima," in Raban – Holum, *Caesarea maritima, cit.,* 146–176.

[37] Kadman, *The Coins of Caesarea Maritima, cit.;* Ringel, *Césarée de Palestine: Étude Historique et Archéologique, cit.,* 151–162.

[38] B. Lifshitz, "Le culte de Jupiter Dolichenus à Césarée. Notes d'épigraphie palestinienne." *RB* 73 (1966), 255–56; Lehman – Holum, *The Greek and Latin Inscriptions of Caesarea Maritima, cit.,* 121–122, inscr. n. 124.

and Serapis, Apollo, Aphrodite, Athena, Asklepius and Hygieia, the Ephesian Artemis, Cybele or Nemesis, and the Dioscuri),[39] one should be precautionary not to interpret each statue as an indication for the existence of a temple for that particular deity. Statues were commonly used for decoration alone, though expressing religious piety.

Herod's temple to Roma and Augustus (*War*, 1.415; *Antiquities*, 15.339),[40] was constructed on top of a U shaped elevated platform, leaving an open esplanade below, to the W, in a lower terrace, along the E mole of the much-silted inner harbor.[41] In ca. 300 twelve vaults were erected on the esplanade, between the arms of the elevated platform. Their roof established an additional square in front of the Roman temple, that was still visible until ca. 400 CE. Certain modifications in the facade of the temple might have occurred in this occasion. But after "the triumph of the cross", the 4th century marked the demise of paganism in Caesarea, as elsewhere. During this period the temple gradually deteriorated, building material being looted. It was replaced by an octagonal church only in ca. 500 CE.

In the SW zone a Mithraeum was installed in the second or third century in one of the vaults underneath the audience hall of the *prae-*

---

[39] R. Gerst, *The Sculpture of Caesarea Maritima*, PhD dissertation (Tel Aviv, 1987) (Hebrew); *Id.*, "The Tyche of Caesarea Maritima," *PEQ* 116 (1984), 110–114; *Id.*, "Seven New Sculptural Pieces from Caesarea," in J. Humphrey (ed.), *The Roman and Byzantine Near East* (The Journal of Roman Archaeology, Supplement Series 14; Ann Arbor, MI: Journal of Roman Archaeology, 1995), 108–120; *Id.*, "Representation of Deities and the Cults of Caesarea," in Raban – Holum, *Caesarea maritima*, *cit.*, 305–324; *Id.*, "Roman Statuary used in Byzantine Caesarea," in Holum, Raban and Patrich (eds.), *Caesarea Papers, 2*, *cit.*, 389–398; A. Frova, "La statua di Artemide Efesia a 'Caesarea Maritima'," *Bollettino d'Arte* 4 (1962), 305–313; R. Wenning, "Die Stadtgöttin von Caesarea Maritima," *Boreas* 9 (1986), 113–129.

[40] Holum et al., *Caesarea Papers*, I, *cit.*, 100–109; A. Raban and K.G. Holum (eds.), *The Combined Caesarea Expeditions: Field report of the 1992 Season* (Haifa: The Recanati Institute for Maritime Studies, 1993), 53–60; A. Raban, *Excavations and Surveys in Israel* 17 (1998), 68–69. For a summary of recent excavations see K.G. Holum, "The Temple Platform Excavation: A Progress Report," in Holum, Raban and Patrich, *Caesarea Papers, 2*, *cit.*, 13–34; K.G. Holum, "Building Power: The Politics of Architecture," *BARe* 30 (2004), 57; *Id.*, "Caesarea's Temple Hill: The Archaeology of Sacred Space in an Ancient Mediterranean City," *Near Eastern Archaeology* 67 (2004), 186–192; Stabler et al., The warehouse quarter (area LL) and the Temple Platform (area TP)," *cit.*, 17–21. For the reconstruction of the temple on the evidence of scattered architectural fragments see L. Kahn, "King Herod's Temple of Roma and Augustus at Caesarea Maritima," in Raban – Holum, *Caesarea maritima, cit.*, 130–45.

[41] See drawing in Y. Porath, *Excavations and Surveys in Israel* 17 (1998), p. 46, Fig. 10. The dimensions of the podium are given in Holum, Raban and Patrich, *Caesarea Papers, 2, cit.*, p. 21.

torium procuratoris (see below).[42] The shrine (*sacellum*) of the hippo-stadium (Herod's *amphitheatron*, see below) was, seemingly, dedicated to Kore according to a dedicatory inscription to her on a marble foot—one of seven—found therein. Four of the ex-voto feet entwined by snakes—a common attribute of Isis—suggest an assimilation between Kore and Isis. It seems that after "the triumph of the cross" this *sacellum* was converted into a Martyrs' Chapel (Fig. 5) (see below).

The foundation feast of Caesarea as a Roman colony, associated with the birthday of the local Tyche, assimilated with Isis, was still celebrated on March 5th–7th in the first half of the 4th c. as is attested for year 306 CE by Eusebius, and by the scenes depicted on the "Louvre Cup" (Fig. 6), the manufacture of which is dated to this period.[43] This feast, still celebrated in the 4th c., had a pronounced pagan flavor.

Of the various synagogues that existed in Caesarea, only one was exposed in the northern part of the city,[44] the site of pre-Herodian Straton's tower. The Late Roman Jewish quarter was presumably located around this 3rd century synagogue. The synagogue was destroyed in the mid 4th century, and rebuilt in the mid 5th. It yielded Jewish inscriptions in Hebrew and Greek, and Corinthian capitals with the *menorah* symbol.[45] A Jewish house of learning (*bêt midrāšâ*) open

---

[42] R. Bull, "Mithraic Medallion from Caesarea," *IEJ* 22 (1972), 187–190; *Id.*, "The Mithraeum at Caesarea Maritima," *Études Mithraiques, textes et mémoires* 4 (1978), 75–89 (at the time when these articles of Bull were written the relation of this sanctuary to the *praetorium* of the Roman procurators was not perceived yet).

[43] On the Louvre Cup see: E. Will, "La coupe de Césarée de Palestine au Musée du Louvre," *Monuments et mémoires* 65 (1983), 1–24. On this feast in Caesarea and its significance see: J. Patrich, "The Date of the Proclamation of Caesarea as a Roman Colony," in J. Geiger, H.M. Cotton and G.D. Stiebel (eds.), Israel's Land. Papers Presented to Israel Schatzman on his Jubilee (Raanana: Israel Exploration Society, 2009), 135–156 (Hebrew).

[44] M. Avi Yonah, "The Synagogue at Caesarea," *Louis M. Rabinowitz Fund for the Exploration of Ancient Synagogues, Bulletin* 3 (1960), 44–48. For the Synagogue inscriptions, all of the Byzantine period, see: M. Schwabe, "The Synagogue of Caesarea and its Inscriptions." In S. Lieberman (ed.), *Alexander Marx Jubilee Volume* (New York: The Jewish Theological Seminary of America, 1950), 433–50, pl. 1–4 (Hebrew); B. Lifshitz, "Donateurs et fondateurs dans les synagogues juives," *CRB* 7 (1967), 50–54, n. 64–68; L. Roth-Gerson, *The Greek Inscriptions from the Synagogues in Eretz-Israel* (Jerusalem: Ben-Zvi, 1987), 11–117, inscr. n. 25–29 (Hebrew). See also I.L. Levine, *Roman Caesarea: An Archaeological-Topographical Study* (Qedem, Monographs of the Institute of Archaeology, Hebrew University 2; Jerusalem: Institute of Archaeology, Hebrew University 1975), 40–45.

[45] Roth-Gerson, *The Greek Inscriptions from the Synagogues in Eretz-Israel, cit.*, 115, inscr. 27. Capitals and architectural fragments with Jewish symbols are illustrated there in pp. 122–124. A marble column with the Hebrew inscription "shalom" (peace) was found by Netser and Levin in their principal area of excavation, to the NW of the

onto the agora of Caesarea is mentioned in the Babylonian Talmud, *Hulin* 86d.

After the death of R. Abbahu—the head of the local Jewish academy—in 309, there was no Jewish leader of his magnitude. The general Jewish revolt against Gallus in 351–52, might have been a decisive factor in this decline. The predominance of Greek inscriptions (even if later than the period under consideration), their content, as well as references in the Rabbinic sources, attest to the high degree of Hellenization and acculturation of the local community.[46]

Several Christian buildings associated with New Testament events and with the persecutions of martyrs, are mentioned in the Byzantine *itineraria*: the houses of Philip (*Acts* 8.40; 21.8) and of Cornelius (*Acts* 10.1–48), the chamber of the four virgin prophetesses—Philip's daughters, the burial place of Pamphilus and Procopius, and the latter's chapel.[47] More chapels and churches are known from literary sources. In the Acts and Miracles of Saint Anastasius (Martyred 627 CE), are mentioned the following churches (besides the 7th c. chapel dedicated to his memory): St. Euphemia, St. Mary the Younger (perhaps not distinct than the unspecified St. Mary), and a building associated with the martyr Cornelius.[48] The church of St. Procopius was set on fire in the Samaritan revolt of year 484. We do not know the location of these

---

inner harbor: I.L. Levine and E. Netzer, *Excavations at Caesarea Maritima 1975, 1976, 1979—Final Report* (Qedem, Monographs of the Institute of Archaeology, Hebrew University 21; Jerusalem: Institute of Archaeology, Hebrew University, 1986), p. 45, Ill. 64. A fragment of a stone slab decorated with a *menorah* was found to the S of the temple platform (Area Z). See A. Raban, "Caesarea Maritima—Land and Sea Excavations," *CMS News, University of Haifa*, Report No. 24–25 (1998), p. 32, Fig. 4.

[46] Beryllos, *archisynagogos* and *phrontistes* (treasurer or administrator), who made a mosaic floor from his own funds, is mentioned in a Greek inscription from the synagogue. See: I.L. Levine, "Synagogue Officials: The Evidence from Caesarea and Its Implications for Palestine and the Diaspora," in Raban – Holum, *Caesarea maritima, cit.*, 392–400. See also J. Geiger, *supra*, note 6.

[47] G. Downey, "Caesarea and the Christian Church," in Ch. T. Fritch, *Studies in the History of Caesarea Maritima* (BASOR Supplement Studies 19; Misssoula, Mont.: Scholars Press, 1975), 23–42; E. Krenz, "Caesarea and Early Christianity," *Caesarea Papers*, I, *cit.*, 261–67; Levine, *Caesarea Under Roman Rule, cit.*, 45–46. Acts 21.13; Jerome, *Ep.*, CVIII.8; PPTS 6, p. 32 (a 13th c. anonymous travelogue referring to the chamber of the four virgin prophetesses). Antoninus of Placentia, *Itinerarium* 45, ed. CCSL 175, p. 174 (reference to the burial place of Pamphilus and Procopius); John Malalas, *Chronographia*, XIV, ed. L. Dindorf (Bonn: Weber, 1831), 93–94; *Chronicon Paschale*, 327, ed. PG 92.840–41 (reference to the chapel of Procopius).

[48] W.E. Kaegi Jr., "Some Seventh-Century Sources on Caesarea," *IEJ* 28 (1978), 177–81; B. Flusin, *Saint Anastase le Perse et l'histoire de la Palestine au début du VIIe siècle* (Paris: CNRS, 1992), 231–243.

churches and when they were constructed. As was mentioned above, it seems that a Martyrs' Chapel replaced the *sacellum* of the stadium after "the triumph of the cross". A chapel dedicated to St. Paul was built above a warehouse of the palatial mansion located to the south of the *praetorium procuratoris* (see below).[49]

On top of the Temple Platform an octagonal church was built over the dilapidated temple of Rome and Augustus only in ca. 525–550 CE, hence it is not at our concern here. It was preceded by an earlier intermediate humbler structure.[50] The process of Christianization of the urban space at Caesarea was slower than assumed. The temple, although ruinous, was replaced by a Christian monument many decades after such a process occurred in Jerusalem (under Constantine), or in Gaza (under Theodosius I and Eudoxia).[51]

The *Praetorium* of the Governor

Herod's palace, constructed on a promontory on the south of the city, becoming the *praetorium* of the Roman governors, was enlarged and elaborated (Fig. 7).[52]

---

[49] See J. Patrich, "A Chapel of St. Paul at Caesarea Maritima?" *LASBF* 50 (2000), 363–382.

[50] Holum et al., *Caesarea Papers*, I, *cit.*, 100–107; Raban et al., *The Combined Caesarea Expeditions: Field report of the 1992 Season, cit.*, 37–42.50–51.53–55. For the date of construction of the octagonal church see: K.G. Holum, "The Temple Platform Excavation: A Progress Report," in Holum, Raban and Patrich, *Caesarea Papers, 2, cit.*, 26, and for the most recent report see: Stabler et al., "The warehouse quarter (area LL) and the Temple Platform (area TP)," *cit.*, 20–30.

[51] See Eusebius, *Vita Const.*, III.cc.xxvi–xl; on the erection of the church of the holy sepulchre in Jerusalem, at the order of Constantine, on the site of the temple of Aphrodite; Marcus Diaconus, *Vita Porphyrii* (ed. H. Gregoire and M.A. Kugener, Paris 1930), about the erection of Eudoxia church at Gaza on the site of the local temple of Marnas. On the conversion of temples to churches and the christianization of the urban space in Palestine see: K.G. Holum, "In the blinking of an eye: the Christianizing of Classical cities in the Levant," in A. Berlin (ed.), *Religion and Politics in the Ancient Near East* (Bethesda, MD: Maryland University Press, 1996), 131–150; Y. Tsafrir, "The Fate of Pagan Cult-Places in Palestine: The Archaeological Evidence with Emphasis on Bet Shean," in H. Lapin (ed.), *Religious and Ethnic Communities in Later Roman Palestine* (Bethesda, MD: Maryland University Press, 1998), 197–218.

[52] On this complex, excavated by several expeditions (Hebrew University of Jerusalem, University of Pennsylvania, and the Israel Antiquities Authority) see: Levine and Netzer, *Excavations at Caesarea Maritima, cit.*, 149–177; E. Netzer, *The Palaces of the Hasmoneans and Herod the Great* (Jerusalem: Ben-Zvi, 1999), 109–114 (Hebrew), E. Netzer, "The Promontory Palace," in Raban – Holum, *Caesarea maritima, cit.*, 193–207; K.L. Gleason, "Ruler and Spectacle: The Promontory Palace," *ibid.*, 208–228;

The *praetorium* extended over two terraces with a difference of elevation of ca. 3.6m. The lower terrace served as the private wing. It occupied a natural promontory, extending 100m into the Mediterranean. The upper terrace, on an upper part of the promontory, and of a slightly different orientation, served as the public wing. It was built around a vast courtyard surrounded by porticoes. A raised square platform, for some monument, or for the emplacement of a outdoor *bema*, stood in its center.

The northern wing of the upper terrace held two suites separated from each other by a service corridor. The western suite faced south, while the eastern one faced north. The western suite, of symmetrical layout, had in its center a basilical audience hall. This was the law court (δικαστήριον) of the *praetorium*. The elevated northern part of the hall accommodated, so it seems, the dais, or the *bema*. It had a heated floor set on stone *suspensurae / hypocaust*.[53] Over this *bema* the Roman governor and his *concillium* of friends and relations held their assizes, including trials of martyrs. A small altar (βωμός) with a sacrificial fire (ἡ πυρά) burning on it was also located inside.[54] This was not found in the excavations.

B. Burrell, "Palace to Praetorium: The Romanization of Caesarea," *ibid.*, 228–247. See also: B. Burrell, K.L. Gleason, and E. Netzer, "Uncovering Herod's Seaside Palace," *BARe* 19 (1993), 50–57.76. K.L. Gleason et al., "The Promontory Palace at Caesarea Maritima: Preliminary Evidence for Herod's Praetorium," *JRA* 11 (1998), 23–52. During 1995–97, in the framework of Israel Antiquities Authority excavations directed by Y. Porath, more parts of the N, S, and E wings of the praetorium were exposed. For a short preliminary note see: B. Rochman, "Imperial Slammer Identified," *BARe* 24/1 (1998), 18; Y. Porath, "Caesarea—1994–1999," *Hadashot Arkheologiyot: Excavations and Surveys in Israel* 112 (2000), 36*. See also J. Patrich, "A Government Compound in Roman-Byzantine Caesarea," in *Proceedings of the Twelfth World Congress of Jewish Studies, Division B, History of the Jewish People* (Jerusalem: World Union of Jewish Studies, 2000) 35*–44* (English section); *Id.*, "The *Praetoria* at Caesarea Maritima," in R. Aßkamp – T. Esch (eds.), *Imperium—Varus und seine Zeit*. Beiträge zum Internationalen Kolloquium des LWL-Römermuseums am 28. und 29. April 2008 in Münster (Münster: Aschendorff, 2010), 175–186.

[53] See plan and reconstruction by K.L. Gleason et al., "The Promontory Palace at Caesarea Maritima: Preliminary Evidence for Herod's Praetorium," *cit.*, 33, 45–48, Figs. 4c, 7, and 13, and discussion in Burrell, "Palace to Praetorium", *cit.*, 229. On the Roman legal institutions referred to in the *Martyrs of Palestine* (and the contemporary Rabbinic literature) see: S. Lieberman, "Roman Legal Institutions in Early Rabbinics and the *Acta Martyrum*," *JQR* 35 (1944), 1–57. I am of the opinion that the law court of the *Acts of the Martyrs* is the same hall as the audience hall (τὸ ἀκροατήριον) of *Acts* 25.23, where the hearing of St. Paul in front of Festus took place. See Patrich, , "A Chapel of St. Paul at Caesarea Maritima?", *cit.* Archaeologically, only a single hall that could fulfill these functions was uncovered in the excavations of the *praetorium*.

[54] *MP* Gr. VIII.7 (p. 146); *MP* Syr. 31 (p. 29).

Under Roman rule Herod's palace was extended farther to the east, adding about 50m along the southern curved end of the hippodrome/ stadium. This wing included offices of military personnel active in the governor's *officium*, mentioned in four Latin inscriptions found in this wing. They mention assistants of the Office in charge of the Prisoners or the Prison (*adiutores custodiarum*), imperial couriers (*frumentarii*), *beneficiarii*—soldiers who received an administrative job from the governor (in this case Tineius Rufus, the governor of Judaea when the Bar Kokhba revolt broke out), numbering as many as 120 in Judaea, and a Club Room of the Centurions (*schola centurionum*).[55] The prison (τὸ δεσμωτηρίον, ἡ εἰκτή, ἡ φυλακή, *beth asyra*) is frequently mentioned in the writings of Eusebius. Presumably, the prison was located nearby, but so far it has not been identified archaeologically. However, an enormous underground water cistern, with two compartments, T-shaped in its ground plan, constructed under the courtyard, was later converted into a vast subterranean space, and a narrow subterranean corridor led into it. This gloomy space apparently served as a prison, as Greek Christian inscriptions were smeared in mud on its walls, by a certain Procopia, seeking help from the Lord (κύριε βοήθι Προκοπία)—a most dramatic find pertaining, perhaps, to another woman confessor.

According to the inscriptions the *praetorium* was still in full activity under the tetrarchy.[56] But immediately thereafter, as a result of the reforms of Diocletian and Constantine, the other *praetorium* of Caesarea—the *praetorium procuratoris*, became the residence of the

---

[55] H.M. Cotton and W. Eck, "Governors and Their Personnel on Latin Inscriptions from Caesarea Maritima," *PIASH* 7/7 (2001), 215–240. For governor's *officiales* see: B. Rankov, "The governor's men: the officium consularis in provincial administration," in A. Goldsworthy and I. Haynes (edd.), *The Roman Army as a Community* (Journal of Roman archaeology. Supplementary series 34; Ann Arbor, MI: Journal of Roman archaeology, 1999), 15–34; B. Palm, "Die *Officia* der Statthalter in der Spätantike. Forschungstand und Perspektiven," *Antiquité Tardive* 7 (1999), 85–133. For a *frumentarius* sent by Sabinus, the prefect of Egypt, to pursue bishop Dionysius in the streets of Alexandria in the persecution under Decius see *Hist. eccl.*, VI.40.2–3 (LCL, p. 97). Also, a *frumentarius* escorted Cyprian, after his arrest, to face trial in Utica (Cyprian, *Ep.*, 81.1).

[56] B. Burrell, "Two Inscribed Columns from Caesarea Maritima," *ZPE* 99 (1993), 287–295; Lehman – Holum, *The Greek and Latin Inscriptions of Caesarea Maritima*, cit., 47–52, inscr. n. 12–17. In one of the three inscriptions on one of the columns, in Latin, the governor (*praes*) of the province of Palaestina—Aufidius Priscus honors Caesar Galerius (293–305). (The earliest inscription on that column, in Greek, was a dedication to a local philosopher Titus Flavius Maximus; its *t.a.q* is the reign of emperor Probus). In another, one of three inscriptions on the second column, in Latin as well, the same governor honors Caesar Constantius.

governor, and the *dux* was dispatched to sojourn nearer to the border zones of the province. Herod's *praetorium* deteriorated during the 4th c.; the northern wing of the upper terrace being washed away by the sea.

The *Praetorium Procuratoris*[57]

Late in the first century CE a second *praetorium* was constructed for the use of the financial procurators of the province. Later, following the administrative reforms of Diocletian and Constantine, this palace became the residence and *officium* of the Byzantine governor. It was located in the first grid block (*insula*) of the city to the south of the temple platform, adjacent to the Harbor, overlooking the sea—a prominent location. The western and southern parts of the *praetorium* were constructed on top of vaults, which served as substructures.

Three major phases were discerned in the architectural history of the complex; phase 2 reflects modifications in the 4th c., seemingly associated with the adaptation of the complex to serve as the new residence and *officium* of the provincial governor (Fig. 8). Phase 3 reflect the layout of the complex during the later Byzantine period, which is not at our concern here.

The complex extended over two terraces. Access was from *cardo* W1 on the east, by means of two stair rooms of similar dimensions that led to the courtyard of the lower terrace, located ca. 2m above street level. It had a circular, domed water cistern in its center. The northeastern corner of the compound comprised of a vast hall surrounded on three sides by seven rooms with mosaic floors. Greek inscriptions identify the complex as a provincial office—σκρίνιον, where an accountant (νουμεράριος) and clerks (καρτυλαρίοι) were in office.[58] In front of this 'revenue office', there was a mosaic-paved arcaded portico

[57] J. Patrich, "A Government Compound in Roman-Byzantine Caesarea," *Acts of The Twelfth World Congress of Jewish Studies, Jerusalem, July 29th–August 5th, 1997*, Jerusalem 1999, 35*–44*; *Id.* et al., "The warehouse complex and governor's palace (areas KK, CC and NN, May 1993–December 1995)," in Holum, Raban and Patrich (eds.), *Caesarea Papers, 2, cit.*, 70–108; *Id.*, "The Praetoria at Caesarea Maritima," in Aßkamp – Esch (eds.), *Imperium—Varus und seine Zeit, cit.*

[58] K.G. Holum, "Inscriptions from the imperial revenue office of Byzantine Caesarea Palaestinae," in *The Roman and Byzantine Near East: some recent archaeological research* (Journal of Roman archaeology. Supplementary series 14; Ann Arbor, MI: Journal of Roman archaeology, 1995), 333–345; Lehman – Holum, *The Greek and Latin Inscriptions of Caesarea Maritima, cit.*, 96–102. The translations given below are from these publications.

of square piers. A Greek inscription in the lowest of three floors reads: "The ὑποβοτηοί (subadjutors) made this in thanksgiving" (tr. Leah Di Segni). The ὑποβοτηοί were assistants of lower rank in the judicial or fiscal administration.[59] To the south, on the south-eastern corner of the compound was a public latrine.

The upper terrace to the west of the courtyard comprised a basilical structure that served as an audience hall, which was surrounded by other offices and installations. The phase 1 marble floor was replaced by a mosaic floor in phase 2 or 3. In phase 1 the hall was surrounded on the south, east and north by a reflection-pool. A square graded fountain was installed to the east of the reflection-pool. The major modification of the compound marking phase 2 was the filling up of the reflecting pool with brown soil (*hamra*), thus converting the reflection-pool into a garden. Also in this phase the rear fountain was reduced in size, and an irrigation water-tank was installed in the strip of land separating the fountain from the rear wall of the audience hall. Nearby, in the small vault 54 underneath was located the latrine of the *praetorium*. A wide staircase was leading down therein from the rear area. It could have been accessed also from the west via a partially vaulted alley (vault no. 3). In phase 2 this vault was separated from vault 19 by a wall, preventing access to the latrine from the west.

To the north, and in ground level there was a rectangular structure paved with colorful mosaic floors of geometric patterns (Fig. 9b). A series of rectangular niches, presumably intended to house wooden cupboards (*armaria*), were installed along its S wall (Fig. 9a). Such niches are common to ancient libraries. This fact, and the proximity of the rectangular structure to the 'law court' and to the 'revenue office' (*skrinion*), give ground to the interpretation that it served as an archive (*tabularium*) or a library for law or finances. Legal or financial records or codices could have been stored in *armaria* set in the niches.[60]

---

[59] Such an official, in a latinized form (*subadiuva* written in Greek—*soubadios*) is mentioned in *The Miracles of St. Artemios*, a collection of 7th century miracle stories by an anonymous Greek author of Byzantium. This *soubadios* or deputy in the office of the eparch assisted a litigant in the law court. See V.S. Crisafulli and J.W. Nesbitt, *The Miracles of St. Artemios* (Leiden – New York – Köln: Brill, 1997), 114–121. I am indebted to K.G. Holum for bringing this interesting and vivid source to my attention.

[60] A record-office (*tablarion*), in Caesarea, perhaps that of the *praetorium* of the financial procurator, is mentioned in a papyrus found in Egypt, but originating from Caesarea, dated to 152 CE. See: J. Rea, "Two Legates and a Procurator of Syria Palaestina, *ZPE* 26 (1977), 217–222, and for a different reading, W. Eck, "Ein Prokuratorenpaar von Syria Palaestina in P. Berol. 21652," *ZPE* 123 (1998), 249–255.

The bath house that had formed a part of this *praetorium*, was partially exposed in the NW corner of the compound. Its layout is diagonal relative to the other components of the *praetorium*, described so far. Whether or not it was added only in phase 3, or it was already a part of the complex in phase 2 is not clear yet. This question deserves farther study.

Other components of the private wing, that might have held the dwelling quarters, and presumably more halls, courtyards and gardens, were almost entirely destroyed by the Islamic / Crusader wall and moat of Qaisariye, located immediately to the north of the area under discussion.

DWELLINGS

Our information about regular dwellings is quite meager for all periods. A palatial mansion was constructed in the fourth century to the south of the *praetorium procuratoris*. Built over a vast first century Roman villa, it was exposed in its entirety, and had an elaborate bathhouse in a good state of preservation (Fig. 10).[61] A more modest dwelling, yet quite spacious, with a smaller peristyle courtyard was uncovered in the north-western zone. A hoard of 99 gold coins of the second half of the 4th c. was uncovered there (Fig. 11).[62]

ENTERTAINMENT STRUCTURES

In the period under discussion Caesarea had several entertainment facilities. A contemporary source praises its pantomimes and its circus.[63]

Herod's theater is located at the southern end of the city. Comprising two blocks of seats, it accommodated ca. 4000 spectators (Fig. 12).[64]

See also: R. Haensch, *Capita provinciarum. Statthaltersitze und Provinzialverwaltung in der römischen Kaiserzeit* (Mainz am Rhein: Zabern, 1997), 556.

[61] Y. Porath, *Excavations and Surveys in Israel* 17 (1998), 42–43, fig. 4. During the IAA excavations this complex was identified as a bathhouse. However, now, after being entirely exposed, it is clear that the bathhouse, being the first part to be exposed, formed just a wing of this palatial mansion.

[62] R.J. Bull and O. Storvick, "The Gold Coin Hoard at Caesarea," *BA* 56 (1993), 116–20; P. Lampinen, "The gold hoard of 4th-c. *solidi* found in 1993," in Holum, Raban and Patrich, *Caesarea Papers, 2, cit.*, 368–388.

[63] Cf. *Expositio totius mundi et gentium*, XXXII (éd. Rougé, SC 124, p. 167).

[64] See A. Albricci, in A. Frova et al., *Scavi di Caesarea Maritima* (Roma: L'"Erma" di Bretschneider, 1966), 93–120; Levine, *Roman Caesarea, cit.*, 23–26. See also J. Patrich, "Herodian Entertainment Structures", in D.M. Jacobson and N. Kokkinos (eds.),

A *kurkar* slab with a Latin dedication of a building to Tiberius by Pontius Pilatus was found incorporated in a 4th century CE floor in the theatre, at the foot of the northern staircase of the Imperial phase, ca. 1m above the orchestra level.[65] Farther east, to the south and outside of the Herodian city wall, were uncovered the remains of another Roman theater, built apparently in the second century CE.[66] It is too large to be a regular *odeum*, and to be identified with the *odeion* installed by Vespasian in a former large Jewish synagogue.[67]

Herod's 'amphitheatre',[68] known as the "Great Stadium" of the city,[69] was located on the seashore.[70] The stadium, together with the adjacent *praetorium*, with its prison and law court, constitute the venue where many of the Acts of the Martyrs of Caesarea took place.

It was a U-shaped structure, comprising a 300m long arena surrounded by seats on the east, south, and west. The estimated capacity was 10.000 spectators. A southern gate under the *sphendone* gave direct access from the *praetorium* to the arena. Starting gates on its northern side, and the writings of Josephus indicate that it was a multi-purpose entertainment structure, where *gymnika*, and *hippika* contests were held, and Roman spectacles of *munera* and *venationes* were held. The term hippo-stadium was coined in order to designate this type of stadium, in which starting gates for chariot races were installed.

Herod and Augustus. Papers Presented at the IJS Conference, 21st–23rd June 2005 (Leiden – Boston: Brill, 2009), 181–213.455–467.

[65] Frova et al., *Scavi di Caesarea Marittima, cit.*, p. 90, Fig. 75; p. 92, Figs. 77 and 78.

[66] Y. Porath, "Caesarea—1994–1999", *cit.*, 36*–37*; *Id.*, "Theatre, Racing and Athletic Installations in Caesarea," *Qadmoniot* XXXVI/125 (2003), 25–42 (Hebrew); M. Peleg and R. Reich, "Excavation of a Segment of the Byzantine City Wall of Caesarea," *Atiqot* 21 (1992), 137–170.

[67] John Malalas, *Chronograph.*, X.338 (ed. Dindorf, *cit.*, p. 261); X.46 (ed. I. Thurn, Berlin: de Gruyter, 2009, p. 197).

[68] *Ant.*, 15.341; *Bell.*, 1.415.

[69] *Bell.*, 2.9; 3.172; in *Ant.*, 18.3; 1.57, simply a stadium is mentioned.

[70] Y. Porath, "Herod's 'amphitheatre' at Caesarea: a multipurpose entertainment building," in J. H. Humphrey (ed.), *The Roman and Byzantine Near East: some recent archaeological research* (The Journal of Roman Archaeology, Supplement Series 14; Ann Arbor, MI: Journal of Roman Archaeology, 1995): 15–27 and 269–72 (color pls.); *Id.*, "Herod's amphitheatre at Caesarea (preliminary notice)," *Atiqot* 25 (1994), 11*–19* (Hebrew); *Id.*, *Excavations and Surveys in Israel* 17 (1998), 40–41; *Id.*, "Herod's "Amphitheatre" at Caesarea," *Qadmoniot* XXIX/112 (1996), 93–99 (Hebrew); J. Patrich, "The *Carceres* of the Herodian Hippodrome/Stadium at Caesarea Maritima, Israel," *Journal of Roman Archaeology* 14 (2001), 269–283; *Id.*, "Herod's Hippodrome/Stadium at Caesarea and the Games Conducted Therein," in L.V. Rutgers (ed.), *What has Athens to Do with Jerusalem. Essays in Honor of Gideon Foerster* (Leuven: Peeters, 2002), 29–68.

In its final phase, perhaps in the mid-third century, the arena was truncated, and the southern third of the structure was converted into a small amphitheatre (Fig. 13). Chariot races could not be held there any more. Such was the shape of this stadium when the local martyrs were persecuted there. In this phase the *loggia* or *pulvinar*, occupied by the dignitaries, was removed from its original location facing the center of the original elongated arena, and placed in the new center of the shortened *cavea*. The *sacellum*, the tiny shrine of this arena, was underneath. Frescoes on the podium wall, depicting hunting scenes, are attributed by Porath to this phase. Identifiable here are the deer, fox, wild boar, tiger, and a right leg of a hunter.[71] A subterranean system of tunnels was also installed in the reduced amphitheatre. It seems that later on, after "the triumph of the Cross", the *sacellum* was converted into a martyrs' chapel (Fig. 5).[72] Three foundation stones for altar legs were found *in situ*, a common find in chapels and churches. At least some of the niches carved in the rock wall are apparently from this phase—the large niche in the middle room serving as an apsidal niche, and the elongated niches in the side room to the north seem to be *loculi* for the emplacement of martyrs' remains, like in the Christian catacombs in Rome.

A "canonical," oval, Roman amphitheater is recognized in aerial photographs on the north-east part of the city. The estimated size of the arena is 62 × 95m; it was not yet properly explored. It is reasonable to assume that it was constructed in the second or third century.[73] It seems that the 306 CE earthquake caused a certain damage that prevented shows to be held at the site. In the south-eastern part of the city a Roman circus was built, under Hadrian. This eastern hippodrome, with obelisks and *metae* decorating its *spina*, continued to function during the Byzantine period, until it went out of use, and systemati-

---

[71] Y. Porath, "The Wall Paintings on the Podium of Herod's *amphitheatron*, Caesarea," *Michmanim* 14 (2000), 42–48, and color pl. 7 (Hebrew with an English summary on p. 17*–18*). The suggested dark-skinned elephant is actually a boar with a typical twisted tail.

[72] The *sacellum* in the amphitheatre of Salonae was likewise converted into a Christian chapel in the 4th c. See: E. Dyggve, *Recherches à Salone*, II (Copenhague: Schultz, 1933), 102–107.

[73] A. Reifenberg, "Archaeological Discoveries by Air Photographs in Israel," *Archaeology* 3 (1950), 40–46; *Id.*, "Caesarea: A Study in the Decline of a Town." *IEJ* 1 (1951), 20–32; A. Negev, "Caesarea in the Roman Period," *Mada* 11 (1966), 144 (Hebrew).

cally demolished, well before the end of that era, perhaps already early in the sixth century.[74]

As was mentioned above, according to Malalas, Vespasian converted a Jewish synagogue into an *odeion*.[75] The location of this *odeion* is unknown.

THE *LUDUS*

The *ludus* was a school or caserne for training gladiators. In the Roman world there were three types of *ludus*, imperial, municipal, and private. It seems that Caesarea had such an imperial institution.[76] This was a part of an imperial system of *munera*. Each imperial *ludus* was headed by a *procurator ludorum*, while the imperial system as a whole was directed (in the Early Empire) by the procurator of the *Ludus Magnus* in Rome.[77] The *procurator ludorum* (Latin), or *epitropos loudon*

[74] J. Humphrey, "A Summary of the 1974 Excavations in the Caesarea Hippodrome," *BASOR* 218 (1975), 6; L.E. Toombs, "The Stratigraphy of Caesarea Maritima," in R.P.S. Moorey and P.J. Parr (eds.), *Archaeology in the Levant: Essays for Kathleen Kenyon* (Warminster: Aris & Phillips, 1978), 229. On this hippodrome of Caesarea in the wider context of Eastern hippodromes see also J. Humphrey, "Prolegomena to the Study of the Hippodrome at Caesarea Maritima," *Bulletin of the American Schools of Oriental Research* 213 (1974), 2–45; *Id., Roman Circuses. Arenas for Chariot Racing* (London: Batsford, 1986), 438–540 (Caesarea: pp. 477–491). See also: J. Jeremias, "Der Taraxippos im Hippodrom von Caesarea Palaestinae," *Zeitschrift des Deutschen Palästina-Vereins* 54 (1931), 279–89, pls. XII–XIII. For the more recent excavations at the site see Porath, "Caesarea—1994–1999", *cit.*, and *Id.*, "Theatre, Racing and Athletic Installations in Caesarea," *cit.*

[75] See *supra*, n. 67.

[76] *MP* Syr. 36; 30 (p. 22); *MP* Gr. VII.4; VIII.2–3 (p. 142.145). For discussion see J. Patrich, "The Martyrs of Caesarea: the urban context," *LASBF* 52 (2002), 321–346. In the Rabbinic sources there are references also to Jews, including the 3rd century sage Reish Lakish, who sold themselves to the *ludus* (*PT Gitt.*, IV.46b and 47a; *Ter.*, VIII.45d; *Pesikta de Rav Kahana*, 12b). See also: M.Z. Brettler and M. Poliakoff, "Rabbi Simeon ben Lakish at the Gladiator's Banquet: Rabbinic Observations on the Roman Arena," *HTR* 83 (1990), 93–98. It is reasonable to assume that this was the same *ludus* at Caesarea.

[77] L. Robert, *Les gladiateurs dans l'Orient grec* (Paris: Champion, 1940; reprint Amsterdam: Hakkert, 1971), 267–268; H.G. Pflaum, *Les procurateurs équestres sous le haut-empire romain* (Paris: Maisonneuve, 1950), 51; G. Ville, *La gladiature en occident des origines à la mort de Domitien* (Roma: École Française de Rome, 1981), 277–287.295–306; J.-C. Golvin, *L'amphithéâtre romain*, I. Texte (Paris: De Boccard, 1988), 148–156. In the eastern provinces imperial *ludi* are known to have existed at Pergamon, Cyzicus, Ancyra, Thessalonike, and Alexandria. Robert, Pflaum, and Ville are aware of the reference to the *ludus* in the *MP* (but not in the Rabbinic sources). See L. Robert, *Hellenica*, III, *cit.*, 120–21; H.G. Pflaum, *Les carrières procuratoriennes*

(Greek), and their staff were in charge of recruiting gladiators for the imperial *munera*, training and feeding them, providing all their needs from the imperial treasury, and dispatching them to the imperial spectacles in Rome or elsewhere.

Any wealthy mansion with a fairly spacious inner courtyard could have served as a *ludus*. In the more elaborate structures, like the *Ludus Magnus* and *Ludus Matutinus* in Rome, an oval or circular arena was inserted into the courtyard.[78] The location and shape of the *ludus* in Caesarea are not known, but the references given above indicate that gladiatorial combats (*munera*) were still a living practice in Caesarea in the early 4th century, and its *ludus* constituted an integral component of the infrastructure established for the imperial *munera*.

The Water Supply System[79]

The Roman city got its water supply from the north by means of two aqueducts (Fig. 14). The high level aqueduct reached the city as a double arcade supporting two channels. The western, later one, is dated by inscriptions to the reign of Hadrian. The earlier channel is attributed, alternatively, to Herod, the Roman procurators, or Vespasian. The lower-level aqueduct is a masonry tunnel, ca. 1.20m wide and 2.00m high, that got its water from an artificial lake that came into existence in the 3rd c. by building a dam across Nahal Tanninim, before its out-

---

équestres sous le Haut-Empire romain (Paris: Geuthner, 1960), 76; Ville, *La gladiature en occident, cit.*, 287, n. 140.

[78] Golvin, *L'amphithéâtre romain, cit. Ludi* with an oval arena resemble small amphitheaters, like the military amphitheater at Dura Europos, with an oval arena 26×32m in dimensions, and a *cavea* 8–10m wide. It is dated by an inscription to 216 CE. See: M.I. Rostovtzeff et al., *The Excavations at Dura Europos. Preliminary Report of the Sixth Season of Work, October 1932–March 1933* (New Haven, CT: Yale University Press, 1936), 72–77, pl. XIV; Golvin, *L'amphithéâtre romain, cit.*, 139.

[79] A. Negev, "The High Level Aqueduct at Caesarea," *IEJ* 14 (1964), 237–249, pl. 17C; Olami-Ringel, *IEJ* 25 (1975), 148–150; Y. Peleg, "The Water Supply system of Caesarea," *Mitteilungen des Leichtweiss-Institut für Wasserbau der Technischen Universität Braunschweig* 89 (1986), 1–15; D. Everman, "Survey of the coastal area of Caesarea and of the aqueducts: preliminary report," in Holum et al., *Caesarea Papers*, I, *cit.*, 184–193; Y. Porath, "The Aqueducts of Caesarea," in D. Amit, J. Patrich and Y. Hirschfeld, *The Aqueducts of Israel* (Journal of Roman Archaeology. Supplement Series 41; Portsmouth, RI: Journal of Roman Archaeology, 2000), 104–129. For the epigraphical evidence see also A. Negev, "A New Inscription from the High Level Aqueduct at Caesarea," *IEJ* 22 (1972), 52–53; L. Di Segni, "The water supply of Roman and Byzantine Palestine in literary and epigraphical sources," in Amit et al., *The Aqueducts of Israel, cit.*, 37–67.

let into the Mediterranean.[80] A network of lead and *terra cotta* pipes running under the paved streets led the water to various public amenities: fountains, *nymphaea*, bath houses, latrines, and gardens. The palaces and rich mansions benefited from this net of pipes, enjoying a private water supply.

BATHHOUSES, NYMPHAEA AND LATRINES

In addition to temples, Eusebius mentions bathing places (τὰ λουτρά).[81] The 'baths of Cornelius' are mentioned in the early 4th century *Itinerarium Burdigalense*.[82] These are hardly the public bath (δημόσιον λοῦτρον) erected by Antoninus Pius in Caesarea.[83] None of the Caesarean bathhouses uncovered so far was a huge *therma* of the Roman imperial type, to be identified with this one.

A network of lead and terra-cotta pipes lead water to street and private fountains, and to the latrines.[84] An elaborate *nymphaeum*, with three niches holding statues, adorned the NW flank of the temple platform.[85] Smaller fountains were located in street corners, and in the private domain fountains and reflecting pools were incorporated in the gardens and courtyards. Being located on the seashore, Caesarea also enjoyed the pleasant and refreshing panorama of the sea.

THE NECROPOLIS

Most graves uncovered so far are dated to the Late Roman and Byzantine periods. They were found beyond the Byzantine city wall, up to

---

[80] 'Abd a-Salam Sa'id, Nahal Tanninim dam, *Excavations and Surveys in Israel* 114 (2002), 34*–36*, Fig. 52–55; 'Abd a-Salam Sa'id and Uzi 'Ad, Nahal Tanninim Dam, *Excavations and Surveys in Israel* 116 (2004)—http://www.hadashotesi.org.il/report_detail_eng.asp?id=11&mag_id=108; P. Gendelman and U. 'Ad, Nahal Tanninim Dam, *Excavations and Surveys in Israel* 122 (2010)—http://www.hadashotesi.org.il/report_detail_eng.asp?id=1578&mag_id=117. The dam created an artificial lake, whence the low-level aqueduct started. The excavations at the dam indicated that it was laid down at the end of the Roman—beginning of the Byzantine periods.

[81] *MP* Gr. IX.7 (p. 148) (baths; bath attendants are also mentioned).

[82] Ed. CCSL 175, p. 13.

[83] John Malalas, *Chronograph.*, XI.367 (ed. Dindorf, *cit.*, p. 281); XI.25 (ed. Thurn, *cit.*, p. 212).

[84] For a list, see Patrich, *supra* n. 23.

[85] Y. Porath, "The Evolution of the Urban Plan in Caesarea's Southwest Zone," in Raban – Holum, *Caesarea maritima, cit.*, 112–113; 121–24; *Id.*, *Excavations and Surveys in Israel* 17 (1998), 45.

several hundred meters away from it.[86] But an earlier cemetery existed outside the Herodian city wall.[87] Burials from the earlier Roman period were uncovered so far only in the south, being built against the Herodian city wall. These were non-Jewish cremation tombs. They date from the end of the first century CE, to the third century.[88]

---

[86] G. Edelstein, "Binyamina," *Excavations and Surveys in Israel* 18 (1998), 114 = *Hadashot Arkheologiyot* 106 (1996), 174 (Hebrew); D. Lipkunsky, "Or 'Aqiva (East)," *Excavations and Surveys in Israel* 20 (2000), 37 = *Hadashot Arkheologiyot* 108 (1998), 53–54 (Hebrew); M. Peilstöcker, "Or 'Aqiva (North)," *Hadashot Arkheologiyot: Excavations and Surveys in Israel* 110 (1999), 35* and 44–45 (Hebrew); A. Nagorsky, "Or 'Aqiva (A-3265)," *Hadashot Arkheologiyot: Excavations and Surveys in Israel* 115 (2003), 33*–34* and 41–42 (Hebrew). See also Levine, *Roman Caesarea, cit.*, 46–47. Many burial inscriptions on stone or marble plates were found dispersed throughout the city, and it is evident that they were carried in from their original location in the Byzantine, or in the Muslim period. For a list of burial inscriptions and details about their finding spots see Lehman – Holum, *The Greek and Latin Inscriptions of Caesarea Maritima, cit.*, 24.

[87] This is implied from the Rabbinic literary sources. See discussion in Patrich, "The Wall Street, the Eastern Stoa, the Location of the Tetrapylon, and the Halakhic Status of Caesarea Maritima", *cit.*

[88] Y. Porath, "Caesarea—1994–1999", *cit.*, 36*–37*.

FOURTH CENTURY CHRISTIAN PALESTINIAN POLITICS: A GLIMPSE AT EUSEBIUS OF CAESAREA'S LOCAL POLITICAL CAREER AND ITS *NACHLEBEN* IN CHRISTIAN MEMORY

Oded Irshai

One of the most famous records and now CDs in rock music history is the Pink Floyd's "*The Dark Side of the Moon*", a title which I adopted for a recent lengthy paper (published late 2006) on the political career and demeanor of one of the most prominent and colorful figures in Late Antique Christianity, Eusebius of Caesarea.[1]

Eusebius was born in Caesarea ca. 260 and died at an advanced age in 339 CE; he served the church for approximately 26 years as the Bishop of Caesarea Maritima, his home town. Eusebius is well known to us via his numerous writings, his encyclopedic knowledge and his ground-breaking literary enterprises, like the *Chronicon* and above all his *Ecclesiastical History*. Almost 17 centuries later he still continues to command great scholarly interest.

Much of the scholarly effort over the centuries has been devoted to deciphering his involvement in some of the major events of his time that shaped the future of the church, in particular his enigmatic liaison with Constantine. A less well-known side of this renowned church father is his political ecclesiastical career particularly within the Roman Palestinian orbit.[2]

---

[1] What follows is a much abridged though slightly updated version of that paper, "The Dark Side of the Moon: Eusebius of Caesarea between Theological Polemics and Struggles for Prestige", *Cathedra* 122 (2006), 63–98 (Hebrew).

[2] Suffice it here to mention some of the leading and influential scholarly studies in the recent decades. T.D. Barnes, *Constantine and Eusebius* (Cambridge, MA – London: Harvard University Press, 1981); A. Cameron and S.G. Hall, *Eusebius: The Life of Constantine* (Oxford: Clarendon Press, 1990), and more recently, A.H. Drake, *Constantine and the Bishops: The Politics of Intolerance* (Baltimore, MD: Johns Hopkins, 2000). On some specific issues pertaining to Eusebius' exegetical as well as apologetic work it is important to the following recent studies, *Eusebius, Christianity, and Judaism*, ed. H.W. Attridge – G. Hata (StPB 42; Leiden – New York – Köln: Brill, 1992); J. Ulrich, *Euseb von Caesarea und die Jüden* (Tübingen: Mohr-Siebeck, 1999); S. Inowlocki, *Eusebius and the Jewish Authors: His Citation Technique in an Apologetic Context* (Leiden: Brill, 2006); M.J. Hollerich, *Eusebius of Caesarea's Commentary on Isaiah: Christian Exegesis in the Age of Constantine* (Oxford: Oxford University

Fate placed Eusebius at a unique juncture, between the days of the greatest onslaught on the church, and its legitimatization and renaissance under Constantine at which stage it was no longer at the mercy of its persecutors. This formidable position enabled Eusebius to achieve two goals: first, he recorded the atrocities of the Roman heathen against his fellow believers in Christ, i.e. *The Martyrs of Palestine*. Second, he compiled his historic *magnum opus*, i.e. the *Historia Ecclesiastica* which set the future tone for the triumphal posture of the church. In that pioneering enterprise he painted in wide brush strokes the path of the church from its modest grass roots beginnings to the point at which it was on the threshold of becoming a universal power. Eusebius was deeply aware of the transformation the Church was undergoing but he did not let these stirring times color his views with shades of eschatology: he did not expect an imminent salvation.[3] Pragmatism was the call of the day and not just vengeance such as evoked and portrayed by Lactantius, in his *De Mortibus Persecutorum*.[4]

Unlike Lactantius, Eusebius adopted a rather reserved posture. He penned the *Martyrs of Palestine*, which was one of the most harrowing and gruesome portrayals of human violence in Late Antiquity.[5] However, the tone of Eusebius' work is not set by the expectation of

---

Press, 1999); A. Kofsky, *Eusebius and Paganism* (Leiden: Brill, 2000); A.P. Johnson, *Ethnicity and the Argumentation in Eusebius' Praeparatio evangelica* (Oxford: Oxford University Press, 2006).

[3] See D.S. Wallace-Hadrill and J. Sirinelli in the sixties and some later followers who postulated that in Eusebius' mind the Constantinian Empire designated the setting in of some sort of a divine *politeia*, see in his exposition on Isaiah, 2.36.44 (J. Ziegler (ed.) *Der Jesajakommentar* (GCS 43, Eusebius Werke, 9, Berlin 1975), 315.334–342). However, more recent studies tend to see in some later works of Eusebius signs of expectations for the *Parousia*, see the discussion in Hollerich, *Eusebius of Caesarea's Commentary on Isaiah*, cit., 161–162.196–199.

[4] See E. Digeser, *The Making of a Christian Empire: Lactantius and Rome* (Ithaca, NY: Cornell University Press, 2000) and in O. Nicholson's study, "'Civitas quae adhuc sustentat omnia': Lactantius and the City of Rome", in W.E. Klingshirn and M. Vessey (eds.), *The Limits of Ancient Christianity: Essays on Late Antique Thought and Culture in Honor of Robert A. Markus* (Ann Arbor, MI: University of Michigan Press, 1999), 7–25.

[5] The fact that Eusebius was able to take a sideline stand though he was at the time a member of the local clergy, is still puzzling, and rumors about his "foul Christian conduct" during the persecutions were circulating in the Church (cf. Paphnutius' accusations levelled at Eusebius during the council of Tyre in 335), but see Ch. Stead, "The Scripture and the Soul of Christ in Athanasius", *VigChr* 36 (1982), 248. More on this unique Eusebian account in E. Penland's study in this volume.

divine retribution.[6] Rather, his text radiates defiance on the part of the martyrs in the face of the enemies of God. From a strictly political stance the implicit message of the text is that the Christian territorial gains and appropriation of the Holy Land have been handed down by God to future generations on a silver platter dripping with the blood of the martyrs.[7]

At the center of my discussion are Eusebius' turf wars as a politician with his opponents Macarius and later Maximus, the bishops of the church of Jerusalem, better known then as the church of Aelia. Scholarly opinion of the last two decades has tended to adopt the view (advanced by my late colleague Zeev Rubin and later from a divergent perspective by Peter Walker) that the tension between these two sees from its start (that is during the early twenties of the 4th century) erupted on political grounds. They say that essentially this was a struggle over primacy within the Palestinian diocese.[8] I would like to present a

---

[6] On the theme of Divine Retribution in the Eusebian historical corpus, see, G.W. Trompf, *Early Christian Historiography: Narratives of retributive justice* (London—New York: Continuum, 2000), 109–157.

[7] In the course of his *Martyrs of Palestine* Eusebius seems to draw a map of the Christian *Holy Land* consecrated by the blood of the martyrs coming from all regions of Palestine. At the heart of this consecrated land of the Martyrs lay Caesarea where these heroes of Christianity were tried and executed.

[8] Rubin's initial work from the early eighties focused on the backstage setting that led to the wording in the Nicean 7th canon. He rightly suspected that the convoluted text of the canon acknowledging the metropolitan rights of the Caesarean see while at the same time granting special honor to the apostolic see of Jerusalem was a product of compromise in the aim of ending the local bitter political strife, see his "The Church of the Holy Sepulcher and the Conflict between the Sees of Caesarea and Jerusalem", in I.L. Levine (ed.), *The Jerusalem Cathedra*, II (Jerusalem: Yad Ben-Zvi Press, 1981), pp. 79–105. Rubin's paper had a lasting influence, and in 1990 Peter Walker in essence following Rubin's lead published his important study on the Jerusalem-Caesarea dispute, however attributing its unique contours to the Holy Places theology advocated by the leading authorities in these sees, Eusebius and later Cyril of Jerusalem. In the process Walker exposed the deep theological underpinnings of Eusebius' theological reservations concerning the "newly acquired holiness" of the Jerusalem see P.W.L. Walker, *Holy City Holy Places? Christian Attitudes to Jerusalem and the Holy Land in the Fourth Century* (Oxford: Clarendon Press, 1990). More recently, Rubin returned to the subject, in the course of which he did not only extend the chronological boundaries of the issue by surveying its post-Nicene manifestations but also reiterated his basic stand that the dogmatic and other matters tied with this conflict were indeed secondary to the ecclesiastical-political issue of the local crown of primacy; see Z. Rubin, "The Cult of the Holy Places and Christian Politics in Byzantine Jerusalem", in I.L. Levine (ed.), *Jerusalem: Its Sanctity and Centrality to Judaism, Christianity and Islam* (New York: Continuum, 1999), 151–162, esp. p. 152.

corrective: I argue that this contest had its roots in the wider picture of 4th century divide between the Arian and Orthodox factions.

The Arian controversy, which broke out in Alexandria ca. 317–318, soon engulfed the entire Christian-Roman near east and eventually spilled over to the church of the Latin west. Without going into a lengthy discussion over theological minutiae, Arius's views which were presented to Alexander of Alexandria comprised the following principles:

A. There is a hierarchy in the Godhead, Christ the Logos is *subordinate* to God the Father who is *the only one without beginning* (thus the Son is not coeternal with the Father, see more in B), and the Son is not of the same *substance* as the Father.
B. Christ the Logos is a *Creature* however, created *"out of nothing"*, but is not like any of the other creatures. He was created before all the aeons [created *"apart from time"*, but *"was not before his generation"*].
C. His form of creation from and by the Father was not in a manner of eructation or issue (προβολή).[9]

These principles might have had (and some would contend that they most probably had) antecedents in 3rd century theology, but they were rejected outright by Alexander of Alexandria. Following some local negotiations, Arius found himself forced to leave Alexandria. In the hope of finding new allies and some support for his views he headed to Palestine.[10] There he befriended Eusebius of Caesarea,

---

[9] These essential principles are to be found in Arius' *Thalia* (the Banquet) as quoted by his foe Athanasius in his *De Synod.* 15. I am well aware that the above presentation of the theological principles guiding Arius' views does not do justice to the lengthy and extremely intricate study of the Arian theology, the history of which (at least in part) can be followed through the short appraisal by A. Ritter, "Arius redivivus? Ein Jahrzwölft Arianismusforschung", *ThR* 55 (1990), 153–187; and later, Ch. Markschies, *Alta Trinità Beata: Gesammelte Studien zur altchristlichen Trinitätstheologie* (Tübingen: Mohr Siebeck, 2000), 95–195; recently a fresh, stimulating and rather comprehensive survey of the historical-theological aspects of the 4th century Trinitarian debate has been offered by L. Ayres, *Nicaea and its Legacy: An Approach to Fourth-Century Trinitarian Theology* (Oxford: Oxford University Press, 2004), 52–61 (on the Eusebian party the supporters of Arius). However, as will become apparent the principles listed here have bearing on the subject at hand.

[10] Much of the recent scholarly effort to trace the details of Arius' biography especially the episodes concerning his exile from and recall to Alexandria until his tragic end have been focused on the period following the Council of Nicaea in 325 CE in the course of which new suggestions have been offered concerning the chronological order of the documents in H.-G. Opitz's now classical dossier, H.-G. Opitz,

Aetius of Lydda (Diospolis) and Paulinus of Tyre, but it was there also that he encountered new opposition in the figure of Macarius, bishop of Jerusalem. By this stage (ca. 320) Eusebius of Nicomedia was Arius's greatest supporter. In an important epistle (preserved in Theodoret's *Ecclesiastical History*, I, 5), sent by Arius to Eusebius of Nicomedia, Arius sketches out the support he has so far encountered outside Egypt (support led among others by Eusebius of Caesarea).

Athanasius Werke III/1. Urkunden zur Geschichte des arianischen Streites 318-328 (Berlin – Leipzig: De Gruyter, 1934-1935) but see now the continuation of Opitz's unfinished work by H.Ch. Brennecke, U. Heil, A. von Stockhausen and A. Wintjes, *Athanasius Werke*, 3.1: Dokumente zur Geschichte des arianisches Streites. 3. Lieferung (Berlin – New York: de Gruyter, 2007) with some modifications on the dating of Arius' fate, *ibid.*, pp. xxxvi–xxxviii. More recently Timothy Barnes has presented a comprehensive corrective to the recently emerging dating of Arius' biography following the Nicene Council, see, his most recent lengthy note, "The Exile and Recalls of Arius", *JThS* n.s. 60 (2009), 109-129. In the course of the above scholarly enterprises, the earlier stages of the Arian controversy following its eruption and within them the Christian Palestinian angle, have on the whole recently received only scanty scholarly attention. Much of the picture portraying the earliest stages of the controversy was and still is based on H.-G. Opitz's classic article, "Die Zeitfolge des arianischen Streites von den Anfängen bis zum Jahre 328", *ZNTW* 33 (1934), 131-159, with modifications offered by R.P.C. Hanson, *The Search for the Christian Doctrine of God: The Arian Controversy 318-381* (Edinburgh: T&T Clark, 1988), 129-138; R. Williams, *Arius: Heresy and Tradition* (London: Darton, Longman and Todd, 1987; rev. ed. Grand Rapids, MI: Eerdmans, 2002), 48-61, and U. Loose, "Zur Chronologie des arianischen Streites", *ZKG* 101 (1990), 88-92. In the lengthy Hebrew version of the current paper (supra note 1) I have essentially followed the chronological framework of the early stages of the Arian controversy provided by the above mentioned scholars with some minor quallifications. However, the publication of my paper somewhat overlapped with Winrich Löhr's major contribution to the decipherment of the very same rather intricate early stages of the controversy, cf. "Arius Reconsidered (Part 1)", *ZAC* 9 (2006), 524-560 and idem, pt. 2, ibid., 10 (2007), 121-157. On the whole Löhr's outline of the events leading to the Nicene council concurs with the one offered by me (with some minor differences, which go beyond the scope of the current paper), there are also however, some variations. While Löhr attempts a very meticulus ordering of the sequence of the events, he refrains from suggesting precise dating to that very same sequence. Also, in a way he much tones down the presence of the Christian Palestinian component of the controversy by claiming that the famous Palestinian synod dealing with Arius' request for support recommended that he should be allowed to convene his congregation: 'as he had done before' refers to his Alexandrian 'headquarters' rather than to the possibility (offered earlier by Williams) to form his own 'émigré congregation in Palestine' (pp. 258-259). If that was indeed the case, and the entire issue at stake discussed by the Palestinian church concerned a geographicaly distant affair, how are we to account for the centrality of Makarios of Jerusalem among the few figures singled out by Arius' as his archenemies and theological opponents? How are we to account for the mounting pressure within the Palestinian church essentially forming a deep rift between its different sub-region? All of this is unfortunately beyond the scope of this paper, see however, a more detailed account in the Hebrew version (supra, n. 1), pp. 67-90; see further *infra*, n. 12.

In the course of that epistle he also describes the opposition he faces, comprising three leading figures in the following order: Philogonius of Antioch, Hellanicus of Tripoli in Phoenicia, and Macarius of Jerusalem. He labels them all as heretics (ἀνθρώπων αἱρετικῶν). Arius did not stop there but proceeded to describe the theological standpoints of his opponents in the following manner: "Some of them say that the Son is an eructation, others that he is an issue, and others that he is also *co-unbegotten (συναγέννητον)*". If, as I assume, we are presented here by Arius with some sort of symmetry, then Macarius, as the last on Arius's list of opponents, was also the holder of the most radical theological stance in that list. Though it is difficult to furnish from the above attribution a clear picture of Macarius' systematic theology, there is enough in the above catchword of labeling the Father and Son as *co-ingenerate* to postulate in the least a substantive similarity between him and Alexander of Alexandria and more so with Marcellus of Ancyra. If, as I presume, we ought to prefer the latter possibility, this might have added additional friction with Eusebius of Caesarea, who was shortly to become Marcellus' archenemy.[11] Thus, already in the early twenties, the two sees of Jerusalem and Caesarea found themselves embroiled in an emerging all-encompassing theological conflict. Eusebius seems to have woken up one morning to find a viper (Macarius) on his doorstep.[12]

---

[11] In the initial stage of his proclaimed theology, that is in the pre-Nicene period, Marcellus targeted Asterius of Cappadocia ("the sophist") views in his work *Contra Asterium*, of which only fragments survived due to Eusebius of Caesarea's extensive writings against it. Central to these fragments is the emphasis on the indivisibility as well as the *ingenerate* nature of both the Father and the Word, as demonstrated by Ayres, *Nicaea and its Legacy, cit.*, 63–64. Compare S. Parvis, *Marcellus of Ancyra and the Lost Years of the Arian Controversy 325–345* (Oxford: Oxford University Press, 2006), 33–36; later on in her study Parvis discusses Theodoret's testimony (*ibid.*, pp. 55–57), exposing the Marcellan views (Philogonius) or agenda (Hellanicus) which Arius singled out as opposing his, while only in the case of Macarius of Jerusalem, similarity is drawn between him and Alexander of Alexandria, though as we have postulated above a pro-Marcellan stance could equally be adduced in this case too. One has still to bear in mind, though, that Eusebius' anti-Marcellan views were essentially formulated later on, see now, Christopher A. Beeley, 'Eusebius' *Contra Marcellum*: Anti-Modalist Doctrine and Orthodox Christology' ZAC 12 (2009), 433–452.

[12] A word about Arius's stance in that critical moment is in order. One can not escape the similarities between Arius' initial journey to Palestine (Caesarea) and that of Origen nearly a century earlier in face of Demetrios, and the Alexandrian bishop's hostility towards him, an episode Eusebius was well acquainted with. Cf. the 6th book of his *Church History*. More on the latter episode, see, R.P.C. Hanson, "Was Origen Banished from Alexandria?", in *StPatr* 17, Leuven 1982, 904–906. Having postulated the similarities between the two episodes, one ought to bear in mind that the conflict

The church of Palestine found itself drifting into a local schism.[13] One of the most interesting aspects of this conflict was its fairly clear geographical, regional dimension. The divide brought about the creation of a Christian Palestinian orthodox south (led by the sees of Jerusalem and Gaza [led by Asclepius]) and a more distinct Eusebian ("Arian") Arian north. The "demarcation line" ran between Jericho in the east and Azotus on the Mediterranean shore. The Arian north was led by the see of Caesarea alongside Scythopolis and Diospolis, though within this region one could discern some small rural orthodox enclaves.

The "great Palestinian divide" manifested itself in the list of signatories to the decisions of the somewhat obscure council of Antioch. This council was convened just a few months before the Nicean great council at the behest of the emerging orthodox party. The council convened right after the demise of the emperor Licinius, Constantine's rival in the east, and under the auspices of Eustathius of Antioch (who was only recently transferred to that see) and Ossius of Cordoba (perhaps by then already the Emperor's envoy).[14] Though the pretext for con-

---

between Alexander and Arius carried also some local political overtones emanating from the gradual shift in the local church towards a monarchial model of episcopacy, whereby the bishop held the ultimate authority in matters of faith, a stance that triggered also the Melitian schism, see recently Ayres, *Nicaea and its Legacy, cit.*, 16–17. In addition, Arius was most probably aware of Eusebius' theological views (voiced in his *Demonstratio Evangelica*) which, though slightly different from his own, stood nonetheless in conflict with those of Alexander. Thus, what we have here on the part of Eusebius amounts to a combination of political (or personal) compassion coupled with partial though essential theological accord in the face of tyranny and theological rigidness.

[13] In the early twenties the initial stages of this escalating conflict involved the admonition of Arius's new allies by Alexander and Eusebius and other attempts to secure pardon from Alexander on Arius's behalf, see for instance Paulinus of Tyre's request from Alexander, Opitz, *Urkunden zur Geschichte des arianischen Streites, cit.*, 14 n. 7. Eusebius also convened ca. 321 a local council in support of Arius, which comprised among others of Paulinus of Tyre and Patrophillus of Scythopolis who were to play major parts as his closest allies in the evolving conflict. The council no doubt aroused the ire of Macarius of Jerusalem and his local followers.

[14] On the somewhat obscure council of Antioch, see F.L. Cross, "The Council of Antioch in 325 AD.", *The Church Quarterly Review* 128 (1939), 49–76. The list of participants in this council has aroused some speculations especially as to its presidency which was most probably held by Ossius of Cordoba alongside Eustathius who was transferred to Antioch following the death of Philogonius in 323 and later that of Paulinus of Tyre who also served in that see for a few months and then passed away, see H. Chadwick, "Ossius of Cordova and the Presidency of the Council of Antioch", *JThS* 9 (1958), 292–304, though it would seem too that active behind the scenes of that council was Macarius of Jerusalem. On some chronological aspects pertaining to this

vening the council (of whose deliberations we know very little) was in violation of certain church regulations, the real reason behind its convening was the growing orthodox concern in the face of the mounting Arian threat.[15] The most tangible decision of the council was to impose a threat of banishment on a small number of bishops, among whom Eusebius the metropolitan bishop of Palestine had the dubious honor of being the most senior.

Two aspects of this council are astonishing. The first is the actual presence of Eusebius at its deliberations. This could be attributed to sheer political *naïveté*: his close ally, Patrophilus of Scythopolis failed to show up at the council which may have indicated that he estimated better than Eusebius the direction the wind was blowing.[16] Alternatively, he might have hoped to induce the council, by his sheer presence and political stature, to reconsider its decisions and re-divert its anxiety to other quarters. The second astonishing phenomenon was the makeup of the aforementioned list of signatories, which comprised 59 names, 9 or 10 of which came from Palestine and all save one came from Macarius' party, seven out of which were from the southern regions of the holy land.

Following the council of Antioch Eusebius' leadership of the Caesarean community was on the line. His political ecclesiastical reputation sunk to its lowest ebb yet. It was, I believe, in the course of the council and in the few ensuing months leading to Nicaea, that Macarius decided to push ahead with his demand to acknowledge the *apostolic* reputation of his see in the hope of gaining supremacy over the metropolitan see of Caesarea. Lurking behind the epithet church of Aelia stood its mythically-charged name, the church of Hierosolyma: after

---

council and its participants, see R.W. Burgess, *The Continuatio Antiochiensis Eusebii: Studies in Eusebian and Post-Eusebian Chronography* (Stuttgart: Steiner, 1999), 164–165 (text) and 183–187 (commentary).

[15] There are at least signs that theological issues that were initially supposed to be discussed in Nicaea (Nicomedia) were pushed forward and discussed in the course of the Antiochean council. There are clear signs that in the course of that council Eusebius confronted aspects of the Marcellan theology, see H.B. Logan, "Marcellus of Ancyra and the Councils of AD 325: Antioch, Ancyra and Nicaea", *JThS* 43 (1992), 428–446, pp. 429–436.

[16] Eusebius' possible *naïveté* led him to accept the initial reason for convening the council and he hastened there with intent to oppose the translation of Eustathius to Antioch which was carried out in violation of church rule.

all, it was there that the entire Christian saga began.[17] Both components of the contention, the theological and the political, were hereby fused.[18] In the course of the Nicene council, Macarius succeeded in securing at least part of his initial wish. The stage was set for a lingering contest between the sees, which continued through the days of Macarius' successors. Maximus the homologethes and Cyril were embroiled in this contest, and to a certain extent it continued into the days of John II, until Juvenal, the assertive 5th-century bishop of Jerusalem, managed to elevate the holy city to the rank of a patriarchate alongside Rome,

---

[17] It would be quite naïve to assume that Macarius perpetrated this move in the wake of the political-theological outcome of the council at Antioch. But it would be quite reasonable to assume that the move to bolster the image of the Jerusalemite Church and claim its supremacy over the local Metropolitan Church of Caesarea was initiated in the earlier stages of the local theological strife involving Arius and his local supporters. The Apostolic aura of the Jerusalem Church was maintained for generations, suffice it to mention the presence of James' *Cathedra* which was being shown to visitors (Eusebius, *Hist. eccl.*, VII.19) alongside the cultivation and dissemination of local traditions regarding the founders of the local church (James, Simeon son of Clopas, Narcissus and others, cf. Eusebius, *ibid.* II.23; VI. All in all the tone emanating from Eusebius' *Church History* in regards to these two sees during the 3rd century was of concord and cooperation. Concerning the history of the Jerusalem Church during the Apostolic era and later, see in the following two studies of mine, O. Irshai, "The Church of Jerusalem—From 'The Church of the Circumcision' to 'The Church from the Gentiles'", in Y. Tsafrir and S. Safrai (eds.), *The History of Jerusalem: The Roman and Byzantine Periods (70–638 CE)* (Jerusalem: Yad Ben-Zvi, 1999), 61–114, esp. pp. 63–93 (Hebrew), on the Apostolic and sub-Apostolic era, *Id.*, "From Oblivion to Fame: The History of the Palestinian Church (135–303 CE)", in O. Limor and G.G. Stroumsa (eds.), *Christians and Christianity in the Holy Land: From the Origins to the Latin Kingdom* (Turnhout – Jerusalem: Brepols – Yad Ben-Zvi, 2006), 91–139.

[18] Though Macarius' move to promote the ecclesiastical image and in the longer run to acquire more power for his see was seemingly unprovoked by Eusebius, a closer look at the Eusebian corpus carrying overtones of local patriotic rhetoric betrays some implicit claims for fame and respect for his own see. These claims can be gleaned as we have already demonstrated above (n. 6) from his *Martyrs of Palestine*. A second though belated and bold testimony in which Eusebius forged an *Apostolic* like image for his see can be found in his later treatise, the *Theophania*, IV, 6 where using the famous dictum by Jesus: "thou art Peter, and upon this rock (= כיפא, petra) I will build my church" (Mt 16.18) he claims that Peter founded the churches of Caesarea, Antioch and Rome (see S. Lee, *Eusebius of Caesarea, on the Theophania or Divine Manifestation of Our Lord and Saviour Jesus Christ* (Cambridge: Duncan and Malcolm, 1843), 219–220). One has only to pay a quick glimpse at the Matthean text to discover that the episode in which Jesus uttered the above took place in Caesarea Philippi in the extreme end of the Galilee., see the discussion in W.D. Davies – D.C. Allison, *The Critical and Exgetical Commentary on the Gospel according to Matthew*, II (ICC; Edinburgh: T&T Clark, 1991), 612–616.

Antioch, Alexandria and the Byzantine capital, Constantinopole, the New Rome.[19]

Paradoxically, from Eusebius' point of view, the same Nicene council which was the high water mark for the orthodox faction also marked a turning point in Eusebius' ecclesiastical political career. In the course of the council he managed to manipulate his opponents and to embark on a new and assertive political path.[20] Some would assert that Eusebius barely managed to scrape through the hazards of the council and survive the animosity he encountered from leading prelates such as Eustathius of Antioch, who was amongst the *proedroi*, the presiding circle of the council.[21] A more nuanced reading of the records shows that Eusebius with his outstanding diplomatic skills managed to draft a document of faith which avoided the pitfalls of contemporary theology, defused the tension and rallied all present in support. In securing this all-encompassing unity at Nicaea, was Eusebius acting upon his better instincts about the need for peace and concord in the church?[22] Earlier, in his preface to the 8th book of the *History*, Eusebius had voiced his view that unity was a deeply desirable objective.[23] His ensuing actions seem to betray another motivation,

---

[19] On Juvenal's political career and achievements see the classic study by E. Honigman, "Juvenal of Jerusalem", *DOP* 5 (1950), 211–279.

[20] Eusebius' fluctuation between two positions in the course of the council is somewhat reflected in his epistle to his own community, apud Opitz, *Urkunden zur Geschichte des arianischen Streites, cit.*, n. 22, pp. 42–47. More on Eusebius' participation in the Nicene council in Williams, *Arius: Heresy and Tradition, cit.*, 69–70; Hanson, *The Search for the Christian Doctrine of God, cit.*, 157–161. See more in n. 22.

[21] Not to mention the possible towering presence and impact of Marcellus of Ancyra on the imperial as well as ecclesiastical agenda of the council, do note that Ancyra was the initial venue of the council, see Logan, "Marcellus of Ancyra and the Councils of AD 325", *cit.*, 436–439 as well as *Id.*, "Marcellus of Ancyra, Defender of the Faith against Heretics and Pagans", in *StPatr* 37, Leuven 2001, 551–564. On Eustathius' role in the council see already R.V. Sellers, *Eustathius of Antioch* (Cambridge: Cambridge University Press, 1928), 24–26, Sellers postulated, though without any proof, that Macarius of Jerusalem might have also had a major role in the presidential committee of the council.

[22] See Eusebius' own reflections on the Nicaea council, *Vita Const.*, III.6–15, where he avoids a detailed description of the actual deliberations and focuses rather on the irenic and conciliatory atmosphere introduced by Constantine. The final document reflects some of the concessions Eusebius was prepared to offer reflecting maybe his genuine views about the need to maintain unity within the Church: see further Drake, *Constantine and the Bishops, cit.*, 252–255.

[23] Reflecting on the recent past he argued that among the causes for the great persecutions were the strife and jealousy between the leaders of the Church (*Hist. eccl.*, VII.1.8–9). Could that statement have been a concealed reflection on his Jerusalem foe's animosity towards himself?

which makes one think that his efforts during the council were geared only to protect his own interests and secure his position as a leading ecclesiastical political figure. If that is the case, peace and concord were used in the most cunning way as a smoke screen to conceal his real aims. In the years after 325 Eusebius became ever more involved in the political and theological aspects of the evolving Arian controversy. Following the re-instatement of Eusebius of Nicomedia and Theognis of Nicaea (deposed by the council), the three embarked on a political vendetta against the leaders of the opposing orthodox faction. Their first victim was Eustathius of Antioch: he was deposed (somewhat between 326 and 330/1) on trumped-up charges of insulting Helena, the Emperor's mother on her way to Jerusalem on pilgrimage, and/ or for his ties with a local Antiochean whore.[24] Their banishment of Asclepius of Gaza, yet another vehemently orthodox leader, seems to betray a much deeper and orchestrated plan to uproot the orthodox leadership from its ecclesiastical strongholds.[25] The banishment of the aforementioned bishops coupled with the translation of Eusebius of Nicomedia to the newly-formed imperial capitol Constantinopole signified a major political shift whereby the Arian territorial gains added political clout to their ever-growing prominence.[26]

Eusebius' fine skills as a politician coupled with his strong urge to maintain an edifying image for posterity are demonstrated by the following anecdote, to which I come now at the closing stages of this

---

[24] To the latter his accusers added that he had leanings towards the heresy of Sabellianism another catchword for linking their foes with Marcellus of Ancyra their theological archopponent. For the various views concerning the confused dating and circumstances of Eustathius' banishment see, H. Chadwick, "The Fall of Eustathius of Antioch", *JThS* 49 (1948), 25–37 (326 CE); R.P.C. Hanson, "The Fate of Eustathius of Antioch", *ZKG* 95 (1984), 173–174 (330–331 CE), and more recently, R.W. Burgess, "The Date of the Deposition of Eustathius of Antioch", *JThS* 51 (2000), 149–160 (end of 328 CE). According to Burgess (*ibid.*, 156–157) Eusebius of Nicomedia was the leading force behind the deposition of Eustathius and not Eusebius of Caesarea. It would seem though that following the events of the Antiochean council in 325 the Caesarean bishop most probably harbored great animosity towards Eustathius and also as things later transpired with the motion to translate Eusebius to Antioch he had the most to gain from Eustathius' banishment.

[25] This took place according to Burgess, (*ibid.*, 158–159) in the course of a council held in Antioch during the year 329, though the exact pretexts for Asclepius' deposition remain unclear.

[26] I strongly believe that Macarius too was on their radar screen but his contemporary privileged position as the prime executioner of Constantine's Holy Land plan (predominantly in Jerusalem and in its adjacent hinterland, Bethlehem and Mamre) spared him.

bird's eye survey of his long political career. Following Eustathius's banishment and later his death, there was a power vacuum in the local church leadership. In an effort to fill it, a struggle broke out between two local parties. The local opponents of Eustathius resolved to invite Eusebius to become the leader of their see and in fact of the entire eastern diocese. This was a most flattering proposal entailing great power.

Surprisingly enough, even though it was nearly tantamount to political suicide, Eusebius declined the offer. His portrayal of the circumstances is even more astounding. In a series of epistles which he published in his late panegyric, *The Life of Constantine*, he described his own actions as driven by two factors: his determination to remain with and faithful to his flock in Caesarea, and his desire to uphold the stringent administrative code of the Church concerning the translation of bishops. This explanation suppresses any mention of the great internal tension in Antioch which on occasion bordered on violence. In a word, what really mattered to Eusebius was his image in the collective ecclesiastical memory, which he himself was so instrumental in forging.[27] The emperor greatly commended Eusebius for his action and praised him to the skies: "You are worthy of being a bishop not of merely one city but of the entire world" he wrote.[28] However, he himself really opposed the translation of Eusebius to Antioch, in fear of the commotion it was bound to cause in the local Christian community.

The truth behind the facade so ably constructed by Eusebius was more prosaic. Indeed there might have been yet another reason for the Emperor's reluctance. Eusebius was to play a key role in one of the Emperor's most ambitious plans. By early 330 CE Constantine was deeply involved in his plan to found his new imperial capital, Constantinople. In order to adorn his "new Rome" with Christian garments, the emperor planned to build several churches and for their future cultic, liturgical needs he had to furnish them with copies of the Bible. He commissioned Eusebius, whose Caesarean library possessed the finest biblical manuscripts, to oversee the preparation of 50 copies

---

[27] Eusebius, *Vita Const.*, III.59–63, and the notes by A. Cameron and S.G. Hall, *Eusebius: Life of Constantine*, Introduction, Translation and commentary, (Oxford: Clarendon Press, 1999), 305–306.

[28] Socrates, *Hist. eccl.*, I.24.

of the Bible, a most formidable task.[29] Eusebius' possible translation to Antioch would have no doubt shattered Constantine's plan.

Eusebius departed this life in 339 CE leaving behind a lingering political legacy of discord and competition within the Christian Palestinian diocese.[30] In spite of all his efforts to preserve his memory for posterity, as a "good citizen" of the church, Eusebius' fell victim at least once to his rivals' vengeful desire to consign him to a status of *damnatio memoriae*. This happened approximately a century after his death at the hands of Cyril of Alexandria, a late successor of Athanasius of Alexandria (who himself was one of Eusebius' great rivals, and suffered a great deal from his wrath).

Towards the end of May 431 en route to Ephesus to take part in the great council to be convened there, Cyril passed through Caesarea and ordered the local Christians to erase Eusebius' name from the Church dyptich commemorating the memory of the saints. If we are to judge by the records in the *Martyrologium Syriacum* from 411, Eusebius' commemoration day was the 30th of May.[31] Ernst Honigman years ago discussed this anecdote and pondered what was it that induced Cyril to go to these lengths and order something that was against the

---

[29] Eusebius himself reports about the royal plan, *Vita Const.*, IV.36–37. Concerning the scope of the project, whether the emperor was interested in the Gospels or in the entire corpus of the Bible, see, G.A. Robbins, "'Fifty Copies of the Sacred Writings', VC 4, 36: Entire Bibles or Gospel Books?", in *StPatr* 19, Leuven 1989, 91–96, who contends that the royal request concerned only the Gospels. More recently however, T.C. Skeat, "The Codex Sinaiticus, The Codex Vaticanus and Constantine", *JThS* 50 (1999), p. 605 n. 28 argued that the emperor commissioned the copyists to produce the entire biblical corpus. On another note, it is tempting to regard this episode as yet an additional and subtle extension of the Moses imagery adopted by Eusebius in several instances throughout his portrayal of Constantine in the *Vita Constantini*. In this case Constantine was seen to be the bearer of the Law to the barren city the newly founded Christian *New Rome*. On the centrality of the Moses typology in Eusebius' Christian political theory and moral ethics, see among others, M.J. Hollerich, "Religion and Politics in the Writings of Eusebius: Reassessing the First 'Court Theologian'", *Church History* 59 (1990), 309–325 esp. pp. 316–324; C. Rapp, "Imperial Ideology in the Making: Eusebius of Caesarea on Constantine as 'Bishop'", *JThS* 49 (1998), 685–695, and Drake, *Constantine and the Bishops*, *cit.*, 376–377 (on Eusebius' predisposition towards the figure of Moses in his portrayal of Constantine's image).

[30] As for instance in the case of his successor in the Caesarean see, Acacius who undermined the authority and tarnished the image of Cyril of Jerusalem, on that chapter in the the history of the Palestinian church see among others, Rubin, "The Cult of the Holy Places", *cit.*, and J.W. Drijvers, *Cyril of Jerusalem: Bishop and City* (SVigChr 72; Leiden: Brill, 2004), 35–41.181–186 (Cyril and Arianism).

[31] Eusebius' name was engraved in the local dyptich most probably by Gelasius of Caesarea (bishop from ca. 367–395 CE), see the testimony of Eulogius of Alexandria (580–607 CE), apud Photius, *Biblioth.*, cod. 227.

church's explicit rule and custom on the matter; he came up with
the most plausible answer. Cyril's action should be regarded as part
of his campaign against Nestorius.[32] He hoped to secure Juvenal of
Jerusalem's support for his actions. In Honigmann's words: "It seems
clear that it was on Juvenal's request that St. Cyril came to Caesarea to
humiliate the metropolitan to whose jurisdiction Jerusalem belonged".[33]
Cyril clearly had his own historical axes to grind. According to Honigmann's reading, what counted was not Eusebius' shady political past
nor his historical involvement with the Arian cause.[34] What really
haunted him in his grave and on the tablets of the local dyptich was
his constant bickering with the Jerusalem bishopric over Palestinian
supremacy. In the collective memory of the Palestinian church, political rivalry counted for more than theological discord.

---

[32] E. Honigman, "Eusebius of Caesarea: The Removal of his Name from the Dyp-
tichs of Caesarea in Palestine in 431 AD", in Id., Patristic Studies (StT 173; Roma:
Biblioteca Apostolica Vaticana, 1953), 66–67.

[33] Ibid., pp. 69–70.

[34] Had Eusebius' slate been clean in the eyes of the orthodox public opinion, the
5th century Christian historian Socrates would not have dedicated a lengthy apology
to exonerate him from the stain of heresy, see, his Historia Ecclesiatica, II, 21. This and
other contemporary efforts seem to have been somewhat futile, for Eusebius' heretical image left its mark in later Byzantine literature, see for instance the entry in the
11th century lexicon, the Souda s.v. Eusebius, in A. Adler, Suidae Lexicon, vol. II,
(Leipzig, 1931) p. 472.

THE PROMOTION OF THE CONSTANTINIAN AGENDA IN EUSEBIUS OF CAESAREA'S *ON THE FEAST OF PASCHA*

Mark DelCogliano

Mention of the Council of Nicaea in 325 most often brings to mind the famous creed it approved to exclude the theology of Arius and his supporters—and rightly so. But at Nicaea resolving the conflict between Arius and Alexander was not the only item on Constantine's agenda. He also wanted all churches throughout the empire to celebrate Easter on the same day. This concern can be viewed as part of Constantine's larger programme to bind the empire together religiously. Religious dissension in all its forms was abhorrent to Constantine (as well as to many other Christians of the period) and, as sole emperor since his defeat of Licinius in late 324, Constantine now had the power and the means to effect religious unity in the empire.

Following Constantine's lead, the Council of Nicaea decided that a single system for computing the date of Easter should be in force throughout the empire.[1] During the celebration of the emperor's vicennalia shortly after the council, Constantine himself wrote a letter to each province announcing this decision and included several arguments for the single celebration of Easter.[2] Some time after the conclusion of the council, Eusebius of Caesarea wrote a treatise on Easter that was dedicated and sent to Constantine, which offered a mystical explanation of the feast.[3] What is likely a fragment of this treatise, entitled *On the Feast of Pascha*, has survived in the catena on the gospel of Luke produced by Nicetas of Heraclea.[4] This little-studied fragment is the subject of the following remarks. An English translation is

---

[1] See the synodal letter to the Egyptians, preserved in Socrates, *Hist. eccl.*, 1.9.1–14 and Theodoret, *Hist. eccl.*, 1.9.2–13; see also H.-G. Opitz, *Athanasius Werke III/1. Urkunden zur Geschichte des arianischen Streites 318–328* (Berlin – Leipzig: De Gruyter, 1934–1935), document 23 (hereafter *Urk.*, cited by document number). My thanks to Aaron Johnson for his help in honing the argument of this essay.

[2] Preserved in Eusebius, *Vita Const.*, 3.17–20 (hereafter *VC*) and Theodoret, *Hist. eccl.*, 1.10.1–12; see also *Urk.* 26.

[3] Eusebius, *VC*, 4.34–35.

[4] See J. Quasten, *Patrology* (Westminster: Newman Press, 1951–1960), 3.339–40. *On the Feast of Pascha* (*De solemnitate paschali*) was first published by A. Mai,

published in its entirety for the first time here, in the hope of fostering further research on this neglected text.[5]

I will argue that Eusebius' treatise was a response to continued opposition to the decision reached at Nicaea and was in fact commissioned by Constantine himself in order to win over persistent dissenters by a scripturally-based theological argument. In other words, in this fragment Eusebius promotes Constantine's agenda for a single celebration of Easter at the emperor's request. This is most clearly seen in how Eusebius consciously interprets scripture in such a way that he takes as his starting point some of the reasons advanced by Constantine for a single observance of Easter. He thus sets the emperor's agenda for religious unity in the celebration of Easter on a solid theological and scriptural basis. This fragment is therefore one of the first examples of how scriptural exegesis and theological discourse developed during the initial stages of the Christianization of the empire in the service of ecclesiastical unity. It furthermore shows that Constantine sought to effect his policies not only through legislation and coercion, but also through reasoned argument.

Constantine's Concern with the Date of Easter

Constantine was scandalized by divergence in the celebration of Easter long before the Council of Nicaea. The bishops at the Council of Arles (314), which was convened by Constantine to resolve the burgeoning Donatist controversy in North Africa, reported in their synodal letter to Sylvester of Rome that the first matter discussed was the celebration of Easter. The prominence given to this issue no doubt reflects the concern of Constantine himself. The bishops write:

> And it seemed that with regard to our life and welfare the first matter to be treated was when *one alone has died for all* and *was raised* (2 Cor 5.14–15), this time should be observed by all with pious minds in such a way that neither divisions nor dissensions would be able to arise in such

---

Novum Patrum bibliotheca, vol. IV (Romae, 1852–1854), 208ss., and was reprinted by J.-P. Migne in PG 24.693–706 (hereafter *Pasc.*).

[5] A partial translation was published in R. Cantalamessa, *Easter in the Early Church: An Anthology of Jewish and Early Christian Texts* (trans. J.M. Quigley and J.T. Lienhard; Collegeville: Liturgical Press, 1993), 65–70.

a great duty of devotion. We therefore decree that the Pascha of the Lord should be observed on one day throughout the whole world.[6]

Though the council decided that Easter should be celebrated on a single day "throughout the whole world," it lacked not only the jurisdiction to issue such a decree, but also the means of enforcing it. Its prescriptions were not accepted.[7] But note the argument it advances against division in the observance of Easter: since there is a single savior, there should be a single celebration of his death and resurrection. Constantine himself would use a variation of this very argument in his letter on Easter.

The emperor remained concerned with the date of Easter after Arles. Constantine is reported to have convened the Council of Nicaea not only to put an end to the religious dissension caused by the dispute between Arius and Alexander that was disturbing the entire east, but also to resolve the long-standing scandal of different Christian communities celebrating Easter on different days because some kept the feast in accordance with Jewish customs.[8] He had charged Ossius of Cordoba, at the time his preferred agent in ecclesiastical affairs, with the resolution of both matters.[9] When Ossius failed in his mission on both counts, Constantine convened the Council of Nicaea,[10] which met

---

[6] Optatus of Milevis, *Libri VII* (*Against the Donatists*), App. 4 (ed. Ziwsa, CSEL 26, p. 207, 24–29); trans. (slightly modified) M. Edwards, *Optatus: Against the Donatists* (Liverpool: Liverpool University Press, 1997), 186–187. The first canon of Arles is considerably briefer: "The first matter concerns the observance of Pascha: we should observe it on one day and one time throughout the whole world, so that according to custom you [sc. Sylvester] may send letters to everyone" (C.H. Turner, *Ecclesiae Occidentalis Monumenta Iuris Antiquissima* (Oxford: Clarendon Press, 1939), 1.384).

[7] See K.J. von Hefele, *Histoire des conciles d'après les documents originaux*, Vol. 1, Pt. 1 (Paris: Letouzey, 1907), 459. Wolfgang Huber considers the solution proposed at Arles "somewhat too simple" (*Passa und Ostern* (Berlin: Töpelmann, 1969), 64).

[8] Eusebius, *VC*, 3.5; Socrates, *Hist. eccl.*, 1.8.2–3; and Sozomen, *Hist. eccl.*, 1.16.4–5. On Constantine's concern for a single celebration of Easter, see A. di Berardino, "L'imperatore Costantino e la celebrazione della Pasqua," in G. Bonamente and F. Fusco, eds., *Costantino il Grande*, vol. 1 (Macerata: Università degli studi di Macerata, 1992), 363–384.

[9] Sozomen, *Hist. eccl.*, 1.16.5. Ossius presided over a council in Antioch in early 324 that dealt with the controversy between Arius and Alexander. It resulted in the provisional excommunication of Theodotus of Laodicea, Narcissus of Neronias, and Eusebius of Caesarea for holding the same views as Arius (*Urk.* 18.14–15). The conciliar letter does not mention any discussion of the date of Easter. See H. Chadwick, "Ossius of Cordova and the Presidency of the Council of Antioch, 325," *JThS* (1958), 292–304, and T.D. Barnes, *Constantine and Eusebius* (Cambridge: Harvard University Press, 1981), 213–214.

[10] Sozomen, *Hist. eccl.*, 1.17.1.

in 325, probably from May to July. As mentioned earlier, the bishops
put the issue on the council's agenda and decided that Easter should
be celebrated at the same time throughout the empire.[11] The actual
decree on Easter does not survive,[12] but in their synodal letter to the
Egyptians, the Nicene bishops write:

> We also have good news for you about an agreement on the most holy
> Pascha because this issue too has been settled through your prayers. All
> the brothers in the East, who until now have observed it with the Jews, will
> from this day forward celebrate Pascha in agreement with the Romans
> and us and all who from the earliest time have kept it with us.[13]

As mentioned above, it was this decision that Constantine endorsed in
his letter to the bishops of all the provinces shortly after the council.[14]
The Nicene decree was intended to resolve the issue of disunity in
the observance of Easter throughout the Roman empire[15] and through
his long letter Constantine indicated that the issue was of immense
importance to him and that he was committed to its enforcement.[16]

The divergence in the celebration of Easter in the empire was due to
two different systems of computing its date.[17] Some eastern Christians

---

[11] Eusebius, *VC*, 3.14 and Sozomen, *Hist. eccl.*, 1.21.6.

[12] The Nicene Easter decree preserved by John the Scholastic in his *Synagoga L
titulorum* (V. Beneeviè, *Iohannis Scholastici synagoga L titulorum* (Munich: Verlag der
Bayerischen Akademie der Wissenschaften, 1937), 156) appears to be nothing more
than a summary of earlier accounts. A translation can be found in Cantalamessa,
Easter in the Early Church, cit., 63–64.

[13] Socrates, *Hist. eccl.*, 1.9.12 (ed. Hansen, GCS n.f. 1, p. 30, 15–19); Theodoret,
Hist. eccl., 1.9.12 (ed. Parmentier – Scheidweiler, GCS 19, p. 41, 10–14); and *Urk.*
23.12 (50.13–51.2). The versions differ slightly from one another. My translation here
follows Socrates.

[14] Eusebius, *VC*, 3.17–20 and Theodoret, *Hist. eccl.*, 1.10.1–12; see also *Urk.* 26. On
this letter, see I. Danieli, *I documenti costantiniani della "Vita Constantini" di Eusebio di Cesarea* (AnGr 13; Roma: Università Gregoriana, 1938), 159–162; H. Dörries,
Das Selbstzeugnis Kaiser Konstantinus (Göttingen: Vandenhoeck & Ruprecht, 1954),
66–68; H. Kraft, *Kaiser Konstantins religiöse Entwicklung* (Tübingen: Mohr, 1955),
223–225; M. Hollerich, *Eusebius of Caesarea's Commentary on Isaiah: Christian Exegesis in the Age of Constantine* (Oxford: Clarendon Press; New York: Oxford University
Press, 1999), 34–36; and J. Ulrich, *Euseb von Caesarea und die Juden: Studien zur Rolle
der Juden in der Theologie des Eusebius von Caesarea* (Berlin – New York: de Gruyter,
1999), 239–244.

[15] The intended force of the Nicene decree on Easter is uncertain. For one, the
decision was not included in the twenty conciliar canons; for further discussion, see
Huber, *Passa und Ostern, cit.*, 64–68.

[16] Kraft, *Kaiser Konstantins religiöse Entwicklung, cit.*, 223–224.

[17] On the ancient systems of calculating Easter, see Hefele, *Histoire des conciles*,
450–488, and the good summaries of Quasten, *Patrology, cit.*, 3.340 and A. Cam-

(mostly in Syria, Cilicia, and Mesopotamia, according to Athanasius) celebrated Easter on the Sunday following the Jewish feast of Pascha, or Passover.[18] According to the Jewish calendar, which was based on the lunar year, Passover began on the evening of the fourteenth day of Nisan, which is to say fourteen days after the first full moon that fell on or followed the spring equinox. This full moon is called the 'paschal full moon' because it is used to calculate the date of Pascha. In the same eastern regions,[19] Christians also observed Easter according to the calculation based on the Julian calendar that was in force throughout the empire. According to this system, the paschal full moon could never occur before the spring equinox, which in the Julian calendar was March 21 in the east (using the Alexandrian standard) and March 25 in the west (using the Roman standard). As a result, whenever the Sunday following the Jewish Passover occurred before March 21, those Christians in the east who followed the Jewish calendar for calculating Easter would celebrate Easter a month before their fellow Christians who used the Julian calendar to determine its date.[20]

Take the year 322 as an example. The fourteenth of Nisan fell on March 20, and thus the Sunday following Passover was March 25. But since according to the Alexandrian calendar the paschal full moon could not occur before March 21, in 322 it was computed to fall a lunar month later on April 17 and thus Easter was celebrated on April 22. Therefore, in 322 some Christians of Syria and Mesopotamia, who followed the Jewish computation for Passover, would have celebrated Easter a full month before their co-religionists in the same regions and elsewhere in the empire. In 325, however, Passover fell on April 15 and the paschal full moon on April 13, so Christians throughout the empire would have celebrated Easter simultaneously on April 18.

The divergent practice which Constantine wanted to eradicate was not that of the 'Quartodecimans,' who ended their pre-Easter fast on

---

eron and S.G. Hall, *Eusebius: Life of Constantine* (Oxford: Clarendon Press, 1999), 259–261.

[18] Athanasius, *Syn.*, 5.1–2. Much the same is said in *Ad Afros*, 2, now considered a pseudo-Athanasian work; see Ch. Kannengiesser, "(Ps.) Athanasius, *Ad Afros* Examined," in H.C. Brennecke, E.L. Grasmück, and C. Markschies (eds.), *Logos: Festschrift für Luise Abramowski* (Berlin – New York: de Gruyter, 1993), 264–280.

[19] Socrates, *Hist. eccl.*, 1.8.2; Sozomen, *Hist. eccl.*, 1.16.4; see also F. Daunoy, "La question pascale au concile de Nicée," *Echos d'Orient* 28 (1925), 424–444, p. 427.

[20] See Cameron and Hall, *Life of Constantine, cit.*, 260, and Barnes, *Constantine and Eusebius, cit.*, 381 n. 86, who both cite other literature on the subject.

the Jewish Passover instead of on the following Sunday.[21] The Quartodeciman observance was widespread in the primitive church in Asia
Minor, but came into conflict with the tradition of celebrating Easter
not on the Jewish Passover, but on the following Sunday. This latter
tradition, heavily promoted by Roman Christians, became standard in
the third century. So by the early fourth century all Christians were
celebrating Easter on a Sunday. Accordingly, it was not the Quartodeciman practice that Constantine sought to eliminate, but rather the
so-called 'Protopaschite' practice which calculated the paschal full
moon according to the Jewish lunar calendar and not the Julian solar
calendar.[22] They are called 'Protopaschites' because they were the first
('proto') to celebrate Easter ('Pascha'), that is, they celebrated Easter a
full month before those Christians celebrating the feast according to
the Julian calendar. And so, this was the practice that was widespread
in the East during Constantine's reign, not Quartodecimanism.

While divergence in the celebration of Easter happened infre-
quently—for example, from Constantine's accession in 306 until 325
this would have happened only three times in 311, 316,[23] and 322—it
nonetheless prompted Constantine to act.[24] Oddly, neither the synodal
letter of Nicaea nor Constantine's letter states precisely what system for

---

[21] On this practice see Eusebius, *Hist. eccl.*, 5.23–24; Daunoy, "La question pascale,"
cit., 428–430; B. Lohse, *Das Passafest der Quartadecimaner* (Gütersloh: Bertlesmann,
1953); Huber, *Passa und Ostern, cit.*; and S. Hall, "The Origins of Easter," in *StPat*
15.1, Berlin 1984, 554–567.

[22] L. Duchesne, "La question de la Pâque au Concile de Nicée," *Revue des questions
historiques* 28 (1880), 5–42. Earlier scholars considered Quartodecimanism the issue
under debate at Nicaea; Duchesne was the first to show that this was not the case. His
position has found widespread acceptance; see, for example, Daunoy, "La question
pascale," *cit.*, 430, V. Grumel, "Le Problème de la date pascale au IIIe et IVe siècles,"
REByz 18 (1960), 163–178, G. Visonà, "Ostern / Osterfest / Osterpredigt I", in *TRE*
25, Berlin – New York, 1995, 517–530, and Cameron and Hall, *Life of Constantine,
cit.*, 260. But the older opinion persists; for example, Hefele, *Histoire des conciles, cit.*,
450–488.

[23] The divergence in the celebration of Easter in 316 happened for a different reason than that outlined above. In this year, Passover fell on Sunday March 25 and the
paschal full moon on March 24. Christians in Syria and Mesopotamia would have
celebrated Easter on the following Sunday, April 1, whereas elsewhere in the Roman
empire it was celebrated on March 25. Thus the celebrations occurred a week apart,
not a month apart.

[24] Listing only three occurrences of the divergence in the celebration of Easter in
the years 306–325 assumes that the date for the Jewish Passover was accurately calculated in these years. There is plenty of evidence, however, of frequent miscalculations;
see Cameron and Hall, *Life of Constantine, cit.*, 259–260. Accordingly, divergences
may have occurred more frequently.

calculating the date of Easter was decided upon at the council.[25] But we can deduce it from his letter and from Eusebius' *On the Feast of Pascha*. Eusebius recounts that when Constantine introduced the issue of the celebration of Easter, a quarter of the bishops—all of them easterners, no doubt mostly from Syria and Mesopotamia—resisted any alteration of their 'ancient custom' of the East for celebrating Easter. This 'ancient custom' was undoubtedly the Protopaschite practice. But the easterners were opposed by the majority of bishops—three-quarters of the assembly—from the other regions of the empire. Both Constantine and Eusebius refer to these bishops as from the northern, southern, and western regions of the empire.[26] Debate ensued, and eventually the easterners yielded, and agreed to celebrate Easter on the same day as all other Christians.[27] Presumably the bishops of Rome and Alexandria were asked to collaborate in determining the date of Easter each year.[28] In practice this meant that Easter would be celebrated throughout the empire on the Sunday following the new moon that occurred on or after the spring equinox in the Julian calendar.[29]

The uniformity in the celebration of Easter that Constantine hoped to secure at Nicaea proved elusive. In his letter Constantine is either unaware of or simply ignores how the different dates assigned for the spring equinox in the Alexandrian and Roman version of the Julian calendar could cause these churches to celebrate Easter on different days a week apart, as happened, for example, in 343.[30] Furthermore,

---

[25] Nor was the Nicene decision on Easter included in its twenty canons; cf. Daunoy, "La question pascale," *cit.*, 435–436.

[26] Eusebius, *VC*, 3.19.1; *Pasc.*, 14.

[27] Constantine reports a unanimous decision (*VC*, 3.18.1), but omits the foregoing debate mentioned in *Pasc.*, 14.

[28] Daunoy, "La question pascale," *cit.*, 440–444; Barnes, *Constantine and Eusebius, cit.*, 217; and di Berardino, "L'imperatore Costantino," *cit.*, 382–383. Daunoy, "La question pascale," *cit.*, 437–440, demonstrates that there is little evidence for the claim that the Council of Nicaea adopted the paschal cycle of nineteen years in use at Alexandria.

[29] Epiphanius (*Pan.*, 70.11.1–2) mentions three criteria for determining the 'harmonized' date of the Pascha, that is, according to the Nicene decree: "The Lord's Day is determined by the course of the sun, and the month by the course of the moon because of the Law's requirement that the Passover be slain on the fourteenth of the month, as the Law said. Thus the Passover may not be celebrated unless the day of the equinox is past" (ed. Holl – Dummer, GCS 37, p. 243, 24–244, 2; trans. F. Williams, *The Panarion of Epiphanius of Salamis* (Leiden – New York – Köln: Brill, 1994), 2.413).

[30] Daunoy, "La question pascale," *cit.*, 436–437; Barnes, *Constantine and Eusebius, cit.*, 217; and Hefele, *Histoire des conciles, cit.*, 464–465.

the Protopaschite practice of celebrating Easter on the Sunday after the Jewish Passover did not cease but continued in defiance of the Nicene decree. The first canon of the Council of Antioch in 341 threatened to excommunicate those who followed the Protopaschite observance.[31] This canon explicitly states that such a practice contravenes the Nicene decree endorsed by Constantine and "celebrates Pascha with the Jews."[32] Furthermore, Epiphanius notes that the Audians, a Syrian ascetical sect named after the early fourth-century Audius, were Protopaschite in their observance of Easter.[33] He even records some of the Audian taunts against the Nicene computation: "You abandoned the fathers' Paschal rite in Constantine's time from deference to the emperor, and changed the day to suit the emperor."[34] With even more sarcasm, the Audians claimed that the Nicene fathers had changed the date of Passover as a gift to Constantine on his vicennalia.[35] Audian resistance to the Nicene practice is a protest against imperial meddling in the church. In addition, John Chrysostom attacked Protopaschite practice in a homily delivered in Antioch in 386–387.[36] In the early fifth century, imperial laws were issued prohibiting the practice.[37] Just as Constantine's hope that Nicaea would mark the final resolution of the conflict between Arius and Alexander was quickly dashed, so too his plan for one celebration of the feast of Easter was unrealized.

The Context and Date of Eusebius' On the Feast of Pascha

It appears that the Nicene decree and imperial letter of 325 were not Constantine's final attempts at securing the observance of Easter

---

[31] P.-P. Joannou, *Discipline Générale Antique (IVᵉ–IXᵉ s.)*, t. I, 2, *Les canons des Synodes Particuliers* (Grottaferrata [Roma]: Tipografia Italo-Orientale "S. Nilo", 1962), 104–105. Also see Canon 7 of the Apostolic Canons from ca. 400 (*ibid.*, 11).

[32] Gk. μετὰ τῶν Ἰουδαίων ἐπιτελεῖν τὸ πάσχα (Joannou, *ibid.*, 104, 20–21).

[33] Epiphanius, *Pan.*, 70.8.2–14.4. For analysis of this passage, see Daunoy, "La question pascale," *cit.*, 432–434, and Hefele, *Histoire des conciles, cit.*, 479–488.

[34] Epiphanius, *Pan.* 70.9.3 (ed. Holl – Dummer, GCS 37, p. 241, 21–24; trans. Williams, *The Panarion, cit.*, 411).

[35] Epiphanius, *Pan.*, 70.9.4; Williams, *The Panarion, cit.*, 411 n. 29, cites Karl Holl's interpretation of this verse, followed here.

[36] *In eos qui primo pascha jejunant* (PG 48.861–872). On this homily, see M. Schatkin, "S. John Chrysostom's Homily on the Protopaschites: Introduction and Translation," in D. Neiman and M. Schatkin (eds.), *The Heritage of the Early Church* (OCA 195; Roma: Pontificium Institutum Studiorum Orientalium, 1973), 167–186.

[37] *Codex Theodosianus*, 16.6.6.1 (21 March 413) and 16.10.24 (8 June 423). The former was directed against Novatianists.

on a single day. Around 335, Constantine wrote a letter to Eusebius thanking him for sending him a treatise he had written on Easter, and Eusebius later included this letter in his *Life of Constantine*.[38] Both the contents of this letter of Constantine and Eusebius' comments upon it suggest (1) that Eusebius' treatise on Easter was polemical, aimed at swaying opponents of the Nicene decree, and (2) that Constantine himself had asked Eusebius to write the treatise.

Before inserting a copy of the emperor's letter, Eusebius writes: "After we had addressed to him a mystical explanation of the account of the festival, the reply with which he honored us in response may be learnt by reading the letter itself, as follows."[39] In this letter, Constantine praises Eusebius for speaking "worthily of the mysteries of Christ" and interpreting "in a suitable way the dispute about and origin of Pascha, and its beneficial and painful fulfillment."[40] Constantine notes that he has read the book himself and, in accordance with Eusebius' own desire, ordered it to be disseminated, both in its original Greek and in a Latin translation.[41] He commends Eusebius' erudition and requests additional treatises from his pen.[42]

By saying that he "addressed" (προσφωνησάς) his treatise to Constantine, Eusebius could mean nothing more than that he decided to write on Easter and dedicated it to the emperor, whom he knew was concerned with its observance. But from the emperor's response, it seems more likely that Constantine requested Eusebius to write it. The fact that he read it himself, as if eagerly waiting for it, and had it disseminated both in its original Greek and in a Latin translation, appears to indicate that he had requested it as the basis of another attempt to resolve the 'dispute' over the date of Easter. When Constantine says that he has disseminated the treatise according to Eusebius' wishes, it could hardly be the case the emperor is a cog in the bishop's plans;

---

[38] Eusebius, *VC*, 4.34–35. For the date, see T.D. Barnes, "Panegyric, History, and Hagiography in Eusebius' Life of Constantine," in R. Williams (ed.), *The Making of Orthodoxy: Essays in Honour of Henry Chadwick* (Cambridge: Cambridge University Press, 1989), 94–123, p. 112, and Cameron and Hall, *Life of Constantine, cit.*, 326. On this letter, see Dörries, *Das Selbstzeugnis Kaiser Konstantinus, cit.*, 81–82, and Danieli, *I documenti costantiniani, cit.*, 169–170.

[39] Eusebius, *VC*, 4.34 (ed. Winkelmann, GCS 7/1, p. 133, 5–7; trans. Cameron and Hall, *Life of Constantine, cit.*, 166).

[40] Eusebius, *VC*, 4.35.1 (ed. Winkelmann, GCS 7/1, p. 133, 10–12; trans. [slightly modified] Cameron and Hall, *Life of Constantine, cit.*, 166).

[41] Eusebius, *VC*, 4.35.2–3.

[42] Eusebius, *VC*, 4.35.3.

rather, the emperor is minimizing his role in the execution of his own agenda. It is more likely that he commissioned the treatise from Eusebius intending to disseminate it throughout the empire in both languages. Constantine's praise of Eusebius' learning points to the reason that the emperor initially asked the bishop to write the work: Eusebius was one of the leading bishops and one of the most accomplished Christian scholars of his era. Constantine must have thought that Eusebius' ecclesio-political prominence and his erudition would have been persuasive to those still hesitant to accept the new Easter policy. Hence it seems likely that Eusebius wrote his treatise on Easter at the request of Constantine in a second attempt on the part of the emperor to promote the Nicene Easter observance.

Furthermore, Eusebius and Constantine must be referring to the fragment entitled *On the Feast of Pascha*.[43] The contents of the extant Eusebian fragment correspond exactly to how Eusebius describes the treatise he wrote and how Constantine describes the treatise he received. In *On the Feast of Pascha* Eusebius speaks of the Jewish prescriptions for Passover (*Pasc.*, 1) and then gives a long explanation of how these ritual prescriptions are types fulfilled by Christ in his passion and mystically celebrated by Christians at Easter, eliminating the need for the Jewish observances (*Pasc.*, 2–13). This first part of the fragment is thus the "mystical explanation" mentioned by Eusebius and "the mysteries of Christ" mentioned by Constantine. The fragment concludes with an exegetical discussion of why Jesus did not celebrate Pascha on the same day as the Jews (*Pasc.*, 14–21), which begins with an account of the Nicene decision (*Pasc.*, 14). This indicates the polemical context of Eusebius' treatise: it is aimed at convincing opponents of the Nicene decree to accept it. Constantine seems to have been pointing to this second part of the treatise when he said that Eusebius had interpreted "in a suitable way the dispute about and origin of Pascha." Therefore the contents of the treatise, as described by Constantine, match perfectly the contents of *On the Feast of Pascha*.

Therefore, *On the Feast of Pascha* must date to somewhere between the Council of Nicaea in 325 and Constantine's letter to Eusebius in

---

[43] This was the opinion of Angelo Mai (see PG 24.693–694), who was followed by Quasten, *Patrology, cit.*, 3.339. Cameron and Hall (*Life of Constantine, cit.*, 326) maintain that the treatise was lost. Note that Mai entitled the fragment based on *VC*, 4.34, where Eusebius describes it as "on the most holy feast of Pascha."

335.[44] Since Constantine's letter to Eusebius thanking him for the treatise was written in 335, it is likely that it was composed shortly before this. Constantine may have planned for a renewed attempt at securing unity in the celebration of Easter during his tricennalia, much as his efforts at the time of Nicaea coincided with his vicennalia. In order to disseminate Eusebius' Easter treatise in both Latin and Greek during the tricennalia, Constantine would have had to initiate his plan some time before it. So Eusebius most likely composed *On the Feast of Pascha* around 333–335.

Constantine's dissemination of the treatise in both Latin and Greek underscores his belief in its usefulness for promoting the imperial agenda. I suggest that in this fragment Eusebius promotes the imperial agenda by drawing on some of the arguments used by Constantine in his letter on Easter written at Nicaea and provides a solid theological and scriptural basis for the claims made therein. As such, it is both an endorsement of the emperor's views and a more persuasive presentation of them. In what follows, I will examine in more detail the arguments that Constantine used in his letter announcing the Nicene decision for a single celebration of Easter and demonstrate how Eusebius in *On the Feast of Pascha* makes similar arguments, in order to prove that Eusebius' treatise was intended to promote Constantine's Easter policy.

THE ARGUMENTS OF CONSTANTINE'S LETTER ON EASTER

In his letter Constantine makes three distinct arguments for a single observance of Easter: (1) it is improper for Christians to follow Jewish calculations for the celebration of their most important festival when the Savior has appointed the proper time for it, (2) it eradicates the scandal of discordant practices and promotes ecclesiastical unity, and (3) it reflects the imperial and divine will.

Constantine's main reason for wanting Easter to be celebrated on the same day throughout the empire was that the Protopaschites were

---

[44] D.S. Wallace-Hadrill twice dates *De solemnitate paschali*: (1) between Nicaea in 325 and Constantine's death in 337 and (2) 325; see his *Eusebius of Caesarea* (London: Mowbray, 1960), 32 and 57. Quasten (*Patrology, cit.*, 3.340) dates it to "before the Emperor's tricennalia (335)."

following Jewish customs.[45] He deals with this issue first in his letter. Constantine wanted Christians to abandon the Jewish calculation
because "having sullied their own hands with a heinous crime, such
bloodstained men are as one might expect mentally blind."[46] "What
could those people calculate correctly," continues Constantine, "when
after that murder of the Lord, after the parricide, they have taken leave
of their sense, and are moved, not by any rational principle, but by an
uncontrolled impulse, wherever their internal frenzy may lead them?"[47]
These claims of Jewish mental deficiency are made to support Constantine's contention that Jewish calendrical calculations are inaccurate.
To demonstrate his position, Constantine points to the Jewish practice
of observing the Pascha a second time in the same year—something
which Christians would never do.[48] What he seems to mean by this is
that sometimes in successive calendar years the Jews observed Pascha
after the spring equinox in the first year and before the spring equinox
in the second year, thereby celebrating two Paschas in the same *solar*
year.[49] This comment of Constantine incontrovertibly indicates that
he was concerned with putting an end to the Protopaschite practice.
Thus, because the Jews are rabid criminals without capacity for logical
thought, Constantine sees Christian dependency on Jewish calculations as inappropriate and humiliating. Therefore Christians should
not associate with such sinners. Constantine abhors any commonal-
ity between Christians and Jews: "Let there be nothing in common
between you and the detestable mob of Jews!"[50] Michael Hollerich has
remarked that Constantine took matters of ritual very seriously and
that "the emperor was deeply convinced that cultic uniformity was

---

[45] Eusebius, *VC*, 3.18.2–4.

[46] Eusebius, *VC*, 3.18.2 (ed. Winkelmann, GCS 7/1, p. 90, 16–17; trans. Cameron
and Hall, *Life of Constantine, cit.*, 128).

[47] Eusebius, *VC*, 3.18.4 (ed. Winkelmann, GCS 7/1, p. 90,27–91,2; trans. Cameron
and Hall, *Life of Constantine, cit.*, 128).

[48] Eusebius, *VC*, 1 3.18.4.

[49] The same point is made by Epiphanius in *Pan.*, 70.11.5–6; see also Cameron and
Hall, *Life of Constantine, cit.*, 269–270. Epiphanius adds the observation that if two
Paschas are celebrated in one solar year, there will be no celebration of Pascha in the
following solar year.

[50] Eusebius, *VC*, 3.18.2 (ed. Winkelmann, GCS 7/1, p. 90, 21; trans. Cameron and
Hall, *Life of Constantine, cit.*, 128); see also *VC*, 3.19.1.

essential to the church's integrity, and the religious commerce with the Jews jeopardized that integrity."[51]

Yet Constantine is making another point as well. When one gets past the bile of his anti-Jewish invective, it becomes clear that he was also arguing that the Christians were already in possession of a better method of calculation that was established by the Savior himself. "We have received from the Savior another way," writes Constantine, "a course is open to our most holy religion that is both lawful and proper."[52] Christians have kept this "truer system" from "the first day of the Passion to the present."[53] The day to celebrate the feast was instituted by Christ himself.[54] Since Easter celebrates the day of the passion of Christ, Christ himself established the precedent for the "decent system" for calculating the day of Easter.[55] Hence it makes no sense for Christians to follow the Jewish calculation when the Savior has already supplied them with the proper time for observing Pascha.

Furthermore, Constantine viewed the discrepant observance of Easter as inimical to ecclesiastical unity for two reasons. The first was the scandal of some Christians feasting while others were fasting. "How dreadful and unseemly it is," said Constantine, "that on the same days some should be attending to their fasts while others are holding drinking parties, and that after the days of Pascha some should be busy with feasts and recreations while others are dedicating themselves to the prescribed fasts."[56] In other words, Protopaschites would have begun their Easter celebrations with food and drink while other Christians were still observing their Lenten austerities. This was an obvious sign of church disunity, whereas a common celebration would express that the universal church is one.[57] Secondly, Constantine objected to the discrepancy on what we might call "historical" grounds. Constantine

---

[51] Hollerich, *Eusebius of Caesarea's Commentary on Isaiah, cit.,* 35–36. Hollerich also notes that in his Jewish legislation Constantine was concerned "to maintain a clear distance between Jews and Christians" (36)—a concern reflected in his letter on Easter.

[52] Eusebius, *VC,* 3.18.3 (ed. Winkelmann, GCS 7/1, p. 90, 22–23; trans. Cameron and Hall, *Life of Constantine, cit.,* 128).

[53] Eusebius, *VC,* 3.18.2 (ed. Winkelmann, GCS 7/1, p. 90, 18–19; trans. Cameron and Hall, *Life of Constantine, cit.,* 128).

[54] Eusebius, *VC,* 3.18.5.

[55] Eusebius, *VC,* 3.19.1.

[56] Eusebius, *VC,* 3.18.6 (ed. Winkelmann, GCS 7/1, p. 90, 17–20; trans. Cameron and Hall, *Life of Constantine, cit.,* 129). See also Eusebius, *VC,* 3.5.2.

[57] Eusebius, *VC,* 3.18.5.

thought that, because the Savior's resurrection took place on one particular day, the feast which celebrated this liberation of humanity should also be celebrated on one particular day: "our Savior has handed down to us that the day of our liberation is one, which is to say the day of his most holy passion, and he wants his universal church to be one."[58] This is a variation of the argument advanced in the synodal letter of the Council of Arles, as noted above. In the years after the Council of Nicaea, its decree on Easter was viewed as an instance of Constantine's promotion of ecclesiastical unity.[59]

Finally, Constantine also claims that the Nicene method of calculating Easter has divine and imperial approbation.[60] Constantine's argument for the divine approval of the Nicene method stems from the fact the Council of Nicaea decided that the whole empire should follow it.[61] "Accept gladly the heavenly grace and this truly divine command," Constantine exhorts the recipients of his letter, "for all the business transacted in the holy assemblies of bishops has reference to the divine will."[62] Constantine views the unanimous decision of the bishops on this matter a sign of divine providence.[63] Constantine also argues for a single celebration of Easter because it reflects his own imperial will.[64] Hence Constantine's Easter agenda is part of a more comprehensive policy of consensus in the ecclesio-political sphere: one God, one emperor, one empire, one church, united in both belief and practice according to a minimal set of standards.[65]

---

[58] Eusebius, *VC*, 3.18.5 (ed. Winkelmann, GCS 7/1, p. 91, 11–14; my translation).

[59] See Epiphanius, *Pan.*, 70.9.5–6, where he responds to Protopaschite resistance to the computational system implemented at Nicaea, and says that Constantine was concerned "for the unity of the church. [...] God accomplished two highly important things through Constantine [...] One was the gathering of an ecumenical council and the publication of the creed [...]. The other was their correction of the Passover for our unity's sake." See also *Pan.*, 70.14.4. This same sentiment is repeated in John Chrysostom's homily against the Protopaschite observance (PG 48.861–872).

[60] Di Berardino, "L'imperatore Costantino," *cit.*, 382.

[61] Eusebius, *VC*, 3.17.2, 3.18.6, and 3.20.1–2; see also Cameron and Hall, *Life of Constantine, cit.*, 269.

[62] Eusebius, *VC*, 3.20.1 (ed. Winkelmann, GCS 7/1, p. 92, 18–21; trans. Cameron and Hall, *Life of Constantine, cit.*, 129).

[63] Eusebius, *VC*, 3.17.2 and 3.18.1. Di Berardino, "L'imperatore Costantino," *cit.*, 382, holds that Constantine deploys the unanimous consensus of the Nicene fathers and the divine authority of the council as two distinct arguments for the adoption of the Nicene Easter policy. It seems to me, rather, that Constantine construes the unanimous consensus of the bishops as a sign of divine approbation.

[64] Eusebius, *VC*, 3.19.1 and 3.20.2.

[65] H.A. Drake, "Constantine and Consensus," *Church History* 64 (1995): 1–15, and *Id.*, *Constantine and the Bishops: The Politics of Intolerance* (Baltimore: The Johns Hopkins University Press, 2000).

In a summary of his letter, Constantine writes: "And to put the most important point concisely, by unanimous verdict it was determined that the most holy feast of Easter should be celebrated on one and the same day, since it is both improper that there should be a division about a matter of such great sanctity, and best to follow that option, in which there is no admixture of alien error and sin (i.e. from the Jews)."[66] This sentence nicely spells out Constantine's three reasons for a single celebration of Easter: (1) the divine will expressed by episcopal unanimity, (2) a concern for ecclesiastical unity, and (3) anti-Jewish sentiment.

Eusebius' Treatise on Easter and the Constantinian Agenda

In the extant portion of his treatise on Easter, Eusebius is wholly concerned with demonstrating that Christians are utterly separate from the Jews in how they observe the feast of Pascha. He does not, at least in the extant portion of the fragment, make an explicit appeal to ecclesiastical unity or to the divine or imperial will as Constantine had done. While Constantine's main objection to Protopaschite practice had been its dependence on the Jews in determining the date of Easter, Eusebius makes a wider anti-Jewish argument than Constantine. He discusses three main areas in which the Christian celebration of Pascha is fundamentally different from that of the Jews: (1) Christians experience the fulfillment of the prefigurations that the Jewish ritual observances of Pascha foreshadowed; (2) Christians celebrate Pascha every Sunday, not once per year; and (3) the Savior himself did not celebrate Pascha on the same day as the Jews. Hence Eusebius has added to Constantine's argument that the Savior set the precedent for the celebration of Pascha apart from the Jews.

Note too that Eusebius also engaged in anti-Jewish polemic much as Constantine had done, accusing the Jews of impurity, murder, and blood-guilt, and alluding to their mental deficiency and lack of truth.[67] But Eusebius did not adopt his negative attitude toward the Jews from Constantine; Eusebius was consistently anti-Jewish throughout his corpus, from his earliest writings, long before he wrote *On the Feast*

---

[66] Eusebius, *VC*, 3.19.2 (ed. Winkelmann, GCS 7/1, p. 92, 13–17; trans. Cameron and Hall, *Life of Constantine, cit.*, 129).

[67] See *Pasc.*, 14; 18–20.

of Pascha.[68] Eusebius and Constantine share an anti-Jewish stance that characterized many Christians of the early fourth century.[69] Hence while Eusebius endorses Constantine's anti-Jewish argument for the single celebration of Easter, he draws on a wider set of anti-Jewish ideas that he developed earlier to make a stronger (that is, a more theological and scriptural) argument than the emperor. Nonetheless, Eusebius' anti-Jewish sentiments do not match the level of the emperor's vitriol, both in the fragment of this treatise that we possess and elsewhere in his corpus.[70]

As mentioned above, *On the Feast of Pascha* contains an account of the debate at the Council of Nicaea over the system for calculating the date of Easter.[71] This narrative indicates the polemical context of the treatise: it is not only an endorsement of the Nicene decree, but also a scripturally-based argument for its correctness. Eusebius has accepted Constantine's anti-Jewish argument, expanded it by aligning it with his own anti-Jewish ideas, and set it on a solid scriptural and theological foundation. There are even striking similarities between Constantine's and Eusebius' account of the debate. Both refer to the fact that some eastern regions were opposed to the practice of observing Pascha in the northern, southern, and western parts of the empire. Similarly, both refer to the Jews as "slayers of the Lord" (κυριοκτόνοι) in the

---

[68] R. Grant, *Eusebius as Church Historian* (Oxford: Clarendon Press, 1980), 97–113; Barnes, *Constantine and Eusebius, cit.*, 171–172.181–186; A.P. Johnson, *Ethnicity and Argument in Eusebius' Praeparatio Evangelica* (Oxford: Oxford University Press, 2006), 107–109.114–119; and S. Inowlocki, *Eusebius and the Jewish Authors: his Citation Technique in an Apologetic Context* (AJEC 64; Leiden – Boston: Brill, 2006), 121–137. J. Ulrich, in his *Euseb von Caesarea und die Juden, cit.*, has called Eusebius' anti-Judaism into question. None of these authors incorporates *Pasc.* in their study of Eusebius' estimation of Judaism.

[69] Ulrich finds Constantine's anti-Judaism to be his own, not Eusebius'; see *Euseb von Caesarea und die Juden, cit.*, 239–254, esp. pp. 241–246. Michael Hollerich has suggested that Eusebius was very much aware of Constantine's hostility toward Judaism and his post-Nicene writings such as the *Commentary on Isaiah* may reflect "the need to state afresh the boundary between Judaism and Christianity, for the benefit of the new Christian emperor" (*Eusebius of Caesarea's Commentary on Isaiah, cit.*, 33). The same would hold true for *On the Feast of Pascha*. See also his "Eusebius as a Polemical Interpreter of Scripture" in H.W. Attridge and G. Hata (eds.), *Eusebius, Christianity, and Judaism* (Detroit: Wayne State University Press, 1992), 585–615, esp. p. 594ss.

[70] See Ulrich, *Euseb von Caesarea und die Juden, cit.*, 245: "im Vergleich zu Euseb hingegen ist Konstantins Einstellung zu den Juden, jedenfalls wenn man die Wortwahl im Osterfestbrief ernst nimmt, deutlich abschätziger als die des Bischofs von Caesarea."

[71] *Pasc.*, 14.

course of the account, though this likely reflects a shared tradition of labeling the Jews as such.[72] In addition, Eusebius highlights Constantine's central role in the debate, a point which Constantine himself makes elsewhere in his letter.[73] But note that while Constantine stresses the unanimity of the bishops in reaching the decision (part of his third argument), in line with his policy of consensus as mentioned above, Eusebius does not hide that agreement was only reached through debate. Hence while Eusebius may have been influenced by Constantine's account of the Council of Nicaea, he was not beholden to it, having himself been in attendance. Nonetheless, by including an account of the Council of Nicaea, even if it is not derived exclusively from Constantine's account, it is clear that Eusebius intended his Easter treatise to defend and win supporters for the Nicene decree.[74] He has taken up the Emperor's cause.

We return now to Eusebius' three arguments. First, the Hebrew prescriptions for Passover, which are observed by the Jews, are prefigurations and foreshadowings of things to come.[75] Christians have the fulfillment of these prefigurations in how they celebrate the Pascha. This argument constitutes the first part of *On the Feast of Pascha*. Eusebius begins by summarizing the ritual observances laid down by Moses, drawing mainly from the book of Exodus (*Pasc.*, 1). But the New Testament teaches us that all these are types; in particular, Christ

---

[72] *VC*, 3.19.1; *Pasc.*, 14. Eusebius uses the same word in reference to the Jews in *Hist. eccl.*, 2.1.1 and *VC*, 3.33.1 and 4.27.1. Constantine uses the cognate κυριοκτονία at *VC*, 3.18.4.

[73] *VC*, 3.17.2; *Pasc.*, 14.

[74] W.L. Peterson has argued that Eusebius' support of the Nicene decree on Easter represents a reversal of his previous sympathy for Quartodeciman observance; see his "Eusebius and the Paschal Controversy" in H.W. Attridge and G. Hata (eds.), *Eusebius, Christianity, and Judaism*, cit., 311–325. But his argument is marred on several counts: belief that the Nicene decree was against Quartodeciman rather than Protopaschite practice, a simplistic view of Eusebius' relation to Origen and Arius, as well as "the anachronistic attribution to Eusebius of an 'autocephalous' ecclesiology and an anti-Roman fixation" (Hollerich, *Eusebius of Caesarea's Commentary on Isaiah*, cit., 34).

[75] Eusebius employs his well-known distinction between Hebrews and Jews in *Pasc.* In *Pasc.*, 1–10 Eusebius contrasts Hebrews and Christians, but in *Pasc.*, 11–21, Jews and Christians. Recent scholarship has noted that Eusebius' distinctions between Hebrews and Jews are more complex, ambiguous, and permeable than is often assumed; see Hollerich, *Eusebius of Caesarea's Commentary on Isaiah*, cit., 117–124; Ulrich, *Euseb von Caesarea und die Juden*, cit., 57–68.79–88; Johnson, *Ethnicity and Argument*, cit., 94–125; and Inowlocki, *Eusebius and the Jewish Authors*, cit., 105–138. Eusebius' use of these ethnic descriptors in *Pasc.*, warrants further study; none of the studies just mentioned incorporates it.

is the Pascha who was sacrificed to take away the sin of the world (*Pasc.*, 2). Eusebius then explains what eating the Pascha, being sealed with blood, and other ritual observances really mean for Christians (*Pasc.*, 3). After an explanation of why spring is the most suitable time for Pascha based on its appropriate weather and the occurrence of the significant events of salvation history during it (*Pasc.*, 4–5), Eusebius discusses how the Passover is doubly fulfilled: by Christ in his passion and by realities that Christians experience even now (*Pasc.*, 6–7). Furthermore, Christians not only celebrate the true Passover, but their celebration of Lent and Pentecost also represent fulfillments of Jewish ritual observances (*Pasc.*, 8–10). Therefore, in every way Christians diverge from the Jews in celebrating their feasts.

Summing up this first argument, Eusebius explains why Moses laid down prescriptions for Pascha:

> Now the reason for the legislation of Moses concerning the Pascha is as follows: since those same Jews were going to lead the Lamb of God like a sheep to slaughter at no other time than at the time already mentioned, and he was going to suffer this for the common salvation of all humanity, God, in order to foreshadow what was going to happen through the symbols by way of prefiguration, commanded the Jews to sacrifice the perceptible lamb at that very time whenever it occurred in the yearly cycle (*Pasc.*, 11).

Hence the prescriptions of Moses were intended solely as a prefigurement of the Lord's passion. The Jews celebrated these rituals every year "until the reality was effected and the ancient prefigurations were terminated." After the passion of the Lord, only Christians observe "the true celebration of the mysteries," while the Jews cannot even retain a memory of the foreshadowings of these true realities because of the destruction of Jerusalem (*Pasc.*, 11). Thus the Jews have entirely missed the point of the Hebrew prescriptions for Pascha, whereas the Christians have penetrated their true meaning. Accordingly, Eusebius concludes, Jews and Christians have nothing in common when they observe Pascha—which is what Constantine hoped for and accused the Protopaschites of not doing.

Eusebius' second argument adopts a different tactic to make the same point: Jews and Christians are utterly divergent in their observance of Pascha because while Jews celebrate it once a year, Christians do so every Sunday: "The Jews, in accordance with Moses, sacrificed the lamb for Pascha only once a year, on the fourteenth day of the first month, toward evening. But we who are of the New Covenant hold our own Pascha on every Lord's day [Sunday]" (*Pasc.*, 12). Thus Christians experience the true fulfillments prefigured by the Jewish Pascha not once a year, but "continually" (ἀεί). Eusebius writes: "Continually we celebrate the Passover. For the word of the gospel wishes us to do all these things not once a year but continually and every day" (*Pasc.*, 12). He principally means the Eucharist: "On every Lord's Day [Sunday] we receive life through the sanctified body of the saving Pascha himself and our souls are sealed through his precious blood" (*Pasc.*, 21).[76] While the Christian practice of celebrating the Eucharist every Sunday may be tangential to the issue of when to celebrate Easter, Eusebius stresses this point in order to offer an additional way in which the Christian observance of Pascha diverges from the Jews.

In his third argument Eusebius takes up the other half of Constantine's anti-Jewish argument, that Christ himself established the celebration of Pascha apart from the Jews and accordingly Christians should follow the precedent of Christ. Eusebius' argument is largely exegetical. Eusebius aims to prove that, in the week Christ was crucified, the Jews celebrated Pascha on Friday (15 Nisan), while Christ did so on Thursday (14 Nisan). For the former, Eusebius appeals to John 18.28, which records the Jews' refusal to enter the Praetorium on Friday morning lest they defiled themselves before eating the Pascha that evening (*Pasc.*, 16, 18, 19). For the latter, Eusebius cites Luke 22.15, the passage which recounts Jesus, reclined at table with his disciples on Thursday, as saying, *With such desire I have desired to eat this Pascha with you!* (*Pasc.*, 16).

Eusebius interprets Christ's actions here as a conscious choice to depart from the Jews. Rather, he wanted to impart to his disciples "the new mystery of his New Covenant" (*Pasc.*, 17). Thus Christ himself established the precedent of celebrating Pascha apart from the Jews: "And so, continually thirsting for the salvation of all, the Word himself handed on the mystery by which all humans would celebrate the feast and confessed that this was what he desired" (*Pasc.*, 17). Christ needed to establish the observance of Pascha apart from the Jews because the Jewish Pascha was only applicable to a certain people (the Jews) and only held in a certain place (Jerusalem),[77] whereas "the new mystery of the New Covenant" was intended by Christ to be celebrated by all

---

[76] See also *Pasc.*, 12 and 19.
[77] A similar argument is made throughout *Dem. ev.*, 1–2; see especially 1.3.

peoples in all places (*Pasc.*, 17). Eusebius drives home his main argument with a rhetorical flourish:

> Do you see how at that time the Savior separated himself from the Jews and withdrew from Jewish blood-guilt? How he brought his disciples into union with himself and celebrated together with them the feast he desired to keep? Accordingly, we too should eat the Pascha with Christ (*Pasc.*, 19).

And so, Eusebius has set Constantine's claim that Christ himself established the date for the celebration on a solid scriptural foundation. Christians should celebrate Pascha, "not with the Jews" (*Pasc.*, 18), but rather "with Christ."

It turns out, however, that in keeping Pascha on Friday Eusebius thinks that the Jews have disobeyed their own law. For they ate the Pascha on fifteenth of Nisan (Friday) rather than the fourteenth (Thursday). This mistake on their part demonstrates how far removed from the truth the Jews are. "They were so preoccupied with the plot against our Savior that they were blinded by their wickedness and fell away from all truth" (*Pasc.*, 20). Hence it would be foolish to follow the Jews in their celebration of Pascha. Thus Eusebius once again echoes Constantine's anti-Jewish polemic.

While Eusebius' *On the Feast of Pascha* has much to say on the subject of the relation between the Jews' Pascha and Christians' Easter that does not specifically concern Protopaschite practice, at its core it elaborates Constantine's anti-Jewish argument against Protopaschite opponents of the Nicene decree on Easter observance. The inclusion of the account of the debate at the council alone suffices to indicate this. Yet Eusebius also adopts and adapts both halves of Constantine's anti-Jewish argument: (1) Christians should have nothing in common with Jews in the observance of Pascha, and (2) Christ has established the true system for its observance. Hence Eusebius has aligned his previous anti-Jewish ideas with Constantine's specific anti-Jewish argument for a single celebration of Easter. Yet Eusebius' explanations of how the Jewish Pascha was a prefiguration of Christian realities and of how Christians kept the Pascha weekly rather than yearly go beyond anything Constantine envisioned in his letter. Nonetheless, Constantine clearly indicates in his letter to Eusebius after receiving the Easter treatise that these "mystical explanations" strengthened his case. Therefore, I conclude, in *On the Feast of Pascha*, Eusebius has promoted the Constantinian agenda for a single celebration of Easter.

Translation

The following translation is based on PG 24.693–706. Roman numerals in square brackets correspond to the paragraph divisions printed by Migne. Arabic numerals indicate my own paragraphization and are intended to facilitate easier reference. *Italics* are used in the translation for scriptural citations or reminiscences; these are always followed by the scriptural reference in parentheses. References to scriptural allusions are given in the footnotes. At times words in square brackets have been supplied by the translator to improve the sense. In a few instances possible sources for Eusebius' ideas are noted.

Eusebius of Caesarea, *On the Feast of Pascha*

1. [I] Perhaps it would not be out of place to offer a fresh discussion of Pascha,[78] which the children of the Hebrews handed down as a prefiguration.[79] Ritually observing the foreshadowings of things to come, the Hebrews would begin their celebration of the feast of Pascha[80] by taking an offspring from the herd, whether it be a lamb or a sheep.[81] They sacrificed it themselves,[82] and then each of them first smeared its blood upon the lintels and doorposts of his own house,[83] blood-staining the sills and frames[84] of their doors in this manner to thwart the destroyer.[85] Then they used the sheep flesh for food,[86] girt their loins with a belt,[87] and participated in a meal of unleavened bread and partook bitter herbs.[88] After this, they passed over from one place to another place, from the land of Egypt to the desert. The Law prescribed

---

[78] Gr. πάσχα. The term can refer to the feast, the meal eaten during the feast, or the lamb eaten at the meal. I shall preserve Eusebius' ambiguous use of the term in this translation.

[79] Gr. ἐκονικῶς.

[80] Gr. φασέκ a transliteration of *psh* employed in the LXX mainly in 2 Chronicles 30; πάσχα is the normal transliteration employed in the LXX.

[81] See Ex 12.5.

[82] See Ex 12.6.

[83] See Ex 12.7.

[84] See 1 Kings 7.41.

[85] See Ex 12.13.

[86] See Ex 12.8–9.

[87] See Ex 12.11.

[88] See Ex 12.8.

that they should ritually observe all these things, as well as the slaughtering and the eating of the sheep. It is because of this passing over from Egypt that among the Hebrews this feast is called Passover.[89]

2. But while *these things happened to them as types, they were written for our sakes* (1 Cor 10.11). Indeed, Paul expounded the true interpretation of these well-known ancient types when he said: *Christ our Pascha has been sacrificed* (1 Cor 5.7). The Baptist communicated the reason for sacrificing him when he said: *Behold! The Lamb of God who takes away the sin of the world!* (Jn 1.29). For the body of the Savior was handed over to death as the sacrificial victim, as the prophylactic of all evils. Like a purifying agent, it took away the sin of the whole world. So it is that Isaiah cried out with great insight: *This one bears our sins, and suffers pain on our behalf* (Is 53.4).

3. [II] And so, when we nourish ourselves on the spiritual flesh of this sacrificial victim by whose blood the entire human race was saved—that is, when we nourish ourselves on his teaching and his proclamation of the kingdom of heaven—we feast on the rational delicacies of God.[90] When our bodies, the houses of our soul, are sealed by faith in his blood,[91] which paid the ransom[92] for our salvation, we drive from ourselves the whole race of treacherous demons. When we ritually observe the feast of the Passover, we engage in the passing over to divine things, as the ancient Hebrews once passed over from Egypt to the desert. So then, this is how we too embark upon that path untravelled and abandoned by many, banishing from the soul itself the ancient leaven of the error of disbelief and partaking the true bitter herbs through a lifestyle full of bitterness and suffering.

4. The time at which the feast is held is suitable, as it does not take place in the middle of winter, a gloomy time indeed. But neither was it appropriate for it to be held in the middle of summer, when the sun is at its highest and burns its hottest, depriving those relaxing in the country of beauty. Plus the hours of daylight are excessive, as they are double those of winter.[93] Nor is the season of autumn a pleasant

---

[89] On viewing Passover as commemorating a migration, or 'passing over,' see Philo, *Spec. Laws*, 2.145–146 and Origen, *On the Pascha*, 1.

[90] On the flesh of the sacrificial lamb as the Word of God, see Origen, *Homilies on Numbers*, 23.6.

[91] See Rm 3.25.

[92] See Mt 20.28; Mc 10.45.

[93] This refers to the ancient practice of dividing daylight into twelve hours in all seasons; as a result, an hour of daylight during the summer was much longer than the same in the winter.

thing to see, with the fields deprived and robbed of household fruits as though of their children. And so, that leaves us with spring, the season of joy. It gives guidance to every year, like the head does the body. Just when the sun traverses the first segment of its path, the moon with its fullness of light acts in parallel and restores the course of the night to the brightness of day. Spring brings an end to the terrifying thunderstorms of winter, brings an end to the long night intervals, and alters the water-tides. The air is fresh and day dawns with clear skies. The waters are calm for those at sea, and those traveling on land enjoy lovely weather. At this time the fields in the countryside are pregnant with seeds, and the trees teem with fruit and delight in God's gifts, and yield to farmers the blessing of recompense for their labors.

5. [III] This opportune time for the feast brought about destruction for the Egyptians, the friends of the demons, but freedom from evils for the Hebrews who were celebrating the feast for God. This same time was reserved even for the first creation of the universe, when the earth sprouted with growth, when the heavenly lights came into being, when heaven and earth and everything in them was fashioned.[94] It was also at this time that the Savior of the whole world accomplished the mystery of his own feast, and the great splendor bathed the world with the rays of true religion, and in fact this time seems to have embraced the birth of the world.

6. Also celebrated at this time was a type,[95] the ancient Pascha, which is also called the Passover. For the slaughter of the sheep is a symbol,[96] and the eating of the unleavened bread is a prefigurement.[97] All of these [figures] have been fulfilled in the Savior's feast. For he is the one who was the sheep, in that he clothed himself with a body. He is also the one who was the *sun of righteousness* (Mal 4.2). After all, the springtime of a divine and saving way of life has surely brought about a change in the conduct of men and women from the worse to the better.

7. Yet even now plagues sent by God are still being hurled down upon the Egyptian demons, and people inhabiting the earth everywhere

---

[94] See Gen 1.11–19. On Pascha as the anniversary of creation, see Philo, *Spec. Laws,* 2.150–152 and Pseudo-Hippolytus, *Homily on the Holy Pascha,* 17.1–3 (*Homélies pascales, 1. Une homélie inspirée du traité sur la pâque d'Hippolyte,* étude, éd. et trad. par P. Nautin [SC 27; Paris: Cerf, 1950, corrected reprint, *ibid.,* 2003]).

[95] Gr. τύπος.

[96] Gr. σύμβολον.

[97] Gr. εἰκόνα.

celebrate their freedom from the egregious error of disbelief in God.
Since those spirits who deceive the people have been checked, and
the evils of winter too, even now there is an abundance of new fruits
which crowns the church of God with the various gifts of the Holy
Spirit. In a word, the entire human race has been converted to our
side. All regions have experienced the cultivating Word's cultivation of
their soul and have sprouted forth the blossoms of virtue. In addition,
as those freed from the evils of darkness, we too have been counted
worthy of the knowledge of the light in the day of God.

8. [IV] Such are the new teachings, formerly obscured through figures, but lately brought to light! And each year, in fact, during the
times dictated by the cycles, we also renew the beginning of the feast.
In accordance with the zeal of the holy Moses and Elijah, we undertake
a forty-day period of training as pre-festivals[98] for preparing ourselves,[99]
but we repeat the feast itself for an enduring age.[100] So then, setting out
upon the journey toward God, we gird our loins securely with the belt
of self-control. Keeping the steps of our soul safe from stumbling as if
by wearing protective sandals, we prepare the course of our heavenly
calling.[101] Using the staff of the divine word by the power of prayer
to ward off the attack of our enemies, with all eagerness we pass over
the passageway that leads to heaven, hastening from here below to the
heavenly regions, from mortal to immortal life. For once we have thus
passed over these passovers from here safely and happily, another, better feast will come upon us. The children of the Hebrews call it by
the name of Pentecost, which is a prefiguration of the kingdom of
heaven.[102]

9. Now Moses says: *When you take up the sickle at harvest-time, you
shall count for yourself seven weeks, and you shall set before God new
loaves from the new harvests* (Deut 16.9+Ex 23.19; cf. Ex 34.26 and
Lev 23.16–17). Hence by a prophetic figure he was disclosing that the

---

[98] Gk. προέορτα. On the significance of this term, see C. Leonhard, *The Jewish
Pesach and the Origins of the Christian Easter* (Berlin – New York: de Gruyter, 2006),
146.

[99] See Ex 34.28; Deut 9.18; 1 Kings 19.8. This is one of the first explicit references
to Lent. Eusebius speaks of ascetical preparations for Easter in *Hist. eccl.*, 2.17.21.

[100] That is, continually through the year. The theme of the continual Pascha stems
from Origen, *Contra Cels.*, 8.22.

[101] See Act 20.24; 2 Tim 4.7; Heb 3.1.

[102] See Hippolytus, *On Elkanah and Anna*, cited by Theodoret of Cyrus, *Eranistes*,
florilegium 2.11.

harvest-time is the calling of the nations and that the *new loaves* are the souls offered to God through Christ, the churches coming over from the nations, on whose account this greatest of feasts is celebrated for our God, the lover of humanity. We are reaped by the rational sickles of the apostles, the churches of the whole world being gathered together under one as if on a threshing-floor; we are made into one body through a harmonious disposition of faith and seasoned with the salt of the teachings derived from the divine oracles; we are reborn through the water and the fire of the Holy Spirit. And so in this way we are offered to God through Christ as nourishing loaves that are a delight to eat and quite satisfying.

10. [V] Therefore, since the prophetic symbols of Moses give way to their realities by means of their more sacred fulfillment, we ourselves have learned to celebrate the feast that is more joyful still, as though we have been gathered to the Savior and enjoy his kingdom. For this reason we agree not to toil any longer [in ascetical labors] during this feast, but are taught to bring forth the likeness of the repose we hope for in heaven. Accordingly we neither bend the knee in our prayers, nor exhaust ourselves through fasting.[103] For it is not fitting that those deemed worthy of the resurrection should ever again fall upon the earth, nor that those liberated from their passions should suffer the same as those who are still enslaved. Therefore after Pascha we celebrate Pentecost for seven full weeks, having fought courageously during the earlier forty-day period of ascetical training before Pascha for six weeks. For six is the number of activity and working, which is why it is said that God made everything in six days.[104] It is fitting that the second feast follows upon the toils of the earlier period for seven weeks because our repose, which is symbolized by the number seven, is multiplied seven times seven.[105] Now it is true that the number of Pentecost, that is, fifty, does not fall within these [seven weeks]. But once the seven weeks have passed, on the first day after these [seven weeks], the most festive day of Christ's ascension seals them.[106] So then during the days of Holy Pentecost we fittingly imagine the repose to

---

[103] Not kneeling during Easter was consistently presented as apostolic; see Cantalamessa, *Easter in the Early Church, cit.*, 147, for references.

[104] See Gen 1.1–2.3; Ex 20.11; 31.17.

[105] On this interpretation of six and seven, see Origen, *Commentary on Matthew*, 14.5.

[106] Here and in *VC*, 4.64 Eusebius is dependent upon Philo, *Spec. Laws*, 2.176. This Eusebian passage is one of earliest pieces of evidence for the celebration of the ascension; see Huber, *Passa und Ostern, cit.*, 163–165.

come when we make our souls happy and rest our bodies, as though we were already dwelling with the Bridegroom himself and so are not able to fast.[107]

11. [VI] Because the sacred evangelists narrate that the passion of the Savior took place during the days of the Jewish Pascha of Unleavened Bread, no one can doubt it. Now the reason for the legislation of Moses concerning the Pascha is as follows: since those same Jews were going to lead the Lamb of God like a sheep to slaughter[108] at no other time than at the time already mentioned, and he was going to suffer this for the common salvation of all humanity, God, in order to foreshadow what was going to happen prefiguratively through symbols,[109] commanded the Jews to sacrifice the perceptible lamb at that very time whenever it occurred in the yearly cycle. The Jews did this every year until the reality was effected and the ancient prefigurations were terminated. Hence from that time the true celebration of the mysteries has prevailed among the nations, but the Jews no longer preserve even the memory of the symbols because they have been deprived of the place in which Law prescribed that they should perform the rites of the feast.[110] So then it is fitting that the sacred text of the gospels says that the Savior suffered at the time of the Jewish feast of Unleavened Bread. For it was at that very time that he was led like a sheep to the slaughter in accordance with the prophetic oracles.[111]

12. [VII] Furthermore, the Jews, in accordance with Moses, sacrificed the lamb for Pascha only once a year, on the fourteenth day of the first month, toward evening. But we who are of the New Covenant hold our own Pascha on every Lord's day [Sunday], and so continually we are filled with the body of the Savior and continually we share in the blood of the lamb. Continually the loins of our soul are girded with purity and self-control;[112] continually *our feet* are readied *with the equipment of the Gospel* (Eph 6.15); continually we have staves in our hands,[113] and rest upon *the shoot sprung forth from the root of Jesse*

---

[107] See Mt 9.15; Mc 2.19–20; Lc 5.34–35.

[108] See Is 53.7; Act 8.32.

[109] Gr. διὰ συμβόλων εἰκονικῶς.

[110] That is, Jerusalem.

[111] See Is 53.7; Act 8.32.

[112] See Ex 12.11; Lc 12.35; Eph 6.14; 1 Pet 1.13.

[113] See Ex 12.11 and 2 Kings 4.29–31. Girding the loins and taking one's staff in hand are indicative of a journey being undertaken for some resolute purpose. See also Mc 6.8, though the parallels in Mt 10.10 and Lc 9.3 advise against taking a staff.

(Is 11.1). Continually we are released from Egypt and continually we pursue the desert where humans can really live. Continually we set out upon the journey toward God and continually we celebrate the Passover. For the word of the gospel wishes us to do all these things not once a year but continually and every day.[114]

13. Hence each week we celebrate the feast of our Pascha on the day of our Savior and Lord, through whom we have been redeemed, performing the mysteries of the True Sheep. We do not circumcise the body with a knife, but remove every evil of the soul with the sharp blade of the word.[115] Nor do we use unleavened bread that is physical, but only that *of sincerity and truth* (1 Cor 5.8). For the grace which has freed us from the antiquated custom bestows upon us *the new man created by God* (Eph 4.24),[116] the new law, the new circumcision, the new Pascha, and makes us someone *who is a Jew inwardly* (Rom 2.29). In this way he has sent us forth liberated from the ancient times.

14. [VIII] When the Emperor most beloved by God was presiding over the Holy Synod from its midst and the issue concerning Pascha was brought forward for discussion, he said what he said. The group of bishops from all over the inhabited world who opposed the bishops of the East gained the day, being three times as numerous as their opponents. For the North together with the South and the people of the West found strength in their mutual agreement and contested those who defended the ancient custom of the East. At the end of the debate, the easterners yielded. And so, there came to be a single feast of Christ when the bishops of the East withdrew from the slayers of the Lord[117] and were joined to those who were of the same opinion. For nature attracts like to like.

15. But what if someone were to say that it is written: *On the first day of Unleavened Bread the disciples came to* the Savior *and said, "Where do you want us to prepare for you to eat the Pascha?"* (Mc 14.12+ Mt 26.17), and he sent those whom he commanded to *go to such-and-such a person and say: "At your house I shall observe the Pascha"* (Mt 26.18)? We would respond that these passages do not constitute

---

[114] The repeated use of 'continually' (ἀεί) in this paragraph spells out Eusebius' understanding of the typological significance of the Exodus narrative, as in *Pasc.*, 8–9; on this, see Huber, *Passa und Ostern, cit.*, 186–189.

[115] See Heb 4.12.

[116] See Eph 4.24.

[117] Eusebius' unfortunate designation for the Jews, which parallels Constantine (*VC*, 3.19.1). See n. 72 above.

a command; rather, they recount the historical event that happened at the time of the Passion of the Savior. It is one thing to narrate an ancient event, and it is another thing to establish a law and leave behind commandments for posterity.[118]

16. [IX] But at the time of his Passion the Savior did not celebrate the Pascha with the Jews. For he did not hold his Pascha with his disciples at the time when the Jews were sacrificing the sheep. After all, the Jews kept their Pascha on the Day of Preparation [Friday], the day on which the Savior suffered. That is why *they did not enter the Praetorium*; rather, *Pilate came out to them* (Jn 18.28–29). A whole day before, on the fifth day of the week [Thursday], the Savior reclined at table with his disciples and while he ate with them, he said: *With such desire I have desired to eat this Pascha with you!* (Lc 22.15). Do you see how the Savior did not eat the Pascha with the Jews? Because this practice was new and strange compared with the usual Jewish customs, he had to draw attention to it, saying: *With such desire I have desired to eat the Pascha with you before I suffer* (Lc 22.15).

17. For what he desired was not their ancient and antiquated customs, according to which he of course used to eat with the Jews. What he desired as suitable for himself was the new mystery of his New Covenant, which he was imparting to his disciples. For many prophets and righteous men before him desired to see the mysteries of the New Covenant.[119] And so, continually thirsting for the salvation of all, the Word himself handed on the mystery by which all humans would celebrate the feast and confessed that this was what he desired. The Pascha of Moses was not applicable to all nations of that time. For how could it be, when the Law prescribes that it should be celebrated in one place, which is to say in Jerusalem? Hence it was not what the Savior desired. What he desired as suitable for himself was the saving mystery of the New Covenant that was applicable to all humanity.

18. [X] Now before he suffered the Savior ate the Pascha with his disciples and celebrated the feast, but not with the Jews. After he finished celebrating the feast that evening, the high priests, accompanied by the traitor, came and *laid hands upon him* (Mt 26.50). For they

---

[118] Christ's observance of Pascha according to the Jewish reckoning does not imply that he commanded Christians to do the same; for a similar argument, see John Chrysostom, *Orations against the Jews*, 3.3. Below Eusebius explains that the real precedent of Christ is his celebration of Pascha apart from the Jews.

[119] See Mt 13.17; Lc 10.24.

were not eating the Pascha that evening; if they were, they would not
have had the time to arrest him. So then, once they had him in cus-
tody, they brought him to the house of Caiaphas, where they spent
the night. At dawn they gathered and examined him for the first time.
After these proceedings, they arose and brought him to Pilate in the
company of the mob.[120] It is then that the Scriptures say that *they did
not enter the Praetorium so that they might not be defiled* (Jn 18.28)
by entering under a Greek roof (as they thought would happen). And
so, remaining pure in this way, the abominably impure would eat the
Pascha when evening came. These Jews, *who strained out a gnat but
swallowed a camel* (Mt 23.24) and had defiled body and soul by their
murder of the Savior were afraid to enter under a Greek roof. And yet,
on the very day of the Passion they ate a Pascha that was destructive
to their souls, having demanded the Savior's blood not for themselves,
but against themselves. So it was not at this time that our Savior held
the feast that he desired, but the day before while he was reclining at
table with his disciples.[121]

19. [XI] Do you see how at that time the Savior separated himself from the Jews and withdrew from Jewish blood-guilt? How he
brought his disciples into union with himself and celebrated together
with them the feast he desired to keep? Accordingly, we too should eat
the Pascha with Christ, cleansing our mind of every *leaven of evil and
wickedness* and filling ourselves with the *unleavened bread of truth and
sincerity* (1 Cor 5.8), having within ourselves, in our souls, *one who is
a Jew inwardly* (Rm 2.29) and the true circumcision, and smearing the
doorposts of our mind with the blood of the sheep sacrificed for our
sake in order to avert the one who seeks to destroy us. And we do this
not once every year, but rather every week. The Day of Preparation
[Friday] should be a fast for us, a symbol of suffering, on account of
our previous sins and in memory of the Passion of the Savior.

20. [XII] From the beginning, I contend, the Jews have been mistaken about the truth. From that very time they have plotted against
Truth himself, driving from themselves the Word of Life. The text of
the sacred gospels clearly communicates this. For they testify that the
Lord ate the Pascha on the first day of Unleavened Bread. As Luke

---

[120] See Mt 26.57–68; 27.1–2; Mc 14.53–65; 15.1; Lc 22.66–23.1.
[121] On Eusebius' ingenious reconciliation of the synoptic and Johannine chronolo-
gies, see Cantalamessa, *Easter in the Early Church, cit.*, 166.

recounts, the Jews did not eat the Pascha when it was customary, on the day *on which the Pascha was supposed to be sacrificed* (Lc 22.7). Rather, they ate it the next day, the second day of Unleavened Bread and the fifteenth of the lunar month, the day on which our Savior was being judged by Pilate and *they did not enter the Praetorium* (Jn 18.28). So they did not eat the Pascha in accordance with the Law, on the first day of Unleavened Bread, the day *on which is was supposed to be sacrificed* (Lc 22.7). Otherwise they would have observed the Pascha with the Savior. Rather, at this very time they were so preoccupied with the plot against our Savior that they were blinded by their wickedness and fell away from all truth.

21. We celebrate the same mysteries throughout the year, and on every Sabbath-eve [Friday] we commemorate the Passion of the Savior by fasting. The apostles themselves were the first to keep this fast when the bridegroom was taken from them.[122] On every Lord's Day [Sunday] we receive life through the sanctified body of the saving Pascha himself and our souls are sealed through his precious blood.

---

[122] See Mt 9.15; Mc 2.20; Lc 5.35.

GOOD HEBREW, BAD HEBREW: CHRISTIANS AS *TRITON GENOS* IN EUSEBIUS' APOLOGETIC WRITINGS

Eduard Iricinschi

Eusebius of Caesarea composed *Praeparatio Evangelica* and *Demonstratio Evangelica* (hereafter *PE* and *DE*) between 313 and 324 CE, as apologetic works for the practice of verbal confrontation with Greeks and Jews.[1] This paper argues that, in his depiction of Christianity as a new ethnic and religious category, Eusebius made room for two new rhetorical locations in the Pauline divide between Greeks and Jews, namely the 'Christians' and 'Hebrews.' He placed fourth-century *Christianismos* in a process developing from the Hebrews of the past, through the intermediary phases of Greeks and Jews, to Christians as

---

[1] See Eusebius of Caesarea, *Preparation for the Gospel*, tr. E.H. Gifford (Oxford: Clarendon Press, 1903); *Id., The Proof of the Gospel*, tr. W.J. Ferrar (New York: The Macmillan Company, 1920). I use the *Sources Chrétiennes* critical edition of *Praeparatio Evangelica*: Eusèbe de Césarée, *La preparation évangélique*, ed. by J. Sirinelli, É. des Places et alii (Paris: Les Éditions du Cerf, 1974ss). For *Demonstratio Evangelica*, see Eusebius, *Werke, Die Demonstratio Evangelica*, ed. I.A. Heikel (GCS 23; Leipzig: Hinrichs, 1913), and Eusebio di Cesarea, *Dimostrazione Evangelica*, ed. P. Carrara (LCPM 29; Milano: Paoline, 2000). For the dates of *PE* and *DE*, I follow the chronological table in T.D. Barnes, *Constantine and Eusebius* (Cambridge, Mass.: Harvard University Press, 1981), 277–279. I am indebted in my research mostly to three recent works on Eusebius apologetic writings: S. Inowlocki, *Eusebius and the Jewish Authors. His Citation Technique in an Apologetic Context* (AJEC 64; Leiden – Boston: Brill, 2006); A.P. Johnson, *Ethnicity and Argument in Eusebius' Praeparatio Evangelica* (Oxford: Oxford University Press, 2006), and J.M. Schott's detailed analysis of the connections between Porphyry's writings and Eusebius' apologetics in his *Christianity, Empire and the Making of Religion in Late Antiquity* (Philadelphia: University of Pennsylvania Press, 2008), 136–165. Besides taking advantage of the wealth of books recently published on religious identity formation in late antiquity (see n. 4), this paper benefited from the rich discussions in Elaine Pagels' seminar on "Historiography and Construction of Identity in Late Antiquity," held in spring 2004 at Princeton University, and from the comments of Krisztina Szilágyi. To this, I must add the felicitous encounter with the questions raised by Ra'anan Boustan, Gregg Gardner, Kevin Osterloh, and Philippa Townsend at the Colloquium on "Antiquity in Antiquity" (Princeton University, 2006) and with those asked by the participants of the conference on "Reconsidering Eusebius: A Fresh Look at His Life, Work and Thought" (Centre Interdisciplinaire d'étude des Religions et de la Laïcité, Université libre de Bruxelles, 2008).

future 'Hebrews' drawn from all the nations. Eusebius' apologetic narrative described these new 'Hebrews,' the Christians, as superseding
the Jews and recovering the moral standards of the ancient Hebrews.

By 314, Diocletian had already reorganized the Roman Empire
into a hundred and four provinces, almost doubling their number,
by dividing up larger imperial administrative units.[2] In spite of this
geographic, ethnic, and religious diversity of the Roman Empire, Eusebius' focused only on how to distinguish Christians from the Greeks
and Jews. Why did Eusebius range Christians among those ἔθνη whose
geography cannot easily match Roman imperial administrative criteria: Greeks, Jews, and Hebrews?

For Eusebius, Christians, Jews, Greeks, and Hebrews represent rhetorical locations on the apologetic map of the Roman Empire, endowed
with deep cultural and religious connections. There weren't only Greeks
and Jews besides Christians in the Roman Empire of the fourth century; yet, *solely* these categories promoted a universally recognizable
narrative of descent.[3] Writing mainly for the pagan converts to Christianity, Eusebius grants the Greeks a higher chance to integrate in the
Christian *politeia*. On the other hand, he assigns the Jews a minor
role in the chain of transmitting the Torah and the other books of the
Hebrew Bible, as well as the 'genetic' information, from the Hebrews
to Jesus Christ, and subsequently to the Christians. As a result, Eusebius guarantees *Christianismos* a place in the οἰκουμένη whereby the
textual category of 'Hebrews' provided *Christianismos* with a secure,
archaic, pre-Jewish character, through 'ethnic argumentation.'[4]

---

[2] A.H.M. Jones, *The Later Roman Empire 284–602*, vol. 1 (Baltimore: The Johns
Hopkins University Press, 1964), 42–46. Eusebius mentions in *DE*, 3.7 other nations
inside and outside the Empire he was part of: Romans, Egyptians, Syrians, Greeks,
Scythians, Persians, Armenians, Chaldeans, and Indians.

[3] Johnson, *Ethnicity and Argument, cit.*, 55–152.

[4] See, for early Christian ethnic self-definition J. Lieu, *Christian Identity in the Jew-
ish and Graeco-Roman World* (Oxford: Oxford University Press, 2004); E. Iricinschi
and H. Zellentin, "Making Selves and Marking Others: Identity and Late Antique
Heresiologies" in *eid.*, eds., *Heresy and Identity in Late Antiquity* (Tübingen: Mohr
Siebeck, 2008), 1–27; D. Kimber Buell, *Why This New Race: Ethnic Reasoning in Early
Christianity* (New York: Columbia University Press, 2005); *Ead., Making Christians:
Clement of Alexandria and the Rhetoric of Legitimacy* (Princeton: Princeton University
Press, 1999); and Johnson, *Ethnicity and Argument, cit.* Various other recent works will
help the interested reader bridge the gap between ancient and modern forms of ethnic
reasoning: P. Townsend, *Another Race? Ethnicity, Universalism, and the Emergence
of Christianity* (PhD Dissertation, Princeton University, 2008); S. Kelley, *Racializing
Jesus: Race, Ideology and the Formation of Modern Biblical Scholarship* (New York:

Eusebius' ethnic mode of argumentation enabled him to create a history for Christians through the Hebrew connection and, at the same time, legitimize it in the cultural frame of 'Hellenicity.'[5] Ethnical ancientness and Greek education allowed Eusebius to depict Christians as belonging to a religious *taxis* at the same time old and new. This is not δεισιδαιμονία, irrational fear of gods, but a specific form of θεοσέβεια, worship of one God, which offers grounds for a thorough reorganization of the *polis*, and its administrative and political structures. Finally, Eusebius' use of *genos* and *ethnos* stresses the formative character of religious identity. His apologetic works describe the process of *becoming* a Christian *ethnos*, as a third religious entity between the Greeks and Jews. With Eusebius' apologetic writings, we are witnessing the process of redrawing the ethnical boundaries: if his Christian map did not represent the Roman territory in 320s, it put in place all the makings of a map for the Christian territory.

Aaron Johnson distinguishes two uses of *genos* in Eusebius' apologetic works: biological connections (Hebrews and Jews), and a common way of life (barbarian races), reflected in 'ethnical, religious, or cultural' associations between the members of a certain community.[6] As opposed to the rather focused use of *genos* in Eusebius' *Praeparatio*, Johnson detects a more liberal application of *ethnos*. Highly appropriate to describe newly converted Christians, *ethnos* for Eusebius covers ancestry, territory, language, and culture, and presents a strong connection to its corresponding theology (*politeuma*): "*Genos* is applied to the more specific, *ethne* to the less specific."[7]

In this paper I use 'ethnicity" and 'ethnic reasoning' to describe Eusebius' attempt to present 'Christianity' both as an ethnic *category* of a third kind (*triton genos)*, and as an 'imagined community.'[8]

Routledge, 2002); B. Isaac, *The Invention of Racism in Classical Antiquity* (Princeton: Princeton University Press, 2004); D.M. Goldberg, *The Curse of Ham: Race and Slavery in Early Judaism, Christianity, and Islam* (Princeton: Princeton University Press, 2003); and G.L. Byron, *Symbolic Blackness and Ethnic Difference in Early Christianity* (New York: Routledge, 2002).

[5] J.M. Hall, *Hellenicity: Between Ethnicity and Culture* (Chicago: University of Chicago Press, 2002).

[6] Johnson, *Ethnicity and Argument*, cit., 35–40.

[7] *Ibid.*, 40–51, esp. p. 50. Johnson finds that the conjunction of *genos* and *ethnos* generates a subtle play of meanings in Eusebius' *Praeparatio* (50).

[8] See below for more on the early Christian motive of the *third genus*. I borrowed the expression 'imagined communities' from Benedict Anderson's *Imagined Communities: Reflections on the Origins and Spread of Nationalism*, rev. ed. (London: Verso,

I argue that Eusebius 'imagined' his Mediterranean Christian communities as brought together by a myth of common descent, fictive
kinship, shared biblical history, and the *absence* of a territory.[9] In a
'naturalized understanding of kinship'[10] Eusebius described Christians
as direct descendents of the 'Hebrews' with whom they share a great
deal of biblical history. Eusebius also presented the *absence* of a clearly
delineated territory as an advantage for Christians, who came to Jesus
Christ as an army drawn from every nation (*PE*, I), and as a disadvan-
tage for Diaspora Jews, who could not follow the halakhic regulations
related to Palestine, Jerusalem, and the Temple (*DE* I). Thus, Eusebius
lent a sharp Christian contour to the 'Hebrews' in order to divorce
the Jews from their books and history. He also aligned the Christian
genos with the Romans, by establishing a common 'other': the Greeks.[11]
Since Eusebius delineated Greek and Hebrew narratives of descent *as*
arguments for a debate with 'Greeks' and 'Jews,' I argue that, in his
apologetic dyptich, they play the role of 'hollow categories'—ethnic
forms of classification derived from Pauline theological concerns and
extended to the description of Greco-Roman *paideia*.[12]

1991). Yet, I distance my use of it from his association of nationalism with kinship
and religion *solely* in modernity as a result of 'capitalism and print technology.' (46)
Following Caroline Johnson Hodge, I also hold that Eusebius 'created' Christian kinship through his apologetic writings: cf. Caroline Johnson Hodge, *If Sons, then Heirs:
A Study of Kinship and Ethnicity in the Letters of Paul* (Oxford: Oxford University
Press, 2007), 42. See also Johnson, *Ethnicity and Argument, cit.*, 25–54.
    [9] The main 'dimensions' of pre-modern ethnic communities include a collective
name, a common myth of descent, a shared history, a shared culture, an association
with a territory, and a certain degree of social solidarity; see A.D. Smith, *The Ethnic
Origins of Nations* (Oxford: Blackwell, 1986), 21–30. Later, Anthony Smith and John
Hutchinson amended the territorial feature into 'a link with a homeland' (J. Hutchinson & A.D. Smith (eds.), *Nationalism* (Oxford: Oxford University Press, 1996), 6–7.
See Jonathan Hall's similar use of this definition (*Hellenicity, cit.*, 9); Johnson adapted
the above taxonomy to Eusebius' case in *Ethnicity and Argument, cit.*, 25–33, esp.
p. 30.
    [10] Johnson Hodge, *If Sons, then Heirs, cit.*, 16.
    [11] Maren R. Niehoff argues that Philo ignored the real Greeks, contemporary with
him, rejected the Egyptians, and went along with the Roman project of assuming
Greek genealogies for ethnic purposes; *Ead., Philo on Jewish Identity and Culture*
(Tübingen: Mohr Siebeck, 2001), 60.
    [12] I use here British anthropologist Edwin Ardener's notion of 'hollow category,'
developed in his 1972 paper, "Language, Ethnicity, and Population," see E. Ardener,
The Voice of Prophecy and Other Essays (New York: Berghahn Books, 2007), 65–71.
Analyzing the African Bantu-speaking ethnicities, Ardener argues that matters of language and ethnicity codify the counting of population to a larger degree that usually
acknowledged. To describe the process by which discrete population units receive a
label and a place on the 'taxonomic place' between self-identification and identification

WHEN APOSTASY FEELS RIGHT

Early Christian apologists employed the motif of the *third genus* in order to claim that two major religious and ethnic entities, *Ioudaismos* and *Hellenismos*, exchanged their best identity features, i.e. worship (*theosebeia*), manner of life (*bios*), and culture (*paideia*), and saved them in a third taxonomic category, *Christianismos*. In the second and third century CE, writings such as *Kerygmata Petrou*, Aristide's *Apology*, and *The Letter to Diognetus* posited *Christianismos* not only as a fusion between *Ioudaismos* and *Hellenismos*, but also as a location from which it refuted both *Ioudaismos*, for failing to live up to prophetical expectations, and *Hellenismos*, for its plurality of gods.[13] In these texts, Greek identity functioned as a passport for Christian groups to enter the Graeco-Roman οἰκουμένη, while Jewish identity provided them with ancient books, biblical heroes, and an admirable

---

by others, Ardener crafts the term 'hollow categories.' To put it in Ardener's surprising prose: "In various places and times the categories 'Norman,' 'Pict,' 'Jew,' 'Gypsy,' 'Irishman' and many others may have become, or be becoming hollow—a mere smile surviving from the vanished Cheshire cat." (*ibid.*, pp. 69–70).

[13] *Kerygma Petri* (hereafter *KP*) is preserved in Clement's *Stromateis* (I.182; II.68.2; VI.39–43; VI.48.1.2.6; VI.128.1–3); see W. Schneemelcher, *New Testament Apocrypha*, vol. 2. *Writings Relating to the Apostles; Apocalypses and Related Subjects* (Louisville: John Knox Press, 1992), 34–41. Aristide's *Apology* is preserved fully in Syriac translation and only partially in Greek, Armenian, and Georgian. See Aristide, *Apologie*, introduction, textes critiques, traduction et commentaire par B. Pouderon, M.-J. Pierre, B. Outtier, M. Guiorgadzé (SC 470; Cerf: Paris, 2003), 42–43. Wilhelm Schneemelcher holds that Aristides, writing in 124/125, at Athens, could have known it or, at least, advanced positions very similar to those in *Kerygma Petri* (*New Testament Apocrypha*, vol. 2, *cit.*, p. 34). Judith Lieu advances the hypothesis that Aristide's *Apology* was composed in Asia Minor, based on the lack of a clear indication in the *Apology* or in Eusebius' *Church History* about it (Lieu, *Image and Reality, cit.*, 164–165). H.I. Marrou, the author of the critical edition of *Ad Diognetum* for the *Sources Chrétiennes* series (*À Diognète*, introduction, édition critique, traduction et commentaire (SC 33bis; Cerf: Paris, ²1965), dates the text to the second century, after Aristides' open letter (post 125) and before 200, leaning toward the end of the second century (*ibid.*, 249–263). Bart Ehrman, in his new edition of the Apostolic Fathers for the Loeb Classical Library, narrows this, and places *Ad Diognetum* as having being "written during the second half of the second century, possibly closer to the beginning than the end of the period"; see *The Apostolic Fathers*, vol. 2, edited and translated by B.D. Ehrman (LCL; Cambridge, Mass. – London: Harvard University Press, 2003), 127. While Ehrman does not venture to indicate any specific place of composition, Marrou clearly connects *Ad Diognetum* to the school of Alexandria.

way of life.[14] Thus, Jewish identity supplied the necessary elements for a Christian cultural critique of the initially coveted Greek identity.[15]

Judith Lieu places the roots of Christian identity as the third race in the apologetic understanding of second- and third-century Roman persecutions through the textual lenses of the earlier Jewish Maccabean experience.[16] She describes the apologetic uses of *triton genos* in early Christianity as attempts to "construct a new identity through textual rewriting" and, at the same time, as efforts to gain control over the process of labeling by reversing outsiders' branding and barring their access to further labeling.[17]

Writing in calmer times, after the end of the persecution in Asia Minor, Eusebius of Caesarea put a new spin on what was by then the two-century old theme of *triton genos*. Together, his *Praeparatio for the Gospel* (*Praeparatio Evangelica*, written between 313 and 318) and the *Proof of the Gospel* (*Demonstratio Evangelica*; 318–324) total twenty-five books and represent the most impressive apologetic efforts of the fourth century. In these works, the ethnic categories of 'Greeks' and 'those of the Circumcision' do not just set the limits for

---

[14] For 'Judaism as a school of self-mastery' and the Christian appropriation of this conception, see S.K. Stowers, *A Rereading of Romans: Justice, Jews, and Gentiles* (New Haven: Yale University Press, 1994), 42–82, esp. pp. 58–66.

[15] Adolph von Harnack's *Expansion of Christianity in the First Three Centuries* (New York: Putnam, 1904; English translation of *Mission und Ausbreitung des Christentums in den ersten Drei Jahrhunderten*, Leipzig: Hinrichs, 1902) holds that the separation between Judaism and Christianity marked the emergence of a distinct political and historical entity in the Roman Empire: the Jesus followers as 'new people' and the 'third race.' In Harnack's comprehensive chapter on the third race, the reader encounters a gripping vision, if not of the Hegelian *Geist* hovering omniscient over early Christian history and reconciling antithetic cultural formations, at least of the birth of a new and distinct social formation, Christianity, out of two other equally discrete units, Hellenism and Judaism. The clarity with which Harnack unearths the origins of "the historical and political consciousness of Christendom" in the creation of "the new people and the third race" powerfully resonates with the nineteen-century European striving toward national identity. For an analysis of the connection between late antique and medieval notions of group identity and German nationalism, see P.J. Geary, *The Myth of the Nations: The Medieval Origins of Europe* (Princeton – Oxford: Princeton University Press, 2002), esp. chapter 1, "A Poisoned Landscape: Ethnicity and Nationalism in the Nineteenth Century," pp. 15–40.

[16] J. Lieu, *Image and Reality: The Jews in the World of Christians in the Second Century* (Edinburg: T&T Clark, 1996), 168–169; see also p. 256: Lieu dissociates the genre of Martyr Acts from Jewish martyrological context: "There is no cry 'I am a Jew' in these other [i.e. the Jewish] traditions."

[17] Lieu, *Christian Identity in the Graeco-Roman World, cit.*, 259–66. See now P. Townsend, "Who Were the First Christians? Jews, Gentiles, and the *Christianoi*," in Iricinschi and Zellentin (eds.), *Heresy and Identity in Late Antiquity, cit.*, 212–230.

Eusebius' definition of Christian identity; they are categories of ethnic reasoning with which he operates a *nominal displacement*. Eusebius acknowledged that the Greeks' status carries higher chances to enter the new Christian *politeia*. He demoted the Jews' status, claiming that they had severed their ties with the Hebrews, following the Egyptian sojourn. Thus, the 'third race' discourse in Eusebius' apologetic writings involves appropriation and displacement of ethnic features. Eusebius employed the Pauline verse "neither Greek, nor Jew" (Gal 3.28) to define the Christian as being 'more than Greek,' due to the Hebrew God, and, at the same time, 'more than Jew,' due to the nations who became followers the Hebrew God. Eusebius weaved together these definitions into the ideal *politeia*, where Christians live as a social body among the Greeks and Romans, legitimized by Jewish ancient books, ethical practice, and a body of divine laws.

The Praeparation for the Gospel describes the nations as the addressees of God's message. The *logos* was dispensed like a ray of infinite light to all the peoples (ἐξ ἁπάντων ἐθνῶν), found equally worthy of the gift of his love, "be they Greeks or barbarians, men, women, or children, poor and rich, wise or uneducated, or even the household slaves, [...] because they are all of the same substance and nature."[18] Light is the natural medium through which the *logos* reaches every *ethnos* on earth; the *logos* itself is portrayed as a "ray of infinite light." Similarly, in Eusebius' *Ecclesiastical History* (hereafter *HE*, I.2.2), God's economy, the plan to infuse the *logos* into human history, begins with the light before the world (φῶς τὸ προκόσμιον) seen as both wisdom and the *logos* of God. Eusebius did not name the ἔθνη touched by the *logos*. Instead, in *Praeparatio* he described the nations according to the Pauline taxonomy (Gal 3.27–29), transforming a shorthand definition of οἰκουμένη as irreducible oppositions (Jew/Greek, slave/free, male/female) into the ideal framework for God's final plans for humanity. The Jews, or at least their earlier and better predecessors, the Hebrews, knew this all along. The Hebrews' children received from God the notion that all the nations will one day turn to the divinity of the Hebrew Bible: according to Eusebius, the *logos* brought this knowledge of God, announced early by pagan 'divine oracles,' to all the nations.[19]

---

[18] *PE*, I.1.6.1–10. Notable here is the absence of the Jews as the receivers of the infinite light of the *logos*.

[19] *PE*, I.1.10; cf. Ps 22.28–9; 46.10, Zeph 2.11.

After he identified the Greeks and Jews as his direct opponents, Eusebius introduced the readers of *Praeparatio* to the most likely questions to come from this double-headed enemy. "Let us then begin the *Praeparation* by bringing forward the arguments which will probably be used against us both by Greeks and by those of the Circumcision, and by every one who searches with exact inquiry into the opinion held among us."[20] His next lines come as a masterstroke of narrative ingenuity in the literary history of the *triton genos* motive. Eusebius imagined that his Greek opponent would ask for a definition of the name 'Christian.' "For in the first place anyone might naturally want to know who are we that have come forward to write. Are we Greeks or Barbarians? Or what can there be intermediate to these?[21] And what do we claim to be, not in regard to the name, because this is manifest to all, but in the manner and purpose of our life? For they would see that we agree neither with the opinions of the Greeks, nor with the customs of the Barbarians. What then may the strangeness in us be, and what the innovation of our life?"[22]

In this paragraph, Eusebius characterized the Christians as an 'intermediate class' between Greeks and Barbarians, without mentioning the Jews. He also referred to the theme of Christians as resident aliens, and reused the motif of "new way of worship" as an "innovative life." Furthermore, according to Eusebius, the Greek opponent would object to the "impious and atheistical" relinquishing of Greek and Barbarian ancestral gods, the main patrons of civic life in the οἰκουμένη. Eusebius' imaginary Greek opponent would perceive such a move as defection to "the foreign mythologies of the Jews," and also as adoption "of the doctrines of the impious enemies of all nations with unreasoning and unquestioning faith."[23]

Next, Eusebius moves to the apologetic topos of *triton genos*. In his introductory remarks to *Praeparatio Evangelica*, Eusebius makes his Greek opponent acknowledge the audacity and loneliness involved in the new vision of *Christianismos*. Next, he turns the Greek's questioning of Christian life into barely disguised admiration. The imaginary Greek interlocutor would praise Christians for "not even to adhere

---

[20] Gifford's version, *PE*, I.1.13.

[21] πότερον Ἕλληνες ἢ βάρβαροι, ἢ τί ἄν γένοιτο τούτων μέσον (*PE*, I.2.1).

[22] τί οὖν ἄν γένοιτο τὸ καθ᾽ ἡμᾶς ξένον καὶ τίς ὁ νεωτερισμὸς τοῦ βίου; (*PE*, I.2.1–2), Gifford's version, modified.

[23] *PE*, I.2.3–4; Gifford's version modified.

to the God who is honored among the Jews according to their customary rites, but to cut for themselves a new and solitary track, that keeps neither the ways of the Greeks not those of the Jews?"[24] This was not the first time that Eusebius used the image of a bold pioneer to attribute the virtue of courage to those who dare to explore new ways of worship. In the first edition of the *Historia Ecclesiastica*, written before 300, hence more than a decade before *Praeparatio*,[25] Eusebius describes his task as that of a historian who explores the virgin territories of the *ekklesia*. "We are the first to enter on the undertaking, as travelers on some desolate and untrodden way."[26]

What would the Jewish opponent say to Eusebius? "The Sons of the Hebrews" would express distress at the usage of their books by "strangers and aliens,"[27] the usurpation of their ancestral rights, and the appropriation and misuse of ancient prophecies regarding the coming of Messiah.[28] Lastly, they would disapprove of the Christian understanding of the Law. "But the most unreasonable thing of all is, that though we do not observe the customs of their Law as they do, but openly break the Law, we assume to ourselves the better rewards which have been promised to those who keep the Law."[29] Willamowitz believes that Eusebius fabricated these accusations. Yet, one may equally suspect that the Christian apologist had either borrowed them from a written text,[30] or attempted to refute them not once in his conversations with real Jews.[31]

Eusebius proceeded to include two more categories ('Hebrews' and 'Christian') into preexistent taxonomies such as Greek/Barbarian, a cultural dichotomy intensely politicized by the opposition Empire/ its borderlines,[32] or Greek/Jewish, an ethnical dichotomy utilized by

---

[24] καινὴν δέ τινα καὶ ἐρήμην ἀνοδίαν ἑαυτοῖς συντεμεῖν, μήτε τὰ Ἑλλήνων μήτε τὰ Ἰουδαίων φυλάττουσαν (*PE*, I.2.4), Gifford's version modified.

[25] T.D. Barnes, *Constantine and Eusebius*, cit., 277–279.

[26] ἐπεὶ καὶ πρῶτοι νῦν τῆς ὑποθέσεως ἐπιβάντες οἷά τινα ἐρήμην καὶ ἀτριβῆ ἰέναι ὁδὸν ἐγχειροῦμεν (*HE*, I.1.3), Kirsopp Lake's version.

[27] ἀλλόφυλοι ὄντες καὶ ἀλλογενεῖς (*PE*, I.2.5).

[28] *PE*, I.2.6.

[29] *PE*, I.2.6; Gifford's version.

[30] U. von Willamowitz-Moellendorff, "Ein Bruchstück aus der Schrift des Porphyrius gegen die Christen," *ZNW* (1900), 101–105. As for Eusebius' other major opponent, Porphyry, his apologetic nemesis, see Sébastien Morlet's paper in this volume.

[31] See A. Jacobs, *The Remains of the Jews: The Holy Land and Christian Empire in Late Antiquity* (Stanford, Ca.: Stanford University Press, 2004), 26–36.

[32] M. Simon, *Verus Israel: Étude sur les relations entre chrétiens et juifs dans l'empire romain (135–425)* (Paris: de Boccard, 1964), 137.

previous Greek Christian apologists. In his new fourfold design, the
Hebrew prophets stand in stark opposition to the Jews and in direct
connection to the Christians. These new Hebrews supersede the Jews
and recover the older, higher moral standards of the ancient Hebrews,
while the Jews diverged from these, and having ignored their own
prophets, put Jesus to death. On the other hand, the *nations* displace
the older dichotomy Greek/Barbarian, breaking the borders of the
Roman Empire to create a new *ethnos*.

The οἰκουμένη itself became a better place to live beginning with the
times of Jesus Christ and Augustus. For Eusebius, the social and political chaos that pitted "nations against nations," in cities governed by
"democracy," "tyrants," or just a "multitude of rulers," vanished when
"Augustus became sole ruler at the time of our Savior's appearance"
(*PE*, I. 4. 4), turning *polyarchia* into monarchy just as Jesus turned
polytheism into monotheism.[33] As for the tribes living beyond the
reach of imperial civility, those Persians who "marry their mothers,"
those Scythians who "feed on human flesh," or those Barbarians "who
have incestuous union with daughters and sisters," or "madly lust after
men," they have all abandoned these immemorial customs under "the
unique salutary law of the power of the gospel."[34]

The providential plan enacted in human civilization by the *logos*
established Augustus and Jesus Christ as forerunners of Constantine,
the first Christian emperor.[35] It also educated the Barbarians out of

---

[33] See D. Martin, *Inventing Superstition from the Hippocratics to the Christians*
(Cambridge, Mass.: Harvard University Press, 2004), 218, discussing *DE*, VII.2.334
and *In Praise of Constantine* 16.5–7: "The reason Augustus signifies universal unity
is because he established monarchy for the world. And monarchy, for Eusebius, is
always equated with monotheism, whereas 'polyarchy' represents polytheism." For
a more elaborate, albeit totally opposite perspective, see Johnson's position: "The
focus is not upon Augustus in the synchronism: it is the spread of Christ's teaching
throughout the world, not the conquest of Rome that causes the profound changes
in customs and ways of life that Eusebius depicts" (Johnson, *Ethnicity and Argument*,
cit., 170–197, esp. p. 185).

[34] *PE*, I.4.6–8, Gifford's version.

[35] See H.A. Drake, *Constantine and the Bishops: The Politics of Intolerance* (Baltimore and London: The Johns Hopkins University Press, 2000), 363–364, for the
chronological correlation between Jesus Christ and Augustus as "one of the most
influential equations in the history of political theory: polytheism equals pluralism,
which equals strife and, of course, moral degeneracy." For Eusebius' "patterning of
Constantine on Moses" see Eusebius, *Life of Constantine*, Introduction, translation,
and commentary by A. Cameron and S.G. Hall (Oxford: Oxford University Press),
35–39; and T.D. Barnes, *Constantine and Eusebius* (Cambridge, Mass.: Harvard University Press, 1981), 271.

their ancestral customs, transforming them and the Greeks into the Christian nation. The energy behind this civilizing process takes the shape of the Christian message formulated in Stoic expressions for a Hellenized audience: it is the "high philosophy" that leads to a "high degree of philosophic life" (*PE*, I.4.9–10). Eusebius borrowed Philo's and Josephus' Hellenized philosophical argument according to which a set of monotheistic notions will unfailingly set the grounds for a more ethical, even ascetical, life wholly denuded of superstitions. "For what do you think of the fact that it [our doctrine] induced the whole human race, not only Greeks, but also the most savage Barbarians, and those who dwell in the utmost parts of the earth, to refrain from their irrational brutality and adopt the opinions of a philosophy?"[36] Eusebius opened his *Praeparatio* with a defensive remark against those who accuse Christians of converting by mere irrational faith: "Those who desire the name [of Christian] confirm their opinion by an unreasoning faith and an assent without examination."[37] He counters this accusation by presenting Christian doctrines as the quintessence of highly rigorous philosophy, and by relegating the argument by faith to the "ignorant and uneducated."[38]

Who are then Eusebius' Christians? Eusebius came full circle to answer both his Greek and Jewish opponents. "Well then, that being Greek by race, and Greek by sentiment, and gathered out of all sorts of nations,[39] like chosen men of a newly enlisted army, we have become deserters from the superstitions of our ancestors."[40] Eusebius made use of the Greek element, present in 'genetic' composition, in Hellenic education, and everywhere else in the nations, as an argument against Greek superstitions themselves. "But also that," Eusebius continues "though adhering to the Jewish books and collecting out of their prophecies the greater part of our doctrine, we no longer think

---

[36] ὁποῖον δέ σοι εἶναι δοκεῖ τὸ πᾶν γένος ἀνθρώπων, οὐ μόνον Ἑλλήνων, ἀλλὰ καὶ τῶν ἀνημερωτάτων βαρβάρων καὶ τῶν ἐν ταῖς ἐσχατιαῖς τῆς γῆς οἰκούντων τῆς μὲν ἀλόγου θηριωδίας ἀνασχεῖν, δόξας δὲ φιλοσόφους ἀναλαβεῖν παρασκευάσαι; (*PE*, I.4.13–14), Gifford's version modified.

[37] *PE*, I.1.11, Gifford's version.

[38] *PE*, I.5.3.

[39] ὅτι μὲν οὖν τὸ γένος Ἕλληνες ὄντες καὶ τὰ Ἑλλήνων φρονοῦντες ἐκ παντοίων τε ἐθνῶν ὡς ἂν νεολέκτου στρατιᾶς λογάδες συνειλεγμένοι τῆς πατρίου δεισιδαιμονίας ἀποστάται καθεστήκαμεν (*PE*, I.5.10), Gifford's version.

[40] *PE*, I.5.10, Gifford's version.

it agreeable to live in like manner with those of the Circumcision."[41]
In a double rhetorical move, Eusebius appropriated the Jewish books
and their prophetic voices and displaced their way of life. I use 'displace' deliberately here, and not 'replace,' since Eusebius used the
Jewish argument that monotheism lends austerity to the subsequent
lifestyle.

What is Christianity for Eusebius? The shadow of *triton genos* hov-
ered over Eusebius' text from its very beginning. At this point, he
came to acknowledge it, rename it, and accommodate it to his own
rhetorical needs. "It will be right [...] in conclusion, to state what is
our account of the Gospel argument, and what Christianity should
properly be called, since *it's neither Hellenism nor Judaism, but a new
and true kind of divine philosophy* [my italics, E.I.], bringing evidence
of its novelty from its very name."[42] Eusebius isolated *Christianismos*
as a logically distinct category and discretely social entity—a process
that postmodern historians would call 'inventing Christianness'—and
established it as related to, yet clearly different from, *Hellenismos* and
Ioudaismos. In the above paragraph, Eusebius' search for historical
coherence transformed confused polytheism into focused monotheism, bad customs into good manners, Greek and Barbarian polyarchy into Roman monarchy, and human philosophy into *theosophia*,
applied divine wisdom. In this process *triton genos* becomes καινὴ καὶ
ἀληθὴς θεοσοφία, a new and true divine philosophy.

For Eusebius, breaking the patrilinear connections to the culture,
religion, and urban politics of the Greek forefathers represented the
indispensable condition for formative Christianity. In the beginning
of *Praeparatio*, Eusebius imagined Greek Christians—"Greeks by race
and by sentiment"—coming out of all the nations as deserters from
various superstitions who gathered to form a single army.[43] Under-
scoring a strong connection between the theology of the Greeks and
the theology of the Egyptians in order to downplay Greek theology,
Eusebius further presented the Christians as "apostates and deserters
from the secrets of Greek and Egyptian theology."[44]

---

[41] ἀλλὰ καὶ ὅτι ταῖς ἰουδαικαῖς βίβλοις προσανέχοντες κἀκ τῶν παρ᾽ αὐτοῖς
προφητειῶν τὰ λεῖστα τοῦ καθ᾽ ἡμᾶς λόγου συνάγοντες οὐκέθ᾽ ὁμοίως ζῆν τοῖς ἐκ
περιτομῆς προσφιλὲς ἡγούμεθα (*PE*, I.5.10–11).

[42] ὁ Χριστιανισμός, οὔτε Ἑλληνισμὸς ὢν οὔτε Ἰουδαισμός, ἀλλά τις καινὴ καὶ
ἀληθὴς θεοσοφία (*PE*, I.5.12), Gifford's version.

[43] *PE*, 1.5.10.

[44] *PE*, 3.13.3; 3.4.5.

Against the Greeks' accusations that Christians do not respect laws, do not worship the legacy of the fathers, and do not follow the religion of their forefathers but love religious novelties, Eusebius invoked the gospel deeds of the Savior. He argued that the "grand mystery of gospel economy" dissipated the error transmitted through fathers about the power of the demons, and replaced the places of the error of all the nations—i.e. temples—with "schools of prayer/worship."[45] In *Praeparatio*, Eusebius directed his polemics against three kinds of Greek theology: mythological (poetry), allegorical (philosophical works), and political theology. Highly esteemed as coming from the Greek forefathers, Greek political theology, with its fine legal, urban, social, and religious armature held the Roman Empire together. Yet, Eusebius contended, it was founded on religious practices articulated by polytheist superstitions. *Praeparatio* targets precisely the religion of the *polis*, which urban traditions and the laws of the fathers accredit and support. Eusebius justified the defection from the laws of the fathers, which instituted matters of worship and made Christian practices illegal, by placing Greek political theology in the same category of error as Greek mythological and allegorical theologies. The 'nations' as collective entities were supported by the laws of the fathers; Christ's message, carried all over the inhabited parts of the Roman empire, changed these 'nations' into 'races,' and converted their polytheistic theologies into 'true worship.'

Eusebius introduces a narrative quality to this process of conversion, and presents it as the search for the most appropriated philosophical school, not unlike Justin's *Dialog with Trypho*. In Eusebius' scenario, "after a wise judgment, and not all of a sudden," the Christians decided to become apostates from the mistaken manner of worship (δεισιδαιμονία), transmitted through the agency of the fathers. Using "the right and true judgment," Eusebius' intellectual Christians adopted the right form of worship (εὐσέβεια). Through "the divine power of the demonstration of the gospel," philosophy enables Eusebius to shatter the patrilinear connection with the "theologies of his fathers" at work in "every city" and rearrange this civic religious formation along the lines of a Christian *paideia*. Eusebius' apologetic

---

[45] *PE*, 4.4.1; cf. 4.1.2–5.

examination of his fathers' theology lends justification to the religious mass-defection from the Greek fathers' δεισιδαιμονία.[46]

'HEBREWS' FOR JESUS

In the first book of *Praeparatio Evangelica*, Eusebius used the ethnic category of 'Jews' to construct *Christianismos*. Accordingly, Judaism moved in and out of focus, according to his argumentative needs. For instance, in discussing the civilizing advancement of Greeks and Barbarians toward a rigorous lifestyle, Eusebius overlooked the Jewish element; yet, similar arguments appear in Philo, Paul, 4 Maccabees, and Josephus.[47] The Jewish element, however, remained an important part of Eusebius' treatment of Christianity as *triton genos*: the 'nations' coming out of the Greeks and Barbarians did *not* convert to Judaism, but to a superior, more rigorous and more philosophic lifestyle, supported by divine wisdom, *theosophia*.

In the first book of *Demonstratio Evangelica*, Eusebius returned to the Jews and the relation of their books to *Christianismos;* in the process, he derived from the Hebrew writings the rationale for the Jewish-Christian history of his time. Eusebius integrated Jesus' story in the Hebrew prophetic tradition, and presented the destruction of the Second Temple, the dispersion of the Jews from Jerusalem, and the obliteration of Jerusalem itself after 135, from a Christian perspective, as a punishment for rejecting the Messiah. "And it is plain even to the blind, that what they [the prophets] saw and foretold is fulfilled in actual facts from the very day the Jews laid godless hands on Christ, and drew down on themselves the beginning of the train of sorrows."[48]

What else did the Hebrew prophets see in the future? Whatever lent ancient authority, hence authenticity and credibility, to the budding Christian communities served Eusebius' apologetic purposes. Eusebius even reversed the traditional roles of *genos* and *ethnos*, opposing the "lost nation of the Jews" to all other nations and races recently turned Christian: "They [the Hebrew prophets] could preach the good news

---

[46] φέρ' οὖν πρῶτον ἀπάντων τὰς παλαιοτάτας καὶ δὴ καὶ τὰς πατρίους ἡμῶν αὐτῶν θεολογίας κατὰ πᾶσαν πόλιν εἰσέτι (*PE*, 1.5.13).

[47] Stowers, *A Rereading of Romans, cit.*, p. 65.

[48] *DE*, I.1.6; Ferrar's version.

that though one nation was lost, every nation and race of men would know God."[49] A few lines further in the text, Eusebius relaxed the strict identification between 'nations' and 'Christian,' and included the latter into the former, only to give this new social formation a different name, *laos*, and a new location, "all over the civilized world." Thus, the Hebrew prophets "could see churches of Christ established by their means among all nations and Christian people throughout the whole world bearing one common name."[50]

When did the Hebrews cease being Hebrews and regress into the state of Jews?[51] Eusebius most surely read his Septuagint and knowingly blamed it all on Egypt. He formulated his answer most clearly in the seventh book of *Praeparatio Evangelica*. According to Eusebius, the race of Hebrews multiplied incessantly and, at some point during this process of dissolution and moral degradation, turned into the Jewish *ethnos*, whose increasing numbers naturally lost any contact with their great ancestors, namely, with "the pious conduct of their godly forefathers of old." Egypt, as the new cultural environment of this disconnected *ethnos*, did not help them improve their lifestyle. On the contrary, the Hebrews/Jews "came round in their modes of living to like customs with the Egyptians, so that their character seemed to differ in nothing from the Egyptians."[52] To put it differently, when the Hebrews lived in Egypt, they became (like) Egyptians to such degree,

---

[49] *DE*, I.1.8; Ferrar's version modified.

[50] ὁ Χριστιανῶν λαὸς καθ' ὅλης τῆς οἰκουμένης ὀνομασθήσεται, *DE*, I.1.7, Ferrar's version.

[51] See N. de Lange, *Origen and the Jews: Studies in Jewish-Christian Relations in Third-Century Palestine* (Cambridge: Cambridge University Press, 1976), 29–37 (esp. p. 29, for "*Hebraioi* as the polite word for the Jews"; and pp. 31–32 for the connection between Origen's styling of Jews as "Hebrews not Egyptians" and Eusebius' tighter association between 'Hebrews' and 'Christians').' See G. Harvey, *The True Israel: Uses of the Name Jew, Hebrew, and Israel in Ancient Jewish and Early Christian Literature* (Leiden: Brill, 1996), 104–147, esp. p. 146 ("A 'Hebrew' is one who claims to be a 'good Jew').". For the uses of Abraham in the controversy between Gentile Christianity and Judaism to justify Jewish exclusion see J.S. Siker, *Disinheriting the Jews: Abraham in Early Christian Controversy* (Louisville: John Knox Press, 1991), 185–198. For the switch from positive to negative pagan views of Moses, see J.G. Gager, *Moses in Greco-Roman Paganism* (Atlanta: Society of Biblical Literature, [2]1989 [[1]1972]). Finally, for a very detailed analysis of Eusebius' use of Jewish authors' citation, see S. Inowlocki, *Eusebius and the Jewish Authors, cit.*, 223–288, esp. p. 288: "The meaning given [by Eusebius] to the different excerpts [from Jewish authors] varied according to the representation of the Jewish authors as 'Hebrews,' as 'Jews,' as sources of Greek testimonies or as sources of Christian history."

[52] *PE*, VII.8.37, Gifford's version.

that they actually turned into Jews. In a fashion similar to Aristides' argument that "since the Jews reject Jesus, the Son of God, they closely resemble the nations" (*Apology*, XIV.4), Eusebius aligned the Jews and the nations, and claimed that these opposites coincide to allow Christianity to emerge as a purely different *triton genos*.

Moses saved the Hebrews/Jews from their Egyptian identity and moral decline by taking them out of the country. He also brought them the Torah as the "the polity that corresponds to their condition, ordaining some things openly and clearly, and implying others enigmatically, by suggesting symbols and shadows, but not the naked truth, for them to keep and observe."[53] Aryeh Kofsky summarized this embodiment of Moses very eloquently: "In other words, Moses was a Hebrew, but wrote his Law for the Jews."[54]

How did Eusebius define *Christianismos* as *triton genos* in *Demonstratio*? He put an unexpected twist to this apologetic motif, by simultaneously ascribing both newness and ancientness to the Christian practices. To create the illusion of a clear separation between three forms of worship, Eusebius described *Christianismos* as "neither a form of Hellenism, nor of Judaism" but "a religion (θεοσέβεια) with its own characteristic stamp," "nor new neither original," but "of great antiquity".[55] On the other hand, Eusebius defined Judaism as "the polity constituted according to the Law of Moses, depending on the one, omnipotent God." He reserved Hellenism a much lower place in the hierarchy of conceptions about divinity, characterizing it as "the superstition of many gods according to the ancestral customs of all nations."[56] Eusebius' terms could not have been more eloquent

---

[53] *PE*, VII.8.39, Gifford's version.

[54] A. Kofsky, "Eusebius of Caesarea and the Christian-Jewish Polemic," in O. Limor and G.G. Stroumsa, eds., *Contra Iudaeos: Ancient and Medieval Polemics between Christians and Jews* (Tübingen: Mohr Siebeck, 1996), 74.

[55] ὁ Χριστιανισμὸς οὔτε Ἑλληνισμός τίς ἐστιν οὔτε ἰουδαισμός, οἰκεῖον δέ τινα φέρων χαρακτῆρα θεοσεβείας, καὶ τοῦτον οὐ νέον οὐδὲ ἐκτετοπισμένον, ἀλλ᾽ εὖ μάλα παλαιότατον (*DE*, I.2.1).

[56] τὸν μὲν Ἰουδαισμὸν εὐλόγως ἄν τις ὀνομάσειε τὴν κατὰ τὸν Μωσέως νόμον διατεταγμένην πολιτείαν, ἑνὸς ἐξημμένην τοῦ ἐπὶ πάντων θεοῦ, τὸν δὲ Ἑλληνισμόν, ὡς ἐν κεφαλαίῳ φάναι, τὴν κατὰ τὰ πάτρια τῶν ἐθνῶν ἁπάντων εἰς πλείονας θεοὺς δεισιδαιμονίαν (*DE*, I.2.2); my translation. W.J. Ferrar smoothes out the asperities of this phrase, hides 'superstition,' plants 'religion' where it is not, and describes 'Hellenism' as worship, somehow similarly to Christianity: "Hellenism you might summarily describe as the worship of many Gods according to the ancestral religions of all nations" (p. 8). On the other hand, Paolo Carrara's Italian version is more economical, but still misses Eusebius' pejorative tone: "La religione dei greci invece—per dirla in

in speaking about three different stages in the great chain of civilized religion. Lowest on this value scale, Hellenism embodies superstition (δεισιδαιμονία). Next, Judaism is best described as a civil polity (πολιτεία), with a twist that regards the Torah as a civic constitution. Finally, Christianity represents the corrected worship of, and positioning toward, God (θεοσέβεια).

Whence came Christianity's great antiquity? Eusebius' new master-stroke found that the long shadow of *triton genos* stretches from the dawn of times until his very own day. The most important innovation of *Demonstratio Evangelica*, not yet developed to such a scale by *Praeparatio Evangelica*, with the notable exception of Book VII, is to place the Jewish patriarchs living before Moses' Law, namely Abraham, Isaac, Jacob, and surprisingly enough, Job, between Greeks and Jews, being in fact neither one, nor the other. In his historical exploration, Eusebius chanced upon the surviving fossil of the Christians, the Hebrews as a *triton genos*. "Would not this be exactly the third form of religion (θεοσέβεια) midway between Judaism and Hellenism which I have already deduced,"[57] wonders Eusebius, "as the most ancient and most venerable of all religions, preached anew to all nations by our Savior?"[58] The definition of Christianity sprang from under Eusebius' stylus as the perennial *triton genos*, divine philosophy, and πολιτεία of worship at the same time, planted in its place long before the two other terms, Judaism and Hellenism, even joined the genetic triad. "Christianity would therefore be not a form of Hellenism nor of Judaism, but something between the two,[59] the most ancient organization for holiness, and the most venerable philosophy only lately codified as the law for all mankind in the whole world."[60]

Eusebius makes the identification of Hebrews as proto-Christians also clear in *Historia Ecclesiastica*, where only the name of 'Christian' is the missing link from the Hebrew writings. "If the line be traced

---

sintesi—è quella credenza in molti dèi che si fonda sulle tradizioni patrie di tutti i popoli" (*Dimonstrazione Evangelica, cit.*, p. 134).

[57] τὸ μεταξὺ ἰουδαισμοῦ καὶ ἑλληνισμοῦ τρίτον ἡμῖν ἀποδεδειγμένον τάγμα (*DE*, I.2.9).

[58] *DE*, I.2.8, Ferrar's translation, modified.

[59] καὶ τοῦτ' ἂν εἴη ὁ Χριστιανισμός, οὔτε Ἑλληνισμός τις ὢν οὔτε Ἰουδαισμός, ἀλλὰ τὸ μεταξὺ τούτων παλαιότατον εὐσεβείας πολίτευμα, καὶ ἀρχαιοτάτη μέν τις φιλοσοφία πλὴν ἀλλὰ νεωστὶ πᾶσιν ἀνθρώποις τοῖς καθ' ὅλης τῆς οἰκουμένης νενομοθετημένη (*DE*, I.2.10), Ferrar's translation.

[60] *Ibid.*

back from Abraham to the first man, anyone who should describe those who have obtained a good testimony for righteousness, as Christians in fact, if not in name would not shoot wide of the truth."[61] Jesus Christ's teaching to the nations, therefore, coincides with "the very first and most ancient and antique discovery of true religion by Abraham and those lovers of God who followed him," namely the Hebrews.[62]

Conclusion

I have presented above a few relevant themes in Eusebius' apologetic argumentation: the proclamation of the gospel has gone out to the Barbarians and the Greeks; this made possible the apostasy from δεισιδαιμονία. Further, the demonstration of the gospel prompted the demise of the fathers' urban religious values through a reasoning process of the new Christian *paideia*.[63] Eusebius' discourse on *triton genos* did not take place in a rhetorical vacuum or in the absence of previous literary traditions. It is reasonable to believe that Eusebius and his predecessors derived their premises of *triton genos* from Jewish authors, like Philo and Josephus, and developed their formal aspects following the requirements of rhetorical schools.[64] Secondly, the discourse on *triton genos* set the field of apologetic debates firmly between two constructed ethnical categories, 'Greek' and 'Jew,' making it almost impossible to derive from the ancient texts how much of it is pure rhetoric and how much is about 'real' encounters between Jews and Christians. Finally, I argued that the discourse on *triton genos* enabled Eusebius to employ the rhetoric of appropriation and displacement of Jewish past. Eusebius appropriated Jewish past through his usage of the Hebrew Bible, and displaced the Jewish claims to use it accordingly. For the fourth-century Christian writer, the category of 'Hebrews' opened the possibility to authenticate Christian social formations and situated them with full civic rights in the Greco-Roman οἰκουμένη.

---

[61] *HE*, I.4.6, Lake's translation.
[62] *HE*, I. 4.10, Lake's translation.
[63] *PE*, II.4.5.
[64] Inowlocki, *Eusebius and the Jewish Authors, cit.*, passim.

EUSEBIUS PHILOSOPHUS? SCHOOL ACTIVITY AT CAESAREA THROUGH THE LENS OF THE *MARTYRS*

Elizabeth C. Penland

> *Eusebius is no philosopher.*
> D.S. Wallace Hadrill, *Eusebius of Caesarea* (London: Mowbray, 1960) 140.

> *Si Pamphile a assurément joué le rôle d'un professeur en sciences bibliques, on hésitera à parler d'une véritable 'école' de Césarée remontant à Origène et dont il aurait pris la tête.*
> René Amacker and Éric Junod, *Apologie pour Origène*, vol. 2 (SC 465), p. 76 n. 8.

These pronouncements about Eusebius and Pamphilus' school by Wallace Hadrill and Amacker and Junod are examples of modern interpretative bias disguised as defenses against misreading. Lest one take Eusebius at his word, some scholars have thought it necessary to protect readers from misunderstanding the philosophical and school-oriented content of Eusebius' work. In the *Ecclesiastical History* and the *Martyrs of Palestine*, Eusebius takes pains to delineate the school around Pamphilus and to show its philosophical merit and connection to the tradition of Origen. From some modern scholarly positions, it is a mistake to believe that this school existed, was connected to Origen or was philosophical in nature. As this article will show, the designation of the school of Pamphilus as philosophical and grounded in the work of Origen at Caesarea are two important organizational themes for Eusebius. If they were compelling to him, although one reads with suspicion as a modern historian, one ought perhaps to begin with what was relevant to the ancient writer and his environment.

MODERN APPROACHES

There have been several compromise positions on the philosophical question and on the school question, both of which have to do with situating Eusebius in relation to modern disciplines. T.D. Barnes has asserted that Eusebius is properly a biblical scholar: "Eusebius was a biblical scholar both by instinct and by training, but he was not by nature a philosopher or theologian."[1] This assertion immediately disqualifies Eusebius from several other roles. It excludes any claim to philosophy and also casts an odd light on Eusebius' status as an historian. Lewis Ayres calls Eusebius "the historian and theologian," pointing to his original theological contributions and his knowledge of Origen.[2] Ayres writes that it was the "usefulness and prominence of the *Historia ecclesiastica* (hereafter *HE*) which led to Eusebius' designation as a historian."[3] This claims Eusebius for theology as well as history, but tells us little about Eusebius' own terminology for his work.

It is questionable what meaning the term "theologian" would have had to Eusebius for his own endeavors. He was certainly "speaking/teaching about God," as θεολόγος designates. However, the term θεολόγος was as an epithet was generally applied posthumously by Eusebius and his sources and to a special class of people. For example, Clement uses it for Moses (*Strom.*, 1.22) and Eusebius uses it for the prophets (*Praep. ev.*, 10.1). The actions designated φιλοσοφία had much wider cultural currency in the early fourth century than those of θεολογία. φιλοσοφία, and the ethical actions that were part and parcel of its practice, would be intelligible to a much wider audience. Eusebius appeals to philosophical traditions in characterizing the school of Pamphilus and even uses the terminology of philosophy when talking about its martyrs.

On the school half of the question, some scholars, such as Charles Kannengiesser, will allow for a "school" of sorts, a circle of biblical copyists at Caesarea.[4] The most recent iteration of this idea appears in Anthony Grafton and Megan Williams, *Christianity and the Transfor-*

---

[1] T.D. Barnes, *Constantine and Eusebius* (Cambridge, Mass.: Harvard University Press, 1981) 94. Barnes uses this opportunity to criticize the notion of a school at Caesarea descended from Origen and points to the differences in Eusebius' and Origen's teaching activities, although he will concede that Eusebius "regarded himself as an intellectual heir of Origen," (p. 95).

[2] L. Ayres, *Nicaea and Its Legacy: An Approach to Fourth-Century Trinitarian Theology* (Oxford: Oxford University Press, 2004), 58.

[3] *Ibid.*, p. 58, n. 43.

[4] Charles Kannengiesser speaks of Eusebius' "semi-monastic curriculum" in the house of Pamphilus, "Eusebius as Origenist," 437, in G. Hata and H. Attridge (eds.), *Eusebius, Christianity, and Judaism* (Detroit: Wayne State University Press, 1992).

mation of the Book.[5] This type of school is often envisioned as a scriptorium, an idea borrowed from medieval monastic institutions. Just as medieval monasteries were not only constituted by their scriptoria, it is difficult to imagine that copying sacred literature was the central raison d'être of Pamphilus' school. There were certainly resources for copying books, and particularly bibles, at Caesarea.[6] By the vagaries of manuscript preservation and academic taste, Caesarean biblical versions became the best preserved work of the school and the central feature of interest to modern scholarship on the Caesarean school.[7] The extant manuscripts led to the characterization of the school as a copying site for biblical manuscripts.

However, the survival of manuscripts does not tell us everything about the activities of the school. For one, the library that the school had access to was much larger. It contained the works of Origen and numerous exegetical and philosophical works.[8] The great amalgam projects of Eusebius, such as the *Preparation for* and *Demonstration of the Gospel*, show the range of philosophical, historical, and exegetical sources available to the author.[9] These collections of materials have a clear school use, as sources for argument and articulation of Christian philosophical positions on the basis of Jewish and Greek sources. Yet even with this comprehensive evidence of the literate activity of the school, the label of "philosophical" is still withheld by some modern scholars. Biblical, theological, or historical seem easier labels to apply than "Christian philosophical."

---

[5] "Eusebius: An Impresario of the Codex"; see A. Grafton and M. Williams, *Christianity and the Transformation of the Book. Origen, Eusebius and the Library of Caesarea* (Cambdrige, Mass. – London : Belknap Press of Harvard University Press, 2006).

[6] As Eusebius himself documents, Constantine sent to Caesarea for bibles, *Vita Const.*, 4.36.

[7] The works of Eusebius are in this context seen as the works of an individual and would perhaps be better seen as the flowering of a school setting.

[8] For one reconstruction attempt of the lists of this library, see A. Carriker, *The Library of Caesarea*. (SVigChr 67; Leiden – Boston: Brill, 2003). For a description of Pamphilus' collecting activities, see *HE*, 6.32.2.

[9] For recent work on the *Praeparatio* and *Demonstratio evangelica* (hence *PE* and *DE*), see S. Inowlocki, *Eusebius and the Jewish Authors. His Citation Technique in an Apologetic Context* (AJEC 64; Leiden – Boston: Brill, 2006) and A.P. Johnson *Ethnicity and Argument in Eusebius' Praeparatio evangelica* (Oxford: Oxford University Press, 2006).

ANCIENT EVIDENCE AND MODERN INTERPRETATION

Eusebius' text on the *Martyrs of Palestine* provides alternate insight into some of these questions. It helps the reader to ask, "Why not philosophy?" and "What if it *was* a school?" We have to ask what the modern stakes in preventing these readings are, as well as the ancient stakes in forging them. That is to say, what it is about the Eusebian corpus that makes such defenses necessary. Why is it important to state that a circle of biblical scholars and teachers is not a "true" school? What is preserved by excluding Eusebius from the ranks of those who earn the title "philosopher"? Why then would he claim the attributes of philosophy for the martyrs of his school?

A true misunderstanding may lie at the heart of the scholarly defenses, a misunderstanding of the scope of schools in antiquity and also of the nature and purposes of ancient philosophy. No less eminent an expert on Platonism than John Dillon encourages us to "think small" when thinking about institutions of philosophical higher learning in late antiquity, using the observations of Porphyry and the school of Plotinus as well as the evidence on Proclus at Athens.[10] Raffaella Cribiore, in her masterful survey of literary and papyrological evidence for Greek schooling in Egypt, has shown that schools could be smaller, less permanent, and more diverse in their curricula that we would think.[11] Centers of learning were smaller and also perhaps more significant than the modern reader might take into account.[12] Neither literacy nor libraries nor high levels of education could taken for granted. This can be difficult to remember in an age of literacy rates approaching 100% and from the milieu of rigorous academic learning.

---

[10] J. Dillon, "Philosophy as a profession in late antiquity," in A. Smith (ed.), *The Philosopher and Society in Late Antiquity: Essays in Honour of Peter Brown* (Swansea: Classical Press of Wales, 2005), 1.

[11] See R. Cribiore, *Gymnastics of the Mind: Greek Education in Hellenistic and Roman Egypt* (Princeton – Oxford: Princeton University Press, 2001), especially Chapter 1, "Models of Schooling," 15–44.

[12] For ancient education in general, see H.I. Marrou, *A History of Education in Antiquity* (tr. Lamb; New York: Sheed and Ward, 1956). For schools in civic context, see E.J. Watts, *City and School in Late Antique Athens and Alexandria* (Berkeley: University of California Press, 2006). On the importance of the family and the household for Christian religious education, see J.N. Bremmer, "The family and other centres of religious learning in antiquity," in *Centres of Learning* (Leiden – Boston: Brill, 1995), 29–38; and Marrou, *Education, cit.*, 314–331.

Another hurdle to understanding Eusebius' philosophical content is the question of what constitutes a philosophical or theological work. Much of philosophical labor in late antiquity was grammarian and text critical in nature: reading, revising, and commenting upon the works of other. No one would deny that Eusebius was an avid collector and user of and commentator on texts. The manuscript evidence of his work with Pamphilus on the Hexapla revisions of the Septuagint and the text-critical interests in his works demonstrate this.[13] He had an enormous collection of literature and information at hand and knew very well how to navigate a highly literate level of culture, in fact, a uniquely productive literate level for this time. The criterion of judgment, from a modern standpoint, seems to be the criterion of "original thought," and this very originality in Eusebius is sometimes difficult to pinpoint.

For one, Eusebius' preservation of ancient sources continues to distract scholars from the surprising nature of Eusebius' works. We have so very much Eusebius, with so many wonderful attributions that provide ways of tracking his sources. He took such great pains to document and to provide material for argument. So much so, in fact, that his own work seems almost invisible at times, as if it were only a tissue of the works of others rather than a surprising corpus of original composition. If his composing and editing hand is invisible to scholarship, how much more so are the circumstances of his literary composition.[14]

THE SCHOOL SETTING IN EUSEBIUS

Despite his obvious text critical acumen and literary achievements, Eusebius has rarely been read as an author engaged in Christian philosophical education and scholastic activity, although his works are suitable for a school setting and there are important indicators

---

[13] On the Caesarean copying tradition, see B. Swete, *An Introduction to The Old Testament in Greek* (Cambridge: Cambridge University Press, 1902; many reprints) and W. Bousset, *Textkritische Untersuchungen zum Neuen Testament*, "Der Kodex Pamphili." (Leipzig: Hinrichs, 1894). See also Grafton and Williams, *Christianity and the Transformation of the Book, cit.*

[14] On Eusebius' citation methods in the *HE*, see E. Carotenuto, *Tradizione e innovazione nella Historia ecclesiastica di Eusebio di Cesarea* (Bologna: Il Mulino, 2001). For a nuanced discussion of Eusebius' citation technique of Jewish Authors, see Inowlocki, *Eusebius and the Jewish Authors, cit.*

of such a context in them. The *Martyrs* is one important source for
modern envisioning of this setting. Elements of the school are preserved among the individual accounts in the *Martyrs*. These elements
include a teacher, students, and a curriculum. Additionally, we know
from other sources that there was a library, a tradition of lives, and a
succession.[15]

Pamphilus as a teacher is at the center of the *Martyrs*. He is also
physically the center of a group of 12 martyrs in Eusebius' telling:
"Yet like the sun, which brings light to the day, among the stars, so
the excellence of my master Pamphilus shone forth from among them
all" (*Mart. Palest.*, 37; hereafter *MP*).[16] He and his students also feature in the longest accounts in the narrative. Together, the story of
Pamphilus and companions and the story of Apphianus, the student
of Pamphilus, form a third of the total work. In the martyr narrative, Eusebius characterizes Pamphilus as excelling in Greek learning,
scripture, and divine thought alike (*MP*, 37). According to Eusebius,
he was also possessed of a power of discernment stemming directly
from divine influence (*MP*, 37). This picture of Pamphilus' erudition
and inspiration is consonant with Eusebius' depiction of Origen in the
HE, VI, as well as Gregory Thaumaturgus' characterization of Origen
in the *Thanksgiving Address*.

In addition to their learning and erudition as scriptural and philosophical teachers, there is another didactic function that Pamphilus
in the *Martyrs* and Origen in the *HE* and *Pan.* share: the example
of their lives. Apphianus, the student of Pamphilus in the *Martyrs*,
is shown "[living] in the same house with us, confirming himself in
divine teachings, and receiving instruction in the Holy Scriptures
from that perfect martyr, Pamphilus. He also acquired from him the
excellence of virtuous habits and conduct" (*MP*, 13). So the curricu-

---

[15] Eusebius' *HE* presents the intellectual succession of Pamphilus' school from the
"catechetical school" at Alexandria. For recent discussions of the Alexandrian school,
see Annewies van den Hoek, "The 'Catechetical' School of Early Christian Alexandria
and Its Philonic Heritage," *HThR* 90 (1997), 59–87 and A. Jakab, *Ecclesia Alexandrina*
(Bern: Peter Lang, 2001). In the *HE*, Eusebius also locates the core of the library in
the lists of Origen's material that Pamphilus gathers. The *Vitae* tradition of the school
is shaped by the *Apology* for Origen and HE 6, which functions as a *Life* of Origen.
There is a lost life of Pamphilus. The *Martyrs* fits into the life tradition, as a subniche.
Gelasius also wrote a *Life* of Eusebius, now lost.

[16] The quotes here from the *Martyrs* are from the Syriac long recension, BL add.
ms. 12, 150, edited and translated by W. Cureton, *History of the Martyrs in Palestine*
(London-Paris: Williams and Norgate, 1861). Translations are based on Cureton's.

lum of Pamphilus' Christian philosophical school is not only composed of teachings about the divine and scripture, but also training in virtue. As Gregory Thaumaturgus writes of Origen, "This man by himself was the first who persuaded me to pursue the philosophy of the Greeks to, convincing me by his own moral behavior to listen to and assimilate moral doctrine (ἠθῶν)" (*Address*, 11, Slusser). Unlike Gregory, Apphianus had already undergone a philosophical conversion in Beirut, before meeting Pamphilus, and had come to Caesarea to pursue specifically Christian philosophy under Pamphilus' tutelage (*MP*, 12–13). However, both students share the training in virtue at the hands of their teachers.

There is a strong case to be made for the practice of ancient philosophy as a method of regulating life in addition to study. Pierre Hadot and André Festugière have argued cogently for the connection of life to philosophy in antiquity.[17] Philosophy was not defined by speculative thought alone but also by behavior. Festugière writes about σχολή in Aristotle and Plato and the meaning of "leisure" as the freedom to lead a life devoted to contemplation.[18] In the case of the *Martyrs*, Eusebius' circle around Pamphilus seems to have engaged in scriptural study and learning and had the luxury to produce textual versions. They may have also done this communally, if the emphasis of Apphianus residing in the same house with Eusebius (and presumably Pamphilus) is any guideline (*MP*, 13). These students also studied virtue under Pamphilus, which Eusebius views as a direct preparation for martyrdom. To borrow from Philo, Pamphilus' school in the *Martyrs* (as Origen's schools in *HE*, VI) is a "school for virtue."[19] There is a substantial ancient literary tradition of representing one's "religious" practices (by modern definitions) as philosophical, and ethical in particular. Philo does so in his characterization of Jewish local assemblies (προσευκτήρια) as schools (διδασκαλεῖα) of virtue.

---

[17] As an introduction, see P. Hadot, *Philosophy as a Way of Life* (Oxford: Blackwell, 1995) and A.J. Festugière "Les trois vies," in *Id.*, *Études de philosophie grecque* (Paris: De Vrin, 1971), 117–156.

[18] Festugière, *ibid.*, 154.

[19] On the Christian school at Alexandria as a "school for virtue," see R.L. Wilken, "*Alexandria: a school for training in virtue*," in *Schools of Thought in Christian Tradition* (Philadelphia: Fortress Press, 1984), 15–30. On Philo in a school context, see G.E. Sterling, "The School of Sacred Laws: The Social Setting of Philo's Treatises," *VigChr* 53 (1999), 148–164.

"For what else are our assemblies throughout the cities but schools of prudence and courage and temperance and justice and also piety, holiness and all virtues by which duties to God and men are discerned and rightly performed?" (*De vita Moy.*, 2.48, Colson)

Just as Moses follows the model of Plato's philosopher-king in the *Life* (e.g. *De vita Moy.*, II.2), the entire polity of the Jewish people is represented as a group of philosophers. The assemblies of worship and learning become instruments of ethical training and instruction in both citizenship and worship. Philo characterizes of Jewish practices as ancestral philosophy (ἡ πάτριος φιλοσοφία) at numerous places in the *Life of Moses*, including the passage before the above excerpt (*De vita Moy.*, II.48). The earthly transmitter of this φιλοσοφία is Moses.

The language of φιλοσοφία can also be found in Josephus' discussion of Jewish philosophical sects. In the *Jewish War*, Josephus states that there are three groups who practice Jewish philosophy: the Essenes, Sadducees, and Pharisees. (*Bell. Jud.*, II.119–166). He spends the bulk of the discussion on the Essenes, but notes the relevant characteristic of each groups. The matrix of philosophy is also handed down in the second-century Christian apologists, notably Justin Martyr. Justin speaks of the "school of Christ" in the Apology (I.4.7), contrasting human wisdom with divine philosophy. He also appeals to the philosophical sensibilities of the Emperor as a leitmotif throughout the work.[20] Eusebius was the heir of this Jewish and Christian "apologetic" tradition of school, philosophy and virtue.[21] The authors who formed part of his intellectual lineage used the terms of philosophy and the ideas of the schools for their understanding of community practices. What is also important for this discussion is the function of apologetic material as a means of self-presentation and the articulation of self-understanding of a group addressed to an (often imaginary) audience. These authors were not just writing about philosophy to help "others" understand them, others who are often identified as Greco-Roman outsiders of high educational standing and often philophers. They were writing to understand themselves and their larger context. Apologetic literature informed and was informed by the experiences of literate, highly edu-

---

[20] See *Apol.* I.1; II.15.5, and Ch. Munier (ed. and trans.), Saint Justin, *Apologie pour les chrétiens* (Par. 39; Fribourg: Editions universitaires, 1995), 368 n. 4.

[21] There are a number of exciting recent studies of Eusebius' apologetic techniques and subjects: A. Kofsky, *Eusebius of Caesarea against Paganism* (Leiden: Brill, 2000) and J. Schott, *Christianity, Empire, and the Making of Religion in Late Antiquity* (Philadelphia: University of Pennsylvania Press, 2008), as well as Johnson, *Ethnicity and Argument, cit.*, and Inowlocki, *Eusebius and the Jewish Authors, cit.*

cated Greek-trained Jews and Christians and was not just honed for the benefit of their opposite numbers and dialectical "others."

In order to understand the school of Pamphilus within the context of Late Antique philosophical education, we have to revisit the question of what a school *was*. The material presented by Eusebius about the teaching tradition at Caesarea is cohesive evidence for school activity during this period. There existed a library, a succession, a master teacher, and students.[22] Eusebius' very writing about the members of his own circle in the *Martyrs* constitutes scholastic activity. Another angle of approach is to ask what is to be gained by reading the school of Pamphilus as a philosophical school. What if, instead of defending against Eusebius' presentation of material, we instead read with him and tried to see his labors on behalf of this particular interpretation? This seems the most fruitful tack to take. Instead of arguing against material and its presentation, we can try to understand *how* it is presented and what might have been at stake.

AN OUTLINE OF POSSIBLE STAKES

1. *The heritage from Origen*

Given the extant evidence of the interest in correcting the Septuagint according to Origen's Hexapla and also in preserving Origen's letters and manuscripts, it seems reasonable that the school around Pamphilus was acting self-consciously in the tradition of Origen. This tradition involved biblical scholarship and also some connection to Alexandrian exegetical traditions, but it also involved the practice of ascetic piety and some sort of voluntary poverty. Although the links to Origen are not quite as direct as Eusebius makes them out, Pamphilus did study under Pierius, "the younger Origen," and then move to Caesarea where Origen had moved his teaching activities.[23] Eusebius wrote an extended biography of Origen in the context of his *Ecclesiastical History*: the material on Origen forms most of Book Six of the *HE*. Pamphilus and Eusebius' school was not so very far away from the source. Did Eusebius emphasize the link to Origen? Of course. Was this relationship to Origen a demonstrable focus of the school? Yes.

---

[22] See J. Mansfeld, *Prolegomena* (Leiden: Brill, 1994) for the discussion and analysis of contexts of ancient texts, including scholastic features and the importance of biographical tradition for interpretation.
[23] Jerome, *De vir. ill.*, 76; Photius, *Biblioth.*, cod. 118.

2. *The picture of the Caesarean school*

Part of the importance of understanding the Caesarean school in Eusebius' time, as presented in the *Martyrs* and also in the material about Origen and Pamphilus in the *Ecclesiastical History*, is to understand the lineage of the Caesarean school in other areas. This is most pertinent for the examination of the Alexandrian school in the *HE*. If one sees the Alexandrian catechetical school and the life of Origen as part of Eusebius' own contemporary school-building project, then the mythical beginnings and qualities begin to take on a more concrete form. So, for example, the weaving together of the Marcan Christians with Philo's Therapeutae and the establishment of Alexandrian Christianity *HE* (II.16–17) as ascetic, apostolic, and philosophical, makes much more sense when one moves ahead a few centuries to look at the fourth-century portraits of the *Martyrs*. Eusebius depicts his own school and other figures in the martyrs as communal, ascetic, philosophical Christians. The literary lineage of ascetic intellectual Alexandrian Christianity presented in the *HE* seems to delineate features of ascetic intellectual *Caesarean* Christianity that Eusebius cherished. This is not to say that his source material and the ideas presented are not Alexandrian, but rather that the manner of presentation, emphasis, and distillation display practical relevance to Eusebius' own time.

3. *The validation of the martyrs*

The text of the martyrs functions as a collective memorial, but also as a validation of the school's endeavors. Origen's work in *HE* VI is justified by the martyrs he produces at Alexandria and then by his own, somewhat attenuated martyrdom that does not seem to have been accepted universally. Pamphilus' work is justified in the martyrdom of his pupils, including his household slave, Porphyrius, and then in his own martyrdom. The status of Pamphilus' martyrdom is so above reproach that Jerome can protect him from association with the *Apology for Origen* by pinning it on Eusebius and accusing Rufinus of besmirching the martyr's name.[24]

The production of martyrs from a school is not a matter of antiquarian interest in a history or set of accounts. It is a charged connection to the special dead, people who have been granted extraordinary deaths

---

[24] *Contra Ruf.*, I.9.

and are considered to be ascended directly into heaven. The presence of martyrs in a teaching lineage justifies the connection of that lineage to the divine. So Eusebius' own teaching lineage was justified by having so many remarkable martyrs in his close association. Eusebius acts as literary executor of the martyrs' memories and, perhaps, curator of their relics. He succeeds Pamphilus as the most senior survivor of the school and controls the library, or at least, possesses special privileges. He also becomes bishop of Caesarea shortly after writing the collection of the *Martyrs*.

CONCLUSION

We know so little of what comes after the *Martyrs* in the school. The *Life* of Eusebius by his successor Acacius is not preserved, nor is the *Ecclesiastical History* of Gelasius. The figures in the school, notably Eusebius and Origen, are reinterpreted in the Arianist controversy and the Origenist Controversy. Then came the supersession of Caesarea as an metropolitan see by Jerusalem in the fifth century. Against a backdrop of ecclesiastical and political tumult, the information about the Caesarean school was dispersed. The *Martyrs* exists in its entirety in Syriac. *The Life of Pamphilus* is lost.[25] *The Apology for Origen* survives as one book out of five in Rufinus' Latin translation. While we seem to have ample lines of transmission for Eusebius' material on philosophical doctrine, universal history, and biblical criticism, the local, situated material on the school and the lives of its members can primarily be reconstructed from the *Martyrs*.

Should we reclassify Eusebius as a philosopher? Perhaps. Perhaps not. It depends on our own criteria and what we mean to achieve in the classification. We should at least recognize his attempts to have his intellectual lineage preserved as a high form of Christian learning and his strategies of equating Christian training in virtue with philosophical ways of life. We should also examine our own historical models of ancient philosophical practice and philosophical schools before we question Eusebius' understanding thereof.

---

[25] The *Life of Pamphilus* is mentioned in the shorter Greek version of the *Martyrs*, *MP*(Syr.), 11.3, and *HE*, VII.32.25. Jerome refers to this life in *Ep.*, 34.1; *De vir. ill.*, 81; *Contra Ruf.*, 1.9.

EUSEBIUS THE EDUCATOR: THE CONTEXT OF THE GENERAL ELEMENTARY INTRODUCTION

Aaron P. Johnson

Modern narratives of late Roman education rarely, if ever, include Eusebius of Caesarea in their enumeration of the great teachers who made their mark on the intellectual and cultural topography of the late antique Mediterranean world. The bishop of Caesarea hardly seems to rank among the shining lights of Origen, Plotinus, or Libanius.[1] Indeed, if Eusebius is mentioned at all, it is usually for his description of Origen's teaching activity.[2] And yet, an educational context provides an illuminating vantage from which to view Eusebius' work as an historian, apologist and biblical scholar.

In what follows, I want to turn attention to a text that has often been neglected in studies of Eusebius,[3] and which will greatly enrich our

---

[1] See J. Dillon, "Philosophy as a Profession in Late Antiquity," in S. Swain and M. Edwards (eds.), *Approaching Late Antiquity* (Oxford: Oxford University Press, 2004), 401–418; R. Cribiore, *The School of Libanius* (Princeton: Princeton University Pres, 2007); E. Watts, *City and School in Late Antique Athens and Alexandria* (Berkeley: University Presses of California, 2006).

[2] Eusebius, *Hist. eccl.*, VI.3, with Gregorius Thaumaturgus, *Pan. Or.*; see H. Lapin, "Jewish and Christian Academies in Roman Palestine: Some Preliminary Observations," in A. Raban and K. Holum (eds.), *Caesarea Maritima: A Restrospective after Two Millenia* (Brill: Leiden, 1996), 496–511; R. Wilken, "Alexandria: A School for Training in Virtue," in P. Henry (ed.), *Schools of Thought in the Christian Tradition* (Philadelphia: Fortress Press, 1984), 15–30. For the possibility of reconstructing Eusebius' educational activity from the evidence on Origen, see A.P. Johnson, "Eusebius' *Praeparatio Evangelica* as Literary Experiment," in S. Johnson (ed.), *Greek Literature in Late Antiquity: Dynamism, Didacticism, Classicism* (Aldershot: Ashgate, 2006), 67–89.

[3] Modern studies of the *General Elementary Introduction* can almost be numbered on one hand; see T. Nolte, "Zu den *Eclogis propheticis* des Eusebius von Cäsarea," *ThQ* 43 (1861), 95–109; W. Selwyn, "Emendations of Certain Passages of Eusebii *Eclogae Propheticae*," *JP* 4 (1872), 275–280; H. Smith, "Notes on Origen and Eusebius," *JThS* 18 (1916–1917), 77–78; G. Mercati, "La grande lacuna delle Ecloghe profetiche di Eusebio di Cesarea," in *Mémorial Louis Petit: mélanges d'histoire et d'archéologie byzantines* (Bucharest: Institut Français d'Études Byzantines, 1948), 1–3; T.D. Barnes, *Constantine and Eusebius* (Cambridge, Mass.: Harvard University Press 1981), 167–174; É. des Places, *Eusèbe de Césarée commentateur. Platonisme et Ecriture Sainte* (ThH 63; Paris: Beauchesne, 1982), 133–134.158–188; A. Kofsky, *Eusebius of Caesarea Against Paganism* (Leiden: Brill, 2000), 50–57; G. Dorival, "Remarques sur les *Eklogai*

understanding of the pedagogical side to the polymath of Caesarea. Apparently sometime during the highpoint of the Great Persecution (ca. 310 CE),[4] Eusebius composed a ten-book introductory manual for the student of Scriptures entitled the *General Elementary Introduction*. Aside from a few scanty fragments, Books Six-Nine of this work have survived under the title of *Eclogae Propheticae* and were edited by Gaisford in 1842 (Oxford) and soon reproduced in the PG series, volume 22 (Paris, 1857).[5] Both the title of the entire work and the subtitle of the extant books are explicitly given in the third book of the *Eclogae Propheticae*: "Let us select the [eclogues] from the other poetic books and the prophetic books after them in this third book of the *Prophetic Eclogues* on Christ, being the eighth book of the General *Elementary Introduction*."[6]

Of these four surviving books, the latter three contain prefaces intact, while the first book seems to have the remains of a preface in the badly damaged first pages.[7] In addition to the obvious lacunae in Books Six and Eight due to physical damage to the manuscript, Book Seven is dramatically shorter than the others and is obviously missing a number of its chapters (the so-called "great lacuna").[8] The contents of the four books comprise a Logocentric reading of the historical books of the Hebrew Scriptures (Book Six), the Psalms (Book Seven),

---

Prophétiques d'Eusèbe de Césarée," in B. Janssens, B. Roosen, and P. Van Deun (eds.), *Philomathestatos. Studies in Greek and Byzantine Texts Presented to Jacques Noret for his Sixty-Fifth Birthday* (Leuven: Peeters, 2004), 203–224. Unfortunately, I have not been able to consult the following thesis, though it should be noted: M. Jaubert Philippe, *Les* Extraits prophétiques au sujet du Christ *d'Eusèbe de Césarée*. Introduction. Traduction. Annotations (Université de Provence, Aix-Marseille I, 2000; Lille: Atelier national de reproduction des thèses, 2000).

[4] For considerations of date, see E. Schwartz, "Eusebios von Caesarea," *RE* XI, Stuttgart, 1909, col. 1387; Dorival, "Remarques sur les *Eklogai Prophétiques* d'Eusèbe de Césarée," *cit.*, 204–205; Barnes, *Constantine and Eusebius, cit.*, 167, suggests an earlier date (c. 303).

[5] The information given there is that the work is from Codex Vindobonensis LV; it is currently catalogued as Cod. Theol.gr. 29 (I am grateful to Ernst Gamillscheg at the ONB for reproduction of the manuscript).

[6] Hereafter *GEI*, 8.1 (1120D). All translations of ancient texts are my own, unless otherwise indicated. Here and throughout, references to the books of the *GEI* will be given according to their placement in the work as a whole, not within the *Ecl. proph.* in order to persistently recall Eusebius' larger project. See also, *GEI*, 9.35 (1261BC), where the fourth book of the *Ecl. Proph.* is equated with the ninth book of the *GEI*.

[7] *GEI*, 6 (1021A–1025A).

[8] See the admirable treatment of Dorival, "Remarques sur les *Eklogai Prophétiques*," *cit.*

the wisdom literature and Prophets (Book Eight), with the prophetic book of Isaiah receiving extended treatment of its own (Book Nine).[9]

Eusebius was by no means the first to write an introduction or εἰσαγωγή for students attempting to master a set of texts, nor was he unique in providing ἐκλογαί or selections from source texts, which could function as the basis for a curriculum.[10] Other teachers had set themselves the task of creating εἰσαγωγαί for students in a number of educational tracks in urban centers across the Roman world. And so, in order to appreciate properly the task Eusebius was performing in his introduction to reading Scripture, we should first consider this widespread educational practice, especially as it was developed among certain prominent Platonic philosophers in the years preceding Eusebius' literary activity. In what follows, I would like to attend to two variant foci present in earlier introductory manuals, before tracing their inextricable entanglement within Eusebius' *Introduction*. We shall then be in a better position to determine his place within the isagogic tradition: there may be a wider range to the polemical edge of Eusebius' pedagogy than might at first be apparent.

Earlier Introductions

Students pursuing any number of fields of inquiry[11] might be perplexed by the great number of writings within the particular field, the intricacies of the varied approaches, the obscurity of essential points requiring mastery, or the ambiguity of key terms. Students of the

---

[9] An enumeration of biblical books omitted from the *GEI* is provided by Dorival, *ibid.*, p. 205. The suggestion that the fragments of Eusebius' *Comm. in Luc.* derive from the missing tenth book of the *GEI* (D.S. Wallace-Hadrill, "Eusebius of Caesarea's *Commentary on Luke*: Its Origin and Early History," *HThR* 67 (1974), 55–63), should probably be rejected based on differences of style, scope and aims (as I hope to argue elsewhere).

[10] E.g., Clement Alexandrinus, *Ecl. Proph.* While the goal of this paper is to locate Eusebius within ancient pedagogical traditions, identifying his place within the anti-Jewish *testimonia* tradition is equally important; the thorough analysis of the *Dem. ev.* in this respect provided by S. Morlet ("Eusebius and the *testimonia*: Tradition and Originality," in A.-C. Jacobsen and J. Ulrich (eds.), *Three Greek Apologists: Origen, Eusebius, and Athanasius* (Frankfurt am Main: Peter Lang, 2007), 93–157) is applicable, *mutatis mutandis*, to the *GEI*.

[11] See the different surveys offered by E. Norden, "Die Composition und Litteraturgattung der horazischen Epistula ad Pisones," *Hermes* 40 (1905), 481–528; A.J. Festugière, *La Révélation d'Hermès Trismégiste*, II (Paris: Gabalda, 1949), 345–350.

medical arts required background training in the tenets of the compet-
ing medical schools, in addition to a survey of anatomical knowledge
that would begin with bones and move on to muscles.[12] Students of
mathematics had first to acquire a basic comprehension of its division
into various branches and the advances made by important thinkers
in each.[13] Students of astrology would need to understand the com-
plicated interconnections between signs of the zodiac and powers of
various planets and constellations, as well as the contributions made
by ancient nations to the science of the stars.[14]

Students of philosophy attempting to master Plato's corpus faced a
number of potential difficulties: the dialogue form, the interconnections between the dialogues, the order of reading them, and (most
daunting of all) the ideas expressed within them on reality, the soul,
love and so on. We are fortunate to possess some rather different specimens of such introductory texts to Plato. The εἰσαγωγαί can be distinguished according to their textual or doctrinal emphases. Whereas
a *textual* approach attempted to help students more effectively engage
with a particular text or set of texts, a more *doctrinal* approach sought
to provide students with an introduction to a system of ideas. This
two-fold distinction is admittedly somewhat simple and overly sche-
matic; but it proves helpful for identifying the dominant concerns and
methods of various introductions, whose basic features are otherwise
interconnected to a greater or lesser degree (as will become evident in
the texts discussed below).

Albinus' *Prologos*, written in the mid-second century CE, centered
its pedagogical attention on the determination of a proper *textual*
approach to Plato.[15] Before reading Plato's works, the student needed
to be informed of the correct definition of *dialogos* as a literary form;[16]
knowledge of the genre was then to be supplemented with recogni-

---

[12] See e.g., Galen, *De libr. prop.*, 23–24; 53–55; for general discussion, see Mansfeld, *Prolegomena, cit.*, 117–176, esp. pp. 126–131.

[13] See e.g., Anatolius, *Arithm. intro.*, (PG 10.231–236); for discussion, see Johnson, "Eusebius' *Praeparatio Evangelica* as Literary Experiment," *cit.*, 78–79, and bibliogra-phy there.

[14] See A. Jones, "Uses and Users of Astronomical Commentaries in Antiquity," in *Commentaries—Kommentare*, G. Most, ed. (Göttingen: Vandenhoeck und Ruprecht, 1999), 147–172.

[15] For the text of Albinus, see K.F. Hermann, *Platonis dialogi* (BiTeu; Lipsiae: Teu-bner, 1853), VI.147–151; for discussion of date, biography and context for Albinus, see T. Göransson, *Albinus, Alcinous, Arius Didymus* (Göteborg: Acta Universitatis Gothoburgensis, 1995), 34–77.

[16] Albinus, *Prol.*, 1–2 Hermann.

tion of the various classifications into which the individual dialogues fell.[17] These preliminaries were followed by serious consideration on the matter of what dialogue to read first—no little deliberation was necessary at this point since the dialogue had to be appropriate to the student's character.[18] The natural ability and age of the student, material circumstances, previous training in philosophy are all to be taken into due consideration in determining the best starting point for reading Plato's dialogues.[19]

Alcinous' *Didaskalikos*, on the other hand, centered its *doctrinal* approach upon determining the knowledge requisite for understanding the master's thought as a coherent system.[20] The broad contours of Plato's thinking in the areas of ethics, physics, metaphysics and theology would provide an adequate basis, Alcinous presumed, for the student about to face the challenge of reading the dialogues without falling into confusion or erroneously neglecting the important truths variously expressed within them.

Depending on educational need or the nature of the text to be taught, the same teacher could opt for either the textual or the doctrinal approaches in composing different introductory manuals. Closer to the time of Eusebius' composition of his own *Introduction*, Porphyry, the prolific author of important texts in a number of areas of enquiry and one of the most significant interlocutor's with whom Eusebius would engage in debate[21] or—strikingly—marshal as a supportive source,[22] also wrote introductory manuals of both kinds as part

---

[17] *Prol.*, 3 Hermann; see Mansfeld, *Prolegomena, cit.*, 74–97.

[18] *Prol.*, 4–6 Hermann; cf. Origen, *Comm. Cant.*, Praef. 1.4–7; I. Hadot, "Les introductions aux commentaires exégétiques chez les auteurs néoplatoniciens et les auteurs chrétiens," in M. Tardieu (ed.), *Les règles de l'interprétation* (Paris: Cerf, 1987), 111–113.

[19] *Prol.*, 5, Hermann.

[20] For the text of Alcinous, see J. Whittaker; a useful translation and introduction are provided by J. Dillon, *Alcinous. The Handbook of Platonism* (Oxford: Clarendon Press, 1993).

[21] The license of many scholars in finding Porphyry as a continual presence in the works of Eusebius (especially the *Praep. ev.* and *Dem. ev.*—hereafter *PE* and *DE*) has been soundly refuted by the thorough analyses of Sébastien Morlet (see the contribution to this volume and "La *Démonstration évangélique* d'Eusèbe de Césarée contient-elle des fragments du *Contra Christianos* de Porphyre? À propos du fr. 73 Harnack," *StPatr* 46, Leuven 2010, 59–64, my own modest contribution, "Rethinking the Authenticity of Porphyry, *c.Christ.* frag. 1," *ibid.*, 53–58, is in complete harmony with Morlet's project).

[22] See R. Goulet, "Hypothèses récentes sur le traité de Porphyre *Contre les chrétiens*," in M. Narcy and E. Rebillard (eds.), *Hellénisme et Christianisme* (Villeneuve d'Ascq: Presses universitaires du Septentrion, 2004) 81; C. Riedweg, "Porphyrios über

of his pedagogical program (if we can speak of a coherent program in Porphyry's case). Aside from anecdotes in his *Life of Plotinus* and the report by Eunapius that he taught in Rome after Plotinus' death,[23] we know almost nothing of Porphyry's role as an educator; these isagogical texts are therefore most valuable in reconstructing what we can of Porphyry's pedagogy. Two works are most obvious here: his *Introduction to Ptolemy's Tetrabiblos* and his *Introduction to Aristotle's Categories*.

The former, which cannot be securely dated, adopts a *textual* approach in its introduction to the great astrological treatise of Ptolemy. Porphyry explains the necessity for an introductory manual to the *Tetrabiblos* by insisting that, though the book exhaustively covered the various classes of its subject, it did so in diction (φράσις) that was "obscure and unclear because of antiquated usage of the words (ὀνόματα)."[24] Porphyry continues: "I thought it necessary to lay out information pertinent to its comprehension for the sake of clarity; it should also be fitting in the present work (πόνημα) to pass over that which was said clearly by Ptolemy in some passages since they possess their meaning clearly, but in the case of those said both summarily (κεφαλαιωδῶς) and unclearly we thought it beneficial to present them clearly so far as this was possible."[25] After enumerating some of the more difficult technical vocabulary that his *Introduction* will seek to explain, he promises that he will also address, "whatever material, left entirely unexplained by him, [which] would be a source of difficulty to the [student] entering upon the paths of astrology (προτελέσεις). For this reason, following our predecessors both concisely and judiciously, we put forth this introduction (εἰσαγωγήν) in a timely manner to be beneficial and easy to use for those uninitiated in literature (or "words," λόγων)."[26]

The discussions that follow this preface more or less remain within the parameters which he has set for his *Introduction*: he explains

---

Christus und die Christen: *De Philosophia ex Oraculis Haurienda* und *Adversos Christianos* im Vergleich," in *L'Apologétique chrétienne gréco-latine à l'époque prénicénienne* (EnAC 51; Genève: Fondation Hardt, 2005), 169.187–188.

[23] Eunapius, *Vit. Phil.*, 456.

[24] Porphyry, *Intro. Tetrab.*, praef., p. 190; I use the text published by E. Boer and S. Weinstock, *Catalogus codicum astrologorum Graecorum* V, fasc. 4 (Brussels: Lamertin, 1940), 187–229.

[25] *Intro. Tetrab.*, praef., p. 190.

[26] *Intro. Tetrab.*, praef., p. 190.

certain assumptions left unexplained by Ptolemy; he provides scientific examples to support some of Ptolemy's claims (e.g., that crabs and other hard-shelled sea creatures grow and decline with the waxing and waning of the moon, or that the female menstrual cycle is parallel with the moon);[27] and he includes the theories of his predecessors (Apollinarius, Thrasyllus, Petosiris and "other elders;"[28] Teucer of Babylon;[29] Antigonus and Phnaēs the Egyptian).[30] Throughout, ambiguities are clarified,[31] difficult terminology receives synonyms and explanations,[32] and complexities are simplified or tabulated for easy understanding and reference. Non-Ptolemaean assumptions are eschewed, as Ptolemy must be interpreted from Ptolemy—a procedure that was "useful for understanding these matters."[33]

Porphyry's *Introduction to Aristotle's Categories*, exhibits similar concerns guiding his discussion. He programmatically states: "I shall attempt, in making you a concise exposition, to rehearse, briefly and as in the manner of an introduction,[34] what the old masters say, avoiding deeper inquiries and aiming suitably at the more simple."[35] The concern to maintain brevity, the pedagogical focus on a student readership, the goal of providing what was beneficial, the invocation of earlier authorities, and the explicit adoption of the label εἰσαγωγή for the work in hand are all features that are shared in these two texts of Porphyry. The *Introduction* to the categories differs in its emphasis, however, throughout his explanatory discussion. While the *Introduction to Ptolemy's Tetrabiblos* was firmly a *textual* approach, the *Introduction to the Categories* offered a more *doctrinal* approach. Aristotle's *Categories* (or even more, his *Topics* 101b, 23–25) functioned as a springboard for Porphyry's own reflections about the five predicables, which would be beneficial, as he explicitly notes, not only for understanding

---

[27] *Intro. Tetrab.*, 2, p. 192.12–20.

[28] *Intro. Tetrab.*, 41, p. 212.14–17.

[29] *Intro. Tetrab.*, 47, p. 221.3–5.

[30] *Intro. Tetrab.*, 51, p. 223.17–20.

[31] E.g, *Intro. Tetrab.*, 54, p. 227.20–21.

[32] E.g., *Intro. Tetrab.*, 49, p. 222.4–9; 51, p. 223.20–21.

[33] *Intro. Tetrab.*, 41, p. 212.26–213.1.

[34] Cf. Porphyrius, *Comm. Sophist.*, fr. 169 Smith (= Boethius, *De Divis.*), p. 195, 5–6.

[35] *Isagoge*, praef., p. 1.7–10; text from A. Busse, *Porphyrii isagoge* (CAG 4.1; Berlin: Reimer, 1887), 1–22; all translations of the *Isagoge* are taken from J. Barnes, *Porphyry: Introduction* (Oxford: Claredon Press, 2003); for useful commentary on this passage with further comparanda, see Barnes, *ibid.*, 32–37.

"the teaching of Aristotle," but also for dialectic in general ("matters of division and proof").[36] Explication of obscure language or unclear assumptions in Aristotle's text are absent from Porphyry's *Introduction*. Obviously, a better grasp of what the predicables of genus, species, and so on meant would have aided the student reading the text of Aristotle; but it is not the text itself that receives Porphyry's primary attention (as it would in his commentaries on the *Categories*).

What should be clear from this brief survey of εἰσαγωγαί within the schools of Platonic philosophers is that, while they shared certain overarching pedagogical aims, there remained a fair amount of fluidity in the particular approaches to the topic they addressed. I have suggested that it might be helpful to see these texts as aligning themselves under either *textual* or *doctrinal* emphases. The distinction is by no means rigid, for texts remain important in introductions of the *doctrinal* sort, and doctrines are obviously essential to introductions of the *textual* sort. Yet, the distinction remains useful for identifying the driving mechanisms of the various introductory manuals, and in highlighting some of their most basic concerns. In addition, this distinction may prove helpful in better appreciating what Eusebius was doing in his *General Elementary Introduction*, to which I know turn.

EUSEBIUS' INTRODUCTION

One of the most disappointing features of Eusebius' *Introduction*—aside from the loss of over half of its books—is the severely fragmentary state of the first few leaves of Book Six, which contained its preface and opening chapters.[37] It is here that he claims to be commencing a new portion of his treatise that takes on a different task from what he had set himself in previous books. This change in his argument led him to give this section of the larger work the subtitle of *Prophetic Eclogues*. In the previous books, the *Introduction* had:

---

[36] *Isagoge*, praef. p. 1.6–7.
[37] PG 22.1021A–1025C (i.e., folios 1–2) seem to be from the first chapter or preface; the damaged beginning of folio 3 (at 1025C) seems to have contained the chapter heading of the second chapter. On Eusebius' employment of chapter headings, see T.D. Barnes, "Constantine's Good Friday Sermon," *JThS* 27 (1976), 418–421; K. Mras, *Eusebius Werke VIII. Die Praeparatio Evangelica* (GCS, 43.1; Berlin: Akademie, 1954), VIII–IX.

...proceeded through the testimonies about our Lord and Savior Jesus
Christ, and was confirmed with clear, faithful and true proofs and syllogisms, only at the end using quite short testimonies from divine Scriptures believed in by both Jews and ourselves; since the argument (λόγος)[38]
was not at all[39] choosing to present abundant confirmations[40] from the
divine Scriptures to those not yet believing in them at all. The present
books, at least, were labored at for those who already ought to believe
from their proof that they are divine and God-breathed, filling up what
remains in those sacred Scriptures, and in short containing a collection
(συναγωγή) [of testimonia]....[41]

The latter part of the sentence is unfortunately punctuated by lacunae.

The earlier books of his *Introduction* had apparently treated the life
and teaching of Christ using some form of rational argumentation.[42]
Only as a slight appendage at the end of his argument had he deemed
it necessary to incorporate scriptural citation, and even then he had
exercised restraint; his presumably pagan audience would not have
granted much authority to such testimony. Unlike his later *Praeparatio Evangelica*, which was explicitly addressed to Christian students,[43]
the first part of the *Introduction* was aimed at the yet unconverted. At
least some non-Christians seem to have been comfortable with their
Christian neighbors during the forty years of peace preceding the
Great Persecution, and thoughtful non-Christians like Porphyry were
rather well-read in the writings of the Christians. Unless we are unduly
skeptical, at least some non-Christian intellectuals took Christianity

---

[38] It is uncertain whether this should refer to a previous work of Eusebius' or to
a previous book in the *GEI*. The difficulty with the latter possibility is that Eusebius
usually prefers words like *suntaxis* or *sungramma* for the individual books of a larger
work; see *GEI*, 7. praef. (1089C); *GEI*, 8. praef. (1120D).

[39] I follow W. Selwyn's suggested emendation of the ungrammatical μὴ δὲ ἄλλος
to μηδαμῶς "not at all" ("Emendations of Certain Passages," *cit.*, 276, cf. *GEI*, 8.23
[1148C]); pace T. Nolte, ("Zu den *Eclogis propheticis*," *cit.*, 99), who suggests μὴ δὲ
ἄλλος "not otherwise."

[40] *Sustaseis* could also mean "accumulations," or even "quotations."

[41] *GEI*, 6. praef. (1021A); I have suggested an ending containing "[of testimonia]"
in accordance with e.g., *GEI*, 7. praef (1089C).

[42] J. Stevenson's claim that *DE* 3 may be a synopsis of the first half of the *Introduction* remains speculation (*Studies in Eusebius* (Cambridge: Cambridge University
Press, 1929), 63); for discussion of the background to *DE*, 3, see the excellent contribution of S. Morlet in this volume. The evidence from the exiguous fragments of Book
One, neglected by Gaisford but included by A. Mai at PG 22.1271–1274, seem to be
limited to a philosophical discussion on human nature and conscience.

[43] See *Praep. ev.*, 1.1.12; J. Sirinelli in J. Sirinelli and É. Des Places, *Eusèbe de Césarée. La Préparation Évangélique* (SC 206; Paris: Cerf, 1974), 43–44; Johnson, "Eusebius' *Praeparatio Evangelica* as Literary Experiment," *cit.*

seriously enough to engage in open debate, whether oral or literary, with Christians.[44] If Eusebius ran a school similar to Plotinus or other philosophers, then there would have been students in his audience of varying levels of interest and attachment. Schwartz suggested that the first part of the *Introduction* was aimed at "auditors" (ἀκροώμενοι), while the second part was directed to full catechumens.[45] Lack of evidence prohibits certainty, but the hypothesis possesses the merit of making sense of the exiguous statements of the *Introduction*, as well as pointing to the continuities of Christian and pagan educational structures and processes. If any discomfort remains with presuming a very large readership among pagans especially after the outbreak of persecution in the early fourth century, it can at least be said that Eusebius wanted his readers to suppose that there were quite rational arguments for the truth claims of Christianity, apart from the biblical texts, sufficient for converting non-believers.

These opening remarks of the *Introduction* thus mark a significant shift from whatever had come before and an abrupt turn towards a new emphasis, form of argumentation, and (potentially) audience. Eusebius presents us with further programmatic reflections about his audience in a later portion of what I take to be his preface:

> The presentation of passages from Scripture would, "be serviceable for comprehending the truly beneficial and healthful orthodoxy. It is necessary to attend to this—not only for those who are…advanced in their disposition, but also those who come below them and have just now, for the first time, come to the divine word; to them I think the treatise (ὑπόθεσις) will be serviceable in different ways, so that from it they might be able to know accurately the stability of the teachings (*logōn*) about which they had been taught (κατηχήθησαν)."[46]

Whereas the philosophical introductions we noted above aimed their explanatory discussions at less-advanced students who were still beginning their studies in the particular topic or corpus of writings, Eusebius considered his *Introduction* to be profitable both for the newly

---

[44] Public debates staged between pagans and Christians would have been perfectly at home within the civic context of the intellectual life exhibited by the eloquent personalities of the so-called Second Sophistic; cf. Galen, *De suis libris*, 14, where written text and oratorical display unite in a single event.

[45] Schwartz, "Eusebios," *cit.*, 1386; for similar divisions of the "student body" in late antiquity, see Watts, *City and School, cit.*, 29–35, passim; Dillon, "Philosophy as a Profession," *cit.*, 403–406; Cribiore, *The School of Libanius, cit.*, 174–196.

[46] *GEI*, 6. praef. (1024C).

converted, as well as for the more mature. It is unclear how exactly his treatise was meant to benefit the advanced student; but no doubt with a corpus of writings as varied, obscure and strange as the Hebrew Scriptures there would still be a number of areas in which continued learning might be necessary—especially with the insidious interpretations of Jews and heretics (whom he would soon mention in his preface).[47]

And yet, in spite of the concern to help readers and the care that was called for in learning to read the Scriptures, there was an equal concern, shared by most contemporary writers of introductions (as already noticed in Porphyry's case), to aim at brevity. Following a badly damaged section, which at one point declares that the *Introduction* will present "a most abbreviated (συντομωτάτην) [discussion]" (PG 22.1024D), Eusebius remarks: "We will also give some moderate exegesis with brevity, at times containing a proof of God's sacred prophecies being fulfilled in the case of our Savior alone, at other times indicating our idea which we have about the things put forth."[48] With an almost rhythmic cadence, Eusebius' assertion that more time is needed to delve deeper into the inner workings of prophetic texts echoes throughout the entirety of the *Introduction*: "While there is need of a great and rather deep investigation (θεωρίας) verse by verse, this is sufficient for the present treatment (ὑπόθεσιν);"[49] or again, "I leave [further exegesis] for those who are lovers of learning to seek, since I have been tedious even in what has been said, not because it [has fit] within the proposed scope (σκοπός) [of this treatise], but nevertheless because it was necessary for the clear narrative of the material passage by passage."[50] Eusebius thus introduces the methods of right reading while pointing the student in fruitful directions for more advanced levels of engagement.

Another salient, though less repeated, feature of Eusebius' *Introduction*, which has already been noticed in earlier introductory manuals, occurs in his drawing upon the discussions of earlier authorities. Some of the sources he cites are not surprising. In developing a proper interpretation of the "seven sevens" of Daniel, a passage that would have certainly been perplexing for the novice reader of Scriptures, Eusebius

---

[47] *GEI*, 6. praef. (1025A).
[48] *GEI*, 6. praef. (1025A).
[49] *GEI*, 6.3 (1036B).
[50] *GEI*, 6.8 (1049B).

provides a key passage from the *Chronography* of Africanus.[51] Other chronological matters are illuminated by passages from both Josephus and Africanus.[52] Much of this material will again receive ample attention in Eusebius' *Demonstratio Evangelica*, and again many of the same passages will be quoted for similar effect (indeed, his own comments and interpretation will contain an abundance of verbally identical material).[53]

A less obvious allusion to his predecessors is provided in the ninth book of the *Introduction*, where, before embarking on a survey of relevant passages from Isaiah, he offers an argument used by those who had come before him that might even carry conviction for those otherwise not disposed to believe in the biblical prophecies.[54] Basing itself on Deuteronomy 18:14–15, which prohibits the Israelites from pursuing augury and divination by daemonic means, while promising that God would send a prophet to them, the argument claims that the Jews would certainly have turned away from their traditions and gone after the oracles of the surrounding nations if they doubted the truth of the promise and the divine inspiration of their prophets.

> On the contrary, they appear to have accepted not only Moses but also many after him as prophets of God when they came to them, and it is entirely clear that they experienced the Divinity in them; for these ones not only foretold things that would take place a long time later, but also predicted some things which were close at hand and in their own lifetimes; for instance, lost donkeys and those dangerously ill, whether they would live or not, and coming prosperity for the people, and a thousand other things, which are related in their histories. If these things did not happen in this very way, let someone answer why, then, did they ever consider and call them prophets, or why did they consider their words [to be] Scripture? Why did they pass on their writings to their own children after them as though they were divine?[55]

---

[51] The same passage would later be quoted at *DE*, 8.2, 389b–391a.

[52] See *GEI*, 8.46 (1181A.C; 1184C; 1184D–1188A; 1189CD).

[53] See *DE* 8.2; rigorous comparison of the treatment of Daniel in the two works remains a desideratum in Eusebian scholarship. Most scholars have assumed that Eusebius is attempting in the *DE* passage to meet the challenge laid down by Porphyry (namely, that Daniel provided *post eventum* prophecy; *Contra Christ.*, frags. 43–44 Harnack), in spite of the fact that the two respective treatments do not seem to deal with the same issues; again, see the rigorous reassessment of S. Morlet in this volume.

[54] *GEI*, 9. praef. (1192C).

[55] *GEI*, 9. praef. (1192D–1193A).

The argument offered by Eusebius unmistakably paraphrases Origen's *Contra Celsum* 1.36.[56] Both the general line of reasoning and the scriptural passages cited are taken from the great apologist of the previous generation. Origen had claimed that this argument would be persuasive even to pagans, invoked the verses from Deuteronomy, and recalled the specific prophecies regarding lost donkeys and sick people.

Eusebius' introduction of this particular argument had only begun with the vague gesture: "And first it is good for us to present the reasoning observed by those who came before us. For they seem to me to have spoken well...."[57] It is unclear why Eusebius preferred not to name the predecessor he had in mind. In other contexts, it seems that he used such a veil of anonymity to protect Origen's identity (whom he esteemed highly) when he was criticizing his views.[58] In this case, however, his predecessor's argument is shown admiration. The anonymity could have been employed since he was not offering a verbatim quotation but only recalling the argument from memory; or, he was remembering Philo's earlier treatment as well as Origen's later adoption of it;[59] or, it was due to the contemporary conflict over Origenism.[60] Though his reasons for leaving Origen unnamed remain obscure, this occurrence offers a salutary reminder that Eusebius' interaction with Jewish and Christian traditions went beyond mere verbatim citations (though this remains the most striking feature) and exhibits a multi-layered and complex engagement with the books in his library.[61]

A final authority invoked in the *Introduction* is one of the more interesting. In elucidating a passage from Hosea, which runs "I am like a panther to Ephraim" (Hos. 5:14), the lost *Physics* of Didymus (most likely the Peripatetic philosopher of the first century) is quoted in order to provide information on the panther, in particular its fragrant smell

---

[56] Cf. *Contra Cels.*, 4.95.

[57] *GEI*, 9. praef. (1192C).

[58] E.g., *Comm. Psalm.*, 73.12–18 (LXX), PG 23.864AB; A.P. Johnson, "The Blackness of Ethiopians: Classical Ethnography and the Commentaries of Eusebius," *HThR* 99 (2006), 197–199. A full-scale re-evaluation of Eusebius' appropriation of Origen, which goes beyond glib assertions that Eusebius uncritically adopted the heritage of his intellectual superior, is necessary; see the valuable analysis of C. Zamagni in this volume.

[59] Cf., Philo, *Spec. leg.*, 1.63–65.

[60] This latter possibility is, however, not entirely credible, since he and Pamphilus had recently collaborated on a written defense of Origen.

[61] See A.P. Johnson, "Philonic Allusions in Eusebius, *PE* 7.7–8," *CQ* 56.1 (2006), 239–248.

which serves as an irresistible allurement to its prey.[62] Indeed, alle-
gorically understood, "the power of the divine Word and the fragrance
that comes forth from it" are irresistible. Those "of the circumcision"
who fail to attend to the verse's deeper meaning (*dianoia*) have fallen
prey to the slander that Christ was born from a panther.[63] This time
ignoring the sort of argument offered earlier by Origen against those
who claimed Christ was the son of a soldier named Pantera,[64] Eusebius
allows his scientific source to point towards the necessity of an allegorical interpretation of the passage. The otherwise unlikely Didymus
thus joins the ranks of predecessors whom Eusebius brought forth as
aids to his audience of apprentice readers.

That these authorities are usually directly quoted (with the important proviso of Origen noted above) raises one of the most salient features of Eusebius' *Introduction*; it is at once the most obvious and the
one that most markedly distinguishes his work from the introductory
manuals discussed above. Eusebius is well-known as a master of the
citational art in his other works. A. Momigliano noted the importance
of his extensive use of documentation in his historical work.[65] S. Inowlocki has recently conducted a thorough analysis of the significance
and complexity of citations in his apologetic work.[66] His polemical
work against Marcellus is littered with quotations from his theological
opponent.[67] The *General Elementary Introduction* marks yet another
expression of this consistent and far-reaching concern to present his
sources to the reader in often lengthy verbatim quotations.

In a passage quoted earlier, we saw that Eusebius labels the extant
part of his *Introduction* a collection, or συναγωγή of scriptural passages.[68] While the earlier portions of the *Introduction* had eschewed

---

[62] *GEI*, 8.10 (1136AB).

[63] *GEI*, 8.10 (1136BC).

[64] See Origen, *Contra Cels.*, 1.32; cf. notes provided by H. Chadwick, *Origen: Contra Celsum* (Cambridge: Cambridge University Press, 1953), p. 31, n. 3; and Barnes,
Constantine and Eusebius, cit., p. 361, n. 41.

[65] A. Momigliano, "Pagan and Christian Historiography in the Fourth Century,"
in *Id.* (ed.), *The Conflict Between Paganism and Christianity in the Fourth Century*
(Oxford: Clarendon Press, 1963), 79–99.

[66] S. Inowlocki, *Eusebius and the Jewish Authors. His Citation Technique in an
Apologetic Context* (AJEC 64; Leiden – Boston: Brill, 2006).

[67] For text, see E. Klostermann (ed.), *Eusebius Werke IV. Gegen Marcell, Über Die
Kirchliche Theologie* (GCS, 14; Leipzig: Hinrich, 1906).

[68] *GEI*, 6. praef. (1021A).

undue reliance upon scriptural testimony, the surviving second part sought to gather together all the passages that a student needed to master if he (or she?) was to proceed to deeper levels of inquiry and hence deeper levels of theological knowledge. It is here that we notice a rather clear merging of what I have earlier distinguished as the *doctrinal* and *textual* approaches to writing an introduction. The quotation of sometimes lengthy segments of biblical passages, accompanied by his sometimes equally brief commentary on the best reading strategies for those passages, manifestly expresses the importance of the source texts for his introductory manual. The texts were the object of exposition and introduction; the task set before the student was learning to read those texts well.[69]

And yet, learning to read Scriptures well depended upon a well-developed theological sensibility. Eusebius' *Introduction* thus had necessarily to adopt an equally *doctrinal* emphasis as well. Indeed, before turning to a survey of key Logocentric passages from Genesis, the master reader presents his student with a fundamental principal that was grounded in the proclamation of the Church: "The Word of God not only was preexistent before the incarnation but also before any generated substance (ὑποστάσεως)."[70] Already rooted in Scripture (namely, the prologue of John's Gospel), the doctrine of the Logos as it was formulated by ecclesiastical tradition was then turned back upon Scripture (in particular, the Hebrew Scriptures) as an interpretive guide for the perplexed student.

> The reader needs to maintain the apostolic proclamation as a standard (κάνονα) and focal-point (σκοπόν), preserving the doctrines of truth as perfect and inviolable, that is, the [doctrine] about the first and ungenerated nature of the God of all, and the [doctrine] of the divine Word's preexistence (προυποστάσεως) and service (ὑπουργίας) in the creation of all generated things.[71]

The concerns of the extant portions of the *Introduction* were thus twofold: first, to provide the student with a firm understanding of the nature and distinctiveness of the Logos relative to the God of all

---

[69] His *Introduction* nevertheless differs from earlier introductions of the textual approach (as typified by Albinus) in that there is no discussion (at least not in the extant portions) of the order of reading.
[70] *GEI*, 6. praef. (1025A).
[71] *GEI*, 6. praef. (1025BC).

or lesser angels, as well as the economy of that Logos;[72] and second, to alert the student to appropriate methods of interpreting the biblical texts, which included sensitivity to what was "fitting" (ἁρμόττειν) to the Logos, the Father, or angels,[73] the relevance of the Hebrew tetragrammaton,[74] and the significance of seemingly minor elements of the text.[75] His consistent concern to guide students in a Logocentric reading of the Hebrew Scriptures—a task both *textual* and *doctrinal* at once—secures the *Introduction* a double movement as an educational *and* apologetic treatise.

The preponderance of direct quotation might seem to be a feature of his text that is unique to Eusebius among composers of elementary textbooks. Eusebius' contribution to the apologetic genre in this regard is well-known.[76] Was the citational method Eusebius' own distinctive contribution to the introductory genre? Two observations should provide sufficient caution in too readily answering this question in the affirmative. The first is that introductions formed a rather loose assortment of texts and preclude easy definitions of a genre that set their limits. Attention to ancient commentaries reveals that they shared many of the features and aims of εἰσαγωγαί of the more textually-focused kind, such as concern for brevity, elucidation of obscure words, invocation of predecessors, and so on.[77] If one compares philosophical or biblical commentaries with a "selections" manual, such as Clement of

---

[72] The complete silence regarding the *GEI* in the standard modern treatments of Eusebius' Logos theology is inexplicable; e.g., H. Berkhof, *Die Theologie des Eusebius von Caesarea* (Amsterdam: Uitgeversmaatschappij Holland, 1939), 67–75; F. Ricken, "Die Logoslehre des Eusebios von Caesarea und der Mittelplatonismus," *ThPh* 42 (1967), 341–358; *Id.*, "Zur Rezeption der platonischen Ontologie bei Eusebios von Kaisareia, Areios und Athanasios," *ThPh* 53 (1978), 321–352.

[73] E.g., *GEI*, 6.2 (1028A); 6.3 (1032A, 1033D–1036D); 6.10 (1053D); 7.8 (1104A); 8.8 (1133C).

[74] E.g., *GEI*, 6.2 (1025C, 1029D); 6.7 (1040D); 6.10 (1053D); 6.11 (1056C); 6.12 (1065A, C, 1068A).

[75] E.g., his emphasizing of the article at *GEI*, 7.1 (1092C); his remarks on the use of the singular rather than plural form of a noun at *GEI*, 9.1 (1197A); or, his discussion of "face" (prosopon and enopios) at *GEI*, 6.12 (1060A–1069A); for context within Eusebius' conception of Jewishness, see Johnson, *Ethnicity and Argument, cit.*, 117–119.

[76] See Inowlocki, *Eusebius and the Jewish Authors; cit.*, Johnson, "Eusebius' *Praeparatio Evangelica* as Literary Experiment," *cit.*

[77] See R. Heine, "The Introduction to Origen's *Commentary on John* Compared with the Introductions to the Ancient Philosophical Commentaries on Aristotle," in G. Dorival and A. Le Boulluec (eds.), *Origeniana Sexta*...(Leuven: Peeters, 1995), 3–12; Mansfeld, *Prolegomena, cit.*; Hadot, "Les introductions aux commentaires exégétiques," *cit.*

Alexandria's *Eclogae Propheticae*, the primary difference only seems to reside in the fact that the latter provides comments on a variety of passages loosely (sometimes, very loosely) organized around a single theme, while a commentary explains passages in a linear fashion from the beginning to the end of the source text. A work that was strictly a "selections" manual (that is, it did not make an explicit claim to be an εἰσαγωγή for beginning students) was a multi-purpose text that could be used variously for theological, polemical, isagogical, or homiletical purposes. The extant portions of Eusebius' *Introduction* are narrower in focus and sometimes contain discussion and argument that seems more extensive than might be expected for a strictly "selections" manual; but the work of the fourth-century bishop certainly marks a strong and sustained trajectory of that tradition.

The second consideration that prevents us from too readily taking Eusebius' *Introduction* to be unique for its extensive quotation comes from a reappraisal of a work of Porphyry that has been receiving a good deal of recent attention in discussions of that author's religious position.[78] Porphyry's *Philosophy from Oracles*, which sadly survives in the fragments gleaned from his hostile opponents,[79] chief of whom was Eusebius himself, has remarkable similarities to the extant portions of the *General Elementary Introduction*.[80] In spite of its fragmentary

---

[78] See especially J. Schott, "Porphyry on Christians and Others: 'Barbarian Wisdom,' Identity Politics, and Anti-Christian Polemics on the Eve of the Great Persecution," *Journal of Early Christian Studies* 13 (2005), 277–314; E. Depalma Digeser, "Christian or Hellene? The Great Persecution and the Problem of Identity," in R. M. Frakes and E. D. Digeser (eds.), *Religious Identity in Late Antiquity* (Toronto: Kent, 2006), 36–57; P.F. Beatrice, "Towards a new edition of Porphyry's fragments against the Christians," in ΣΟΦΙΗΣ ΜΑΙΗΤΟΡΕΣ. *'Chercheurs de Sagesse.' Hommage à Jean Pépin* (Paris: Institut des Études Augustiniennes, 1992), 347–55; *Id.*, "Antistes Philosophiae: Ein christenfeindlicher Propagandist am Hofe Diokletians nach dem Zeugnis des Laktanz," in *Aug.* 33 (1993), 31–47; *Id.*, "On the Title of Porphyry's Treatise Against the Christians," in Ἀγαθὴ ἐλπίς. *Studi storico-religiosi in onore di Ugo Bianchi*, ed. G. Sfameni Gasparro (Roma: L'"Erma" di Bretschneider, 1994), 221–235.

[79] It should be remembered that many of the fragments of this work are in fact quoted by their Christian source as *positive* evidence against other (anonymous) pagans; see Goulet, "Hypothèses récentes," *cit.*, 81, and Riedweg, "Porphyrios über Christus und die Christen," *cit.*, 169.187–188.

[80] The text of the *Phil. ex orac.* edited by A. Smith, *Porphyrius. Fragmenta* (BiTeu; Stuttgart: Teubner, 1993), surpasses that of G. Wolff, *Porphyrii de Philosophia ex Oraculis Haurienda Librorum Reliquiae* (Berlin: Springer, 1856). The best modern treatment is that of A. Busine, *Paroles d'Apollon: Pratiques et traditions oraculaires dans l'Antiquité tardive* (Religions in the Graeco-Roman world 156; Leiden: Brill, 2005); also particularly helpful are the critical analyses of misleading modern assumptions about the *Phil. ex orac.* and its relation to Porphyry's other works and thought offered

state, Porphyry's work shows a clear pattern of quoting often lengthy verse oracles of Apollo, Hecate and other divinities, followed by the philosopher's own brief comments that seek to alert the reader to features of the oracle that may otherwise have escaped their attention or posed a difficulty in appreciating the oracle for its more philosophical indications.[81]

An oracle, for instance, that was delivered in response to an enquiry about the mysterious deaths of a group of woodsmen revealed in a rather straightforward way the cause of their death (Pan's sudden arrival in the woods) and proper preventative measures that were to be taken (the survivors must make supplication to Artemis).[82] Rather than emphasizing the cultic aspects of the oracle, Porphyry's comments seem to focus instead on the initial lines of the oracle that show Pan as a servant of Dionysus, hence evincing a divine hierarchy that might easily be situated within a neoplatonist hierarchical system. In another fragment, Porphyry cites another oracle that outlines an extensive list of sacrificial procedures, and again focuses on the divine hierarchy underlying the variety of sacrifices.[83] At the very outset, then, the general tenor and method of Porphyry's work seem to resonate with the processes of Eusebius' own *Introduction*: quotations of sacred texts are followed by doctrinally-charged comments that attempt to maintain brevity and point the reader to a correct interpretative framework.[84]

The remains of Porphyry's preface to the *Philosophy from Oracles* provide further confirmation of the parallels between the two works.

> The present collection (συναγωγή) will contain a record of many of the teachings according to philosophy, since the gods prophesied that they possessed the truth. And I shall briefly adjoin a useful (χρηστική)[85]

---

by Goulet, "Hypothèses récentes," *cit.*, and C. Riedweg, "Porphyrios über Christus und die Christen." *cit.*

[81] On the provenance of the oracles, see Busine, *Paroles d'Apollon, cit.*, 246–256

[82] *Phil. ex orac.*, fr. 307 Smith (= Eusebius, *PE*, 5.5.7–5.6.2).

[83] *Phil. ex orac.*, frs. 314–315 Smith (= Eusebius, *PE*, 4.8.4–4.9.2–7); on this oracle, see the two differing emphases in Busine, *Paroles d'Apollon, cit.*, 259–261, I. Tanaseanu-Döbler, "'Nur der Weise ist Priester:' Rituale und Ritualkritik bei Porphyrios," in *Ead., Religion und Kritik in der Antike* (Münster: LIT Verlag, 2009), 109–155.

[84] See A.P. Johnson, "Arbiter of the Oracular: Reading Religion in Porphyry of Tyre" in *The Power of Religion in Late Antiquity*, A. Cain and N. Lenski, eds. (Aldershot: Ashgate, 2009), 103–115.

[85] Modern scholarship has almost unanimously (but mistakenly) taken χρηστική as referring to divination; the translation of the term as "useful," however, better fits the immediate context: his "useful discussion" will be profitable (ὀνήσει) for contempla-

discussion, which is profitable for contemplation and any other purifica-
tion of life. What benefit the collection (συναγωγή) has those ones will
especially know who are giving birth[86] to truth.[87]

The guiding principles of Porphyry's work bear close resemblance to
those of Eusebius. Both authors devote themselves to the drafting of a
collection (συναγωγή) of oracular source texts, accompanied by their
own brief, yet beneficial, explication of important details of those texts.
Both provide a manual that assists the student in making progress
towards salvation (Porphyry) or orthodoxy (Eusebius) derived from
oracular texts.

In light of such strong resonance between these two texts (damaged
and fragmentary though they both are), one cannot help but be struck
by the possibility that Eusebius was attempting to develop a rival pedagogy to that of Porphyry. Aside from the shared methodological features, the basis of their introductions in oracular texts, whether these
were the oracles of Hebrew prophets or of pagan divinities, makes it
sufficiently difficult to dismiss the possibility too easily. In a provoca-
tive discussion, A. Busine has recently suggested that the *Philosophy
from Oracles* aimed to offer a revelatory basis for philosophy in pagan
oracles so as to rival Christian appeals to the Hebrew oracles (*logia*)—
indeed, the very title of Porphyry's treatise uses the term *logia* for his
pagan oracles (an unusual usage for what would normally have been
named χρησμοί).[88] If she is right, then the work of Eusebius discussed
here may be located within an ongoing struggle between pagans and
Christians that refused to be confined within the narrow boundaries of
overtly polemical treatises. The *Introduction* may stand as a Christian
response that develops a distinctively Christian pedagogy for reading
oracles which counteracted, or rather usurped, the pedagogy and oracles of his anti-Christian rival.

---

tion and will benefit (ὠφέλειαν) the person who is giving birth to truth. See Busine,
Paroles d'Apollon, cit., 256–258; Johnson, "Arbiter of the Oracular," *cit.*
  [86] The metaphor is platonic; see Plato, *Symp.*, 206d; *Phaedr.*, 251e; *Rep.*, 6.490b.
  [87] *Phil. ex orac.*, fr. 303 (= Eusebius, *PE*, 4.6.2–4.7.2).
  [88] A. Busine, "Des *logia* pour philosophie. À propos du titre de la *Philosophie
tirée des oracles* de Porphyre," *Philosophie Antique* 4 (2004), 149–166. The claim by
H. Lewy, *Chaldean Oracles and Theurgy* (Cairo: Institut français d'archéologie ori-
entale, 1956), that many of the oracles of Porphyry's collection were taken from the
Chaldean Oracles is untenable; see E.R. Dodds, "New Light on the *Chaldean Oracles*,"
HThR 54 (1961), 263–273; Busine, *Paroles d'Apollon, cit.*, 200–202.247.

Such a framework for understanding the discursive location of Eusebius' *Introduction* (as well as Porphyry's *Philosophy from Oracles*) does
not entail subsequent discovery of Porphyry behind every bush, so
to speak, of Eusebius' literary garden[89] (nor that Christians should be
found behind every bush in Porphyry's garden). Both thinkers crafted
their introductory manuals in distinctively Christian or Platonic ways
and kept themselves from debasing their pedagogies to mere polemics
or apologetics against the criticisms or doctrines of the opposition.[90]
What is shared by the two is the common understanding of what they
were attempting to do as educators, their common search for a rap-
prochement between the inspired words of oracles and the rationally
concluded doctrines of the lover of wisdom (or of God), their shared
interweaving of the *textual* and *doctrinal* approaches to the composition of their introductory manuals, and their awareness of rival ways
of reading that were insidious to the reasoned exegeses of those who
sought wisdom and true piety.

Though otherwise disconcerting in its fragmentary form and in the
absence of a critical edition or modern translation, Eusebius' *General Elementary Introduction* rewards its patient reader; for it directs
us along paths of enquiry that remain largely untapped in Eusebian
studies, as well as pointing us to other possibilities in delineating his
precise relationship to his predecessors and opponents. Pedagogical
concerns are abundantly attested (albeit neglected in modern scholarship) in his other works—from his biblical commentaries to his *Onomasticon*, the apologetic works, and the *Question and Answer* letters.
In a volume that has set itself the task of rethinking old approaches
to Eusebius and of locating more fruitful approaches for the future, I
hope that this modest contribution might point to the importance of
reading Eusebius as an educator.

---

[89] Eusebius' own metaphor, which prompted this one, is slightly different: his *Introduction* (or at least the *Ecl. Proph.* portion) was a bouquet of flowers plucked from
scriptural gardens; *GEI*, 6. praef. (1024BC).

[90] This is not to say that Eusebius does not engage in full-scale polemic against
Jewish interpretation, however; see my unpublished paper, "Without an Introduction:
Eusebius' *General Elementary Introduction* on the Jews" NAPS Annual Meeting, Chi-
cago, IL, May 23, 2008.

EUSEBIUS' POLEMIC AGAINST PORPHYRY: A REASSESSMENT

Sébastien Morlet*

Eusebius is often considered as the 'Anti-Porphyry'.[1] Two reasons may account for this reputation: first, the fact that Eusebius wrote a *Contra Porphyrium*, now lost; second, and above all, the fact that his master work, composed of the *Praeparatio euangelica* (= *PE*) and the *Demonstratio euangelica* (= *DE*), is often considered as an answer to Porphyry's *Contra Christianos*.[2] This way of reading the whole apology is prior to A. von Harnack. Lenain de Tillemont, in the 18th century, already stated that in his apology, Eusebius "refutes Porphyry almost everywhere, often without mentioning him."[3] This was also the opinion of J.B. Lighfoot,[4] J. Geffcken,[5] J. Bidez[6] and so many scholars till today.[7] Harnack's decision to include among the fragments of the

---

* I am very grateful to Aaron Johnson whose precious remarks helped me to enrich this paper.

[1] We owe this phrase to J. Geffcken, *Zwei griechische Apologeten* (Leipzig – Berlin: Teubner, 1907), p. 309.

[2] Many problems have recently been raised concerning the date of this work, its content and its relationship with other works of Porphyry. In this paper, I consider that Porphyry wrote a work probably entitled Κατὰ χριστιανῶν and different from any of Porphyry's other works. I do not accept P.F. Beatrice's hypothesis that this work is to be identified with the *Philosophy from oracles* (see "On the Title of Porphyry's Treatise against the Christians", in Ἀγαθὴ ἐλπίς. *Studi storico-religiosi in onore di Ugo Bianchi*, ed. G. Sfameni Gasparro (Roma: L'"Erma" di Bretschneider, 1994), 221–235), nor R.M. Berchman's hypercritical view that Porphyry never wrote an independent work against Christianity (*Porphyry Against the Christians* (Leiden: Brill, 2005), pp. 2–3), and I agree with R. Goulet's more reasonable conclusions ("Hypothèses récentes sur le traité de Porphyre, *Contre les chrétiens*", in *Hellénisme et Christianisme*, ed. M. Narcy – É. Rébillard (Villeneuve d'Ascq: Presses universitaires du Septentrion, 2004), 61–109).

[3] "[Eusèbe] y refute Porphyre presque partout, souvent sans le nommer" (*Mémoires pour servir à l'histoire ecclésiastique des six premiers siècles*, VII (Paris: C. Robustel, 1700), p. 53).

[4] "Eusebius", *DCB*, II, London 1880, p. 329.

[5] *Zwei griechische Apologeten*, *cit.*, p. 309.

[6] "V. Christian Apologetics: Eusebius", *CAH*, XII, Cambridge 1939 (repr. 1961), p. 642.

[7] To mention only the most recent scholars: D. Rokeah, *Pagans and Christians in Conflict* [Leiden – Jerusalem: Brill – Magnes Press, 1982], p. 76; H. Schreckenberg,

Contra Christianos no less than six extracts from Eusebius,[8] three of which are from the *PE*[9] and three from the *DE*,[10] had a heavy consequence on subsequent research: it solidified the idea that Eusebius' apology was an answer to Porphyry's work. Using Harnack's edition uncritically, almost every scholar, from that date, has taken this hypothesis as an indisputable truth. However, only two fragments from Eusebius' apology, taken from the *PE*, are explicitly presented by the bishop of Caesarea as quoted from Porphyry's work.[11] In the *DE*, there is no such explicit fragment. Despite this lack of direct evidence, many scholars still consider, paradoxically, that Porphyry is "everywhere" in the *PE* and the *DE*. Two reasons may explain this conviction:

- First, though Eusebius' work contains only two explicit allusions to Porphyry's treatise, the bishop of Caesarea quotes many texts from other works of Porphyry (*Philosophy from oracles*, *On abstinence*, *On*

Die christlichen Adversus-Judaeos-Texte und ihr literarisches und historisches Umfeld (1.–11. Jh.) (Frankfurt am Main: Peter Lang, 1982), p. 263; M. Frede, "Eusebius' Apologetic Writings", in *Apologetics in the Roman Empire: Pagans, Jews and Christians*, ed. M. Edwards – M. Goodman – S. Price (Oxford: Oxford University Press, 1999), p. 242; E.V. Gallagher, "Eusebius the Apologist: the Evidence of the *Preparation* and the *Proof*", StPatr 26, Leuven 1993, p. 259; J.G. Cook, *The Interpretation of the New Testament in Greco-Roman Paganism* (Tübingen: Mohr Siebeck, 2000), p. 134; M. Fiedrowicz, *Apologie im frühen Christentum. Die Kontroverse um den christlichen Wahrheitsanspruch in den ersten Jahrhunderten*, 2ᵉ ed. (Paderborn: F. Schöningh, 2001), p. 73; C. Kannengiesser et alii, *A Handbook of Patristic Exegesis*, II (Boston – Leiden: Brill, 2004), p. 675.

[8] See *Porphyrius, "Gegen die Christen", 15 Bücher. Zeugnisse, Fragmente und Referate, Abhandlungen der preussischen Akademie der Wissenschaften, Philosophisch-historische Klasse*, Berlin, 1916.

[9] *PE*, I.2.1–5 (fr. 1 Harnack); I.9.21 (fr. 41 Harnack); V.1.10 (fr. 80 Harnack).

[10] *DE*, I.1.12 (fr. 73 Harnack); III.5.95–100 (fr. 7 Harnack); VI.18.11 (fr. 47 Harnack).

[11] See *PE*, I.9.21 (= X.9.12); V.1.10. I am aware that P. Nautin attributed to Porphyry three fragments taken from Philo of Byblos' *De Iudaeis* quoted in *PE*, I ("Trois autres fragments du livre de Porphyre *Contre les chrétiens*", RB 57 (1950), 409–416). However, this hypothesis seems doubtful and a few studies have argued that Eusebius quotes these texts directly from Philo of Byblos, and not from Porphyry (T.D. Barnes, "Porphyry *Against the Christians*: Date and the Attribution of Fragments", JThS 24 (1973), p. 426; A.[J.] Carriker, *The Library of Eusebius of Caesarea* (SVigChr 67; Leiden – Boston: Brill, 2003), p. 150). To reject P. Nautin's hypothesis would not automatically contradict the Porphyrian origin of the texts quoted from Philo of Byblos, if one considers, as some scholars did, that Eusebius draws his quotations of Philo's *Historia Phoenicia* from Porphyry's *Contra Christianos*, and that the *De Iudaeis* was a section of the *Historia Phoenicia* (see the *status quaestionis* in Carriker, *ibid.*, pp. 149–150). But the first hypothesis cannot be demonstrated. Moreover, there seems to be some evidence that Eusebius knew first hand the *Historia Phoenicia* (Carriker, *ibid.*, p. 149).

the soul, On the divine statues, Letter to Anebo, Philological lesson,
and perhaps *Philosophical history).*[12] Certainly, Eusebius was a good
connoisseur of Porphyry. But that does not entail that his apology is
an answer to the *Contra Christianos* or to any of Porphyry's works.
In his recent analysis, A. Kofsky showed that Eusebius does not use
Porphyry to answer his objections, but either as an "auxiliary witness", or as a "self-contradictory author".[13] Yet, the same scholar
agrees with the traditional idea that Eusebius' apology, though not
an answer to the *Contra Christianos*, was at least raised by Porphyry's attack against Christianity.[14] Kofsky went as far as to consider
the dual composition of the apology as a reflection of Porphyry's
accusation against the Christians.[15]
- A more modern reason why Eusebius' apology was considered as
  an answer to the *Contra Christianos*, despite the lack of evidence, is
  related to Harnack's edition. Two fragments from Harnack's collection seem to have had a strong influence on modern interpretation
  of Eusebius' apologetic.

1) Fragment 1 is taken from the first pages of the *PE*, where Eusebius
is reproducing pagan accusations against Christianity. Pagans accuse
Christians for supporting an irrational faith and for being apostates
from Hellenism and from Judaism. The accusation of being apostates
from Judaism is then reproduced again, but this time in the mouth
of Jewish opponents to Christianity.[16] Harnack, following Wilamowitz' analysis,[17] was convinced that the pagan accusations were taken
from the prologue of the *Contra Christianos*, though, once again, no
external argument may support that attribution.[18] A.P. Johnson[19] and

---

[12] See Carriker, *ibid.*, pp. 115–123.

[13] *Eusebius of Caesarea Against Paganism* (Leiden: Brill, 2002), p. 273. This analysis
is, of course, not contradictory with the idea that there is a real polemical intention
in Eusebius' debate with Porphyry. Eusebius' ironical remarks show that he also aims
at ridiculing the philosopher. The question is to know whether Eusebius also seeks to
answer his objections against Christianity.

[14] *Ibid.*, p. 275.

[15] *Ibid.*, p. 250ss.

[16] See *PE*, I.2.1–5.

[17] "Ein Bruchstück aus der Schrift des Porphyrius gegen die Christen", *ZNW* 1
(1900), pp. 101–105.

[18] See *Porphyrius, "Gegen die Christen", cit.*, p. 45.

[19] "Rethinking the Authenticity of Porphyry, *c.Christ.* fr. 1", in *StPatr* 46, Leuven
2010, 53–58.

myself[20] have recently, though on different grounds, demonstrated that Wilamowitz' assumption was very disputable; Eusebius is reproducing common accusations against Christianity, primarily taken from Origen's *Contra Celsum*.[21] Harnack's decision had two consequences on subsequent research: first, many scholars took for granted that irrational faith and double apostasy were key concepts of Porphyry's polemic against Christianity;[22] second, the twofold plan of Eusebius' apology was sometimes considered as responding to the accusation of double apostasy.[23] I personally tried to show that the plan of the apology has its logic in itself. Eusebius' aim is to offer a complete defense of Christianity. The plan of the work is not a reflection of a true and precise pagan accusation. More probably, the pagan accusation has been constructed by Eusebius so as to announce his argument.[24]

2) In the very first pages of the *PE*, Eusebius reproduces a pagan accusation that Christians cannot prove their faith.[25] This accusation appears at least three times in *PE*, I,[26] and recurrs at the beginning of the *DE*.[27] It is obvious that Eusebius considers it as a major criticism against Christianity. Since Harnack, who thought that Eusebius was quoting exact words from Porphyry,[28] this accusation has generally been considered as Porphyrian.[29] This hypothesis immediately gives an anti-Porphyrian turn to Eusebius' entire apologetic work. Yet, the accusation of irrational faith has nothing distinctively Porphyrian in

---

[20] *L'apologétique chrétienne à l'époque de Constantin. La* Démonstration évangélique *d'Eusèbe de Césarée* (thèse de doctorat, Université de Paris IV-Sorbonne, 2006), pp. 43–50; see now *La Démonstration évangélique d'Eusèbe de Césarée. Étude sur l'apologétique chrétienne à l'époque de Constantin* (Paris: Études augustiniennes, 2009).

[21] One could also compare *PE*, I.2.1–4 and *Diogn.*, 1.

[22] T.D. Barnes, *Constantine and Eusebius* (Cambridge, Mass.: Harvard University Press, 1981), p. 178; Frede, "Eusebius' Apologetic Writings", *cit.*, p. 249.

[23] Barnes, *Constantine and Eusebius*, *cit.*, p. 178; Frede, "Eusebius' Apologetic Writings", *cit.*, p. 242; Kofsky, *Eusebius of Caesarea Against Paganism, cit.*, p. 250ss.

[24] *L'apologétique chrétienne à l'époque de Constantin, cit.*, p. 51ss.

[25] *PE*, I.1.11.

[26] *Ibid.*, I.2.4; I.3.5; I.5.2.

[27] *DE*, I.1.12; I.1.15.

[28] See *Porphyrius, "Gegen die Christen", cit.*, p. 91.

[29] Harnack's hypothesis is implicitly accepted by recent translators of the supposed fragments of *Contra Christianos*; see R.M. Berchman, *Porphyry Against the Christians, cit.*; E.A. Ramos Jurado et alii, *Contra los Cristianos: recopilación de fragmentos, traducción, introducción y notas* (Cádiz: Publicaciones de la Universidad de Cádiz, 2006).

itself. We can find echoes of it in Lucian,[30] Epictetus,[31] Galen[32] and above all, Celsus.[33] In a paper read in August 2008 at the International Conference of Patristic Studies, I have shown that the wording of Harnack's fr. 73 echoes Celsus' style.[34] As a consequence, it is much more reasonable to think that Eusebius draws his pagan material here from Celsus, not from Porphyry. This conclusion is related to my analysis of Eusebius' argumentation in the *DE*. A precise study of the work shows that Eusebius' dependence on Origen's *Contra Celsum* is important and that most of the anti-Christian criticisms in the *DE* stem from Celsus, not from Porphyry.

These are the main reasons why, nowadays, the *PE* and the *DE* are considered as a direct answer to Porphyry. It encouraged scholars to consider any critique against Christianity in that work as belonging to Porphyry's argumentation, and to analyse any demonstration of Eusebius in terms of anti-Porphyrian polemic. This double approach of modern research opened the way to uncritical and ill-founded conclusions. It recently culminated in M.B. Simmons' repeated attempt to analyse almost every page of Eusebius as an answer to Porphyry.[35] Some scholars, including Simmons himself, have also tried to find traces of anti-Porphyrian polemic in other works of Eusebius, such as the *Panegyric for the Tyre Basilica*,[36] or the *Praises of Constantine*.[37] My aim is not to demonstrate that there is no polemic against Porphyry in the double apology, but to show that this polemic has been exaggerated and has led scholars in wrong directions. I will concentrate primarily on the *DE*. I will first deal with the plan and content of the

---

[30] *Peregr.*, 13.

[31] *Diatr.*, IV.7.6.

[32] Cf. P. Krauss – R. Walzer, *Plato Arabus*, I (London: Warburg Institute, 1951), fr. 1, pp. 99–100.

[33] *Cels.*, I.9; I.42; I.67; III.27.

[34] See preceding note and *Cels.*, I.61; II.31; III.39; V.61; VI.7; VI.10–11; VI.74.

[35] See M.B. Simmons, *Arnobius of Sicca. Religious Conflict in the Age of Diocletian* (Oxford: Clarendon Press, 1995). For an analysis of the universalism theme in the work of Eusebius as a reaction to Porphyry, see *Id.*, "Via universalis animae liberandae: The Pagan-Christian Debate on Universalism in the Later Roman Empire (A.D. 260–325)", *StPatr* 42, Leuven 2006, 245–251; *Id.*, "Universalism in the *Demonstratio Evangelica* of Eusebius of Caesarea", *StPatr* 46, Leuven 2010, 319–324.

[36] M.B. Simmons, "Eusebius' Panegyric at the Dedication of the Church at Tyre AD 315: Anti-Porphyrian Themes in Christian Rhetoric of the Later Roman Empire", in *StPatr* 37, Leuven 2001, 597–607.

[37] M. Amerise, *Elogio di Costantino: Discorso per il trentennale, Discorso regale* (Milano: Paoline, 2005), pp. 83–84.

work, so as to show that the general intention of Eusebius has nothing
(or very little) to do with Porphyry. Then, a critical examination should
show which passages of that work have been held or are held as 'anti-
Porphyrian', and what we should think about that interpretation.

General Remarks

The *DE* contained originally twenty books, from which only the first
ten have survived, to which one must add some fragments from Book
XV, and a testimony of Jerome about Book XVIII.[38] After explaining
in the *PE* why the Christians have abandoned Paganism and turned
to the traditions of the Hebrews, Eusebius aims at showing why the
Christians have abandoned Judaism and adopted a new way of understanding God's Revelation. If we accept, as many scholars do, that
Harnack's fr. 1 contains Porphyry's key argument against Christianity, then we could analyse the plan of *PE-DE* as a reaction against that
argument. But if, as it appears, fr. 1 has nothing, or very little, to do
with Porphyry, then we have to turn to another analysis. Here is a brief
sketch of the content of the work:

PE	I–VI	Refutation of Paganism
	VII–IX	Defense of the Hebrew-Jewish tradition
	X–XV	Attack against Greek philosophy
DE	I	The Law and the Gospel
	II	The call of the Nations / The rejection of Israel
	III–X	Jesus-Christ

It is easy to observe that the *PE* deals with the general topics of anti-
pagan polemic: condemnation of the oracles, the gods and the demons
(I–VI); praise of the pious and 'philosophical' character of the Jewish
tradition (VII–IX); demonstration of the dependence of philosophy
towards the Bible (X–XIII) and of the contradictions within the philosophical schools (XIV–XV). Likewise, the plan of the *DE* is based on
the main topics of anti-Jewish polemic: the Law (I), the promises of
Scripture (II) and Christ (III–X).[39] Consequently, it is obvious that

---

[38] *In Os.*, Prol., p. 5.128–129.
[39] I suggested that the last books of the *DE* (XVI–XX) may have contained a second
discussion about the rejection of the Jews, the call of the nations, and the birth of the
Church (*L'apologétique chrétienne à l'époque de Constantin, cit.*, pp. 157–158).

Eusebius deals with the most traditional topics of Christian apologetic. The *PE/DE* is not innovative in that respect. Rather, it appears as a kind of 'apologetic summa',[40] drawing freely on previous apologetic. It is essentially a work of scholarship, not a reaction to a particular book written against Christianity. In the first pages of the *PE*, Eusebius explains that he wants to show "what Christianity is to those who are ignorant of it."[41] Then he justifies the twofold plan of the work by defining the *PE* as an "introduction", adressed to the beginners, and the *DE* as a "more complete teaching", intended for the more advanced readers.[42] Eusebius' first aim is not polemical, but didactical, and this is one of the most original aspects of his apologetic project.

That does not mean that *PE/DE* is not a real polemical work. In the prologue of the *DE*, Eusebius mentions three virtual opponents: first, the Jews; second, the Pagans; third, the heretics.[43] Once again, the apology stands as a summa: Eusebius does not only want to answer one kind of opponent, but every opponent of Christianity. Some scholars tended to minimize the anti-Jewish character of the work, considering that Eusebius' real target was actually pagan.[44] But this view is contradicted by the evidence, and must be dismissed as hypercritical.[45] By showing why Christianity has abandoned Judaism, it is true that Eusebius not only answers Jewish criticisms, but also pagan criticisms against the Christians. It is also true that the anti-pagan polemic reappears more explicitly in Books III and IV. But that is not enough to contradict the fact that Eusebius is mainly dealing with Judaism. The heretics seem to be less present in Eusebius' mind, but some observations prove that there is a real anti-heretical polemic in the *DE*.[46] We should not forget that point in our inquiry.

Let us summarize some preliminary results: at first sight, the *PE-DE* cannot be considered as a general answer to Porphyry's *Contra Christianos* because 1) the content of the work is traditional; it is not

---

[40] See J. Ulrich, "Wie verteidigte Euseb das Christentum?", in *Three Greek Apologists. Origen, Eusebius and Athanasius*, ed. A.-C. Jacobsen – J. Ulrich (Frankfurt am Main: Peter Lang, 2007), p. 61.

[41] *PE*, I.1.1.

[42] *Ibid.*, I.1.12.

[43] *DE*, I.1.11–13.

[44] Cf. Barnes, *Constantine and Eusebius, cit.*, p. 178; Rokeah, *Pagans and Christians in Conflict, cit.*, p. 76; Frede, "Eusebius' Apologetic Writings", *cit.*, p. 241ss.

[45] Eusebius constantly refers to the Jews in his demonstration and is eager to refute Jewish interpretations of the Bible (see Morlet, *L'apologétique chrétienne à l'époque de Constantin, cit.*, pp. 470–471; 476–478; 502–506).

[46] See Morlet, *ibid.*, pp. 39–41.

dictated by Porphyry's arguments; 2) the work stands as a didactical summa, not a reaction to any specific opponent; 3) Eusebius targets at least three kinds of adversaries, of which the Pagans are only one. However, that does not mean that Eusebius may not polemize against Porphyry on a smaller scale.

BOOK I

In the first book of the *DE*, Eusebius tries to show why Christianity has abandoned the Jewish Law. This is a typical anti-Jewish discussion, but some passages of the book have been thought as being anti-Porphyrian.

DE, I.1.12; I.1.15. These passages reproduce a pagan accusation that the Christians cannot prove their faith. They correspond to Harnack fr. 73. As I have shown in the introduction, one can no longer speak plainly of a 'Porphyrian accusation': 1) that accusation has nothing Porphyrian in itself; 2) the two passages from the *DE* seem to stem from Celsus, not Porphyry; 3) as a consequence, though Porphyry may have used the same argument against Christianity, there is no particular reason to think that Eusebius had *also* Porphyry in mind. This is of course possible, but must remain an open question.

DE, I.2; I.6. Simmons considers these two chapters, where Eusebius is supposed to emphasize the rapid spreading of Christianity throughout the world,[47] as an answer to what he calls "Porphyry's quest to find [a universal way of salvation]".[48] It is well known that Augustine, in the tenth book of the *De ciuitate Dei*, presented Christianity, against Porphyry, as "the universal way of freeing the soul" (*uniuersalis animae liberandae uia*).[49] Simmons, without really justifying his view, considers that Eusebius aimed at the same kind of demonstration. But nothing can support this hypothesis. Simmons tries to give the impression that the theme of the *uia salutis* was as important in Eusebius' mind as in Augustine's by refering to some Porphyrian texts

---

[47] It is difficult to know which passages Simmons has precisely in mind.
[48] *Arnobius of Sicca, cit.*, p. 280. In more recent contributions, Simmons tried to sustain his hypothesis that the universalism theme in Eusebius is a reaction to Porphyry (see n. 35).
[49] *Ciu.*, X.32.

quoted by Eusebius. But those texts are taken out of their context;[50] they are interpreted in an erroneous (and tendentious) way;[51] and they are artificially put together so as to serve Simmons' purpose. Nowhere does Eusebius explicitly polemize against Porphyry's view of salvation as Augustine would do after him.[52] The Porphyrian text extracted by Augustine from the *De regressu animae* is never quoted by Eusebius and nothing can prove that the bishop of Caesarea even knew that text.[53] Moreover, G. Clark has recently argued that the idea of a Porphyrian quest for a *universal* way of salvation depends entirely on Augustine's paraphrase of *De regressu animae*.[54] She tried to show that the theme of universalism is an augustinian addition to Porphyry reflecting Augustine's own concerns about salvation. In any case, reading Eusebius from Augustine is certainly a historical and philological error: Augustine's readings and concerns are not necessarily the same as Eusebius', and Augustine does not necessarily inform us about Porphyry's actual doctrine.

DE, I.9–10. At the end of book I, Eusebius discusses two problems which may undermine his defense of Christianity: if the Christians are the real heirs of the Hebrews,[55] why do they not indulge in polygamy,

---

[50] When quoting the oracle of Apollo cited in *PE*, XIV.10.4–5 (but also in *PE*, IX.10.2–4 and *DE*, III.3.6), Simmons could have explained that Eusebius refers to the text only to demonstrate that the Pagans aknowledge their dependence on the barbarian wisdom (*Arnobius of Sicca, cit.*, p. 280).

[51] Contrary to Simmons' opinion, the text from the *Phil. ex orac.* quoted in *PE*, IV.10 does not entail that "traditional polytheism was the true way of salvation" (*Arnobius of Sicca, cit.*, p. 279). Porphyry simply says that the sacrifice of animals is not convenient to the gods.

[52] If there is an Eusebian polemic against a Porphyrian conception of salvation, it is more clearly attested in Eusebius' attacks against the pagan oracles, considered by Porphyry as full of "hopes of salvation" (see *PE*, IV.7.1). Simmons knows that text (*Arnobius of Sicca, cit.*, p. 26, n. 235).

[53] J.J. O' Meara tried to show that the *De regressu animae* was part of the *Philosophy from oracles*: *Porphyry's Philosophy from Oracles in Augustine* (Paris: Études augustiniennes, 1959). Though accepted by some scholars, that hypothesis has been rejected by the best specialists of Porphyry (P. Hadot, "Citations de Porphyre chez Augustin [À propos d'un ouvrage récent]", *REAug* 6 (1969), 205–244). Simmons supposes that the text from the *De regressu animae* reflects a search for a way of salvation which culminates in the *Phil. ex orac.* (*Arnobius of Sicca, cit.*, p. 26, n. 235), because he dates the *Phil. ex orac.* to a later period of Porphyry's life (*ibid.*, p. 26, n. 235). But this chronology is disputable.

[54] "Augustine's Porphyry and the Universal Way of Salvation", in *Studies on Porphyry*, ed. G. Karamanolis – A. Sheppard (London: University of London, 2007), 127–140.

[55] The reader must keep in mind that Eusebius distinguishes between the old 'Hebrews', who lived before Moses, and the 'Jews', who followed the Law.

like their ancestors (*DE*, I.9)? Why do they not sacrifice animals like the Hebrews (*DE*, I.10)? Since Porphyry is often supposed to have stressed the contradictions within Scriptures or Christian doctrine, do we have any reason here to think that Eusebius is discussing Porphyrian criticisms?[56] Those who try to detect an important pagan background behind the Christian *quaestiones* literature[57] will probably be tempted to recognize Porphyrian ἀπορίαι behind Eusebius' demonstration. But the question is difficult, and no decisive conclusion can be drawn here. The first problem is not attested among the pagan attacks against Christianity; a polemical use of the argument is first attested, as it seems, among the Manicheans, at least from Augustine's time.[58] This polemical use of the argument may stem from a (probably) Marcionite collection of ἀπορίαι.[59] On the other hand, the problem of the polygamy of the patriarchs had been an exegetical commonplace

---

[56] The Porphyrian origin of the problem raised in *DE*, I.10 is taken for granted by X. Levieils, *Le regard des nations. La critique sociale et religieuse du Christianisme des origines au concile de Nicée (45–325)* (thèse de doctorat, dir. P. Maraval, Université de Paris IV – Sorbonne, 2003), p. 171; see now Contra Christianos. *La critique sociale et religieuse du Christianisme des origines au concile de Nicée (45–325)* (Berlin – New York: de Gruyter, 2007). See also Cook, *The Interpretation of the Old Testament, cit.*, p. 269 n. 135.

[57] See for instance G. Bardy, "La littérature patristique des 'Quaestiones et responsiones' sur l'Écriture sainte", *RB* 41 (1932), p. 353; P. Courcelle, "Critiques exégétiques et arguments antichrétiens rapportés par Ambrosiaster", *VigChr* 13 (1959), 133–169; G. Rinaldi, "Tracce di controversie tra pagani e cristiani nella letteratura patristica delle 'quaestiones et responsiones'", *ASEs* 6 (1989), 99–124.

[58] See *Conf.*, III.7.13; *Faust.*, XXII.47; *Sec.*, 22.

[59] Jerome, who discusses the same problem in the course of a demonstration against the Marcionites, may give an argument in favour of this hypothesis (*Ep.*, CXXIII.2). We know that Manicheans drew some arguments from Marcion's *Antitheses* (see M. Tardieu in A. von Harnack, *Marcion, l'Évangile du Dieu étranger*, french translation of *Marcion. Das Evangelium from fremden Gott*, Leipzig, 1921 (Paris: Cerf, 2003), p. 183). There is no evidence that Eusebius knew that collection, though Origen (see *ibid.*, p. 100) seems to have used it (Carriker, *The Library of Eusebius of Caesarea*, *cit.*, does not raise the problem). On the other hand, Eusebius had a knowledge of Apelles' *Syllogisms*, which aimed at showing the absurdity of the Old Testament (see *HE*, V.13). One may assume that Apelles' work was available to Eusebius at Caesarea, since Origen appears to have known it during his Caesarean period (see *Cels.*, V.54; *Hom. in Gn.*, II.2). For other opinions, see Carriker, *ibid.*, p. 256 (Eusebius did probably know Apelles' work thanks to Rhodon's refutation, quoted in *HE*, V.13) and É. Junod, "Les attitudes d'Apelles, disciple de Marcion, à l'égard de l'Ancien Testament", *Aug.* 22 (1982), 113–133 (the few passages in Origen would not be sufficient to assume that the book was available to him). It is less probable that Eusebius depends on Tatian's *Problemata*, since he does not appear to have had a direct knowledge of that work (see Carriker, *The Library of Eusebius of Caesarea*, *cit.*, pp. 260–261).

from Philo to the Fathers.[60] Consequently, it is impossible to know if
Eusebius is here answering to a criticism against Christianity or if he
simply discusses an exegetical problem for the sake of it. Eusebius does
not mention any adversary and simply presents the question as one
that somebody may ask (ζητῆσαι ἄν τις εἰκότως).[61]

The second problem is of a different kind. It is also attested among
the Manichean criticisms against Christianity.[62] One may suppose once
again that these criticisms were dependent on Marcionite collections
of ἀπορίαι. But this time, the argument is also well attested among
pagan criticisms against the Christians.[63] Harnack thought it had been
used by Porphyry.[64] On the other hand, there is no evidence, to my
knowledge, that this problem could have been raised within the 'official' Church before Eusebius.[65] However, it remains difficult to agree
with Harnack's hypothesis: 1) the Porphyrian origin of the argument
remains uncertain;[66] 2) even if it had been used by Porphyry, nothing
proves that Eusebius has Porphyry in mind,[67] since he may be trying

----

[60] See Philo, *Virt.*, 207; Justin, *Dial.*, 134; 141.4; Tertullian, *Cast.*, 6–7; Clement, *Str.*,
II.19.99.1; Origen, *Hom. in Gn.*, X.5; XI.1–2; Ambrose, *Abr.*, IV.22–30; Augustine,
Conj., 15; *Faust.*, XXII.47; *Sec.*, 22; Jerome, *Ep.*, CXXIII.2.

[61] *DE*, I.9.1.

[62] Augustine, *Faust.*, XXII.17.

[63] See Julian, *Gal.*, fr. 83 Masaracchia; Augustine, *Ep.*, CII.16ss.; CXXXVIII.1.2.
In *Faust.*, XXII.17, Augustin mentions the argument as one a Pagan may object
(*obiceret*).

[64] See *Christ.*, fr. 79 Harnack (= Augustine, *Ep.*, CII16ss.).

[65] The *quaestio* recurrs in the *Dialogue of Athanasius and Zacchaeus*, 128–129 and
in Ps.-Justin, *Quaest. ad orth.*, 83 (PG 6.1324C–D). Those two works are posterior to
Eusebius and may be drawing on the *DE*. I showed that the former certainly depends
on Eusebius (see Morlet, *L'apologétique chrétienne à l'époque de Constantin*, cit.,
p. 532). The same conclusion may be drawn concerning Ps.-Justin, who explains, like
Eusebius, that the primitive sacrifices were prophecies of the future events: he may
thus depend, directly or indirectly, on the *DE*.

[66] Augustine himself seems sceptical about the Porphyrian origin of the *quaestiones* discussed in *Ep.*, CII, saying that the Pagans which used these *quaestiones* "say
they are taken from Porphyry's arguments against the Christians, so as to make them
more strong" (*item alia proposuerunt, quae dicerent de Porphyrio Contra Christianos
tamquam ualidiora decerpta*, *Ep.*, CII.8, p. 551, 5–6). The first direct evidence of a
pagan use of the *quaestio* reproduced in *DE*, I.1.10 is found among Julian's critics
(see note 63).

[67] The fact that Eusebius quotes Porphyry (without giving his name) before his
demonstration (*Abst.*, II.5; I.19) cannot be considered as a clue of an anti-Porphyrian
polemic, since Porphyry is not quoted here as the adversary, but as a source about
the Greek conception of primitive sacrifice. Eusebius includes his testimony in an
'ethnographical' discussion opposing Greek and biblical views on sacrifice. Contrary
to Simmons' opinion, he is not at all quoting Porphyry "to justify the Christians' rejection of it" (*Arnobius of Sicca*, cit., p. 309). Porphyry's statement is given by Eusebius as

to answer a heterodoxical use of the argument,[68] or simply discussing it for the sake of exegetical speculation.

As a conclusion, three hypotheses may be suggested in both cases: 1) Eusebius is analysing exegetical problems which he raises himself for the sake of his demonstration; 2) Eusebius is answering Marcionite (?) ἀπορίαι;[69] 3) Eusebius is answering pagan criticisms, possibly from Porphyry. These three hypotheses are not mutually exclusive.[70] On the basis of the available evidence, the first one is the most reasonable, and the question of a polemical intention in *DE*, I.9–10 must remain an open question. My analysis would agree with C. Zamagni's study on the *Questions on the Gospels* (probably contemporaneous with the *DE*) which showed that Eusebius' work was not intended against Porphyry, and that even if Eusebius had Porphyry in mind here and there, the kernel of his *quaestiones* does not stem from the *Contra Christianos*.

---

a document on the Greek conception of primitive sacrifice. He does not try to prove that "men of Old Testament time did not consider sacrifice to be sinful because they had not been taught that the souls of men and beasts are alike, that is to say, rational and intelligent" (*loc. cit.*). This is an erroneous (and absurd) translation of *DE*, I.10.7, which should rather be translated that way: "they had been taught that the soul of the irrational beings is in no way analogous to the rational and intelligent power of men" (μηδὲ τῇ τῶν ἀνθρώπων λογικῇ καὶ νοερᾷ δυνάμει παραπλησίαν εἶναι τὴν ψυχὴν τῶν ἀλόγων ἐπαιδεύοντο). Porphyry's view, in the passages quoted by Eusebius, is that there is no difference between the souls of beasts and the souls of men (*DE*, I.10.2). Consequently, far from using Porphyry's statement to support his demonstration, Eusebius quotes it in order to stress the discrepancy between two conceptions of sacrifice.

[68] It is interesting to note that some elements of Eusebius' demonstration may be derived from Ireneus (*Haer.*, IV.17–19), who stresses, against the heterodox, the continuity of both sacrificial practices.

[69] Another possibility would be that Eusebius had heard of Gnostic or Manichean criticisms against the Old Testament: the objections dealt with in *DE*, I.9–10 are well attested among the Manicheans at least in Augustine's time (see notes 58 and 62), and some Gnostics, like the Marcionites, criticized the difficulties of the Old Testament; see G. Filoramo – C. Gianotto, "L'interpretazione gnostica dell'Antico Testamento. Posizioni ermeneutiche e tecniche esegetiche", *Aug.* 22 (1982), 53–74.

[70] Eusebius may be raising two problems he considers as important for his demonstration, and at the same time answering critics against the Bible. Concerning hypothesis 2 and 3, one must keep in mind that some of Porphyry's arguments echo Marcionite critics (see for instance G. Rinaldi, *La Bibbia dei pagani*, II (Bologna: EDB, 1998), p. 89, who suggests a parallel between fr. 42 Harnack and an objection used by Apelles concerning Gn 2.17). It thus remains possible that Porphyry had acquired some knowledge of the heterodoxical argumentation, either directly or indirectly. R.M. Grant suggested that Porphyry may have drawn some of his objections from Origen's *Stromateis*, probably dealing in part with heretical arguments against Scripture ("The Stromateis of Origen", in *Epektasis. Mélanges Daniélou* (Paris: Beauchesne, 1972), 285–292).

Book II

The second book of the *DE* is certainly not among those which would incline scholars to detect an anti-Porphyrian polemic in Eusebius' work. Eusebius states explicitly that this book will be devoted to refuting the Jews who criticize Christians for using the Scriptures though they do not belong to the chosen people.[71] The book contains primarily four collections of testimonies which are traditional in the anti-Jewish tradition.[72] Yet, that has not prevented scholars from seeing anti-Porphyrian passages in that book.

DE, II.Prol.1. The Jews accuse the Christians of using the Scriptures, though they are not intended for them. H. Schreckenberg thinks that Eusebius knew this Jewish accusation from Porphyry.[73] But this hypothesis is unfounded, and very probably erroneous.

DE, II.2. Simmons finds in this chapter another trace of a Porphyrian polemic against the irrational faith of the Christians and another demonstration of the rapid spreading of Christianity,[74] which he considers as an answer to Porphyry's view of salvation.[75] I refer the reader to my previous analysis.

Book III

The third book of the *DE* is a defence of Jesus' teaching and action during his human life. It is often considered as the anti-Porphyrian kernel of the work. In his introduction to his translation, W.J. Ferrar wrote:

> The great mass of the *Demonstratio* is an elaborate *réchauffée* [sic] of past apologetics, but in this book we feel the touch of something fresh, free, original, something that springs from keen, personal interest, warm perception, and ardent conviction [...]. Its finish, completeness in itself, and contrast with the *Demonstratio* as a whole might suggest that it was a separate essay, written in actual controversy with an opponent who

---

[71] *DE*, II.Prol.1.
[72] About those collections, see Morlet, *L'apologétique chrétienne à l'époque de Constantin, cit.*, pp. 396–400.
[73] *Die christlichen Adversus-Judaeos-Texte, cit.*, p. 264.
[74] *Arnobius of Sicca, cit.*, p. 280, n. 58.
[75] *Ibid.*, p. 280, n. 77.

drew out Eusebius' keenest logic and dialectical skill, and that this essay was eventually incorporated in the greater but more academic work.[76]

The same scholar was convinced that the Eusebian allusion, in that book, to "the sons of our modern philosophers" (τῶν νέων φιλοσόφων παῖδες) was an allusion to the "followers of Porphyry".[77] J. Stevenson went as far as to suggest that many parts of Book III were derived from Eusebius' *Contra Porphyrium*[78] though we do not even know when that work was written.[79] Harnack also thought that the main part of *DE*, III.4–5 was intended against Porphyry.[80] Recent scholars, such as T.D. Barnes[81] or M.B. Simmons,[82] took for granted that *DE*, III as a whole is mainly directed against Porphyrian accusations.

However, a precise study of this book seriously undermines that hypothesis. First, we should not be misled as was W.J. Ferrar by the "fresh style" of Book III. A stylistic observation is not sufficient to reconstruct the genesis of a work. It is obvious in the whole book that Eusebius adapted his style to the specific (essentially anti-pagan) polemic of Book III.[83] Besides, we should not overestimate the stylistic

---

[76] *Eusebius. The Proof of the Gospel* (London: Society for promoting Christian knowledge – New York: The Macmillan Company, 1920 [repr. 2001]), p. xviii.

[77] *Ibid.*, p. 119, n. 3. It is difficult to know if the phrase refers to the Neoplatonists, since the same phrase is used elsewhere to refer to the philosophers who introduced the physical interpretation of the myths, and who are not the Neoplatonists (*PE*, II.6.16; III.1). Consequently, I would tend to think that "the sons of the new philosophers" (or simply "the new philosophers") are not strictly speaking contemporaneous to Eusebius. In my doctoral thesis, I suggested that the phrase may refer to the philosophers in general; the word "new" could be understood as opposed to the antiquity of the Revelation (see Morlet, *L'apologétique chrétienne à l'époque de Constantin, cit.*, pp. 296–297, n. 179). A similar problem has been raised by Arnobius' allusion to the *uiri noui* (*Adu. nat.*, II.15.2ss.). Some scholars think that Arnobius alludes to Neoplatonists, especially Porphyry, but other interpretations have been put forward (see the state of research in M.B. Simmons, *Arnobius of Sicca, cit.*, pp. 216–217).

[78] *Studies in Eusebius* (Cambridge: Cambridgte University Press, 1929), p. 63. The same scholar also thought that the matter of Book III could correspond to the first books of the *General Elementary Introduction*, also probably derived, he thought, from the *Contra Porphyrium* (*ibid.*).

[79] See *infra*.

[80] *Porphyrius, "Gegen die Christen", cit.*, p. 48.

[81] *Constantine and Eusebius, cit.*, p. 184.

[82] See *infra*.

[83] He sometimes adresses an anonymous adversary (see *DE*, III.6.31; 6.34) behind whom we do not need to recognize any specific figure. This kind of address is obviously a literary device. The subject of Book III naturally led Eusebius to adopt the polemical tone of his previous controversy with Hierocles. Such a similarity between the style of the *DE*, III, and the *Contra Hieroclem* offers a new argument against

discrepancy between Book III and the other books of the work.[84] Moreover, the analysis of Book III must take as a starting point Eusebius' explicit statement that he intends to answer three pagan accusations: 1) Christ is a γόης[85] and a deceiver;[86] 2) Christ's miracles never happened;[87] 3) if they happened, they were not performed by a god, but by a sorcerer.[88] I have shown that these three accusations may be found in Celsus, and that Eusebius' argumentation in Book III is often derived from Origen's *Contra Celsum*.[89] The fact that Book III often appears as a rewriting of the *Contra Celsum* contradicts the hypothesis that it could be at the same time a rewriting of the *Contra Porphyrium*. Eusebius may be responding here and there to Porphyry[90] (as he also seems to be responding to Hierocles[91] and probably other sources),[92] but one should not forget that Celsus lies behind most of Eusebius' demonstrations, and that his polemic is mainly a repetition of Origen's controversy with Celsus.

DE, III.1. According to Simmons, this chapter contains another text against "Porphyry's accusation that Christians cannot prove their beliefs."[93]

T. Hägg's hypothesis that Eusebius could not be the author of the *Contra Hieroclem* ("Hierocles the Lover of Truth and Eusebius the Sophist", *SO* 67 (1992), 138–150 = *Parthenope: Studies in Ancient Greek Fiction* (Copenhagen: Museum Tusculanum Press, 2004), 405–416). The fresh style of that work appears to be a rhetorical choice and it would be absurd to think that Eusebius, as a writer, could not make rhetorical choices. In that respect, I agree with C.P. Jones, *Philostratus. Apollonius of Tyana. Letters of Apollonius. Ancient Testimonia. Eusebius' reply to Hierocles* [LCL; Cambridge, Mass. - London: Harvard University Press, 2006], p. 152.

[84] I tried to show that Eusebius was actually as 'scholastical' in Book III as in the other books (*L'apologétique chrétienne à l'époque de Constantin, cit.*, p. 217).

[85] This term is difficult to translate. It means at the same time 'sorcerer' and 'charlatan'.

[86] *DE*, III.2.78.

[87] *Ibid.*, III.4.31.

[88] *Loc. cit.*

[89] *L'apologétique chrétienne à l'époque de Constantin, cit.*, pp. 298–303.

[90] *Ibid.*, pp. 303–304.

[91] *Ibid.*, pp. 305–306.

[92] *Ibid.*, pp. 306–307.

[93] *Arnobius of Sicca, cit.*, p. 275, n. 58.

DE, III.2. Simmons detects in this chapter another echo to a Porphyrian criticism against irrational faith,[94] and a new trace of an answer to Porphyry's conception of salvation.[95]

DE, III.3. This chapter is a defence of Jesus' doctrine. According to Simmons, it is an answer to an Hecatean oracle and its commentary by Porphyry, which presented Jesus as a mere man, thus negating his divinity.[96] The proof of this is, according to Simmons, that Eusebius quotes the oracle four chapters after this one (!).[97] But Simmons clearly exaggerates the importance of the Hecatean oracle in Eusebius' defense of Christ's divinity (reading Eusebius, once again, from Augustine).[98] First, Eusebius does not quote the oracle in chapter 7 to refute it, but on the contrary to serve his purpose (the oracle attesting that Christ was a superior man). Second, it would be erroneous to think that the Hecatean oracle is responsible for Eusebius' attempt to demonstrate Christ's divinity. Simmons does not pay attention to the context of chapter 3. Eusebius explicitly states that he will defend Jesus' teaching against "most of the unbelievers", who think that Jesus is "a γόης and a deceiver".[99] One could assume that Porphyry used that accusation,[100] but Eusebius more probably has Celsus in mind.[101]

In another passage from the same chapter (*DE*, III.3.18), Simmons thinks that the exposition of Jesus' doctrine on the angels is

---

[94] *Ibid.* The Porphyrian passage is extracted from the *Philosophy from oracles* (fr. 345 Smith). About the Hecatean oracle, see A. Busine, *Paroles d'Apollon. Pratiques et traditions oraculaires dans l'Antiquité tardive (IIᵉ–IVᵉ siècles)* (Leiden – Boston: Brill, 2005), 280–281.

[95] *Arnobius of Sicca, cit.*, p. 280, n. 77.

[96] *Ibid.*, p. 234.

[97] *Ibid.*, p. 235 (see *DE*, III.7.1–2). Simmons erroneously refers to *PE*, IV.7, but the Hecatean oracle does not appear to be quoted in any part of *PE*.

[98] See the discussion of Augustine against the Hecatean oracle in *Ciu.*, XIX.23.2 and F. Culdaut's commentary ("Un oracle d'Hécate dans la Cité de Dieu de saint Augustin: 'Les dieux ont proclamé que le Christ fut un homme très pieux' (XIX, 23, 2)", *REAug* 38 (1992), 271–289).

[99] *DE*, III.2.78.

[100] Aaron Johnson convincingly explained to me that such an assumption would contradict some fragments from the *Phil. ex orac.* where Porphyry seems to praise Christ as a wise man (fr. 345–346 Smith). Unless of course one supposes that Porphyry has changed his mind in the *Contra Christianos*.

[101] The association of the words γόης and πλάνος does not occur in Porphyry's work. It is only attested in Celsus (see *Cels.*, IV.33; VII.36). Note that almost all the 'Porphyrian' fragments which attack Jesus' teaching are derived from Macarius Magnes (see fr. 52; 54; 58; 61; 62; 69; 70; 72). The accusation also occurs in Jerome, but the latter does not refer to any pagan author (see fr. 56).

a response to another oracle and its Porphyrian commentary.[102] But Eusebius does not refer to this oracle, and he never quotes it in any of his works. Besides, the connection between Porphyry's commentary and Eusebius' text is not apparent. Unlike Porphyry, Eusebius does not distinguish between three orders of angels. His description of the angelic powers has nothing original in itself, and expresses the common Christian view on the subject. Besides, I have shown elsewhere that Eusebius' chapter on Jesus' teaching was in part inspired by Origen's *On Principles*.[103] This is particularly true of his passage dealing with Jesus' teaching about the angels and the demons.[104]

Porphyry's presence in this chapter (one text from the *Phil. ex orac.*[105] and one text from *Abst.*)[106] must not lead us to misunderstand Eusebius' polemic here. Each time, Porphyry is quoted as an 'auxiliary witness', to illustrate the pagan dependence on the Hebrew wisdom.[107] In no way does he appear as an adversary.

DE, III.4–7.[108] Simmons considers this section as being a retorsion against the (supposedly Porphyrian) accusation that there is "a wedge between Christ and his followers".[109] In opposition to that accusation, Eusebius is supposed to have insisted on the continuity between Christ and his disciples. But once again, Simmons does not understand the context of Eusebius' argumentation. The theme of a continuity between Christ and his followers is dealt with in two sections of *DE*, III:

1) In *DE*, III.4.39–41, Eusebius states that the disciples continued to consider Jesus as God even after his slanderous death.
2) In *DE*, III.6.1–2, Eusebius argues that the disciples never abandoned Jesus; in *DE*, III.6.7–8 and 11–25, he says that the disciples, like Jesus, were not γόητες.

---

[102] *Arnobius of Sicca, cit.*, pp. 233–234.

[103] Morlet, *L'apologétique chrétienne à l'époque de Constantin, cit.*, p. 275, n. 69.

[104] Compare *DE*, III.3.18 and *PE*, VII.16.7 with *Princ.*, I.5.5.

[105] Fr. 324 Smith (*DE*, III.3.6).

[106] *Abst.*, II, 34 (*DE*, III.3.10).

[107] Simmons admits himself that in *DE*, III.3, *Abst.*, II.34 is quoted "to justify the Christian's rejection [of sacrifice]" (*Arnobius of Sicca, cit.*, p. 309).

[108] Simmons refers once to *DE*, III.4–8 (*Arnobius of Sicca, cit.*, p. 30, n. 284), but this is an error, since there is no chapter 8 in Book III.

[109] *Ibid.*, p. 30. See also p. 20, n. 180; p. 232; p. 239.

In context 1, the idea of a continuity between Christ and the disciples is clearly an answer to the accusation that the disciples were liars (the argument being: why would they have lied, if they had been convinced that Jesus was truly God?). In context 2, this continuity enables Eusebius to defend Jesus from the accusation of γοητεία: if the disciples never abandoned Jesus, it is because they considered his teaching as being true; if they were not γόητες, it is because they had not been taught to become so. Consequently, Eusebius does not aim at responding to the accusation that there is a wedge between Christ and his followers. In the one case, he wants to show that the disciples were not liars; in the second one, he wants to demonstrate that they were not charlatans.

DE, III.5.95–100. In this passage, Eusebius alludes once again to the accusation that the disciples were liars. Harnack considered this text as a 'fragment' of Porphyry's *Contra Christianos*,[110] though it is not, strictly speaking, a fragment.[111] The problem is not whether Porphyry did or did not accuse the disciples of being liars, since other evidence demonstrates that he did.[112] The question is whether Eusebius has Porphyry in mind and whether *DE*, III.5.95–100 can be considered as a Porphyrian fragment. A stylistic analysis would probably shed some light on that problem. But two observations need to be made here: 1) the accusation is not specific to Porphyry, since it may be found in Celsus[113] and Hierocles;[114] 2) when answering this accusation, Eusebius, as he does throughout Book III, appears to be drawing his inspiration from Origen's *Contra Celsum*.[115] Consequently, it seems that Eusebius, once again, had primarily Celsus in mind,[116] not Porphyry.[117] In any

---

[110] See *Christ.*, fr. 7 Harnack.

[111] Fr. 7 does not only include the accusation against the disciples, but also Eusebius' refutation of it.

[112] *Christ.*, fr. 2, 6, 11, 55 Harnack.

[113] *Cels.*, I.38; 31; 40; II.48.

[114] See Eusebius, *Hier.*, 2.

[115] See my discussion, *L'apologétique chrétienne à l'époque de Constantin, cit.*, pp. 284–290.

[116] Note that the way Eusebius reproduces the two pagan objections in *DE*, III.4.31 (Christ's miracles did not happen; or if they happened, they were the work of a sorcerer) exactly reflects Celsus' objections according to the *Contra Celsum* (*Cels.*, I.38; 68).

[117] It remains to explain why Eusebius insists on the disciples' συμφωνία throughout Book III: is this a clue that he did not know the argument of the discrepancy of the evangelists (supposedly Porphyrian, but possibly also used by Hierocles, according to Lactantius, *Inst.*, V.2.13), or on the contrary that he aims at answering that argument

case, we cannot conclude with Simmons that Eusebius is responding to Porphyry when he defends the evangelists.[118]

DE, III.6–7. The final demonstration of Book III is a defense of Jesus' miracles. Simmons thinks that Porphyry "undoubtedly is the enemy behind [...] *DE* 3.5 ff."[119] (in fact, Simmons refers to *DE* III.6–7). The accusation that Christ performed no real miracle is attested in Porphyry,[120] but one can also find it in Celsus[121] and Hierocles.[122] There are some clues that Eusebius has, once again, Celsus in mind: when reproducing the pagan accusation, he alludes to the couple γόης— πλάνος,[123] to be found only in Celsus;[124] in the course of this demonstration, he echoes many times Origen's *Contra Celsum*, as Heikel already observed (but surprisingly, Simmons ignores Heikel's edition, and quotes from the PG).[125] Once again, the presence of a Porphyrian

---

by stressing the harmony of the disciples (see my discussion, *L'apologétique chrétienne à l'époque de Constantin, cit.*, pp. 300–301)? In any case, this discussion on the concord of the disciples appears to be the counterpart of *PE*, XIV–XV, where Eusebius stresses the discord of the Greek philosophers. I am grateful to Aaron Johnson for reminding me this parallel and I refer to his book *Ethnicity and Argument in Eusebius' Praeparatio Evangelica* (Oxford: Oxford University Press, 2006), pp. 142–149.

[118] *Arnobius of Sicca, cit.*, p. 240 (and note 133). Among the passages concerned, Simmons quotes *DE*, III.6 (p. 29), but the reference is erroneous. *DE*, III.6 is an answer to the third accusation examined by Eusebius, that Christ is not a divine being. Simmons should rather have quoted *DE*, III.4.32–5.109, where Eusebius does answer the accusation that the disciples have forged Jesus' story. In *DE*, III.5, Simmons thinks Eusebius defends the evangelists from using magic (*Arnobius of Sicca, cit.*, p. 275), apparently against a Porphyrian accusation (see p. 240, note 132). But the term πλάνοι, as employed by Eusebius, does not denote here a magical deception. The only passage where Eusebius does defend the disciples against the charge of using magic is *DE*, III.6.–11, a passage probably inspired by Origen, *Cels.*, I.6. The idea of an anti-Porphyrian intention is here unnecessary (see *Arnobius of Sicca, cit.*, p. 237, where Simmons seems to detect an anti-Chaldean polemic behind Eusebius' text). For other undemonstrated statements about Eusebius' defense of the disciples, see Simmons, *ibid.*, p. 282 and 283 (about a Porphyrian accusation against Peter).

[119] *Ibid.*, p. 238. See also p. 28, n. 262.

[120] See fr. 49, 60, 63 (primarily from Macarius Magnes).

[121] *Cels.*, I.38; VI.42.

[122] See Lactantius, *Inst.*, V.3.9.

[123] γοητείᾳ δὲ ἄλλως ἐπὶ πλάνῃ (III.4.31).

[124] See n. 101.

[125] Heikel detected the following parallels: *DE*, III.6.1ss. = *Cels.*, II.7; II.50; *DE*, III.6.26 (in fact 26–27) = *Cels.*, I.29; *DE*, III.6.35 = *Cels.*, III.36; *DE*, III.6.37 = *Cels.*, I.68; *DE*, III.7.9 = *Cels.*, I.29; *DE*, III.7.22 = *Cels.* I.62. One could mention a passage where Eusebius defends Jesus against having Egyptian masters (*DE*, III.6.29). Simmons thinks he may have in mind the same enemy as Arnobius (*Adu. nat.*, I.43.1–5), namely Porphyry (*Arnobius of Sicca, cit.*, pp. 237–238). But Eusebius certainly has Celsus in mind, since his text is clearly a rewriting of *Cels.*, I.38.

text in Eusebius' argumentation (the Hecatean oracle, quoted from the *Phil. ex orac.*) cannot induce us to agree with Simmons, since the oracle is quoted to support Eusebius' view, not to be refuted by him.[126]

BOOK IV

The fourth book of the *DE* is devoted to Christ as a divine being. It falls into three parts: 1) demonstration of the 'theology' of Christ (1–6); 2) answer to the question 'why did he not come before?' (7–9); 3) demonstration concerning his Incarnation (10–14).

In each part of the book one might be tempted to detect new answers against Porphyry... But a careful analysis, once again, leads to the conclusion that Eusebius depends heavily on Origen (*On principles* and *Contra Celsum*).[127] This undermines the hypothesis of a strong anti-Porphyrian intention in Book IV. Each of its three parts have been thought, however, as being anti-Porphyrian.

DE, IV.1–6. In chapter 2, Eusebius seeks to demonstrate the unicity of Christ. A.A. Garcia considers the corresponding section of the *Theophany* as an answer to the Neoplatonic conception of the revelation of the One in the universe, and thinks that Eusebius has Porphyry in mind.[128] But this interpretation is unfounded and probably erroneous. C.T.H.R. Ehrhardt more convincingly suggested that in the corresponding part of the *Laudes Constantini*, Eusebius was answering Celsus.[129] When Eusebius refers to the pagan belief of several gods attached to each part of the body,[130] he may have in mind the Egyptian belief praised by Celsus against Christian monotheism.[131] In any case, the demonstration of the unicity of Christ is a common place of early apologetic.[132] We do not need to assume that Eusebius has Porphyry

---

[126] Simmons agrees that Eusebius quotes this oracle to support his demonstration (*ibid.*, p. 224).

[127] See Morlet, *L'apologétique chrétienne à l'époque de Constantin, cit.*, p. 316ss. That conclusion agrees with Ehrhardt's analysis of the corresponding part of the *Laudes Constantini* (see n. 129).

[128] "Eusebius' Theophany: a Christian Neoplatonist Response", *PBR* 6 (1987), 230–237.

[129] "Eusebius and Celsus", *JAC* 22 (1979), 40–49.

[130] *DE*, IV.5.4.

[131] *Cels.*, VIII.58. See also VIII.55.

[132] See Justin, *Apol.*, II.6.3; Athenagoras, *Leg.*, 8. See also *Tripartite Tractate*, 51.

in mind here. In the same chapter, one could notice that Eusebius also seeks to explain the phrase 'son of God' attached to Christ.[133] We may be tempted to suggest that Porphyry hides behind Eusebius' demonstration, since he probably objected to the Christians that God cannot have a son.[134] But that objection is also (and better)[135] attested among Celsus' accusations.[136]

DE, IV.7–10. In the second part of Book IV, Eusebius aims at answering the following question: "Why has he made his appearance to all men now, and not before and what is the reason why he began the call of the nations, not in days long past, but now after the length of ages?"[137] Do we have to assume that Eusebius is here responding to Porphyry? The philosopher appears to have mentioned the delay of the Incarnation in his anti-Christian polemic.[138] But so did Celsus before him.[139] The words used by Eusebius clearly recall Celsus' way of posing the question.[140] And once again, Eusebius' answer is, at least in part, inspired by Origen's *Contra Celsum*.[141] Consequently, there is no necessary reason to see an anti-Porphyrian polemic in that section of the *DE*.

DE, IV.10–15. In these chapters, Eusebius deals with several problems concerning the Incarnation. Simmons thinks he is again answering Porphyry. In chapter 10, he thinks Eusebius stresses both the humanity and the divinity of the incarnate Christ, to answer Porphyry's commentary on the Hecatean oracle saying that Christ was

---

[133] See the κεφάλαιον of *DE*, IV.2.

[134] See fr. 85. About that fragment, taken from Augustine's *Letter CII*, see P. Courcelle, "Critiques exégétiques et arguments antichrétiens rapportés par Ambrosiaster", *VigChr* 13 (1959), p. 163 ("l'origine porphyrienne est stipulée").

[135] Fr. 85 is extracted from Augustine's *Letter CII*, the content of which seems to me problematical (see note 66). In the fragment, the accusation is not clearly and directly attributed to Porphyry. Moreover, Aaron Johnson tells me that the idea of a son of God seems to be implicitly accepted in some Porphyrian fragments (284; 297; 376 Smith).

[136] *Cels.*, II.31; VIII.14. One could also think that Eusebius is answering Jewish objections against the Christian conception of Christ as 'son of God' (see Aphr., *Dem.*, XVIII, 12; *Dialogue of Philo and Papiscus*, 2).

[137] The question occurs at the end of Book II (II.3.178).

[138] See fr. 81–82.

[139] *Cels.*, IV.7; VI.78.

[140] Compare the phrase μετὰ τὸν μακρὸν αἰῶνα (*DE*, II.3.178) with μετὰ τοσοῦτον αἰῶνα (*Cels.*, IV.7) and ἐκ τοῦ μακροῦ ὕπνου (*ibid.*, VI.78).

[141] Cf. *Cels.*, IV.3–4; 8–9; V.31. See also *Com. Rm.*, V.1, PG 14.1017C, 7–15 (Morlet, *L'apologétique chrétienne à l'époque de Constantin, cit.*, pp. 326–329).

only a mortal.[142] It is actually much more probable that he is answering Celsus' criticism of the Incarnation. Celsus objected against the Christians that the Logos could not become man without changing his nature.[143] Origen answered that the Incarnation does not imply any change of the divine nature, because 1) the descent of the Logos was an act of condescension (συγκατάβασις) which did not imply in itself any change of nature;[144] 2) the physician, to which the Logos may be compared, is not affected by the sufferings of his patient.[145] Now, Eusebius makes it very clear that he is answering such objections.[146] And his argumentation is, once again, obviously derived from the *Contra Celsum*.[147]

BOOK V

Book V contains a collection of testimonies about the divinity of Christ. Two texts from this book have been thought as being directly related to Porphyry.

DE, V.Prol.3–5. At the beginning of his prophetical collection, Eusebius gives the opinion of the Pagans concerning divination. I give the text in Berchman's translation:

---

[142] *Arnobius of Sicca, cit.*, p. 224. The passage in the *DE* is the following (*DE*, IV.10.19): τάς τε κοινὰς ἡμῖν ὑπέμεινεν διατριβάς, οὐδαμῶς μὲν τοῦ εἶναι ὃς ἦν ἐξιστάμενος, ὁμοῦ δ' ἐν τῷ ἀνθρώπῳ φυλάττων τὸν θεόν ("And he led the life which we lead, in no way forsaking the being that he had before, and at the same time retaining the God in the man").

[143] See *Cels.*, IV.14.

[144] *Ibid.*, IV.15; VI.77.

[145] *Ibid.*, IV.15.

[146] The passage of *DE*, IV.10.19 is already explicit. Eusebius deals again with the same problem in chapter 13, which is entitled: ὡς ἀπαθὴς καὶ ἀβλαβὴς καὶ ἀσώματος διέμεινεν καὶ καθ' ὃν ἐνηνθρώπει ("He remained impassive, unharmed and incorporeal, even when he was made man" as W.J. Ferrar suggests). At the beginning of chapter 13, he makes very clear that he has in mind such objections as that of Celsus (*DE*, IV.13.1): οὕτω δὴ τούτων ἐχόντων οὐ δεῖ ταράττεσθαι τὸν νοῦν, γένεσιν καὶ σῶμα καὶ πάθη καὶ θάνατον περὶ τὸν ἄυλον καὶ ἀσώματον τοῦ θεοῦ λόγον ἀκούοντα ("And since this is so, one must not be disturbed on hearing of birth, body, passions and death as regards the immaterial and incorporeal word of God").

[147] The Logos suffered no change (*DE*, IV.10.19; IV.13.6). The Incarnation was only an act of condescension (*ibid.*, IV.10.18; 13.6). Eusebius also compares the Logos to a physician (IV.13.4). But he insists on three other examples: when a lyre is struck, the musician is not affected (IV.13.7); when a wise man is punished, his soul is not affected by the punishment of his body (*loc. cit.*); the rays of the sun are not defiled by touching the material world (IV.13.8). This last example is traditional (see Tertullian, *Apol.*, XXI.12–14), but Eusebius may owe it to Origen (*Cels.*, VI.73).

Greeks and barbarians alike testify to the existence of oracles and oracular responses in all parts of the earth and they state they were revealed by
the creator's providence for the use and benefit of men. Thus there is no
need for an essential difference between Hebrew prophecy and the other
nations' oracles since the supreme God gave oracles to the Hebrews
through their prophets, and suggested that which was to their advantage.
So also he gave them to other nations through their local oracles. For
he was not only the God of the Jews, but also of the rest of humanity.
He cared no more for these than those, but his providence was over all
similarly just as he has given the sun ungrudgingly to everyone, and not
for the Hebrews only, and the supply of needs according to the seasons,
and a similar bodily make-up for everyone, and one mode of birth, and
one type of rational soul. And thus, they say, he provided to all men the
science of foretelling the future ungrudgingly, to some by prophets, to
some by oracles, to some by the flight of birds, or by examining entrails,
or by dreams, or by omens contained in word or sound, or some other
sound. For these they say were given to all men by God's providence, so
that the Hebrew prophets should not seem to have an advantage over
the rest of the world.

R.M. Berchman made this text fr. 18 of his collection of Porphyry's
anti-Christian fragments, thus adding a new text to Harnack's collection. It is worth noting, first, that it is difficult to know what the
opinion of the Greeks and barbarians exactly is in this text. According
to Eusebius, they say that God has given divination to all mankind, *so
that there is no difference between the Jews and the other men.* If one
thinks that the consecutive clause is an extrapolation by Eusebius, one
should limit the Greek and barbarian statement to the idea that the
gifts of God are universal. But it remains possible that the statement
about the Hebrews does belong to the Greek and barbarian λόγος. In
any case, the question of the Porphyrian origin of this text must be
examined. Three facts may support Berchman's hypothesis:

– There is a parallel between the discussion on divination in *DE*,
   V.Prol. and the discussion on sacrifices in *DE*, I.10. In each case,
   Eusebius reproduces an anonymous pagan opinion on the subject,
   before giving his own conception. Now, we can check that in *DE*,
   I.10, the Greek λόγος is derived from Porphyry.[148] It is thus probable
   that the Greek and barbarian opinion in *DE*, V.Prol. is also derived
   from Porphyry.

---

[148] See *Abst.*, II.5; I.19.

- Porphyry is Eusebius' main source in the *PE* when dealing with divination.
- Some passages in the text may indicate a Porphyrian source. 1) First, the text admits the reality of a Hebrew prophecy. This cannot be a reproduction of Celsus' view,[149] but may correspond to Porphyry's supposedly positive attitude to Jewish tradition.[150] 2) The allusion to God's providence (πρόνοια) may indicate a neoplatonic background.[151] 3) The text refers to a conception of divination which echoes some parallels in the *Letter to Anebo*.[152]

On the other hand, it is clear that this text cannot be considered as a Porphyrian 'fragment'. The first words of the text (μαντεῖα καὶ χρηστήρια) are directly taken from the *Contra Celsum*.[153] The list of the divinatory practices, though finding echoes in Porphyry, more probably stems from the same work.[154]

In the *Prophetical Extracts*, Eusebius had tried to defend the Hebrew prophets from the accusations of the Pagans.[155] His demonstration was almost entirely derived from the *Contra Celsum*.[156] In *DE*, V, Eusebius has reworked his previous text, and his polemic has changed. He still wants to prove the superiority of the prophets, but his demonstration is not intended to those who think the Hebrew prophets are inferior to the pagan prophets (as Celsus thought), but to those who consider there is no difference between both prophetical trditions. If Porphyry hides behind Eusebius' text, two possibilities may be suggested: either the *Contra Christianos*, or the *Philosophy from oracles*. If the statement about the Jewish prophets belongs to the pagan λόγος, then the *Contra Christianos* may be a possible source. But if this statement is a Eusebian extrapolation, then the *Philosophy from oracles* would appear to me as a more probable source (if one admits, of course, that the

---

[149] On Celsus' negative conception of Hebrew prophecy, see *Cels.*, VII.3; 9.

[150] See M. Stern, *Greek and Latin Authors on Jews and Judaism*, II (Jerusalem: Israel Academy of Sciences and Humanities, 1980), p. 427.

[151] See Porphyry, fr. 277–282F Smith. The example of the sun as a sign of divine providence also recalls Porphyry, fr. 477F–478F Smith; *In Tim.*, II.51,63.

[152] The idea that divination has been given to men by the Gods echoes *Aneb.*, 2, 2d. The list of divinatory practices in Eusebius' text may recall *Aneb.*, 2, 2f.

[153] *Cels.*, I.36.

[154] *Loc. cit.*

[155] See *Ecl. proph.*, IV.Prol. (hereafter *EP*).

[156] See my discussion, *L'apologétique chrétienne à l'époque de Constantin, cit.*, pp. 365–369.

Contra Christianos and the *Philosophy from oracles* are different works and that the latter was not an anti-Christian work). As a 'confirmation' of this hypothesis, one should note that in the demonstration following the text, Eusebius alludes to his previous attack against the pagan oracles in *PE*, IV–VI,[157] where the *Philosophy from oracles* was extensively quoted. The idea that divination was given to all men may have been put forward by Porphyry in the prologue of the work.[158]

DE, V.22. This text is a Eusebian commentary on Hos 11.9–10. Simmons finds in it a new answer to the Hecatean oracle about Christ, because Eusebius attacks "those who confess he was a holy man, not God".[159] But Simmons' interpretation is unfounded. Eusebius aims at showing Christ's divinity not only in this passage, but throughout Book V. Why detect an anti-Porphyrian polemic here and not elsewhere in the same book? More probably, Eusebius is defending Christ's divinity against any adversary, either Pagan, Jewish or Christian, who might be inclined to negate it.[160] Besides, Hos 11.9–10 is a famous testimony about Christ's divinity. It was quoted for that purpose by the Christians before Porphyry.[161]

BOOK VI

DE, VI.18.11. After commenting on Zec 14.1–10 as a messianic prophecy, Eusebius seeks to refute another exegesis of the text, which applies the passage to the time of Antiochus Epiphanes. Following

---

[157] See *DE*, V.Prol.6; 9; 19.

[158] See *PE*, IV.7.2.

[159] *Arnobius of Sicca*, cit., p. 224, n. 55.

[160] In the *DE*, Eusebius uses the text against "those who confess he was a holy man, but not God" (V.22.1). In the *EP*, where Eusebius already commented on the same text, he accuses those who think that "he was a mere man (ψιλόν τινα ἄνδρα), like one of the just and holy men of old" (III.12). The phrase ψιλὸς ἀνήρ is a clear allusion to the adoptianist heresy: in another chapter of the *EP*, Eusebius links it to the names of the Ebionites, Artemon and Paul of Samosata (IV.22). There is no particular reason to think that Eusebius' adversaries have changed in the *DE*.

[161] See Cyprianus, *Quir.*, II.6. We may add the *Letter of the six bishops* against Paul of Samosata (§ 3), if one admits that the letter is authentic (see P. de Navascues, *Pablo de Samosata y sus adversarios. Estudio histórico-teológico del cristianismo antioqueno en el s. III* (SEAug 87; Roma: Institutum Patristicum "Augustinianum", 2004), pp. 29–32).

J. Geffcken,[162] A. von Harnack thought this was an allusion to a Porphyrian commentary.[163] Some scholars have held that hypothesis as
probable.[164] It apparently relies on the fact that Porphyry applied some
of Daniel's prophecies to the time of Antiochus Epiphanes. But no
evidence indicates that he made the same kind of exegesis in a commentary on Zechariah. Eusebius' adversary remains anonymous (εἰ
δὲ λέγοι τις...). P. Carrara suggested that he may have had in mind
a Jewish exegesis of the text.[165] But we may also think of a Christian
interpretation, such as those of the heretics who did not accept the
harmony (συμφωνία) of the two Testaments.[166]

Book VIII

In this book, Eusebius collects the prophecies concerning the time of
Christ's coming. In the prologue of the book, he once again deals with
the question, "why has he come so late?".[167] I will not come back to
the question whether Eusebius has here Porphyry in mind. As far as I
know, only one passage of Book VIII has been thought as being anti-
Porphyrian: the Eusebian commentary on Dn 9.

DE, VIII.2. This chapter contains an important commentary on
the famous prophecy of the Seventy weeks (Dn 9.20–27). It has been
supposed that if Eusebius spends so much time on that passage, it is
because he has in mind Porphyry's criticism of the Book of Daniel.[168]
What should we think about that interpretation?

The only passage from Dn 9.20–27 which appears to have been
criticized by Porphyry is the passage concerning the 'abomination of

---

[162] *Zwei griechische Apologeten, cit.*, p. 309, n. 1.

[163] See Porphyry, *Christ.*, fr. 47 Harnack.

[164] A. Benoît, "Le *Contra Christianos* de Porphyre: où en est la collecte des fragments?" in *Paganisme, judaïsme et christianisme: influences et affrontements dans le
monde antique. Mélanges offerts à M. Simon*, ed. A. Benoît (Paris: De Boccard, 1978),
261–275, p. 272; Rinaldi, *La Bibbia dei pagani*, II, *cit.*, n° 289.

[165] *Eusebio di Caesarea. Dimostrazione evangelica* (Milano: Paoline, 2000), pp.
515–516 n. 29.

[166] See *DE*, I.1.13. Eusebius more explicitly attacks those heretics in some pages of
the *EP* (I.3; III.19).

[167] *DE*, VIII.Prol.5–12.

[168] See M.J. Hollerich, "Myth and History in Eusebius' 'De vita Constantini': 'Vit.
Const. 1. 12' in Its Contemporary Setting", *HThR* 82 (1989), 421–445, p. 438.

desolation' (Dn 9.27).[169] Porphyry may have commented on other parts of that section, but we cannot speculate on what we do not know.[170] On the other hand, Dn 9.20–27 had been used by the Christians, long before Eusebius, as a famous *testimonium* about the time of Jesus' coming.[171] By quoting that text in a collection about the time of the Incarnation, Eusebius is simply the heir of an apologetic tradition. Moreover, the commentary contains no allusion either to Porphyry or to the Pagans. The only adversaries mentioned by Eusebius are the Jews, who refuse to consider that the prophecy is accomplished.[172] Finally, we should stress the fact the Eusebius' commentary is not always polemical. The apologist admits that the interpretation of the Seventy weeks is difficult, and he refuses to draw any definite conclusion, letting the reader find the best interpretation.[173] He himself puts forward three exegeses of the passage, of which the first one is taken from Africanus.[174] It is clear that Eusebius primarily aims at commenting on a difficult text, not answering any criticism against its Christian readings.

Porphyry's exegesis of the 'abomination of desolation' has not survived. Jerome tells that the Pagan devoted a copious discussion on that passage, and that Eusebius responded to him in three books of his *Contra Porphyrium* (books XVIII, XIX and XX).[175] J.G. Cook assumes that "Porphyry almost certainly interpreted the desolation to be the actions taken against the temple in Jerusalem by Antiochus. Consequently he would have criticized the NT use of this figure to refer to an event in the future"[176] (J.G. Cook has Mt 24.15 and Mk 13.14 in mind,

---

[169] See Cook, *The Interpretation of the Old Testament, cit.*, pp. 217–218.

[170] I am aware of A. Magny's hypothesis that the *Contra Christianos* contained a throrough commentary on Daniel, but that hypothesis, even if it is possibly true, seems impossible to demonstrate (*Porphyre et le livre de Daniel: réaction à la tradition exégétique chrétienne du IIIe siècle*, Mémoire de maître ès Arts, dir. E. De Palma Digeser, Université McGill, Montréal, 2004).

[171] See F. Fraidl, *Die Exegese der siebzig Wochen Daniels in der alten und mittleren Zeit* (Graz: Leuschner und Lubensky, 1883); R. Bodenmann, *Naissance d'une exégèse. Daniel dans l'Église ancienne des trois premiers siècles* (Tübingen: Mohr, 1986); W. Adler, "The Apocalyptic Survey of History Adapted by Christians: Daniel's Prophecy of 70 Weeks," in *The Jewish Apocalyptic Heritage in Early Christianity*, ed. J.C. Vanderkam – W. Adler (Assen – Maastricht – Minneapolis: Van Gorcum – Fortress Press, 1996), 201–238.

[172] *DE*, VIII.2.127.

[173] *Ibid.*, VIII.2.58.

[174] *Ibid.*, VIII.2.46–54.

[175] See Cook, *The Interpretation of the Old Testament, cit.*, p. 218.

[176] *Ibid.*, p. 218.

where Jesus foretells the coming of the abomination of the desolation predicted by Daniel). It is difficult to know if Porphyry's exegesis of the text was part of his criticism against Daniel, or rather part of his objections against the NT.

According to the *DE*, the 'abomination of desolation' is an allusion to several events after Jesus' Passion: the time when the veil of the temple tore and God's power departed from the temple;[177] Pilate's decision to introduce Caesar's images in the temple;[178] finally, the destruction of the temple and the desolation which followed.[179] It is difficult to consider this commentary as an answer to Porphyry. The fact that Eusebius cites the text as a messianic prophecy is not original in itself. The quotation of Jesus' prophecies, in Eusebius' commentary, is more original,[180] but does not necessarily reflect an anti-Porphyrian polemic.[181] We may even wonder whether Eusebius knew Porphyry's criticism against Daniel at that date, since when he accuses the Jews of not being able to show any accomplishment of the prophecy before his own time,[182] one may reasonably assume that he would have mentioned Porphyry's view that the greater part of the prophecy was accomplished in Antiochus' time if he had known it. This is of course a mere hypothesis, and one may also consider this omission as deliberate. Whether he knew of Porphyry's criticism against Daniel or not, it seems clear that Eusebius did not intend to answer Porphyry in his commentary on Dn 9.[183]

BOOK IX–X

Book IX deals with the prophecies of Jesus' deeds during his lifetime. Eusebius raises several difficulties concerning the gospels' narrative. For instance, he seeks to show the reason why Scripture mentions the

---

[177] *DE*, VIII.2.111–121.
[178] *Ibid.*, VIII.2.122–123.
[179] *Ibid.*, VIII.2.124.
[180] *Ibid.*, VIII.2.126–127.
[181] Eusebius was particularly interested in Jesus' prophecies. He quotes them many times in the *DE* and devoted a special work to them (see Kofsky, *Eusebius of Caesarea Against Paganism, cit.*, p. 151 n. 63). The link between this interest in Jesus' prophecies and Porphyry's criticisms against them must remain an open question.
[182] *DE*, VIII.2.127.
[183] Likewise, the corresponding commentary in the *EP* (III.45–46) does not reflect any clear polemic against Porphyry.

appearance of a star at the birth of Christ[184] or why the Savior fled to Egypt to escape Herod's plot.[185] In these two instances, one can easily notice that Eusebius draws on Origen's *Contra Celsum*.[186] He also deals with other passages of the gospels which do not appear to have been attacked by Celsus. In some cases, one may be tempted to assume that Eusebius is answering Porphyrian objections. But the question of an anti-Porphyrian polemic in *DE*, IX must remain open: the Porphyrian origin of the objections is also not certain, and it is often difficult to know if Eusebius is actually seeking to answer objections.[187]

Three times in books IX–X, Eusebius tries to explain a few discrepancies between some Septuagint texts and their quotation in the New Testament.[188] Porphyry is known to have criticized similar discrepancies.[189] But do we have to think that Eusebius is reacting to Porphyrian objections? The answer is probably no. The discrepancies mentioned by Eusebius do not appear to have been used by Porphyry or any Pagan against Christianity. On the other hand, they are already dealt with by Christian writers before Eusebius.[190] Moreover, there are some clues that Eusebius is here drawing on Origen.[191]

BOOK XV

The fragments of book XV contain interpretations on two passages from the book of Daniel commented on by Porphyry: the vision of the statue composed of gold, silver, bronze, iron and clay (Dn 2); the vision of the four beasts and of the son of man (Dn 7). In Dn 2.35, the stone which destroys the statue was read by Porphyry as an allusion to the Jewish people.[192] As he dated the book of Daniel to the time of Antiochus Epiphanes, he must have considered this passage as a (false) prophecy about the supposed everlasting triumph of the Jews

---

[184] *DE*, IX.1.
[185] *Ibid.*, IX.4.
[186] *Ibid.*, IX.1.13 = *Cels.*, I.58–59; *DE*, IX.4.3–5 = *Cels.*, I.66.
[187] See Morlet, *L'apologétique chrétienne à l'époque de Constantin, cit.*, pp. 527–528.
[188] See *DE*, IX.15 (Is 42.1 quoted in Mt 12.18); *DE*, IX.18.14 (Ps 117.25 quoted in Mt 21.9); *DE*, X.4.13 (Zech 11.12ss. quoted in Mt 27.9).
[189] See *Christ.*, fr. 9–10 Harnack.
[190] See Morlet, *L'apologétique chrétienne à l'époque de Constantin, cit.*, pp. 528–530.
[191] Compare *DE*, IX.18.4 and Orig., *Com. Mt.*, XVI.9; *DE*, IX.15.4–6 and Jerome, *In Is.*, XII.42.1/4 (probably from Origen); *DE*, X.4.13 and Orig., *Ser. in Mt.*, 117.
[192] *Christ.*, fr. 43d Harnack (= Jerome, *In Dan.*, 2.35).

in the future.[193] As to Dn 7, Porphyry interpreted the last two beasts as an allusion to the realm of the Macedonians (the leopard being Alexander, and the other beast being Alexander's successors).[194] He may have interpreted the first two beasts as allusions to the Babylonians on the one hand, and the Medes and the Persians on the other hand.[195] Eusebius' commentaries on both passages are lacunose, but the available evidence does not reflect any polemic against Porphyry.[196] First, no pagan adversary is mentioned in the commentaries. Second, Eusebius does not seek to refute any other interpretation of the texts. He gives his own exegesis without contrasting it to other ones. The stone mentioned in Dn 2.35 would be the kingdom of God.[197] The four beasts would refer to the Assyrians, the Persians, the Macedonians and the Romans.[198] Finally, the Son of Man would be Christ who will come back at the end of time.[199] Unsurprisingly, Eusebius comments on both texts as eschatological prophecies. This way of reading Daniel is of course contrary to that of Porphyry, but has nothing anti-Porphyrian in itself: it corresponds to the common Christian reading of Daniel, well attested before and after Porphyry.[200]

Concluding Remarks

The preceding analysis leads us to reassess Eusebius' polemic against Porphyry. The *PE* and the *DE* cannot be considered as an answer to the *Contra Christianos*. Eusebius does not aim at responding to the most innovative objections of the Pagans. The kernel of the pagan arguments he answers stems from Origen's *Contra Celsum*. Interpreting Eusebius' demonstration as a reaction against Porphyry leads to obvious misinterpretations. It remains possible that Porphyry's work

---

[193] See Cook, *The Interpretation of the Old Testament, cit.*, p. 208.

[194] *Christ.*, fr. 43m Harnack (= Jerome, *In Dan.*, 7.8.14).

[195] See Cook, *The Interpretation of the Old Testament, cit.*, pp. 211–212.

[196] One could draw the same conclusion about the corresponding commentaries in the *EP* (III.42; 44).

[197] *DE*, XV, fr. 1.

[198] *Loc. cit.*

[199] *Ibid.*, XV, fr. 3.

[200] Eusebius' exegesis of the four beasts reappears later in Jerome and Theodoretus (see. Cook, *The Interpretation of the Old Testament, cit.*, p. 211, n. 341). For eschatological exegeses of Dn 2 before Porphyry, see Cyprianus, *Quir.*, II.17; Hippolytus, *Dan.*, II.13. About Dn 7, see Justin, *I Apol.*, 51.9; Tertullian, *Marc.*, IV.10.9; Hippolytus, *Dan.*, IV.2–5.

encouraged Eusebius to write a thorough apology of Christianity, and even that Eusebius has Porphyry in mind here and there, but his apology can in no way be considered as a direct answer to Porphyry. Likewise, Eusebius' polemic against the *Philosophy from oracles*, though important, must not be exaggerated. It is reasonable to think that, apart from the explicit passages where Eusebius mentions Porphyry's work (that is to say, essentially in the *PE*),[201] the polemical intention in the *PE—DE* reduces itself to opposing the pagan prophecy praised by Porphyry.

As a consequence, one must admit that the Porphyrian material in the apology is much less important than it is often thought to be. Only two texts from the *PE* are explicitly extracted from Porphyry's anti-Christian work. In both cases, Eusebius does not quote Porphyry to refute him, but on the contrary to use him as an auxiliary witness.[202] These concluding remarks imply that we can no longer be sure that Eusebius knew Porphyry's whole pamphlet when he wrote the *PE—DE*, nor can we use the *PE—DE* to reconstruct the overall argument of the *Contra Christianos*.[203] Most scholars take for granted that Eusebius had written the *Contra Porphyrium* long before the *PE—DE*.[204]

---

[201] The only exception in *DE* is *DE*, III.6.39, to which one may add *DE*, V.Prol., where Eusebius refers to his polemic against Porphyry's work in *PE*.

[202] In *PE*, I.9.21, he uses Porphyry as a source for Phoenician history. In *PE*, V.1.10 he uses Porphyry's testimony to support the idea that the demons have disappeared since Jesus' arrival.

[203] In works supposedly written before *PE—DE*, one finds only one allusion to the fourth book in the *Chronicle* (II.4 Schoene) and one fragment of the third book in the *HE* (VI.19.2). It is interesting to note that from the *PE*, one fragment is taken from the fourth book (*PE*, I.9.21; X.9.12); Eusebius does not mention the book from which he quotes the second one (V.1.10). Consequently, at the time when Eusebius wrote *PE—DE*, the only certainty is that he knew books III and IV of the *Contra Christianos*. The fact that at the beginning of the *Contra Hieroclem*, Eusebius says that almost every objection of his adversary is taken from other polemists does not necessarily entail that Eusebius has Porphyry in mind, and that he had a good knowledge of Porphyry's anti-Christian work at that time. The interpretation of Eusebius' polemic against Porphyry must also take into account the *Questions on the Gospels*, and the possible (but marginal?) presence of Porphyry in that work.

[204] According to Harnack, such a work could not have been written after the triumph of the Church. Eusebius may have considered it an unsatisfying book, since he never refers to it, and the book may date before 300 (*Geschichte der altchristlichen Literatur bis Eusebius. Teil I* [Leipzig: Hinrich, 1893], pp. 118–119). Schwartz thought the work could not have been written after Constantine had become the only master of the Roman empire ("Eusebios von Caesarea", *RE*, VI/1, München 1907, col. 1395). F. Winkelmann supposed that the *Contra Porphyrium* was written before Pamphilus' death (310) and that Eusebius was the polemist of the group (*Euseb von Kaisareia. Der Vater der Kirchengeschichte* (Berlin: Verlags – Anstalt Union, 1991), p. 33). J. Moreau

But the date of that work is actually totally unknown.[205] In any case, Eusebius does not seem liable to have used that work in the *PE—DE*. Nothing prevents from dating the *Contra Porphyrium* to a late period of Eusebius' life. We do not even know if the bishop of Caesarea had direct access to Porphyry's work before writing the *Contra Porphyrium*.[206] This remark raises several questions: was the *Contra Christianos* kept in Eusebius' library? If that is so, was it part of a 'Porphyrian corpus'? When, why and by whom would this Porphyrian corpus have been acquired?[207]

---

thinks that the work could not have been written after Constantine's supposed order to destroy the copies of the *Contra Christianos* (*DHGE*, XV, Paris 1963, col. 1149).

[205] The arguments put forward to support the idea that the *Contra Porphyrium* is one of the first works of Eusebius are very disputable (see preceding note). The fact that Christians did write works against Porphyry after Constantine's supposed edict proves that Eusebius may have written his *Contra Porphyrium* towards the end of his life. The idea that Eusebius' answer to Porphyry was related to his defense of Origen, as Harnack suggests, may imply that the *Contra Porphyrium* was written before Pamphilus' death, but this idea, though attractive, is not certain.

[206] It remains possible that the few fragments which lie in Eusebius' work stem, at least in part, from intermediary sources, such as Methodius' refutation of Porphyry.

[207] Some years ago, R.M. Grant assumed that all the Porphyrian works known to Eusebius (except *Contra Christianos*, *De Abstinentia* and *Chronicle*) had been brought to Caesarea around 279 by an Anatolius mentioned in the *HE* (VII.32.20) ("Porphyry among the Early Christians", in *Romanitas et Christianitas. Studia I.H. Waszink a. d. VI kal. Nov. a. MCMLXXIII XIII lustra complenti oblata*, ed. W. den Boer – P.G. van der Nat – C.M.J. Sicking – J.C.M. van Winden (Amsterdam: North Holland Publishing Company, 1973), 181–188). More recently, A.J. Carriker defended another view: because of the allusion to Porphyry in the *Chronicle*, he supposed that Eusebius had acquired the whole work (with the *History of philosophy*) by 306. He thinks Eusebius acquired the rest of Porphyry's works around 315 (when he was working on the *PE—DE*) and that Plotinus' tractates were acquired on that occasion. He admits that Porphyry's works may have been acquired at Caesarea before 300, but considers that it is an unlikely hypothesis. Finally, he supposes that the persecution prompted Eusebius (and Pamphilus) to make a suitable response to Porphyry (*The Library of Eusebius of Caesarea, cit.*, p. 123). A recent analysis of Eusebius' quotations of Plotinus' tractates led M.-O. Goulet-Cazé to the conclusion that, despite the traditional view, Eusebius knew them through Porphyry's edition ("Deux traités plotiniens chez Eusèbe de Césarée", in *The Libraries of the Neoplatonists*, ed. C. D'Ancona (Leiden: Brill, 2007), 63–97; see also M. Zambon, "Edizione e prima circolazione degli scritti di Plotino: Porfirio ed Eusebio di Cesarea", in *Plotino e l'ontologia. Sostanza, assimilazione, bellezza*, ed. M. Bianchetti (Milano: Albo versorio, 2006), pp. 55–78). This conclusion, if true, would suggest a strong link between the acquisition of Plotinus' tractates and the possible 'Porphyrian corpus' at Caesarea. Another way of linking the two groups of works would be to accept P. Kalligas' hypothesis that Eusebius knew Plotinus' tractates and most of Porphyry's works from Longinus' library ("Traces of Longinus' Library in Eusebius' *Praeparatio Evangelica*", *CQ* 51 (2001), 584–598).

EUSEBIUS' EXEGESIS BETWEEN ALEXANDRIA AND ANTIOCH: BEING A SCHOLAR IN CAESAREA (A TEST CASE FROM *QUESTIONS TO STEPHANOS* I)

Claudio Zamagni*

Eusebius' Exegesis between Alexandria and Antioch

Since the last comprehensive monograph on Eusebius by David Wallace-Hadrill, the exegesis of the bishop of Caesarea has been understood through his auspicious definition: Eusebius as an exegete has to be placed, like his city, between Antioch and Alexandria, halfway between the literal and the allegorical exegesis.[1] Within such a framework, Carmel Sant has tried to settle a developing line in Eusebius' career as an exegete. At its outset, under the influence of Pamphilus and Origen, Eusebius' exegesis leans mainly toward the allegorical reading. Later, in the period between his appointment to the episcopacy of Caesarea and the Council of Nicaea, there is a tendency to balance in Eusebius, and allegorical exegesis is perfectly offset by the 'literal' exegesis. Finally, in his last phase, which includes the

* I am grateful to Aaron Johnson, University of Chicago, for his helpful suggestions about this paper and for his precious revision of my English. A big part of this essay is based on my dissertation, *Les Questions et réponses sur les évangiles d'Eusèbe de Césarée. Étude et édition du résumé grec* (Lausanne – Paris, 2003).

[1] D.S. Wallace-Hadrill, *Eusebius of Caesarea* (London: Mowbray, 1960), 96–97 (American edition: Westminster, MD: Canterbury Press, 1961). These convictions are driven by an analysis of Eusebius' philological and exegetical works related to the Bible (see *ibid.*, pp. 59–99). This comprehension of Eusebius' exegesis has also been recently confirmed by the remarkable study on the *Commentary on Isaiah* by M.J. Hollerich, *Eusebius of Caesarea's Commentary on Isaiah. Christian Exegesis in the Age of Constantine* (OECT; Oxford: Oxford University Press, 1999), 70–102 (especially pp. 94–102) and 610 n. 1. See also C. Sant, "Interpretatio Veteris Testamenti in Eusebio Caesarensis", *VD* 45 (1967), 77–90, p. 80; *Id., The Old Testament Interpretation of Eusebius of Caesarea: The Manifold Sense of Holy Scripture* (Malta: Royal University of Malta, 1967), xiii–xiv; C. Curti, "L'esegesi di Eusebio di Cesarea: caratteri e sviluppo", in *Le trasformazioni della cultura nella tarda antichità...*, I (Roma: Jouvence, 1985), then in *Id., Eusebiana I, Commentarii in Psalmos* (Saggi e testi classici, cristiani e medievali 1; Catania: Centro di studi sull'antico cristianesimo, Università di Catania, [1]1987 = *ibid.*, [2]1989), 193–213, pp. 195–196; M. Simonetti, *Lettera e/o Allegoria. Un contributo alla storia dell'esegesi patristica* (SEAug 23; Roma: Institutum Patristicum "Augustinianum", 1985), 113–124.

commentaries on the Psalms and on Isaiah, the allegorical meaning tends to disappear completely, while the literal exegesis expands disproportionately; in these commentaries, Eusebius shows all his erudition, his philological interests, his knowledge on ethnography, geography, and ancient history. Carmel Sant identifies exactly four steps in this development of Eusebius' exegesis:[2] in a first stage, Eusebius is greatly influenced by Origen's exegesis (e.g., in the *Prophetic excerpts*); in a second successive phase, he gives more importance to the historical facts, because of his enlarged interest in apologetics (e.g., in the *Evangelical demonstration*); in a third step, Eusebius mainly uses his philological competences to attack some works by other theologians or adversaries (e.g., in his *Against Marcellus* and *Ecclesiastical theology*); and finally, in a last period (when he comments on Isaiah and Psalms), Eusebius reaches the maturity of his widely-known 'historical' exegesis, which is to be regarded as a prelude to the forthcoming Antiochene exegesis. According to Sant, this course clearly shows that Eusebius' interests in historical matter increases during his life.[3]

Later, Carmelo Curti has proposed virtually the same kind of intellectual journey for Eusebius' exegesis, defining an increasing interest on any 'historical' aspects,[4] except that he does not consider the third stage proposed by Sant.[5] Recently, studying Eusebius' exegesis of Isaiah 8.4, Sébastien Morlet has subjected Curti's conclusions to a close inquiry, proposing to consider such an approach in Eusebius' exegesis not in a merely mechanical way.[6]

---

[2] Sant, "Interpretatio Veteris Testamenti in Eusebio…", *cit.*, 87–88.

[3] Cf. Sant, *ibid.*, 80 and *Id.*, *The Old Testament Interpretation…*, 118–119 and 124.

[4] Curti, "L'esegesi di Eusebio di Cesarea…", *cit.*, 202–213.

[5] The work of Sant is mentioned only once by Curti (*ibid.*, 196 n. 7), and apparently disregarded thereafter.

[6] S. Morlet, "Le commentaire d'Eusèbe de Césarée sur Is 8,4 dans la *Démonstration évangélique* (VII, i, 95–113): ses sources et son originalité", *Adamantius* 13 (2007), 52–63, especially pp. 61–63. There is, in any case, a peculiar aspect of Origen's influence on Eusebius that cannot be fitted into this scheme, and concerns the way of argument using quotations and biblical allusions. According to Hollerich, this even represents the most notable issue of Eusebian exegesis (Hollerich, *Eusebius of Caesarea's* Commentary on Isaiah, *cit.*, p. 10). He uses for such conclusions (based on the *Commentary on Isaiah*) the remarks proposed by T.D. Barnes, *Constantine and Eusebius* (Cambridge, MA – London: Harvard University Press, 1981) especially pp. 106–125, although this phenomenon has been many times observed in Eusebius: see for example Sant, "Interpretatio Veteris Testamenti in Eusebio", *cit.*, 85 (in reference to *Quaest. ad Steph.*, VII); M. Simonetti, "Esegesi e ideologia nel commento a Isaia di Eusebio", *RSLR* 19 (1983), 3–44, pp. 4–12.41–44 and *Id.*, "Eusebio e Origene. Per una storia dell'Origenismo", *Aug.* 26 (1986), 323–334, pp. 327–330; F. Winkelmann, *Euseb*

EUSEBIUS' EXEGESIS AT WORK: AN EXAMPLE FROM THE EXTRACT
(ἐκλογή) OF THE QUESTIONS TO STEPHANOS

I also think there are good arguments to tweak a little our comprehension of Eusebius' exegesis, and I will start by studying a precise
example, coming from the central period of Eusebius' production, the
Questions and answers on the gospels, one of his first texts completely
devoted to biblical exegesis. Unfortunately, this book is actually lost
in its original form, but many parts survive in disparate sources; one
of them is an ἐκλογή, a patchwork composed by literary extracts (not
summed up) from the original work.[7]

The *Questions* were begun at about the same time as the *Evangelical
demonstration*, and were finished possibly later. I will here analyze the
first question addressed to Stephanos, which was for sure composed
alongside the *Evangelical demonstration*, or shortly before, as some
cross-references show.[8]

Eusebius tries here to solve a problem concerning Jesus' genealogy
and about the significance of such a genealogical table as a proof of
his Davidic descent. The genealogies had without doubt a great importance in Late Antiquity, and this is reflected not only in the text of
1 Tm 1.4,[9] but also from several studies about this topic in a Christian

---

von Kaisareia. Der Vater der Kirchengeschichte (Biographien zur Kirchengeschichte;
Berlin: Verlags-Anstalt Union, 1991), 41–43; M.J. Hollerich, "Eusebius as a Polemical
Interpreter of Scripture", in *Eusebius, Christianity, and Judaism*, ed. H.W. Attridge –
G. Hata (StPB 42; Leiden – New York – Köln: Brill, 1992), 585–615, pp. 589–594
(American edition: Detroit: Wayne State University Press, 1992) and *Id.*, "Origen's
Exegetical Heritage in the Early Fourth Century: the Evidence of Eusebius", in *Orige-
niana Quinta...*, Ed. by R.J. Daly (BEThL 105; Leuven: Peeters, 1992), 542–548, pp.
543–547; M. Amerise, *Eusebio di Cesarea* (Brescia: Morcelliana, forthcoming), chapter III.5. The most interesting studies on this topic are probably those by Wallace-
Hadrill, *Eusebius of Caesarea*, cit., 72–99; Barnes, *Constantine and Eusebius*, cit.,
97–105, and Hollerich, *Eusebius of Caesarea's* Commentary on Isaiah, cit., 46–57 (cf.
also pp. 74–78, 87–88, 184–185), because they underline the differences between Eusebius and Origen.

[7] I have published a first modern edition of this ἐκλογή: Eusèbe de Césarée, *Questions évangéliques*. Introduction, texte critique, traduction et notes par C. Zamagni
(SC 523; Paris: Cerf, 2008).

[8] *Dem. ev.*, VII.3.18 refers to this first question to Stephanos, while the seventh
question to Stephanos is referred to at *Dem. ev.*, I.2–9; on these cross-reference, cf.
R. Bohla, *Dating Eusebius' Quaestions ad Stephanum*, in *La Littérature des Questions
et reponses dans l'antiquite* (forthcoming).

[9] "...and not to occupy themselves with myths and endless genealogies that promote speculations rather than the divine training that is known by faith" (New Revised
Standard Version).

context,[10] as well as in Jewish and in Near East contexts.[11] Therefore, it is not to be regarded as out of the ordinary that Eusebius' *Questions* deeply concern problems dealing with Jesus' genealogy, together with other questions, apparently much more crucial, as it is the problem of the resurrection of Jesus, treated in the questions dedicated to Marinos. I propose here a translation of the beginning part of this first question to Stephanos (hereafter ESt), taken from the extract (ἐκλογή) of this work, ESt I.1.

I. Why do the evangelists trace Joseph's genealogy, instead of Mary's?

1. For what reason do they trace the genealogy of Christ as a son of David? Probably because of Joseph, who comes from David. However Christ is not son of Joseph, but of the Holy Spirit and Mary, as the Scripture says. It was therefore imperative to trace the genealogy of Mary, if they really wanted to trace a genealogy of Christ, and not that of Joseph, with whom Christ is not related in any way according to the flesh, since he was not generated by him. And, if he is not his descendent, but from Mary only, he cannot come from David, because no text indicates that Mary is a descendant of David. So it is in vain that they repeat that

---

[10] Cf. on this W. Speyer, "Genealogie", *RAC*, IX, 1976, 1145–1268, and especially pp. 1201–1265, as well as R.E. Brown, *The Birth of the Messiah*. A commentary on the infancy narratives in Matthew and Luke (The Anchor Bible Reference Library; Garden City, NY – London: Doubleday – Chapman, [1]1977), 64–66; G. Broszio, *Genealogia Christi. Die Stammbäume Jesu in der Auslegung der christlichen Schriftsteller der ersten fünf Jahrhunderte* (Bochumer Altertumswissenschaftliches Colloquium 18; Trier: Wissenschaftlicher Verlag, 1994) and K.-H. Ostmeyer, "Der Stammbaum des Verheißenen: Theologische Implikationen der Namen und Zahlen in Mt. 1.1–17", *NTS* 46 (2000), 175–192, pp. 182–183.

[11] Cf. for example O. Eissfeldt, *Einleitung in das Alte Testament*, unter Einschuß der Apokryphen und Pseudepigraphen sowie der apokryphen- und pseudepigraphenartigen Qumran-Schriften. Entstehungsgeschichte des Alten Testaments (NTG; Tübingen: Mohr, [3]1964), 31–33 ([1]1934); M.D. Johnson, *The Purpose of the Biblical Genealogies*. With Special Reference to the Setting of the Genealogies of Jesus (MSSNTS 8; Cambridge: Cambridge University Press, [1]1969), especially 77–82.115 ([2]1988); R.R. Wilson, "The Old Testament Genealogies in Recent Research", *JBL* 94 (1975), 169–189, pp. 169–173; B.E. Scolnic, *Theme and Context in Biblical Lists* (SFSHJ 119; Atlanta, GE: Scholars Press, 1995), 3–9 and K.L. Sparks, *Ancient Texts for the Study of the Hebrew Bible*. A Guide to the Background Literature (Peabody, Mass.: Hendrickson, 2005), 344–360. In the same sense, we should also see the parallels to the New Testament texts reported by H.L. Strack – P. Billerbeck, *Das Evangelius nach Matthäus erläutert aus Talmud und Midrasch* (Bill. 1; München: Beck, 1922), 1–6, as well as those reported by J. Jeremias, *Jerusalem zur Zeit Jesu*. Kulturgeschichtliche Untersuchung zur neutestamentlichen Zeitgeschichte, II. Teil, Die Sozialen Verhältnisse, B. Hoch und niedrig [2. Lieferung] (Göttingen: Vandenhoeck & Ruprecht, 1937), 150–168, by Johnson, *The Purpose of the Biblical Genealogies, cit.*, 146–208.240 and by R. Bauckham, *Jude and the Relatives of Jesus in the Early Church* (Edinburgh: T. & T. Clark, 1990), 315–326.

Christ is from the family of David, because he is not the son of Joseph, and because the genealogy of Mary is not derived from David. This is more or less the contents of the first question, and here is the solution that is proposed.

In proposing and developing such a question, Eusebius certainly did not ignore that this issue was also the topic of a strong criticism proposed by Celsus at the end of the second century, in a work that has partly survived in its refutation written by Origen, the *Contra Celsum*. Eusebius' answer contains a comprehensive response to such delicate problem, and his original issue is built, as we will see, on a frame of scattered observations that he was able to read in different works of Origen.

Celsus had expressly noted the contradiction that arises in the gospels about the fact that Jesus is presented as a descendant of David through Joseph, while Joseph is actually not his father. He wondered why Mary, if she were also from the same royal lineage, has ignored her family tree (Origen, *Contra Cels.*, II.32).[12] On this particular point, Eusebius responds in ESt I.12, but it is more than likely that the criticism of Celsus was more developed and complex than this sole remnant. Another part of the same Celsus' critique was the charge against Jesus as an illegitimate child, and the assertion that Mary had in fact been banned by Joseph (in this regard, see Origen, *Contra Cels.*, I.28; I.32; I.39). Even if Eusebius does not take into account these points, I think that such a set of criticisms concerning the birth of Jesus shows that Celsus had clearly noted also that the Davidic descent could not be proved by the genealogy of Joseph. We can therefore reasonably conclude that, even though there is no evidence of that, Celsus' criticism included also the main problems discussed by Eusebius in this question, as we will see in detail. It counts as some kind of evidence

---

[12] On this point, cf. Theodor Zahn: *Das Evangelium des Matthäus*, ausgelegt von T. Zahn (KNT 1; Leipzig: Deichert, 1903), 65–68; Brown, *The Birth of the Messiah, cit.*, 535–536; J.G. Cook, *The Interpretation of the New Testament in Graeco-Roman Paganism* (Studien und Texte zu Antike und Christentum 3; Tübingen: Mohr, 2000), 28; G. Rinaldi, Biblia gentium. *Primo contributo per un indice delle citazioni, dei riferimenti e delle allusioni alla Bibbia negli autori pagani, greci e latini, di età imperiale. A First Contribution Towards An Index of Biblical Quotations, References and Allusions Made by Greek and Latin Heathen Writers of the Roman Imperial Times* (Roma: Libreria Sacre Scritture 1989), as well as *Id., La Bibbia dei pagani*, II. Testi e Documenti (La Bibbia nella storia 20; Bologna: EDB, 1998), n° 442.

also if we remember, together with Enrico Norelli,[13] that Celsus relies directly on the text of Matthew for this criticism (Mt 1.19 is behind Celsus' critiques in this case, of course).

The points that have been the subject of criticism by Celsus were very likely also taken into account by Porphyry, but we have no testimony from him on that. After them and after Eusebius too, this problematic was in any case resumed in a thorough manner by Julian, especially concerning the contradictions between the two genealogies and the fact that they demonstrate at least the non-Davidic origin of Jesus. Several fragments remain of this criticism by Julian, probably connected with each other, as was noted for example in Migne (PG 10.63 n. 27) as well as, more recently, by John Cook.[14] Traces of Julian's text are found primarily in *Adv. Gal.*, fr. 62, l. 18–32,[15] which asserts that the prophecy of a perpetual royal offspring from Judah had already been achieved (before Jesus); that Jesus, being the son of Mary and not of Joseph, is not even a descendant of Judah, and that in any case Joseph's genealogy is controversial because the two evangelists are in great disagreement on this. There is also another question that arises in *Adv. Gal.*, fr. 64, l. 9–12[16] about Nb 24.17, which is referring to the prophecy of a Davidic reign that cannot concern Jesus. Finally, there is *Adv. Gal.*, fr. 90,[17] a passage about the discrepancy between the two genealogies, especially about the fact that Jacob is the father of Joseph according to Matthew, while according to Luke it is Heli. To sum up, the criticism of Julian are very near to the entire problematic treated in Eusebius' first question to Stephanos. The same is also true for the case of the scarce fragments of Celsus. The fact that, between Celsus and Julian, the same questions have also been developed by Porphyry is a hypothesis which is certainly possible, but that we cannot

---

[13] E. Norelli, "La tradizione sulla nascita di Gesù nell' ΑΛΗΘΗΣ ΛΟΓΟΣ di Celso", in *Discorsi di verità, paganesimo, giudaismo e cristianesimo a confronto nel* Contro Celso *di Origene*. Atti del II Convegno del Gruppo Italiano di Ricerca su "Origene e la Tradizione Alessandrina". A cura di L. Perrone (SEAug 61; Roma: Institutum Patristicum "Augustinianum", 1998), 133–166, p. 154.158.

[14] Cook, *The Interpretation of the New Testament in Graeco-Roman Paganism*, cit., 289–290.

[15] Ed. Masaracchia 1990, pp. 157–158.

[16] Ed. Masaracchia 1990, p. 159. Text coming from Cyrillus of Alexandria, *Contra Iul.*, VIII (PG 76.900D–901C).

[17] Ed. Masaracchia 1990, p. 184. Text coming from Jerome, *Comm. in Mt.*, I.1.16; cf. Rinaldi, *Biblia gentium*, cit., and *Id.*, *La Bibbia dei pagani*, II., cit., n° 319.

prove further, in spite of all the tests that have been carried out in this direction.[18]

In the first part of his answer, Eusebius says that there was a divine plan to let the people consider the origin of Jesus as an ordinary one. Actually, if it were otherwise, the child could not escape the infamy, as he would have been considered son of Mary and without a father. This could also result in a death sentence for his mother, because of the mosaic laws (ESt I.2–9). Having built this coherent framework, Eusebius gives also his main solution to the question. The answer will be obvious, and will join the statements already proposed by other Christian authors: this is because Mary also is descendant from the seed of David, like Joseph (ESt I.10–12).[19]

Apparently, nothing is new, as several ancient Christian texts say explicitly or implicitly that Mary also is from the Davidic lineage or in any case from the tribe of Judah. However, as we will see later in detail, no other known text contains the main arguments appearing in Eusebius' exegesis. In sum, we can argue that the question and its final solution were not original in themselves, but the way Eusebius chose to resolve this problem differs from any other previous explanation and it goes, in fact, much more deeply inside the question. Let's start with the first part of the solution, stating the necessity that the origin of Jesus had to be widely known as ordinary in its times (ESt I.2–3).

> 2. Among the actions of our saviour Jesus Christ, it was necessary that some were hidden from people in that time and that others, on the contrary, were delivered to the ears of many, all those that should be beneficial

---

[18] Cf. W. Nestle, "Die Haupteinwände des antiken Denkens gegen das Christentum", *ARW* 37 (1941), 51–100, then in *Id., Griechische Studien. Untersuchungen zur Religion, Dichtung und Philosophie der Griechen* (Stuttgart: Hannsmann, 1948), 597–660, p. 612 (reprint, Aalen: Scientia Verlag, 1968) and Rinaldi, "Tracce di controversie tra pagani e cristiani nella letteratura patristica delle 'quaestiones et responsiones'", *ASE* 6 (1989), 99–124, p. 106, especially n. 23.

[19] Cf. on this matter already P. Poussines, *Diallacticon Theogenealogicum, sive de genealogia Iesu Christi Dei ac Domini nostri*, liber singularis [Tolosae 1646], 567–574; Johann Bengel: *D. Joh. Alberti Bengelii Gnomon Novi Testamenti. in quo ex nativa verborum vi, simplicitas, profunditas, concinnitas, salubritas, sensuum coelestium indicatur. Editio octava stereotypa. Ed. III.* (1773) per filium superstitem Ernestum Bengelium quondam curata, sexto recusa, emendata et e ceteris Bengelii scriptis—posthumis ex parte—suppleta et aucta opera Pauli Steudel (Stuttgartiae: Steinkopf, 1891), 8–10.233–234 ([1]1742), and lately, for example, Brown, *The Birth of the Messiah, cit.*, 62–64, as well as the dissertation by J. Masson, *Jésus fils de David dans les généalogies de saint Matthieu et de saint Luc* (Paris: Téqui, 1982), 483–511.

for listeners. For example, the fact that Jesus, in the thirtieth year of his embodied age, came to the baptism of John and that, therefore, he began his teaching and prodigious works; however, what he achieved during all of thirty years before baptism, is revealed by no narrative, and one cannot learn from any divine Scripture what his previous life was. But, even after he was known to all, there are things he proclaimed to the ears of all, and others in which he initiated his disciples only. Sometimes, when he performed miracles, he recommended not telling anyone; sometimes he performed his miracles without this recommendation. For example, one of the things on which he had decided to observe the greatest silence was the prodigy of his birth; among those who were contemporaries of the time when he became a man, nobody, with the exception of a few, had acquired this knowledge. 3. The holy man named Ignatius, who was the second bishop of the church of Antioch after the apostles, says somewhere that the virginity of Mary and the birth of the saviour remained hidden even to the prince of this age. He says: "Mary's virginity, his birth and also the death of Christ have remained hidden to the prince of this age: three resounding mysteries, which took place in the silence of God." The reason must be that all those who lived in the flesh, when they saw the Christ of God himself, living with men as an ordinary man, were unable to believe that he was born from an unmarried girl, without having a father.

The quotation from Ignatius, *Eph.*, XIX.1, is the only known quotation from another author in the *Questions*, apart from a long extract taken from Julius Africanus.[20] Its presence here is interesting because it seems to point directly to Origen.

Ignatius is said here to be "the second bishop of the church of Antioch after the apostles" but, regarding the episcopal succession in Antioch, our sources are partly contradictory.[21] One of the oldest testimonies about the episcopacy of Ignatius is that of Origen, *Hom. in Luc.*, VI.4, which says that Ignatius is the second bishop of Antioch after Peter,

---

[20] Both quotations are omitted from the census by A. Carriker, *The Library of Eusebius of Caesarea* (SVigChr 67; Leiden – Boston: Brill, 2003), 215–217.219–220.

[21] See on this subject the reports by Theodor Zahn, *Ignatii et Polycarpi Epistulae, Martyria, Fragmenta*, recensuit et illustravit T. Zahn (= *Patrum Apostolicorum Opera*...instruxerunt, O. De Gebhardt – A. Harnack – T. Zahn, II; Lipsiae: Hinrichs, 1876), 261–262 as well as A. von Harnack, *Geschichte der altchristlichen Litteratur bis Eusebius*, II. Chronologie des altchristlichen Litteratur bis Eusebius, 1. Die Chronologie der Litteratur bis Irenäus nebst einleitenden Untersuchungen (Leipzig: Hinrichs, 1897), 118–129.208–213 and Franz Funk: *Patres Apostolici*. Ed. F.X. Funk, I... (= *Patres Apostolici*...I; Tubingae: Laupp, ²1901), LV.

"episcopum Antiochiae post Petrum secundum",[22] or, in an original Greek fragment, μετὰ τὸν μακάριον Πέτρον τῆς Ἀντιοχείας δεύτερον ἐπίσκοπον.[23] Eusebius follows possibly the same origenian tradition in *Hist. eccl.*, III.36.2, where he says that Ignatius was the second bishop after Peter, Ἰγνάτιος, τῆς κατὰ Ἀντιόχειαν Πέτρου διαδοχῆς δεύτερος τὴν ἐπισκοπὴν κεκληρωμένος.[24] With the support of Origen, one interprets the Πέτρου διαδοχή in the sense that, according to Eusebius, Ignatius would stand as the second bishop of Antioch after Peter;[25] but this expression of Eusebius could also be understood as simply indicating the episcopal dignity and not an immediate succession. In fact, in *Hist. eccl.*, III.22, Eusebius says that Ignatius was the second bishop of Antioch after Evodius.[26] In the two last cases, he just says he was the second bishop, as he does in *Chronicon*, a. CCXII Olymp.: "Antiochiae secundus episcopus ordinatur Ignatius", and *ibid.*, a. CCXXI Olymp.[27] In my opinion, in *Hist. eccl.*, III.36, Eusebius did not intend to affirm that Peter was really the first bishop of Antioch and, even if we can assume, with Walter Bauer,[28] that he used two different sources in *Hist. eccl.*, III.22 and III.36, without spotting the contradiction, this does not sound truly convincing, as also noted by Enrico Norelli.[29] Eusebius obviously knows the origenian tradition and tries not to contradict it, but he seems clearly to prefer the other tradition, that he considers

---

[22] Ed. Crouzel – Fournier – Périchon, SC 87, p. 144.

[23] Ed. Rauer, GCS 49, p. 34.

[24] Ed. Bardy, SC 31, p. 147.

[25] So for example Pierre Camelot in his introduction for Ignace d'Antioche, Polycarpe de Smyrne, *Lettres*; *Martyre de Polycarpe*, texte grec, intr. tr. et notes de P.T. Camelot (SC 10), Paris ⁴1969, pp. 9–10 or Enrico Norelli in C. Moreschini – E. Norelli, *Storia della letteratura cristiana antica greca e latina*, I. Da Paolo all'età costantiniano (Letteratura cristiana antica. Strumenti; Brescia: Morcelliana, 1995), p. 166.

[26] Evodius is rather unknown, but he is mentioned in the interpolated letters of Ignatius, *Philad.*, IV, and *Antioch.*, VII, as well as in the Roman martyrium of Ignatius, *Mart. Ign.*, I (texts ed. by Zahn, *Ignatii et Polycarpi Epistulae, Martyria, Fragmenta, cit.*, p. 234.260.207 and Franz Diekamp in F.X. Funk – F. Diekamp, *Patres Apostolici...II...(= Patres Apostolici...II.*; Tubingae: Laupp, 1913), p. 176.218.341.

[27] Ed. Helm, GCS 24, p. 186.194–195.

[28] W Bauer, *Rechtgläubigkeit und Ketzerei im ältesten Christentum*. Zweite, durchgesehene Auflage mit einem Nachtrag, hrsg. von G. Strecker (BHTh 10; Tübingen: Mohr, ²1964), 119–120.

[29] E. Norelli, "Ignazio d'Antiochia combatte veramente dei cristiani giudaizzanti?", in *Verus Israel. Nuove prospettive sul giudeocristianesimo*. Atti del Colloquio di Torino (4–5 novembre 1999), a cura di G. Filoramo – C. Gianotto (Biblioteca di cultura religiosa 65; Brescia: Paideia, 2001), 220–264, p. 259 n. 93.

genuine and that he probably learned from Julius Africanus.[30] It is
likely that the traditions knowing Peter as the first bishop of Antioch
and knowing Ignatius as his direct successor are both secondary traditions, as many scholars have already remarked, Bauer among others.[31]

Both traditions have been harmonized by another great personage of
the patristic age, someone who deeply knew the work of Origen as well
as the work of Eusebius, Jerome of Stridon. In his *De vir. ill.*, XVI.1,
Jerome states: "Ignatius, Antiochenae ecclesiae tertius post Petrum
apostolum episcopus".[32] Jerome certainly knew the text of Origen and
the two passages of the eusebian *Chronicon* because he is the author
of their Latin translations; he also knew *Hist. eccl.*, III.36, because he
drew two ignatian quotations from this passage of Eusebius (cf. *Hist.
eccl.*, III.36.7–11 and *De vir. ill.*, XVI.3–8), but, if he does not follow
exactly any of these four passages, it is because he had clearly in mind
the tradition of *Hist. eccl.*, III.22 mentioning Evodius. Besides, other
old testimonies attempt to bring the two traditions together, including those of the *Apostolic. constitut.*, VII.46, and John Malalas.[33] Our
passage from ESt I.3, telling that Ignatius is "the second bishop of the
church of Antioch after the apostles", uses an expression that can be
easily interpreted as excluding the possibility that Peter was the predecessor of Ignatius, because the phrase μετὰ τοὺς ἀποστόλους, in its
plural form, seems to refer to the time of the episcopacy of the predecessor of Ignatius (i.e., Evodius), and excludes any other reference.

This excursus on Peter, Evodius and Ignatius only apparently has
nothing to do with the general interpretation of Eusebius' question.
We know that the influence of Origen was great on Eusebius, but in
his texts concerning this episcopal succession (to me, even in *Hist.
eccl.*, III.36), Eusebius shows that he is capable of disposing of Origen's convictions when he has the certitude that the story has gone

---

[30] On this point, cf. Harnack, *Geschichte der altchristlichen Litteratur bis Eusebius*,
II./1., *cit.*, 124.
[31] Cf. for example Bauer, *Rechtgläubigkeit und Ketzerei im ältesten Christentum*,
cit., 120, and, for example, R. Aubert, "Evodius, Εὐόδιος, premier évêque d'Antioche",
in *DHGE*, XVI, Paris 1967, 133.
[32] Ed. Ceresa-Gastaldo, BPat 12, p. 106.
[33] Quoted by Norelli, "Ignazio d'Antiochia combatte veramente dei cristiani giudaizzanti?", *cit.*, 259–260. Cf. also the sources mentionned by Zahn, *Ignatii et Polycarpi
Epistulae, Martyria, Fragmenta, cit.*, 262 et Funk, *Patres Apostolici*, I., *cit.*, LV–LVI.

in another way.[34] This is very softly made, but, as Origen was a well known reference, there was no necessity for Eusebius to highlight his convictions against him: with Origen, this is a minimum fair play.

But there is also another reason to point to the fact that Eusebius did know this passage of Origen's *Homilies on Luke*, VI, and that Eusebius has consciously decided not to follow him in concerning the apostolic succession in Antioch. In fact, Eusebius has clearly taken inspiration from Origen's *Hom. in Luc.*, VI (especially VI.4)[35] when writing his passage of ESt I.2–9. There are many parallels between the two texts, but one of the most significant is that both share the same quotation from Ignatius. This means that Eusebius quotes Ignatius by the way of Origen's *Homilies on Luke*. This particular quotation of Ignatius, *Eph.*, XIX.1, has had a great fortune in the Christian literature, as a large amount of scholars have noted,[36] but in reality the widespread knowledge of this passage by Ignatius is only the result of its quotation by Origen and later by our passage of Eusebius. For example, Ambrose, *Exp. in Luc.*, II.3, quotes this passage in a context that is clearly influenced by both the homilies of Origen and the *Questions* of Eusebius. The same conclusion can be inferred for Jerome, *Comm. in Mt.*, I.1.18.76–78, who lacks the explicit mention of Ignatius,[37] as well as for other authors.[38] Most of these authors quoted Ignatius from Eusebius' text rather than from his source Origen, as is evidenced by their use of the arguments that are taken from Eusebius' question. The textual form of *Eph.*, XIX.1 quoted by Eusebius has a minor variant

---

[34] For another example concerning Eusebius' free attitude towards Origen, cf. A.P. Johnson, "The Blackness of Ethiopians: Classical Ethnography and Eusebius's Commentary on the Psalms", *HThR* 99 (2006), 179–200, pp. 192–200.

[35] See in general *Hom. in Luc.*, VI.4–6 as well as fragment 20b of the same work (ed. Rauer, GCS 49, p. 235), and the text of Origen's *Comm. in Mt.*, fr. 13/I–II (ed. Klostermann – Benz, GCS 41/1, pp. 20–21).

[36] See the references from Camelot in Ignace d'Antioche, Polycarpe de Smyrne, *Lettres; Martyre de Polycarpe, cit.*, 74–75 n. 4.

[37] Ed. Bonnard, SC 242, p. 78.

[38] See Ps.(?)-Basil of Caesarea, *In sanct. Christi gener.*, 3 (PG 31.1464A-C); Ps.-Origen, *Hom. in Mt.*, I.1.3 (ed. Klostermann – Benz, GCS 41/1, p. 239, p. 243); II (PLS 4, p. 853); and Theophylact of Bulgaria, *En. in Mt.*, 1.18, who also does not even mention the name of Ignatius in their exegesis. This list is not exhaustive; see also R. Weijenborg, *Les lettres d'Ignace d'Antioche, étude de critique littéraire et de théologie.* Mis en français par B. Héroux (Leiden: Brill, 1969), 27.30–31 and J. Rivière, "Le démon dans l'économie rédemptrice d'après saint Ignace d'Antioche", *RevSR* 2 (1922), 13–25, later in *Id., Le dogme de la rédemption. Etudes critiques et documents* (BRHE 5; Louvain: Bureau de la Revue d'histoire ecclésiastique, 1931), 61–77, pp. 68–72.

compared to the direct tradition of Ignatius,[39] and seems to retain some traditions concerning the theme of the *descensus absconditus* of the saviour, as Heinrich Schlier has pointed out.[40]

So actually, the text of Eusebius takes some ideas from Origen's *Hom. in Lc.*, VI.4–6, and develops them, making a larger discussion and including for instance topics that are not taken from this passage of Origen, but are developed directly by Eusebius, or even other origenian texts, as is the case with ESt I.5–6, whose translation follows.

> 5. If it had happened that she became pregnant while she was still with her parents, it is likely that the fact that she had not conceived by a husband would have been disclosed and that she would have been immediately put to death according to law. Or, if this is not the case, it is likely that she would have been considered reprehensible, because she was certainly not a credible witness for herself and for what had happened to her. Nobody would have believed if she had spoken of the appearance of an angel and of the words addressed to her by Gabriel. On the other hand, Joseph, who is witnessed as an upright man, would not have been able to accept her in his home, when she was already pregnant. That is why, quite rightly, she became pregnant not when she was with her parents, but when she was at home with him, living with him, so to speak, according to the status of marriage. Indeed, before "they united", as evidenced by Scripture, "she was found pregnant". 6. By whom was she

---

[39] It reads τοῦ χριστοῦ in place of τοῦ κυρίου. Such a variant is reported and discussed by Weijenborg (*Les lettres d'Ignace d'Antioche, cit.*, 30), who erroneously does not find it relevant because of the ἐκλογή could not really go back to Eusebius and his era in his opinion. Weijenborg makes clear reference to the fact that the author of the ἐκλογή has summed up the original text, but this is actually not the case, because the ἐκλογή consists instead of literal excerpts, as is illustrated by a comparison with the text of the tradition of Nicetas (I have discussed upon this matter in the introduction of Eusèbe de Césarée, *Questions évangéliques, cit.*, 19–26).

[40] Cf. H. Schlier, *Religionsgeschichtliche Untersuchungen zu den Ignatiusbriefen* (BZNW 8; Gießen: Töpelmann, 1929), 5–32. This question has been largely studied: cf. for example Weijenborg, *Les lettres d'Ignace d'Antioche, cit.*, 274–275; W.R. Schoedel, *A Commentary on the Letters of Ignatius of Antioch*. Ed. by H. Koester (Hermeneia; Philadelphia, PA: Fortress Press, 1985), 88–91. The topic itself is very complex, and is linked to the idea of the passage of the dead souls through the skies, on which see the remarks by Norelli in his commentary on *Ascension of Isaiah* 10.16–31: *Ascensio Isaiae*. Commentarius, cura E. Norelli (Corpus Christianorum. Series Apocryphorum 8; Turnhout: Brepols, 1995), 529–533, as well as the statements on the Orphic shelves by C. Calame, "Orphik, Orphische Dichtung", in *Der Neue Pauly. Enzyklopädie der Antike*. Hrsg. von H. Cancik – H. Schneider, IX (Stuttgart – Weimar: Metzler, 2000), 58–69, especially p. 67.

'found', other than by Joseph? The text itself will teach why and how this became known to Joseph, saying that it was by the Holy Spirit that this became known to him also, in the following manner. Joseph was indeed an upright man, and, as he was upright, it is no wonder that he has been judged as worthy of God's Spirit, to understand the pregnancy of her who was to become his wife, and to suspend the relationship of the husband. Having readily understood, and struck with fear, "he wanted to dismiss her secretly", judging that what had happened was too high for a common life with him. This was precisely the reason why, as he was an upright man, he did not just expose her, but "he wanted to dismiss her secretly". Of course, if he had not been convinced that she had conceived by the Holy Spirit, knowing that she was not pregnant by him, why then, as the man was upright, would he not drag her in front of everyone, at that very moment, the one that had corrupted herself before the marriage, and why would he not deliver her to those who judge such actions, to expose her as guilty? How can it be upright for one who is willing to cover and conceal the illegal action? It would certainly not have been likely that the evangelist call him upright, if he had done so. But, as it was aware that the special divine conception of the Virgin Mary had been received by the Holy Spirit, and considering that this design was higher than a life with him, the evangelist rightly said that "he wanted to dismiss her secretly", without being exposed by him, and that her condition become apparent to the public. It thus appears that the evangelist has rightly said "he did not want to expose her". Indeed, he did not say "not wanting to defame her" but "not wanting to expose her", and there is a lot of difference between these two words, as well as "to write down" and "to interpolate"[41] do not mean the same thing nor "to set down" and "to defraud",[42] or "to vote" and "to vote deceptively", and as does not "to expose" and "to defame". Indeed, "defame" makes one think of a public disclosure and of an indictment of someone who acted improperly; "expose" brings to mind the simple act of demonstration.

---

[41] As Aaron Johnson suggests me, this couple and the following seem to have a legal sense. In this way, "to write down" (or "register") someone is opposed to "change an entry" of someone in the court proceedings, i.e. "to accuse falsely". Hereafter the Greek text of the final section of this paragraph: οὐ γὰρ ἔφησε μὴ θέλων αὐτὴν παραδειγματίσαι, ἀλλὰ μὴ δειγματίσαι θέλων· πολλῆς οὔσης ἐν τούτοις διαφορᾶς· ὡς γὰρ οὐ ταυτὸν σημαίνει τὸ γράψαι καὶ παραγράψαι, καὶ τὸ λογίσασθαι καὶ παραλογίσασθαι, καὶ ψηφίσαι καὶ παραψηφίσαι· οὕτως οὐδὲ τὸ δειγματίσαι καὶ παραδειγματίσαι· τὸ μὲν γὰρ παραδειγματίσαι, τὴν ἐπὶ κακῶς πράξαντι εἰς πάντας φανέρωσίν τε καὶ διαβολὴν ὑποβάλλει νοεῖν· τὸ δὲ δειγματίσαι, τὸ φανερὸν ἁπλῶς ποιῆσαι.

[42] In a legal sense, "to set down" to one's account (or "audit the accounts" of someone) is opposed to "defraud" someone.

The considerations in paragraph 5 are mainly distinctive to Eusebius, and show his attitude in elaborating a topic, inspired in this case from the lecture of Origen. At the end of this passage, Eusebius settles the reasons for the justice of Joseph and the links between this justice and his behaviour towards the pregnant Mary (Mt 1.19), an issue developed in the following two paragraphs (ESt I.6–7).

At the beginning of paragraph 6, the phrase "by whom she was 'found', other than Joseph?" (τίνι δ᾽ ἄρα εὑρέθη, ἀλλ᾽ ἢ τῷ Ἰωσήφ;) is very close to that of Jerome, *Comm. in Mt.*, I.1.18, Ps.-Origen, *Hom. in Mt.*, I.2,[43] and Theophylact of Bulgaria, *En. in Mt.*, 1.19. Regarding these three texts, it may be noted also that they are coming very close in another way. They all list among the causes of the marriage of Mary, besides the fact that in this way her virginity was hidden from the devil, also the fact that Mary needed a husband during the flight to Egypt.[44] Unless these three authors have inferred this element from ESt XVI, which is unlikely, this accordance means that they have had another common source that is not Eusebius. That source could also be the origin of a third argument used to defend Mary from stoning because of adultery, that Eusebius ESt I.5 also shares with two of these sources, i.e. Jerome, *Comm. in Mt.*, I.1.18 and Ps.-Origen, *Hom. in Mt.*, I.2–3.[45] These three arguments might be found in a lost work of Origen, probably the commentary on Luke, a text which we know in fragments only:[46] it is likely that this commentary was the source of these traditions.

But there are also other works of Origen that remain behind this exegesis of Eusebius. One of these has to deal with the reading chosen and commented on by Eusebius for Mt 1.19, "he did not want to expose her" (μὴ θέλων αὐτὴν δειγματίσαι). Actually, this reading is mainly attested in the Vatican Manuscript, B, and is also the reading

---

[43] Ed. Klostermann – Benz, GCS 41/1, pp. 240–241.

[44] Jerome, *Comm. in Mt.*, I.1.18; Ps.-Origen, *Hom. in Mt.*, I.3 (ed. Klostermann – Benz, GSC 41/1, p. 242); Theophylact of Bulgaria, *En. in Mt.*, 1.18.

[45] Ed. Klostermann – Benz, GCS 41/1, p. 241.243.

[46] Cf. the state of our knowledge on this text by C. Gianotto, "Luca (scritti esegetici su)", in *Origene. Dizionario, la cultura, il pensiero, le opere*, a c. di A. Monaci Castagno (Roma: Città Nuova, 2000), 243–245, p. 244.

chosen by major modern editors of Matthew.[47] On the other side, the reading that Eusebius expressly disclaims (οὐ γὰρ ἔφησε μὴ θέλων αὐτὴν παραδειγματίσαι), is supported by the first hand of the Sinaitic (ℵ¹) and by a large majority of manuscripts,[48] and, although discarded by Eusebius and by the modern editors, it is the most widely known by the ancient Christian authors.

An interesting parallel to this exegesis occurs in Origen, *Comm. in Mt.*, fr. 15,[49] a fragmentary text that is assigned both to Eusebius and Origen by a *catena* and edited by Erich Klostermann and Ernst Benz. Apart from a brief introduction and conclusion, it corresponds closely to that of the ἐκλογή, to the point that the editors of Origen's *Commentary on Matthew* have put that entire part in brackets.[50] It might be that this fragment really comes from Eusebius' *Questions*, but in any case its tradition suggests that Origen should be the origin of this exegesis. It is interesting to notice that Eusebius elsewhere, in *Dem. ev.*, VII.1.54, quotes another time this passage of Mt 1.19, using this time the reading παραδειγματίσαι.[51] This fact also allows us to infer that, as the fragment published by Klostermann and Benz clearly implied, this textual exegesis of Mt 1.19 derives from Origen's *Commentary on Matthew*.

After further developments, Eusebius come finally to an answer of the main subject of this question (ESt I.10–12), arguing that Mary is also a descendant of David. Here is the main part of this section (I.10–11).

---

[47] Cf. for example the texts by Tischendorf or the late Nestle – Aland (*Novum Testamentum Graece*, ad antiquissimos testes denuo recensuit, apparatum criticum omni studio perfectum apposuit, commentationem isagogicam praetextuit Constantinus Tischendorf, I (Lipsiae: Giesecke & Devrient, ⁸1869) and *Novum Testamentum Graece*, post Eberhard et Erwin Nestle, editione vicesima septima revisa communiter ediderunt Barbara Aland – Kurt Aland – Joannes Karavidopoulos – Carlo M. Martini – Bruce. M. Metzger. Apparatum criticum novis curis elaboraverunt B. et K. Aland, una cum Instituto Studiorum Textus Novi Testamenti Monasterii Westphaliae (Stuttgart: Deutsche Bibelgesellschaft, ²⁷1993). Cf. also the commentary by Zahn, *Das Evangelium des Matthäus*, cit., 72–73.

[48] This reading has been chosen only in Hermann von Soden's and Heinrich Vogels' editions, as recorded by Nestle – Aland, *Novum Testamentum Graece*, cit., 748.

[49] Ed. Klostermann – Benz, GCS 41/1, pp. 21–23.

[50] *Ibid.*, 22.

[51] On this text, cf. É. des Places, *Eusèbe de Césarée commentateur. Platonisme et Ecriture Sainte* (ThH 63; Paris: Beauchesne, 1982), 146 and S. Nielsen, *Euseb von Cäsarea und das Neue Testament*. Methoden und Kriterien zur Verwendung von Kirchenväterzitaten innerhalb der neutestamentlichen Textforschung (Theorie und Forschung 786—Theologie, 43; Regensburg: Roderer, 2003), p. 107.

10. For those who have received in our time these facts and who have also experienced his superhuman nature, everything else and what concerns his birth are rightly recognised as being trustworthy. But however the admirable evangelists necessarily wrote at that time, among the Jews, the genealogy of Joseph, the one who was proclaimed by all as the father of Jesus. In fact if they, being careless about that, had written his genealogy through his mother, that would have been inappropriate and alien to the simplicity of divine Scripture, because nobody previously has been described as having received his genealogy from a woman: the one whose genealogy they write could have appeared as someone who had no father and was of humble origin; this, as I said, would have been the cause of a substantial injury and at the same time a cause of reprimand. Therefore, setting up properly the genealogy of Joseph from David for the reason explained, they also have established that Mary is descendant from David, saying it by the spouse [who stands] behind his wife. The law of Moses prescribed that it is not allowed to choose someone for marriage outside their own family and tribe, so that the family heritage would not be transferred from tribe to tribe. The record about the man was therefore also sufficient to identify the woman. In fact, as he lived by law, he would first of all have married a woman from elsewhere but his father's tribe which in this case was that of Judah, and then from his "demos" and his lineage, that is David's. These were indeed the commandments of the law. Therefore, as Joseph is identified as being descended from the tribe of Judah, from the inheritance and the family of David, how can Mary not also be seen as coming from the same? 11. However, don't be surprised if, being from the tribe of Judah, it has been said that she is a relative of Elizabeth, who was from the tribe of Levi. All Jewish people are from one offspring, and all the tribes had relatives among them, that is why the divine apostle also calls all Jews kindred, saying: "I want to be anathema to my brothers, my fellow creatures in the flesh, those who are the Israelites",[52] although his kindred were only those of the tribe of Benjamin. So Paul called his brothers and relatives absolutely all descendants of Israel. Thus the angel calls also Elizabeth from the same family as Mary, since both were the progeny of Israel. In addition, it is reasonable for Elizabeth to be called of the same family of Mary because of the place, as she lived among the tribe of Judah, whom Mary was born. Luke certainly witnesses it, saying: "Rising up in those days, Mary walked in a hurry to the mountain, to a city of Judah, and she came into the house of Zechariah and greeted Elizabeth".[53] In fact, the law of Moses has not reserved an inheritance to the tribe of priests because the Lord God is their part, but has disposed for them to live among other tribes, and, because Zechariah and Elizabeth were located

---

[52] Rm 9.3–4.
[53] Lk 1.39–40.

in a city of the tribe of Judah, of which Mary was born, it was reasonable that both are declared kindred. Indeed, this is also not implausible because of the similarity of the characters, in which the two were considered worthy of the economy of the salvation, one having hosted the Saviour, the other the forerunner of the Saviour, and both having a share of the same Holy Spirit. Therefore, they shared in the highest level of one family, the one according to God.

The fact that Mary is of Davidic descent had often been stated by the Christian authors, although nobody else before Eusebius seems to know his arguments.[54] Known texts preceding Eusebius on this point are Ignatius of Antioch, *Eph.*, 18.2 and *Trall.*, 9.1 (see also *Smyrn.*, 1.1); *Acta Pauli*, III.1 and X.4.5[55] [= *III Cor.*, 2.5];[56] *Test. Jos.*, 19.8;[57] *Asc. Es.*, 11.2;[58] Justin, *Dial. cum Tryph.*, 43.1, 45.4, 68.6, 100.3; *Prot. Iac.*, 10.1; probably the *Diatessaron* of Tatian (and, in any case, Ephrem of Nisibis, *Comm. in Diat.*, I.25–26 and II.1); Irenaeus, *Adv. haer.*, III.9.2; III.21.5 and *Dem. praed. ap.*, 36, 40 and 63; Hippolytus, *Ben. Isaac et Iacob*, XVI;[59] Tertullian, *Adv. Marc.*, III.20.6–7, IV.1.7; *De carne Chr.*, XXI.5–XXII.6, as well as the disputed work *Adv. Iud.*, IX.26–27; and, finally, Victorin of Poetovio, *Comm. in Apc.*, IV.4.[60] All these texts preceding Eusebius merely affirm that Mary is from the Davidic descent. Only *Prot. Iac.*, 10.1 has a small explanation more that we find in

---

[54] Cf. the remarks by Theodor Zahn, *Das Evangelium des Lukas*, ausgelegt von T. Zahn (KNT, 3; Leipzig – Erlangen: Deichert, ³/⁴1920), pp. 208–211; Walter Bauer, *Das Leben Jesu im Zeitalter der neutestamentlichen Apokryphen* (Tübingen: Mohr, 1909), pp. 9–16, as well as the texts mentioned by José A. de Aldama, *María en la patrística de los siglos I y II* (BAC, 300; Madrid: La Editorial Católica, 1970), pp. 63–80 (and especially pp. 78–83).

[55] Reference to the new chapters by W. Rordorf, avec la coll. de P. Cherix et R. Kasser, "Actes de Paul", in *Écrits apocryphes chrétiens*, I. Édition publiée sous la dir. de F. Bovon – P. Geoltrain (Bibliothèque de la Pléiade 442; Paris: Gallimard, 1997), 1115–1177, p. 1129.1163 (Rordorf's critical edition is forthcoming in Corpus Christianorum series).

[56] See the new commented edition in *Terza lettera ai Corinzi*—Pseudo-Giustino, *La resurrezione*, a cura di A. D'Anna (LCPM 44; Milano: Paoline 2009), 170.

[57] On this text, cf. Norelli, *L'Ascensione di Isaia. Studi su un apocrifo al crocevia dei cristianesimi* (Origini. Nuova Serie 1; Bologna: EDB 1994), 121 n. 226.

[58] This passage is not a rewriting coming from the gospel of Matthew, as both texts use a common lost source, as has been demonstrated by Norelli, *ibid.*, 116–142.

[59] PO 27/1-2, pp. 76–78.

[60] Ed. Dulaey, SC 423, p. 66.

Eusebius too, when it affirms that Mary is from the "tribe of David".[61] In any case, Eusebius is the first known exegete to affirm the Davidic roots of Mary arguing from a specific paradigm of the Jewish law.

For Eusebius, the comprehension of this passage (ESt I.10) lies upon a Mosaic law that prohibits marriage between people coming from two different tribes when this would cause the transfer of a real estate holding from one tribe to another, as explained in Numbers 36.1–12. This particular case could effectively apply to the marriage of Mary and Joseph, because these requirements affect women who are the sole heirs of the property of their father (cf. Nb 27.1–11), and, according to the tradition of *Prot. Iac.*, 1–5, Mary has no brother or sisters, although Eusebius does not explicitly refer to such tradition, possibly because he regards the protogospel of James as a suspect text. To my knowledge, there are only two other texts, much more recent than Eusebius' one, that expressly explain the Davidic ascendance of Mary because of this reason, those of Bruno di Segni, *Comm. in Mt.*, I.1, and of Rodrigo Jimenez de Rada, *Brev. hist. cath.*, IX.1. They also do not refer explicitly to *Prot. Iac.*, while knowing for sure Eusebius' *Questions*, at least indirectly. In any case, this law should require from Mary a marriage within her own tribe, but not within a particular family, unlike the claims of Eusebius. As Eduard Schwartz had noted,[62] Eusebius illustrates the same argument also in *Hist. eccl.*, I.7.17, in a much more succinct way. This does not mean that Eusebius is repeating himself as he thinks, because no certain chronological claim can be established from the comparison of these two passages. Proof of this is that Eusebius takes even this argument from Origen. In his *Comm. in Rm.*, I.7.66–68,[63] Origen explains that "Maria quae desponsata Iosef antequam conueniret inuenta est in utero habens de Spiritu Sancto

---

[61] According to a hypothesis proposed by George Zervos, this is a theme that comes from a source used also by the *Ascension of Isaiah*, a source that he calls *Genesis Marias*. See G.T. Zervos, "An Early Non-Canonical Annunciation Story", in *Society of Biblical Literature, 1997 Seminar Papers*. One hundred Thirty-third Annual Meeting…, San Francisco, California (SBL.SPS 37; Atlanta, GE: Scholars Press, 1997), 664–691, pp. 666–668, 674–675, 686 and *Id.*, "Seeking the Source of the Marian Myth: Have We Found the Missing Link?", in *Which Mary? The Marys of Early Christian Tradition*. Edited by F. Stanley Jones (SBL, Symposium Series 19; Atlanta, GE: Society of Biblical Literature, 2002), 107–120, pp. 114–118.

[62] E. Schwartz, "Eusebios von Cesarea", *PRE*, VI/1, Stuttgart 1907, 1370–1439, p. 1388.

[63] Ed. Hammond Bammell, VL.AGLB 16, pp. 59–60.

secundum legem sine dubio contribuli suo et cognato coniuncta est". This phrase echoes the same ambiguous wording used by in Eusebius ESt I.10: ἢ πρῶτα μὲν ἐκ τῆς φυλῆς τῆς πατρικῆς αὐτοῦ, αὕτη δὲ ἦν ἡ τοῦ Ἰούδα· ἔπειτα ἐκ τοῦ δήμου καὶ τῆς αὐτῆς πατριᾶς, αὕτη δὲ ἦν ἡ τοῦ Δαβίδ ("[He was not going to marry a woman from elsewhere] but first, from his father's tribe, which in this case was that of Judah, and then from his "demos" and his lineage, that is David's").[64] These statements from Origen and Eusebius introduce the idea—which in no way comes from the normative text of Numbers—that the marriage should have been celebrated not only between persons of the same tribe, but also ἐκ τοῦ δήμου καὶ τῆς αὐτῆς πατριᾶς, or, using the formula of *Hist eccl.*, I.7.17, τῶν ἐκ τοῦ αὐτοῦ δήμου καὶ πατριᾶς τῆς αὐτῆς.[65] The dependence on Origen's thought "secundum legem sine dubio contribuli suo et cognato coniuncta est" is, to me, sure and there are even other points in common, as we will see later.

This argument about Mary's genealogy was echoed by several authors, such as Ambrose, *Exp. in Lc.*, III.4 (which explicitly refers to Nb 36.7–8); Jerome, *Comm. in Mt.*, I.18; John Chrysostom, *In Mt. hom.* II.4; IV.2.[66] Among these texts, the homily by Chrysostom, *In Mt. hom.* II.4, is a very interesting one, because it uses all the key terms discussed in Eusebius' argument (φυλή, πατριά, οἶκος), but in a passage that seems closest to the arguments of Origen, *Comm. in Rm.*, I.7. This passage of Chrysostom does not show the common arguments that Eusebius borrowed from Origen's *Hom. in Lk.*, VI, and it is thus possible that the source followed here by John Chrysostom is not Eusebius, but a more developed text written by Origen himself and now lost.

---

[64] It is difficult to translate the technical words used here by Eusebius; I have chosen to transliterate δῆμος and rendered πατριά and οἶκος following the remarks and translations found in *La Bible d'Alexandrie*, [IV.] Les Nombres. Tr. du texte grec de la Septante, Intr. et notes par G. Dorival, avec la collaboration de B. Barc – G. Favrelle – M. Petit – J. Tolila (Paris: Cerf, 1994), p. 210 (and 192); G. Dorival, "La traduction de la Torah en grec", in *La Bible des Septante. Le Pentateuque d'Alexandrie*, texte grec et traduction. Ouvrage collectif sous la direction de C. Dogniez – M. Harl. Avec une intr. par M. Alexandre – J.-M. Auwers – M. Casevitz, et al. (Paris: Cerf, 2001), 31–59, p. 34; J. Moatti-Fine, "La tâche du traducteur", *ibid.*, 67–76, p. 71; and, finally, in *La Bible d'Alexandrie*, [II.] L'Exode. Traduction du texte grec de la Septante, Introduction et notes par A. Le Boulluec – P. Sandevoir (Paris: Cerf, 1989), p. 114.

[65] Ed. Bardy, SC 31, p. 29.

[66] PG 57.28[A]–29[C].41[A]–42[C].

Eusebius' argument seems to continue arguing that, if the reader accepts that Mary is from the tribe of Judah, a contradiction arises concerning the passage of Luke saying that Mary and Elizabeth have a blood relation (Lk 1.36), since, in the same way that Mary comes from the tribe (and the family) of Joseph, Elizabeth, married with a priest, is clearly defined by Luke 1.5, as a descendant of Aaron. Actually, Eusebius also borrowed this question and at least the first solution he proposes from Origen, *Comm. in Rm.*, I.7. Only the last part of the argument as proposed by Eusebius is absent in the text of Origen. Nevertheless, the passage of Origen may indicate that his discussion was continued elsewhere, as we will see hereafter. In any case, it is also worth mentioning that even the quotation of Rm 9.3 came to Eusebius from this page of Origen.

These remarks do not mean that there is nothing original in Eusebius' question. On the contrary, I have focussed here on the explanations that he borrowed from others; but there are many other parts of Eusebius' larger question that have no known parallel before him. For example, this is the case with another explanation proposed as a solution of the problem of the relationship between Mary and Elizabeth, which consists in considering the fact that her living in the midst of the tribe of Judah brings Elizabeth also someway into that same tribe. Certainly, this is not a particularly felicitous explanation, as Eusebius forgets that, according to Lk 1.26, Mary lived in Nazareth of Galilee, outside the territory of Judah. On the contrary, according to the tradition of Mt 2, the residence of Joseph before the flight to Egypt seems to be Bethlehem; and particularly, according to Mt 2.22, it appears that Joseph is unable to return from Egypt to Judea because of Archelaus, Herod's successor, and this is the reason why, as a result of a divine warning, he settled in Nazareth. Worth mentioning here is that the tradition of the *Prot. Iac.*, 15.1, sets the house of Joseph in Jerusalem. In fact, all these narratives are clearly an attempt to restore an image of the family of Jesus, who appears to have very little to do, if anything, with historical facts.[67]

---

[67] Cf. E. Norelli, "La Vergine Maria negli apocrifi", in *Maria. Vergine Madre Regina. Le miniature medievali e rinascimentali*, a cura di C. Leonardi – A. Degl'Innocenti (s.l.: Centro Tibaldi [2000]), 21–42, pp. 21–23.

The paragraph of ESt I.11 has an interesting parallel in another textual tradition of Eusebius' questions, the *Fragment of the Questions to Stephanos* 14, edited by Angelo Mai[68] from an unpublished Vatican *Catena*. It presents an argument that is not recorded in the tradition of our ἐκλογή: according to this fragment the apparent contradiction concerning Mary and Elizabeth coming from the tribes of Judas and of Levi is a mark of the divine economy, which shows in this way that the Christ was in fact descendent of both tribes, the tribe of the kings and the tribe of the priests, and that—like Melkisedek, obviously—he was therefore king and priest.

Martin Routh has noted that this argument is very similar to a passage of ESt IV.1, a text from the ἐκλογή that consist of a large excerpt from the *Epistle to Aristides* by Julius Africanus.[69] It is probably starting from this observation of Routh that Friedrich Spitta decided to ascribe the fragment of the *Questions to Stephanos* 14 to Julius Africanus.[70] But such a hypothesis is not adequately demonstrated, as also Walther Reichardt has pointed out.[71] According to him, even the attribution of this fragment to Eusebius by the manuscript published by Mai is to be discarded.[72] Reichardt does not consider the proximity between the passages of ESt I.11 and ESt IV.1, which makes it difficult to completely reject the attribution to Eusebius of fragment 14. What is interesting for our purpose here is that, if this fragment 14 really comes from this first question to Stephanos, we would have another argument (Jesus is king and priest) to explain the proximity between Mary and Elizabeth and, of course, we would have found in Julius Africanus another source for this question of Eusebius.

---

[68] *Scriptorum veterum nova collectio*, e Vaticanis codicibus edita ab A. Maio, tomus I [pars prior] (Romae, Typis Vaticanis, 1825), 83–84; PG 22.973A–B.

[69] M.J. Routh, *Reliquiae sacrae, sive auctorum fere jam perditorum secundi tertiique saeculi post Christum natum quae supersunt...*, II (Oxonii, Typis Academicis, ²1846), 331. On Julius Africanus and his *Epistle to Aristides*, see also the dissertation by Ch. Guignard, *La lettre de Julius Africanus à Aristide sur la généalogie du Christ. Analyse de la tradition textuelle, édition enrichie d'un fragment inédit, traduction et étude critique* (Strasbourg – Bari, 2009), forthcoming in the TU series. For the present paper, I have not been able to consider this major new study on Julius Africanus.

[70] F. Spitta, *Der Brief des Julius Afrikanus an Aristides*, kritisch untersucht und hergestellt (Halle: Buchhandlung des Waisenhauses, 1877), 46–53 and 108–109.

[71] *Die Briefe des Sextus Julius Africanus an Aristides und Origenes*, hrsg. von W. Reichardt (TU 34/3; Leipzig: Hinrichs, 1909), 36–42.

[72] *Ibid.*, 37–38.

To sum up, there are several ancient Christian texts that claim that Mary belongs to the descendants of David. The larger part of the exegesis developed by Eusebius does not, however, come from those authors. In fact, Eusebius seems not even to consider these texts, but is mainly inspired by Origen. Two origenian texts appear to have been used to frame this passage of Eusebius. They are, *Hom. in Lc.*, VI.3–6[73] and *Comm. in Rom.*, I.7.61–96.[74] In the first passage, Origen, quoting Ignatius of Antioch, explains that the choice of a virgin who was already betrothed, but not really married, was made by God in order to avoid any possible reason for shame when the pregnancy became noticeable, and hide in this way the miraculous birth of Jesus from the prince of this age. This plan had been possible thanks to Joseph and the marriage with him. The second passage explains in what sense Jesus is a descendant of David, though not being a son of Joseph; Origen suggests that even Mary is from the Davidic line because she probably had to marry someone from his tribe and from his family according to the law. With regard to the fact that she is said to be akin to Elizabeth, Origen explains that all Israelites are part of the same family, the descendants of Israel (and he quotes Rm 9.3), and he continues suggesting that other explanations may be found on the subject: "Haec et alia quidem his similia respondentur".[75] In any case, Origen does not seem to like very much such a literal explanation (which is preferred by Eusebius) and prefers rather a spiritual and allegorical reading; unfortunately, he does not really enter more deeply into the question, saying that these arguments are very complex and that they ask for a specific analysis: "quae non est nobis nunc in transitu pulsanda; in suo enim loco requiretur".[76] If Origen refuses to discuss further such a problematic issue in his *Commentary on Romans*, his references to another discussion suggest, I believe, that he had already handled it or that he was willing to treat the same arguments in a more ample way elsewhere. This other place should obviously have been his commentaries on Matthew and Luke. Such texts from Origen are likely to have been the source also for John Chrysostom, *In Mt. hom.* II.4 and IV.2.

---

[73] Ed. Rauer, GCS 49, pp. 34–37; chapters according to the edition of Crouzel – Fournier – Périchon, SC 87, pp. 144–148, cf. also *Comm in Lc.* fr. 20a–b, ed. Rauer, GCS 49, p. 235.

[74] Ed. Hammond Bammel, VL.AGLB 16, pp. 59–61.

[75] *Comm. in Rm.*, I.7.75; ed. Hammond Bammel, VL.AGLB 16, p. 60.

[76] *Comm. in Rm.*, I.7.90–91, *ibid.* p. 61.

There are, indeed, some other origenian texts that seem the possible sources for other eusebian remarks. For instance, in *Comm. in Mt.*, fr. 10,[77] Origen affirms that it would be strange for the scriptures to suggest a genealogy for Jesus' mother (see ESt I.10); in *Comm. in Mt.*, fr. 13/I (which refers specifically to Ignatius and which is also attributed to Eusebius by the author of the *catena* that contains this passage) and in *Comm. in Mt.*, fr. 13/II,[78] Origen also treats the question of the hidden virginity of the pregnant Mary.[79] The same can be said about the other texts of Origen which have been mentioned above. This is the case of *Comm. in Mt.*, fr. 15, of some passages of *Contra Cels.* (I.28; I.32; I.39; II.32), and, possibly, the lost *Commentaries on Luke* and *on Matthew*. Therefore, although less significant, other passages exist which may have inspired Eusebius, for instance when Origen affirms that the birth of Jesus, integrated in the first census, seems to indicate a mystery (*Hom. in Lc.*, XI.6),[80] or when he states the same about the miraculous conception of Jesus (*In Lc.*, fr. 12d),[81] or, finally, when he asserts that Mary and Elizabeth shared a similar spirit (*In Lc.*, fr. 33b).[82]

Even though Origen is surely the main reference for such questions, there are other possible references, as noted above. Eusebius could have had at his disposal the whole book of Celsus, instead of barely Origen's discussion on it. Eusebius certainly had at his disposal Porphyry's polemic work on the Christians and their scriptures, which he read carefully at some point in his life and, as the comparison with Julian's *Against the Galileans* shows, it is possible that many of the problems here discussed were also to be found in that lost work of Porphyry. Eusebius, finally, could have borrowed a last argument from the *Letter to Aristides* of Julius Africanus, a text that he also knew very

---

[77] Ed. Klostermann – Benz, GCS 41/1, p. 19.

[78] Ed. Klostermann – Benz, GCS 41/1, pp. 20–21.

[79] According to Klostermann and Benz (*ibid.*, 21), the text of fr. 13/II has probably to be associated with a scholion attributed to Theodore of Heraclea, fr. 5 on Mt 1.24–25, published by Joseph Reuss: *Mattäus-Kommentare aus der Griechischen Kirche*, aus Katenenhandschriften gesammelt und hrsg. von J. Reuss (TU 61; Berlin: Akademie-Verlag, 1957), 57–58, a text sometimes falsely attributed to John Chrysostom according to John Cramer: *Catenae Graecorum patrum in Novum Testamentum*, I. *Catenae in evangelia s. Matthaei et s. Marci*, ad fidem codd. mss. ed. J.A. Cramer (Oxonii, E Typographeo academico, 1840), 20.

[80] Ed. Crouzel – Fournier – Périchon, SC 87, pp. 194–196.

[81] Numbering according to Crouzel – Fournier – Périchon, *ibid.*, 474.

[82] *Ibid.*, 240.

well and that he quotes at length in his questions (ESt IV and parallels) as well as in his *Ecclesiastical history* (I.7.2–16).

Within this test case, Eusebius as an exegete clearly shows his debts, but, still, he gives also a personal synthesis of all the material he read in Origen or elsewhere. His result is neither the poor and shortened version of an origenian exegesis, nor a text lacking originality in its conclusions. He is able to put together different origenian passages, noting his differences from the model when requested, as in the case of origenian tradition about the episcopacy of Ignatius, which is clearly rejected by Eusebius. The bishop of Caesarea tries to consider all major sources available to him, and he works as if he were trying to compile a complete *status quaestionis* about the problem discussed, considering all possible questions and solutions involved, as they had been discussed before him—not by Origen only. A demonstration of the Davidic descent of Mary that is a summary of the best available exegesis at his time, written in a form of original report made from them, and expressly excluding what he thought were errors (even in the case where they were defended by Origen, as is the case with the episcopacy of Ignatius). This method is not so distant, I suppose, from the way in which Eusebius writes his major and more complex works like the *Ecclesiastical history* or the *Preparation of the Gospel*: he always tries to be as complete as possible, tends to use the most number of sources available to him in the big library of Caesarea inherited by Pamphilus, tries to compare different versions of a story or of an exegesis, without taking a position except in the cases where he he sure of his evidence or is willing to demonstrate something that is for him a theological truth.

CONCLUSION

While the definition of Wallace-Hadrill certainly remains interesting, the *cursus* defined by Sant and Curti seems to me less convincing. Considering the text of ESt I, it is difficult to place it in a kind of scheme that starts from Origen and finishes with historical exegesis, while it perfectly fits within the picture I have of Eusebius as a scholar, reading books in one of the major Christian libraries of his time, making cardfiles based upon his lectures, and eventually also using copyists and secretaries to prepare his works. Some other texts pointed out by Manlio Simonetti are interpreted as if Eusebius, initially trying to follow the footsteps of Origen, under the influence of Pamphilus, tends increasingly to reduce his allegorical readings,[83] but this has nothing to do with Eusebius' historical sensibility, which is supposed to increase. Even considering the case independently studied by Sébastien Morlet, who has a slightly different perspective than mine, it is interesting to see that he arrives at similar conclusions in re-examining two texts (*Ecl. proph.*, IV.5 and *Dem. ev.*, VII.1.95–113) that Curti also had directly studied.[84]

Clearly, these are only limited examples, but the same kinds of hesitations arise when we consider that the first phase of the *cursus* of Sant and Curti, when Eusebius should have been mainly a partisan of allegorical exegesis, is actually the period of some texts that, like the *Chronicon* and the *Ecclesiastical history*, are astonishingly historical in their scheme. These works are already full of Eusebius' historical convictions (in the broadest sense), and they show to what extent they were present from the beginning of his literary activity; these works have certainly been conceived and written only thanks to the vast readings that only Caesarea's library could permit at that time, and I see no real difference between the way they were composed and the way Eusebius, at the same time as well later, used to compose his exegesis.

And, on the opposite side, we find, together with Jerome, the Eusebius never abandoned allegory: although the bishop of Caesarea claims that his commentary on Isaiah has been written by means of purely historical exegesis, the fine reader that Jerome of Stridon was contests these claims, and not without reason.[85] If there really was a genuine origenian phase, such as envisioned by Curti and Sant, it should concern the time when Eusebius had not yet started his literary activity at the school of Pamphilus; but this is unlikely, and we cannot in any case say anything about it.

Returning to the field of exegesis, I think that we have to acknowledge that there are some constant traits during his life. From the

---

[83] See the conclusions and the examples proposed by Simonetti, *Lettera e/o Allegoria, cit.*, 114–124.

[84] Cf. Morlet, "Le commentaire d'Eusèbe de Césarée sur Is 8,4", *cit.*, 56–63.

[85] See Jerome, *Comm. Is.*, V.prol.; V.18.2 (CC.SL 73–73A, p. 160, l. 25–30 and p. 190, l. 29–35). See on this point especially Hollerich, "Eusebius as a Polemical Interpreter", *cit.*, 590–592 and *Id., Eusebius of Caesarea's* Commentary on Isaiah, *cit.*, 54–57.68–70, although the words of Jerome are not to be taken literally according to the remarks by Wallace-Hadrill, *Eusebius of Caesarea, cit.*, 82–84, Sant, "Interpretatio Veteris Testamenti in Eusebio", *cit.*, 88, Simonetti, "Esegesi e ideologia", *cit.*, 4–6 and *Id., Lettera e/o Allegoria, cit.*, 117.119–120.

beginning of his literary activity, for example, he demonstrated an attitude that can be described as "literal" concerning the reading of Scriptures. This is in part already the case in the *Ecclesiastical history*, where,
even if it is not an exegetical text, he shows an attitude of compliance
with any venerable tradition, and this attitude is a major principle
which simply cannot be withdrawn through any kind of allegorical
reading.[86] This arrives always without fail when Eusebius is convinced
on a particular point concerning an old tradition.

What is certain is that Eusebius seems to prefer literal exegesis, but
enhanced by a broad spectrum of cultural interests: if compared to
his predecessors, Eusebius shines out for his formidable erudition. It
is therefore not surprising that a man as clever as him, without very
strong interests in theological speculation,[87] focussed his interests on
what can be proved with certainty, all that is "literal". In this sense,
Michael Hollerich gave us another key for a possible explanation of the
attitude of Eusebius on exegesis and on its development. For Eusebius,
there is a strong difference between literal and allegorical interpretations, the same difference that passes between a fact and its interpretation.[88] Eusebius likes more the *data*, the enunciations that the erudite
man can dominate and master; but this does not mean that he, at any
time in his career, has disliked allegorical exegesis, exactly in the same
way that he has never avoided to offer his *interpretations* of the facts,
from the time of his *Ecclesiastical history* to his late panegyrics on the
Emperor Constantine.

---

[86] This of course does not mean that Eusebius is unable to influence the traditions
according to his intentions when interpreting them, as it has been many times noted.
On this topic, see for example L. Perrone, "Eusèbe de Césarée face à l'essor de la littérature chrétienne au IIe siècle: Propos pour un commentaire du IVe livre de l'Histoire
Ecclésiastique", *Zeitschrift für antikes Christentum* 11 (2007), 311–334, p. 327 (and
references in n. 47), as well as the two cases discussed by Norelli regarding Eusebius'
reconstitution of Christian origins in E. Norelli, "La mémoire des origines chrétiennes:
Papias et Hégésippe chez Eusèbe", in *L'historiographie de l'église des premiers siècles*,
sous la dir. de B. Pouderon – Y.-M. Duval. Préface de M. Quesnel (ThH 114; Paris:
Beauchesne, 2001), 1–22, pp. 9–21, and *Id.*, "Il VI libro dell'*Historia ecclesiastica*:
appunti di storia della redazione", in *La biografia di Origene fra storia e agiografia…*,
a cura di A. Monaci Castagno (Biblioteca di Adamantius 1; Villa Verucchio, Rimini:
Pazzini, 2004), 147–174, pp. 155–170.

[87] This is the case even in his approach to the Council of Nicaea, where, although he
had precise feelings on the ongoing discussions—convictions that were easily reconcil-
able with those of Arius—Eusebius seemed not really involved in putting thoroughly
his ideas on question, while his epistle to the church in Caesarea shows that he has
just tried to reconcile its positions with those of the Council.

[88] Hollerich, *Eusebius of Caesarea's* Commentary on Isaiah, *cit.*, 67.

EUSEBIUS' *PANEGYRIC ON THE BUILDING OF CHURCHES* (*HE* 10.4.2–72): AESTHETICS AND THE POLITICS OF CHRISTIAN ARCHITECTURE

Jeremy M. Schott

Eusebius of Caesarea is best known to modern scholars as church historian and scholar. As bishop, however, he was also a prominent public intellectual. Though he must have delivered numerous sermons and speeches, only three of Eusebius' performance pieces survive: a panegyric for the dedication of the cathedral basilica at Tyre, another delivered at the dedication of the basilica of the Holy Sepulchre, and a panegyric composed for Constantine's tricennalia and delivered in the emperor's presence in Constantinople.[1] Eusebius accorded these orations a special place within his own literary corpus. When Eusebius added the tenth book to his *Ecclesiastical History*, he included the oration he had delivered at Tyre to illustrate the new peace and prosperity enjoyed by Christian communities in the East upon the defeat of Maximinus and the restoration of church properties by the *Augusti* Constantine and Licinius. Over a decade later, Eusebius combined his Holy Sepulchre oration and his tricennial panegryic into a single text and appended it to his *Life of Constantine*. Thus, Eusebius' orations have tended to be read as Eusebius wanted them read—as speeches of Christian victory and triumph.

It is all too easy to read Eusebius' orations as documents illustrating the power and prestige of Christianity in the Constantinian empire. In fact, Eusebius' orations belong to a crucial transitional period in the histories of the later Roman empire, early Christianity, and early

---

[1] Fragments from Marcellus of Ancyra's *Contra Asterium* cite very short fragments of sermons Eusebius delivered in Ancyra (*C. Marc.*, 1.4.26–27) and Laodicea (*C. Marc.*, 1.4.26). Additionally, that Eusebius reproduced much of the *Theophania* in his Tricennial Orations suggests that some of the material served as Fodder for his homilies; the stylistics of portions of the *Theophania*, moreover, suggest oral delivery. On the *Theophania* and the Tricennial Orations see H.A. Drake, *In Praise of Constantine: A Historical Study and New Translation of Eusebius' Tricennial Orations* (University of California Publications: Classical Studies vol. 15; Berkeley: University of California Press, 1975) and H. Gressman, *Studien zu Eusebs Theophanie* (TU 23.3; Leipzig: Hinrichs, 1903).

Christian architecture. Christian church building in the years following 313 CE was an agonistic process in the formation of civic and
imperial identities.[2] Rather than reading monumental building as the
result or commemoration of already-accomplished cultural and political transformations, monumental building is better seen as a means of
negotiating and effecting such transformations.

The oration Eusebius delivered at Tyre, probably in 315 CE,[3] was
likely one of his first major public performances. The oration com-
memorated the re-construction of the church at Tyre after its destruction during the Great Persecution. Eusebius had become a bishop
only recently, probably in 313 CE, upon the cessation of persecution.
Constantine had not yet assumed sole rule of the empire—thus this
construction project and Eusebius' oration did not have the timbre
that subsequent imperially funded projects—like the Basilica of the
Holy Sepulchre and Eusebius' dedicatory oration for it—would have
two decades later. The Tyrian oration thus presents an opportunity to
explore the theology as well as the socio-economics of early Christian
architecture as it was emerging in the East after the Great Persecution but before the accession of Constantine. The oration also offers
a glimpse of early fourth century identity politics as it was played out
in the context of early fourth century urbanism. In the *Ecclesiastical
History,* Eusebius titled the oration a "Panegyric on the Building of
Churches, offered to the bishop Paulinus of Tyre" (*HE,* 10.4.2);[4] it was,
in other words, a panegyric of Paulinus as well as the basilica. The oration thus also provides important evidence for the roles of bishops in
early fourth century ecclesiastical and urban life.

---

[2] On early Christian architecture in the city of Rome see, for example, D. Trout,
"Damasus and the Invention of Early Christian Rome," *Journal of Medieval and Early
Modern Studies* 33 (2003), 517–536 and more recently, R. Van Dam, *The Roman Revolution of Constantine* (Cambridge: Cambridge University Press, 2007), esp. 130–141;
on church-building and the identity politics of civic space see especially A. Whar-
ton, *Refiguring the Post Classical City: Dura Europus, Jerash, Jerusalem, and Ravenna*
(Cambridge: Cambridge University Press, 1995).
[3] Eusebius praises Constantine and Licinius as co-emperors and gives no indication
of turmoil between them (*Hist. eccl.,* 10.4.59–60; hereafter *HE*)—this indicates a date
between 315–317 CE; see T.D. Barnes, *Constantine and Eusebius* (Cambridge, Mass.:
Harvard University Press, 1981), 162–163.
[4] Text: E. Schwartz, et al., GCS 6.1–3 n.f. (Berlin: Akademie Verlag, 1999); English
translations of the *HE* throughout the paper are those of J.E.L. Oulton, *Eusebius. The
Ecclesiastical History.* Vol. II (LCL 265; Cambridge, Mass.: Harvard University Press,
1932, repr. 1994), with modifications.

1. The Cathedral of Tyre and Early Christian Architecture

The church of Tyre was destroyed by order of Diocletian's first perse-cuting edict, issued 23 February, 303. The edict ordered the destruc-tion of Christian books, the confiscation of church property, and the destruction of Christian buildings.[5] Diocletian's edict presumed that certain urban buildings were identifiable as Christian structures. The archaeological evidence suggests that the late third century was marked by a period of transition in Christian architecture. The house church, or *domus ecclesiae*, of earlier generations, remained the primary Christian liturgical space in the late third century.[6] These house churches were established in both private homes and in rented residential spaces. By the late third century, however, some house churches were enlarged and embellished. These transitional structures—church halls, or *"aulae ecclesiae"*—were more formal, dedicated gathering spaces, and some were large enough to constitute small Christian complexes.[7]

In the mid 260's CE Paul of Samosata, for example, is reported to have embellished the church at Antioch with a raised platform (βῆμα) and a throne (θρόνος ὑψηλὸς) for the bishop. Paul also had a private office, or *secretum* (σήκρητον) (*HE*, 7.30.9). These features, as well as the vocabulary used to describe them, were characteristic of the architec-ture of Roman provincial administrative architecture—of a governor's audience hall and private chamber, for instance. The description of the church at Antioch comes from a letter denouncing Paul to the bishops of Rome and Alexandria, and his accusers clearly view these features as presumptuous innovations. The architectural elements introduced by Paul at Antioch were an exception rather than the rule. Nonethe-less, Paul's embellishments also anticipate some features seen in later Constantinian basilicas: the elevation of the bishop and, perhaps, the orientation of the gathering towards him as opposed to earlier house churches, arranged in traditional seating arrangements for dining.

---

[5] Our primary source on the edicts of persecution is Lactantius, *Mort.*, 12 and Euse-bius, *HE*, 8.2.4–5. For a narrative account see Barnes, *Constantine and Eusebius, cit.*, 22–24.

[6] R. Krautheimer, *Early Christian and Byzantine Architecture* (London: Penguin, 1965), 23–38; L.M. White, *The Social Origins of Christian Architecture. Volume I: Building God's House in the Roman World: Architectural Adaptation Among Pagans, Jews and Christians* (Valley Forge, PA: Trinity Press International, 1997), 125–126.

[7] White, *ibid.*, 127–139.

By the end of the third century, however, the house church was in some locales giving way to more formal church halls. The late third-century *Didascalia Apostolorum*, for example, suggests a hierachical arrangement oriented towards the bishop, who sits on a throne (ܩܘܩܝܐ), and the presbyters, all of whom sit at the eastern end of the hall.[8] Eusebius suggests that this period of renovation and expansion was a result of the growth of the Christian population and the period of peace preceding the Great Persecution.[9] "Because they were no longer satisfied with the old buildings," he writes, "you could find churches being rebuilt from their foundations throughout every city" (*HE*, 8.1.5). Writing at the turn of the fourth century, Porphyry of Tyre, moreover, mocked Christians because "imitating the arrangement of temples they build great buildings, in which they gather to pray, even though nothing prevents them from doing this in their homes, for it is clear that the lord can hear them anywhere."[10] Porphyry's polemic makes an explicit distinction between private homes and larger structures that stood out in the urban cityscape.

The first church destroyed on the authority of Diocletian's edict was that in the imperial capital of Nicomedia. Lactantius reports that Diocletian ordered the structure demolished, rather than burned, lest the fire spread to other structures.[11] In deciding to demolish the church at Nicomedia instead of burning it, Diocletian may have been as interested in salvaging raw materials (*spolia*) as he was in avoiding a wider conflagration. According to Lactantius, Diocletian and Galerius watched the spectacle from the imperial palace. Indeed, he says that the Christian building was located on elevated ground in sight of

[8] L. Michael White, *The Social Origins of Christian Architecture. Volume II: Texts and Monuments for the Christian* Domus Ecclesiae *in its Environment* (HThS 42; Valley Forge, PA: Trinity Press International, 1997), no. 18.
[9] On estimating growth in the Christian population see K. Hopkins, "Christian Number and Its Implications," *Journal of Early Christian Studies* 6 (1998), 185–226.
[10] *Contra Christianos* fr. 76. Text: Ed. A. von Harnack. *Porphyrius, 'Gegen Die Christen.' 15 Bücher, Zeugnisse, Fragmente und Referate*. In Abhandlungen der K. Preuß. Akad. Der Wiss. Phil. Hist. Klasse, 1916, 1–115. This fragment of *Contra Christianos* comes from Macarius, *Apocriticus*, 4.21. That Macarius' anonymous pagan appears to be critiquing pre-Constantinian Christian architecture suggests that this is a genuine fragment of a late-third or early-fourth-century anti-Christian polemicist, rather than a purely literary "fiction" constructed by Macarius or a fragment derived from the work of a later polemicist, such as Julian.
[11] Lactantius, *Mort.*, 12.

the palace.[12] Not all Christian structures suffered destruction. In their rescript of 313, Constantine and Licinius ordered any property seized by the fisc and/or subsequently sold returned to the Christian community (*HE*, 10.5.9–11). Clearly then, some Christian sites had not been demolished, but sold or given as gifts and then put to new uses during the ten years of intermittent persecution in the East.

There is, unfortunately, no archaeological record of the early fourth-century basilica at Tyre. Since Eusebius' panegyric stresses that the rebuilt church is much larger and more ostentatious than its predecessor, one can infer that the earlier structure may have been a modified house church or a simple *aula ecclesiae*. Eusebius' description of the implementation of the edict at Tyre suggests that the church was burned and despoiled.

> This desert, this dry place, this defenseless widow, whose gates they chopped down with axes like a grove of trees, together they smashed it with hatchets and hammers, and destroying her books, put the sanctuary of God to the flame, trod to the earth the dwelling of his name, whom all those who pass by pick at, having knocked down her gates, whom the boar of the grove ravaged and a lone beast fed upon…. (*HE*, 10.4.33).

Eusebius' description consists of a patchwork of quotations from Psalm 73 and 79, which reference the destruction of the Jerusalem Temple. Eusebius' use of biblical quotation and exegesis in his oration will be discussed in what follows. Here it is interesting to note that Eusebius has inserted the detail about burning the church's books into the middle of his quotation of verses 6 and 7 of Psalm 73, suggesting, perhaps, that the books were burned inside the church hall in the area reserved for the altar. Although Eusebius is most interested in demonstrating that the destruction of the church and its reconstruction fulfill scripture, the parallels with Lactantius' account of the destruction of the Nicomedian church would suggest that he has chosen his quotes to describe a similar process of demolition and spoliation.

The Christian community of Tyre would have received whatever remained of the structure along with the land upon which it stood thanks to the imperial rescript of 313. The "Edict of Milan," as the rescript is known, was issued in the names of both Constantine and Licinius. Thus, although the cathedral of Tyre is often cited in

---

[12] Lactantius, *Mort.*, 12.

discussions of "Constantinian" architecture,[13] the rebuilding took place not under the rule of Constantine, but Licinius. Unlike the basilicas begun in Rome on land and with funds granted by Constantine fairly soon after his victory in the West, the reconstruction at Tyre was funded solely by the community itself. Eusebius praised the Tyrian Christians for being generous donors, and singles out Paulinus himself as the principal patron. The virtues of the wealthy Tyrians— "greatmindedness," "ambition," and "great-heartedness"—are those traditionally ascribed to civic euergetists.

Inscriptions from two other churches built immediately after the cessation of persecution testify to similar euergetism on the part of local bishops. Theodore, Paulinus' contemporary in Aquileia, presided over the construction of an *aula ecclesiae*. An inscription suggests that Theodore, like Paulinus, served as the primary patron but was assisted by donations from other members: "Theodore, Happy One, with the help of almighty God and of the flock bequeathed to you from heaven, you have made everything happily and dedicated it gloriously."[14] Closer to Tyre, the epitaph of Eugenius, bishop of Laodicea Combusta in Phrygia, indicates a building project similar to that in Tyre. Eugenius was a member of the βουλή and as such would have been a man of some means. The inscription credits Eugenius with "rebuilding the entire church from its foundations." Like the church Eusebius describes at Tyre, Eugenius' church had a forecourt, *stoae*, a fountain, and was adorned inside with paintings and mosaics.[15]

Rebuilding the church, then, was an act of civic benefaction similar to other privately contracted building projects in Tyre. Paulinus would have had to contract with local artisans. A letter written by Gregory of Nyssa in the early 380's provides a glimpse of a bishop's negotiations with masons and other workers. Gregory finds the going rate for stonedressers in Nyssa too high: one *aureus* plus board for a crew of thirty. Gregory would prefer to hire less skilled brick masons and pay his workers based on output, rather than a fixed daily wage.[16] Eusebius also praises Paulinus as the architect of the structure. We

---

[13] As, for example, in Krautheimer, *Early Christian and Byzantine Architecture, cit.*, 45–46.

[14] White, *Social Origins Vol. II, cit.*, no. 51.

[15] White, *ibid.*, no. 48.

[16] Gregory of Nyssa, *Ep.*, 25.12,15, translated in A. Silvas, *Gregory of Nyssa: The Letters. Introduction, Translation, and Commentary* (SVigChr 83; Leiden: Brill, 2007).

probably should not imagine Paulinus sitting at a draftsman's table; the bishop would likely have provided a general description to his contractors who would have worked up plans.[17] As Gregory put it in his letter, "We shall of course provide the materials; the form that is to be impressed on the material skill will bestow."[18]

Eusebius rhetorically "walks" his hearers through the Christian complex and the new cathedral (*HE*, 10.4.37–45). The Christian complex was enclosed by a wall, analogous to the marking out of a τέμενος in traditional Greek temple architecture. A πρόπυλον, or formal entry-porch, stood at the eastern end of the complex and communicated with traffic on the street. One then entered an atrium enclosed by colonnaded *stoae* adorned with wooden lattice-work. In the middle of the atrium and opposite the entry to the main church building were fountains. A central doorway flanked by two smaller doorways marked the entrance to the main structure. The building itself was colonnaded along the outside walls, and windows, again decorated with wooden lattice-work, provided interior illumination. A number of outbuildings communicated with the main structure. The interior space was arranged hierarchically, with thrones for the bishop and presbyters and benches for the rest of the congregation. The altar was separated from the rest of the interior space by a wooden lattice-work chancel screen.

There is some debate over the precise architectural form of the cathedral. Eusebius terms the structure a "basilica (βασίλειος οἶκος)" (*HE*, 10.4.42). On the one hand, Krautheimer sees the *propylaeum, atrium*, and clerestory (all features upon which Eusebius focuses in his description of the cathedral) as conscious references to the architecture of imperial audience halls.[19] L. Michael White, on the other hand, suggests that Eusebius' description is of an *aula ecclesiae*.[20] White focuses on Eusebius' apparent lack of reference to a colonnaded nave. White points out that *HE*, 10.4.42 ([...] ταῖς παρ' ἑκάτερα τοῦ παντὸς νεὼ στοαῖς τὸν τῶν προπύλων ἀριθμὸν διατάξας [...]) most likely refers to *stoae* along the building's sides, rather than internal colonnades.[21]

---

[17] The value of skilled labor is evidenced by two of Constantine's rescripts, one granting freedom from public service to architects, stonecutters, and so forth (*Cod. Theo.*, 13.4.2) and a second encouraging apprenticeships (*Cod. Theo.*, 13.4.3).

[18] Gregory of Nyssa, *Ep.*, 25.14.

[19] Krautheimer, *Early Christian and Byzantine Architecture, cit.*, 46.

[20] White, *Social Origins. Vol. I, cit.*, 136.

[21] White, *ibid.*, 199, n. 119.

Most late-third and early-fourth century Roman basilicas, however, did not have colonnaded interiors. A "basilica" in this period was defined primarily by its function as an official, imperial audience hall.[22] In terming the new cathedral a "basilica," then, Eusebius was likening the experience of the grandeur of the Christian structure to the awe inspired by the splendor of imperial architecture. If White's suggestion concerning flanking *stoae* is correct, however, he may be right in his suggestion that the cathedral at Tyre is more likely to have resembled Krautheimer's reconstruction of S. Crisogno in Rome than the later Lateran Basilica or the basilica of the Holy Sepulchre/Anastasis.[23]

2. THEOLOGY, AESTHETICS, AND THE POLITICS OF CHURCH BUILDING

At the time of the dedication festival for the rebuilt cathedral church, Paulinus and Eusebius were only beginning their episcopal careers. Eusebius was likely elected bishop of Caesarea in the immediate aftermath of the persecution in 313. Paulinus, a native of Antioch, seems to have assumed the See of Tyre under similar circumstances.[24] Many communities in the Eastern provinces were undergoing similar transitions during this period as a new generation filled sees vacated by the deaths of older bishops and those martyred during the Diocletianic persecutions.[25] It was time to network; this new cadre of leaders scrambled to solidify friendships and alliances. Some of these men were familiars already—Eusebius of Nicomedia and a number of his allies had studied in Antioch in the circle of the scholar Lucian.[26] Pau-

---

[22] Krautheimer, *Early Christian and Byzantine Architecture, cit.*, 42. The Constantinian basilica at Trier is a well-preserved example of a non-collonaded basilica from this period.

[23] White, *Social Origins. Vol. I, cit.*, 136, 199, n. 199. See also Krautheimer's renderings of S. Crisogno (*Early Christian and Byzantine Architecture, cit.*, 37, fig. 8), the Lateran Basilica (47, fig. 11), and the basilica of the Holy Sepulcher/Anastasis (63, fig. 27[a]).

[24] Eusebius notes that Tyrannion of Tyre was martyred during the Diocletianic persecution (*HE*, 8.13.3), but Eusebius does not name his immediate successor. Paulinus was bishop by 315, but the date of his consecration is not certain.

[25] Theodotus of Laodicea (*HE*, 7.32.23), Alexander of Alexandria (*HE*, 7.32.31), Eusebius, first of Berytus, then of Nicomedia (Theodoret, *HE*, 1.18), Philogonius of Antioch (John Chrysostom, *De beato Philogonio* [=*Contra Anomoeos hom.* 6] PG 48.751, 14–26), and Eusebius himself all succeeded to the episcopate during or immediately after the Diocletianic persecution.

[26] Philostorgius, 2.14; text: J. Bidez, *Philostorgius. Kirchengeschichte.* 3rd ed. rev. by F. Winkelmann (GCS 21; Berlin: Akademie-Verlag, 1981), English translation:

linus, while he was not a "fellow-Lucianist" of Eusebius of Nicomedia, likely moved within the same social circles during his time in Antioch. He certainly would have known and worked with Eusebius of Nicomedia during the latter's tenure as bishop of neighboring Berytus. It is not clear whether or not Eusebius knew Paulinus before both were elected bishops. During his days as a member of Pamphilus' circle of Christian intellectuals in Caesarea, Eusebius traveled to Antioch and was familiar with intellectual circles there, including that of Lucian.[27] In Eusebius' oration, we glimpse the beginnings of a lasting alliance between Paulinus and Eusebius that would prove crucial in the theological controversies of the early fourth century.[28]

Eusebius would have had several rhetorical models available as he composed his oration for the cathedral and its bishop.[29] Speeches in praise of cities had been part of the classical rhetorical tradition since Isocrates.[30] Early examples focus on the virtues of the collective social body of citizens, but geographers adapted the classical tradition of urban encomium, adding extended discussions of architecture.[31] Panegyrics for individuals could also include sections in praise of their architectural patronage. During the Second Sophistic, moreover, rhetoricians such as Lucian and Aelius Aristides praised specific structures for their aesthetic value.[32]

Rather than analyzing Eusebius' speech as an example of classical rhetoric, however, I would like to examine it as both an exegetical text and a "spatial practice." How, that is, does Eusebius deploy both exegetical techniques and aesthetic theories to make sense of the new church for his audience? Michel de Certeau describes the negotiation of space as an enunciative practice homologous to other rhetorical

---

Ph. Amidon, *Philostorgius. Church History. Writings From the Greco-Roman World.* (Atlanta: Society of Biblical Literature, 2007).

[27] *HE*, 8.13.2.

[28] Paulinus was also the dedicatee of Eusebius' *Onomasticon*. In a letter to Paulinus, Eusebius of Nicomedia appealed to Paulinus' friendship with Eusebius of Caesarea in an effort to encourage Paulinus to emulate his friend in taking a more active role in opposing Alexander of Alexandria (H.-G. Opitz, *Athanasius Werke III.1–2, Urkunden zur Geschichte des arianischen Streites* [Berlin: de Gruyter, 1934–1941], Urk. 8). On Paulinus see Gustave Bardy, "Sur Paulin de Tyr," *RevSR* 2 (1922), 35–45.

[29] Ch. Smith ("Christian Rhetoric in Eusebius' Panegyric at Tyre," *VigChr* 43 (1989), 226–247) does a fine job situating Eusebius' speech in the context of the classical rhetorical tradition. The paragraph that follows is indebted to her piece.

[30] Smith, *ibid.*, 228; see for example Isocrates *Or.* 4.

[31] Smith, *ibid.*, 228.

[32] Smith, *ibid.*, 230–231.

practices and having its own grammar and figures of speech. In pointing to the broad homologies between speech-acts and spatial-acts, de
Certeau's insights help to elucidate the complex relationships between
texts and architectural spaces.[33] Rhetoric, spatial or otherwise, is never
politically neutral. If, as de Certeau argues, "spatial practices [...]
structure the determining conditions of social life,"[34] I suggest that we
consider the spatial practices and attendant social conditions Eusebius
sought to effect with his oration.

From the outset, the church prompts Eusebius to consider the nexus
of text and event, of the biblical past and the Christian present. "Long
ago," Eusebius intones, "we heard from the holy reading of the miraculous signs and the benefits for humanity of God's wondrous deeds." But
now, he continues, "by deeds [...] and with our very eyes we observe
that what was transmited by memory long ago is faithful and true..."
(*HE*, 10.4.5–6). Christine Smith has argued that Eusebius' method of
composition was based not primarily on classical rhetorical models
but in the techniques of allegorical exegesis. Eusebius construes biblical references to architecture as signifiers of transcendent signifieds.
Eusebius then "reads" the church of Tyre as signifying the same transcendent realities.[35] Smith's analysis does help to elucidate Eusebius'
rhetorical technique as an extension of methods he had honed in his
biblical scholarship. Eusebius sees the reconstruction of the church as
a typological fulfillment of the construction of the Second Temple following the Babylonian Exile. In this reading, the Tyrian congregation
is cast as the "city of God" of Psalms 48.8 and 87.3, the new church
as the Jerusalem Temple, and bishop Paulinus as "a new Bezalel the
architect of a divine tabernacle, or a Solomon the king of a new and far
better Jerusalem, or a new Zerubbabel who bestowed upon the temple
of God glory much greater than the former" (*HE*, 10.4.2–3).

The church at Tyre, however, was not a *written* text. The church
neither replaces the biblical text, nor does the "textualization" of the
church efface its imminent material, historical presence. Rather, the
church serves to signpost the intersection of past and present. This
mode of exegesis, then, is also a spatial practice. De Certeau distinguishes between place—the differential relationships that constitute

---

[33] M. de Certeau, *The Practice of Everyday Life*, trans. S. Rendall (Berkeley: University of California Press, 1984), 91–110 *passim*.
[34] de Certeau, *ibid.*, 115.
[35] Smith, "Christian Rhetoric in Eusebius' Panegyric at Tyre," *cit.*, 236.

the *here* and *there* of the spatial field—and space—the effects produced as places get worked over. Space is "a practiced place," homologous to reading as the operation which works over the text.[36] The church serves as the place in and through which Eusebius negotiates the expanse between the *here* of a triumphal Christian present and the *there* of a scriptural, prophetic past. Simultaneously, he reads in and through the text of scripture to bridge the fissures between his narrative of salvation history and the church.

If the church stands as a typological fulfillment of biblical texts, it is also a monument to contemporary events. The new church, built on the ashes of the old, stands as a trophy of Christ's victory over the demons and Constantine's and Licinius' victories over the persecutors. The persecutors, egged on by demons, had attacked "the stones of the prayer-houses and the soulless matter of the buildings" (*HE*, 10.4.14). Now, however, with Christ having dispelled the demons, the Emperors "style him as savior on monuments [...] in the midst of the city that is Empress among the cities of the world" (*HE*, 10.4.16). This is likely an allusion to a statue of Constantine dedicated in Rome accompanied by an inscription that Eusebius quotes earlier at *HE*, 9.9.11: "By this saving sign (σωτηριώδει σημείῳ), the true proof of bravery, I saved (διασωθεῖσαν) and delivered (ἠλευθέρωσα) your city from the yoke of the tyrant [Maxentius]; and moreover I freed and restored to their ancient fame and splendor both the senate and the people of the Romans."[37] In referencing the statue and inscription in the oration, Eusebius likens the church to an imperial monument. Like the statue, which served to memorialize victory and restoration, the church functions by metonymy to represent the entirety of a globally reworked geography. Of Christ's triumph Eusebius writes:

> who among emperors rules so powerfully, leads his army after death, and sets up trophies of victories over his enemies, and sets up votive offerings in every place, region, and city, both Greek and barbarian, with his basilicas and divine temples, such as the beautiful ornaments and offerings of this temple? (*HE*, 10.4.20).

---

[36] de Certeau, *The Practice of Everyday Life, cit.*, 117.
[37] The statue referenced by Eusebius may be the colossal statue placed in the Basilica Nova (originally constructed by Maxentius); see Van Dam, *Roman Revolution, cit.*, 48, n. 17, 86–87.

With this strophe and antistrophe between past and present, text and event, Eusebius places the construction of the new cathedral within a larger narrative of Christian triumph and Manifest Destiny. The Christian τέμενος stands-in for imperial space. The empire, like the church's property, had been oppressed by demons but liberated and repatriated by Christ/the emperors. The oration functions similarly within the tenth book of the *Ecclesiastical History*, where this local reconstruction project is placed as emblematic of an ecumenical Christian triumph over demons and persecutors.

But, the triumphal tone achieved by this blurring of local and global space also effects distraction. By leading his audience back and forth, from the Tyrian church to the οἰκουμένη and back again, Eusebius obscures the politics of local, civic space. The reconstruction of the church was almost certainly controversial. One need only think of contemporary debates surrounding reconstruction plans in lower Manhattan to get a sense of what is at stake in the refashioning of cityscapes. Altering urban geography prompts questions: whose city is this, whose buildings are these. To ask what a city will look like is always to ask what a city *means*. No transformation of a city's topography is politically innocent.

The demolition of the earlier Christian structure at Tyre, as much as its reconstruction, had constituted a refashioning of the Tyrian cityscape. Our sources do not indicate exactly what had become of the earlier Christian complex after its destruction. As noted above, some churches were demolished for *spolia*, others were simply confiscated and sold. The site could also have been repurposed, or left desolate. In any case, the implementation of Diocletian's edict involved a dramatic enunciation of the cityscape.

That the new basilica should be rebuilt on the site of the earlier ruined church was not a given. Paulinus rebuilt on the original site, Eusebius notes, even though he "might have lighted upon another spot (*for the city supplied countless other sites*), and thus found relief from toil and freedom from trouble" (*HE*, 10.4.26, my emphasis). After Galerius rescinded Diocletian's edicts and restored church properties in 311, some in the community had petitioned Maximinus Daia asking that Christians be banished from Tyre. The Tyrian βουλή had Maximinus' rescript inscribed on a pillar for public display, thus making the conflict over religious and civic identities part of the cityscape. Eusebius had seen this inscription, recording it in his *Ecclesiastical History* (*HE*, 9.7.3–14). Despite this evidence for competition over civic space and civic identity, however, Eusebius represents Paulinus' efforts to rebuild on the site of the ruins as only natural. Yet it is possible to glimpse the local politics that underlie Eusebius' comments.

Not only did Paulinus reclaim the site, he also enlarged the entire complex and oriented the structure so as to reshape the experience of the urban geography, and in turn, refashion the identity of its residents. Paulinus made the entrance to the complex tall and wide, Eusebius writes, "providing even those who stood outside the sacred precincts with an unobstructed view of the interior, and as it were turning the gaze even of strangers to the faith towards the first entrances [...] He hoped that perhaps being moved by the mere sight would turn people and propel them towards the entrance" (*HE*, 10.4.38). Where Eusebius previously globalized the space of the Christian τέμενος he here stresses its distinction from other Tyrian spaces. The gates through which gentile Tyre communicates with the interior of the Christian complex gesture towards possible transformation. Eusebius claims that the πρόπυλον welcomes those outside to enter the interiority of the Christian complex. One might infer other, more hostile readings of this entryway, however. For those who had petitioned Maximinus for the expulsion of Christians, might the gates have represented a threat—the possible infiltration of Christian outsiders into the urban spaces of Tyre?

From the entrance, Eusebius leads his hearers through the complex, past the fountains of the courtyard, and into the church. Rather than stopping to take in the adornment of the church, he moves his audience away from the building and back to the prophetic texts of scripture—specifically, a sequence of passages from Isaiah concerning God's restoration of Israel, but which Eusebius casts as a conversation between the Church, as Bride, and Christ, as Bridegroom. Thus, Eusebius represents Paulinus' project not as an incursion on the local urban geography of Tyre, as it may well have been viewed by some in the community, but rather as a textualized, exegetical space (*HE*, 10.4.53–54).

As its title suggests, Eusebius' oration is as much a panegyric for Paulinus as for the new cathedral. Drawing on the Song of Songs, Eusebius portrays Paulinus as the paranymph ("best man") who facilitates the union of the Bridegroom (the *Logos*) and his Bride (the Church) and who "restored [the church] to be such as he learned from the record of the sacred oracles" (*HE*, 10.4.54). Paulinus is also cast as God's "servant and interpreter (θεραπευτὴς καὶ ὑποφήτης) [...] the

new Aaron or Melchizedek, who has become like the Son of God"
(*HE*, 10.4.23). During the same period in which he wrote and delivered this panegyric of Paulinus, Eusebius was working out a synthesis
of Philonic and Platonic philosophy in his *Praeparatio Evangelica*. In
Book 7 of the *Praeparatio*, in particular, Eusebius draws from Philo to
articulate his theology of the Son as "second cause (δεύτερος αἴτιος)."
Eusebius preserves an otherwise unknown fragment of Philo's *Questions and Answers* that elucidates his characterization of Paulinus.

> Why as if speaking of another God does He say, "In the image of God I
> made man," and not in the image of Himself? With consummate beauty
> and wisdom is this oracle expressed. For nothing mortal could be made
> in the likeness of the Most High God and Father of the universe, but
> in the likeness of the second God, who is the *Logos* of the former. For
> it was right that the rational character in the soul of man should be
> impressed on it by the divine *Logos*; since the God who is prior to the
> *Logos* is superior to every rational nature; and it was not lawful for any
> created thing to be made like to Him who is set above the *Logos* in the
> most excellent and unique nature.[38]

Eusebius claims that Paulinus, "bearing in his soul the image of the
whole Christ, *Logos*, and Wisdom, established this exalted temple of
the Most High God like in nature to the paradigm of that [heavenly
one] which is better, as that which is visible is to that which is invisible" (*HE*, 10.4.26). Eusebius' description of Paulinus as an architect
working from the blueprint provided by intelligible reality is indebted
to Philo's *Life of Moses*. According to Philo, Moses prescribed the layout of the temple based on the paradigm (παράδειγμα) stamped in
his mind by God on Sinai.[39] The layout of the tabernacle was based on
Pythagorean mathematical symbolism, and serves as a figurative representation of human psychology, with the inner reaches of the temple
symbolizing mind and the outer courts sense-perception.[40] Eusebius'
panegyric of Paulinus, however, also buttresses his theology of the Second Cause. In his likeness to the Son, Paulinus' role is demiurgical.

---

[38] *PE*, 7.13.1–2 (323a), trans. (with slight modifications): E.H. Gifford, *Eusebius.
Preparation for the Gospel* (Oxford: Oxford Unviersity Press, 1903; repr. in 2 vols.
Eugene, OR: Wipf and Stock, 2002).
[39] Philo, *V. Mosis*, 2.76. Text and English translation: F.H. Colson, *Philo. Volume
VI.* (Cambridge, Mass.: Harvard University Press, 1935).
[40] Philo, *V. Mosis*, 2.76–83.

Our first and great High Priest says that the Son does exactly what he sees the Father doing. While he [Paulinus] too, looking to the first as to his master with the pure eyes of his mind, as if using whatever he sees [the master] making as archetypes and paradigms, has made images of them, as if crafting (δημιουργῶν), as far as is possible for him, what is most similar (*HE*, 10.4.25).

Thus, like the Second Cause, Paulinus plays a mediating role between the intelligible *Logos* and the congregation analogous to the *Logos'* mediation between the First Cause (the Father) and the sensible world.

Eusebius uses his reading of Philo together with the Letter to the Hebrews to support a monarchic episcopate. Only Christ, the "Great High Priest," Eusebius writes, is able to see into "this living temple of the living God that has been comprised out of ourselves [...] whose innermost recess is unseen by the common herd" (*HE*, 10.4.22). Christ, however, has granted Paulinus "to be second after [Him], as one alone among equals" (*HE*, 10.4.23). The Christian community must submit their souls to the supervision of Paulinus, who alone is able "to see and examine the innermost recesses of your souls; for through long experience he has made a thorough test of every person, and by his eager care he has set you all in a beautiful and rational order...." (*HE*, 10.4.24).

Eusebius' description of Paulinus as a soul endowed with direct, unmediated knowledge of intelligible reality also involves an engagement with Platonic political philosophy. In the *Praeparatio Evangelica*, Eusebius sets passages from Exodus and Hebrews alongside a quotation from Plato to compare the work of Moses with that of the philosopher-king of the *Republic*. According to Eusebius, both Moses and Plato's philosopher-king craft a πολιτεία based on paradigms in the intelligible realm.

> The answer of God said to Moses: "See, thou make all things after the pattern which was shown thee in the mount" (Ex 15.40). And the sacred word stated more plainly, "Who served a copy and shadow of the heavenly things" (Heb 8.5); and taught that the symbols in the writings of Moses plainly contain an image of the more divine realities in the intelligible world. Now then listen how Plato also gives a similar interpretation in the sixth book of the *Republic*, writing as follows:

> The philosopher then by communing with God and with the order of the world becomes both orderly and divine, as far as is possible for humans[...] If therefore, said I, it ever become necessary for him to study how to introduce what he sees in that realm [i.e. the intelligible

world] into the habits of humankind both in private and in public life,
and so to mould others as well as himself, do you think that he will be
found a bad artificer of temperance and justice and civic virtue in general? [...] And will [the multitude] disbelieve us when we say that a State
can never be prosperous, unless it be planned by artists who follow the
divine pattern? [...] Then, I suppose, in working out [the constitution
of the πολιτεία] they would frequently look to this side and that, both
to what is essentially just and beautiful and temperate and everything of
that kind, and then to the other side, to what is found in humans, and
would put upon their tablet the likeness of a human being by making
a combination and mixture of the various ways of life, and taking their
design from that which, when embodied in humans, Homer called the
form and likeness of God (Rep. 500d–501c)[41]

I have quoted this long passage from the *Praeparatio* to illustrate the
extent to which Eusebius' aesthetic thought derives both from his
reading of scriptural texts, like Hebrews, and reflection on the Platonic
corpus itself. Eusebius' construal of a soteriological political philosophy based on his interpretation of Plato, moreover, is similar to his
late-Platonic near-contemporaries' interpretations of Platonic political
philosophy.

In his recent study of late-Platonic political philosophy, Dominic
O'Meara has shown how political philosophy was integrally related
to soteriology in later Platonism.[42] For philosophers such as Plotinus
and Porphyry, the ideal ruler was one who, like the prisoner of Plato's
cave, having been freed from ignorance and enjoying knowledge of
the intelligible, must be compelled to return from the realm of intellection to assist those still bound in the world of sense-perception.[43] As
Plotinus puts it, "having been with that [One] and having adequately
conversed with it, [the soul] must come and announce, if possible,
to another the conversation it has had there [i.e. in the intelligible
world]."[44] The philosopher-ruler assists in the ascent of his or her subjects' souls by cultivating the virtues, beginning with the "practical"
or as Porphyry terms them, the "political" virtues. Insofar as becoming a virtuous social being was a preparation for the transcendence of

---

[41] Eusebius, *PE*, 12.19.1–9 [592c–593d], trans. Gifford.

[42] D. O'Meara, *Platonopolis. Platonic Political Philosophy in Late Antiquity* (Oxford: Clarendon Press, 2003).

[43] Plato, *Rep.*, 519c–520c.

[44] Plotinus, *Enn.*, VI.9 [9]. 7, 20; though Plotinus goes on to note that some who have had vision of the Good will prefer to "remain above"; text: P. Henry and H.-R. Schwyzer, *Plotini Opera*, 3 vols (Leiden: Brill, 1951–73).

embodiment and noetic ascent, then, salvation was at its most fundamental level communal.[45] As Porphyry puts it "it is only after one has
been set in order in accordance with [the political virtues] that one can
abstract oneself from performing any act in concert with the body."[46]

Aesthetic theory also plays an important role in Plotinus' doctrine
of the soul's ascent.[47] First, in its perception of a beautiful object, the
soul recognizes something akin to itself—like is drawn to like.[48] As a
result, the soul is induced to intellection and begins to contemplate the
source of its beauty. The soul must then transcend sense perception
and intellection to achieve absolute unity with the One. The perception of beauty, then, prompts a process of contemplation that is itself
a spatial practice. The soul's ascent to the One begins discursively in
the *here* of sense perception, proceeds to knowledge *there* (ἐκεῖ) in
the intelligible world, but ends in epoptic vision—the absolute unity
of the individual's soul with the One that is beyond being—in which
all spatial distinction, indeed all difference between the *here* of subject
and the *there* of object, is obliterated.

We can see Eusebius developing a similar aesthetic in his oration.
Eusebius denies the ultimate efficacy of words and redirects his hearers towards the beauty of Paulinus' craftsmanship. "Why need I speak
more particularly of the perfect wisdom and art with which the building has been ordered and the surpassing beauty of every part," he
intones, "when the witness of the eyes leaves no need for the instruction through the ears" (*HE*, 10.4.44). Thus Eusebius marks an important turning point in the oration—away from a discursive aesthetic
towards an epoptic aesthetic.

Eusebius directs sense perception away from changeable, material beauty (φαντασία), towards the contemplation of the immaterial
archetypes, prototypes, and paradigms that lie behind the beauty of
the church. This aesthetic reorientation also involves redirection of his
hearers away from the macrocosm of the monumental church to the

---

[45] Porphyry, *Sent.*, 32, trans. J. Dillon and L. Gerson, *Neoplatonic Philosophy* (India-
napolis, IN: Hackett, 2004), 182–188.

[46] Porphyry, *Sent.*, 32; Dillon and Gerson, *Neoplatonic Philosophy*, *cit.*, 182.

[47] See the recent article by J. Noel Hubler, "The Role of Aesthetics in Plotinus'
Ascent of the Soul," in A. Alexandrakis and N. Moutafakis (eds.), *Neoplatonism and
Western Aesthetics* (Albany: State University of New York Press, 2002), 193–203.

[48] As Plotinus puts it, "…if [the soul] sees anything kindred or the trace of anything
kindred, it rejoices and takes flight and returns to itself and recalls itself and its own"
(Enn. I.6 [1]. 2).

microcosm of the individual soul, which Eusebius describes as "the divine and rational building in our souls" (*HE*, 10.4.55). Philo had described the soul as "an animate shrine of the Father," in which an individual can achieve a vision of God.[49] Plotinus also used construction metaphors to articulate his aesthetic theory in *On Beauty*. For him, beauty in the sensible world derives from the intelligible forms.

> But how does the beauty in the body harmonize with that which is prior to body? How can the architect, harmonizing the external house with the form of the house internal to him, claim that the former is beautiful? In fact, it is because the external house is, apart from the stones, the inner form divided by the external mass of matter.[50]

The vocabulary of temples and religious iconography as a metaphor for the soul was also a favorite of both Plotinus and Porphyry. Plotinus urges, "If you do not yet see yourself as beautiful, then be like a sculptor, making a statue that is supposed to be beautiful."[51] Porphyry likens the philosopher's soul and mind to a temple and its statue.

> Reason (*logos*) states that the Divine is everywhere universally, but among human beings only the discursive faculty of the wise person has been sanctified as its temple, and that the honor due to God is most properly rendered by the one who knows God most; and this would naturally be the wise person alone, by whom the Divine must be honored through wisdom, and through wisdom adorn for It a temple in his thought with a living statue—the mind—when God, represented in it, adorns it.[52]

Much as the Plotinian soul is beautiful by virtue of its participation in the intelligible forms, Eusebius describes the soul as a temple within that takes its order and beauty from God via the demiurgical *Logos*.

> This building the divine offspring himself fashioned according to his own image, and in everywhere and in every respect he endowed it with likeness to the divine, ... Such then is the perfect and purified soul, created from the beginning to bear the image of the heavenly *Logos* (*HE*, 10.4.56).

---

[49] Philo, *Quaest. in Ex.*, 2.51.
[50] Plotinus, *Enn.* I.6 [1]. 3; trans. Dillon and Gerson, *Neoplatonic Philosophy, cit.*, 21.
[51] Plotinus, *Enn.*, I.6 [1]. 9; trans. Dillon and Gerson, *Neoplatonic Philosophy, cit.*, 29.
[52] Porphyry, *Marc.*, 11; text: W. Pötscher, *Porphyrios, Πρὸς Μαρκέλλαν* (Leiden: Brill, 1969): λέγει δὲ ὁ λόγος πάντῃ μὲν καὶ πάντως παρεῖναι τὸ θεῖον, νεὼν δὲ τούτῳ παρ' ἀνθρώποις καθιερῶσθαι τὴν διάνοιαν μάλιστα τοῦ σοφοῦ μόνην, τιμήν τε προσήκουσαν ἀπονέμεσθαι τῷ θεῷ ὑπὸ τοῦ μάλιστα τὸν θεὸν ἐγνωκότος· τοῦτον δὲ εἶναι εἰκότως μόνον τὸν σοφόν, ᾧ τιμητέον διὰ σοφίας τὸ θεῖον καὶ κατακοσμητέον αὐτῷ διὰ σοφίας ἐν τῇ γνώμῃ τὸ ἱερὸν ἐμψύχῳ ἀγάλματι τῷ νῷ ἐνεικονισαμένου ἀγάλλοντος θεοῦ.

Just as the earlier church building had been demolished by the persecutors, so too has the demonic host profaned souls—the temples within (*HE*, 10.4.58). And, just as the site of the new church had to be cleared of refuse, so too have souls been prevented from salvation, burdened by the detritus of materiality (*HE*, 10.4.58).

Plotinus saw the soul's recognition of its beauty as a prompt to intellection and ultimately, to transcendent unification with the One. Eusebius, in contrast, retreats from interiority to situate the individual soul within the salvation history that the new church inscribes in the Tyrian cityscape. The ascent of the individual soul to God is effected *not* primarily through an individualized aesthetic practice, but in and through the community. Paulinus, as the philosopher-ruler of the congregation, must structure the social body of Christians in appropriate proportion. According to Porphyry's *Sententiae*, the political virtues were fourfold—prudence, courage, moderation, and justice. This last virtue, justice (δικαιοσύνη) is concerned with balance and proportion—especially between rulers and those ruled.[53] Eusebius deploys similar terminology to describe Paulinus, who "building with justice, divided the whole people according to their particular abilities (δικαιοσύνῃ δῆτα οἰκοδομῶν, κατ' ἀξίαν τοῦ παντὸς λαοῦ διῄρει τὰς δυνάμεις) maintaining the balance and proportion of the church as well as ordering the community of souls that use the space of the church (*HE*, 10.4.63).

The individual soul, or to borrow Eusebius' metaphor, each temple within, is situated in relation to the interior temples of others. Thus, the architectural space of the church maps the inner-soulscape of the congregation. The outer enclosure of the complex represents those whose "unerring faith" differentiates the Christian community from those souls outside it, just as the wall of the compound separates Christian space from the rest of the Tyre. More advanced Christians serve as doormen or support the colonnades of the courtyard. Those souls within the church itself are those who have attained sight of the divine. All, however, are led by Paulinus, in whom "the entire Christ has taken his seat" (*HE*, 10.4.63–68).

The ecclesiology and soteriology of Eusebius' oration constitute integrally related spatial rhetorics. By directing hearers' back and forth, from the beauty of the church to an interiorized aesthetic of the soul as the image of the *Logos*, and out again, Eusebius seeks to

---

[53] Porphyry, *Sent.*, 32.

mediate a spatial practice that structures the community hierarchically. The oration provides an itinerary that is enunciated on interrelated planes. To congregate in the cathedral is to map the progress of
souls on their ascent to God. But, to congregate in the church is also
to instantiate a hierarchical ecclesiology that naturalizes a monarchic
episcopate and other asymmetrical relations of power. The oration
describes a community under the direct authority of a bishop who
enjoys the patronage and protective care of emperors who reside in
distant metropolitan centers but who are present in their effects on
the local cityscape. Thus, being in the space of the church is homologous to being in imperial space. Finally, the analogies Eusebius draws
between Paulinus and God the Son effect a movement that seeks to
position his hearers not only in the *here* of monarchic-episcopal and
imperial space, but simultaneously in the *there* of Eusebius' "Arian"
cosmology that envisions the Second Cause as a mediator between the
intelligible and sensible worlds.[54]

At the same time that these spatial practices situate the Tyrian congregation within a Christian salvation history and within the empire,
however, they simultaneously disorient and dislocate. We have seen
that the oration obscures the local politics of urban space by eliding the
here and now of Tyre's present with the there and then of a scriptural
past. For that matter, Eusebius also distorts the economic conditions
of the church's construction—he focuses on the product rather than
the process of construction, on the patronage of emperors and the
euergetism of Paulinus rather than the labor of the church's construction, on Paulinus' demiurgy rather than Paulinus' hired craftspeople.

Traditional histories tend to read the remains of material culture
as stable and univocal in contrast to texts as rhetorical, tendentious,

---

[54] See, for example, Eusebius, *C. Marc.*, 1.1.32–34: "For it is not fitting that the
mediator be limited to one nature. Therefore this [mediator] is not of one [nature],
but of necessity a middle is two, and it is neither of those things of which it is the middle—with the result that he is not thought to be the God who is over all nor one of the
angels, but a mediator and middle between them, when he mediates for the Father and
the angels; and once again, when he is "mediator between God and humans," being
established as a middle between each of them, he is neither of those things of which he
is the middle—he is neither the one and only God, nor a human similar to the rest of
humans. What is he then, if he is none of these, but Only-begotten Son of God, having
become now the mediator between God and humans, but earlier, at the time of Moses,
being mediator between God and angels?"; text: G.C. Hansen and E. Klostermann,
*Eusebius Werke, Band 4: Gegen Marcell. Über die kirchliche Theologie. Die Fragmente
Marcells* (GCS 14, 2nd ed.; Berlin: Akademie Verlag, 1972), my translation.

biased, and manipulative. We tend to want to get at the "real" building behind the rhetoric of Eusebius' oration. But, as I have hoped to show in this paper, the relationship between the context of the Tyrian church and the text of Eusebius' oration is neither simple nor unproblematic. There are no fixed, stable sites that are politically neutral. Places, like texts, are sites of meaning production. As such, places, like texts, are sites of multiplicity and instability. In drawing from de Certeau's notions of spatial rhetoric to explore the relationships between texts on the one hand, and art and architecture, on the other, I have been reading art and architecture as texts. Although walking, congregating, and viewing may be practices homologous to reading, they are not identical to reading. To understand the art-text nexus less myopically, therefore, it may also be fruitful in future studies of early Christian aesthetics to draw from theoretical approaches that take viewing, walking, sitting, and so forth, *rather than* reading, as their point of departure. Such an interdisciplinary approach may also in turn better elucidate aspects of textuality that may be otherwise obscured.

EUSEBIUS' CONSTRUCTION OF A CHRISTIAN CULTURE IN AN APOLOGETIC CONTEXT: READING THE *PRAEPARATIO EVANGELICA* AS A LIBRARY

Sabrina Inowlocki

INTRODUCTION

Eusebius' methodology in the *Praeparatio*, which consists in the accumulation of excerpts, is characteristic of the imperial period: as J. König and T. Whitmarsh point out in their book *Ordering Knowledge in the Roman Empire*, "It is hard to avoid the impression that accumulation of knowledge is the driving force for all imperial prose literature."[1] What is the significance of this observation regarding the *Praeparatio*?

At the time when Eusebius was writing the *Praeparatio*, between 312 and 325, the Roman empire was being transformed into a Christian Empire. Eusebius attended this transformation with great expectations. He was acutely aware of the necessity of constructing and empowering a Christian culture that would match the accomplishments of divine providence. In order to do so (at least in the *Praeparatio*), he resorted to the same methodology as other ancient prose writers such as Pliny or Athenaeus of Naucratis, whose encyclopedic writings were built a libraries of sorts. Yet at the same time he subverted this methodology by using it against the Greek cultural hegemony. In order to achieve this goal, I will argue, he presented the *Praeparatio* as a library and what I would call a 'performance of erudition'. By 'performance of erudition', I mean that Eusebius deliberately theatralized acts of reading and writing, turning them into cultural statements supporting his construction of a Christian literary culture. This, I believe, was a deliberate apologetic strategy on his part.

In this paper, I will attempt to demonstrate that Eusebius' *Praeparatio*, is a complex cultural project which intertwines Christian apologetics and one of the most comprehensive reflection on the place of the

---

[1] In J. König and T. Whitmarsh (eds.), *Ordering Knowledge in the Roman Empire* (Cambridge: Cambridge University Press, 2007), 3.

Greek (and Jewish) texts within the Christian culture. I will also try to clarify Eusebius' construction of his own status as a Christian author in this project. In order to do so, I will first examine the linguistic and literary strategies through which Eusebius presents the *Praeparatio* as a library and a performance of erudition; I will then proceed to the analysis of that which is at stake in the presentation of the *Praeparatio* as a library, focusing on the relationship between library and power, piety, and memory.

THE PRAEPARATIO AS A LIBRARY AND AS A PERFORMANCE OF ERUDITION

Although in his introduction to book VII of the *Praeparatio* G. Schroeder has presented the *Praeparatio* as an architectural construction, a cathedral made of 5 naves,[2] I think that Eusebius' handling of citations suggests in a more direct way the image of a library.

In the ancient world, especially the Christian world, the library par excellence was that of Alexandria.[3] Initially, it had been conceived as a totalizing project aiming to universal knowledge, a microcosm of sorts.[4] If libraries could somehow become miniature universes, for Eusebius, as for other Christian writers, books could also be conceived as libraries.[5]

---

[2] G. Schroeder et É. des Places, Eusèbe de Césarée. *Préparation évangélique* VII (SC 215; Paris: Cerf, 1975), 15–16.

[3] On which secondary literature is huge. See, e.g., *s.v.* 'Bibliotheken', in *PRE*, V, 1897, col. 405–424. The best modern history of the Alexandrian library is L. Canfora, *The vanished library. A wonder of the ancient world* (London: Vintage, 1991); see also U. Jochum, "The Library of Alexandria and Its Aftermath," *History* 15 (1999), 5–12 (http://www.ub.uni-konstanz.de/fileadmin/Dateien/Fachreferenten/Jochum/alexandriaaftermath.pdf); L. Collins, *The Library in Alexandria and the Bible in Greek* (VT.S 82; Leiden – Boston: Brill, 2000); R. MacLeod (ed.), *The Library of Alexandria, Center of Learning in the Ancient World* (London – New York: ib Tauris, 2000); W.V. Harris and G. Ruffini (eds.), *Ancient Alexandria between Egypt and Greece* (Columbia Studies in the Classical Tradition 26; Leiden – Boston: Brill, 2004); A. Hirst and M. Silk (eds.), *Alexandria Real and Imagined* (Aldershot – Burlington: Ashgate, 2004); A. Le Boulluec et C.G. Conticello, *Alexandrie antique et chrétienne—Clément et Origène* (EAug, Série Antiquité 178; Paris: Études Augustiniennes, 2006).

[4] See the *Letter of Aristeas*, 9; for secondary literature, see, e.g., L. Canfora, *Il viaggio di Aristea* (Bari: Laterza, 1996); S. Honigman, *The Septuagint and Homeric Scholarship in Alexandria*, (London – New York: T&T Clark, 2003).

[5] On the history of libraries, see especially the writings of the two Italian specialists L. Canfora and G. Cavallo: e.g., L. Canfora, *The Vanished Library, cit.*; G. Cavallo (ed.), *Le biblioteche nel mondo antico e medievale*, (Bari: Laterza, 1988); *Id.* (ed.), *Libri, editori e publico nel mondo antico. Guida storica e critica* (Bari: Laterza, 1989), and

Jerome, for instance, called scriptures a 'divine library';[6] Photius' reading notes were called the *Bibliothèkè*, and so is Diodorus Siculus' work. Eusebius even calls Diodorus the συναγαγὼν βιβλιοθήκας, 'the collector of libraries',[7] an expression which refers to book collections. There also existed a work entitled Περὶ συναγωγῆς βιβλίων (*On the collection of books*), written by Artemon of Cassandreia and used by Athenaeus of Naucratis.[8] It was a manual for book collectors.[9] Such a genre is attested otherwise: for example, according to the Suda,[10] Philo of Byblos, who was extensively cited by Eusebius in the *Praeparatio*,[11] also wrote a book on book collection.

In the *Praeparatio*, the extensive number of citations calls up the image of a collection of books, not only because of the quantity of authors quoted, but also because of the large size of the quotations. To some extent, the *Praeparatio* may be seen quite literally as a portable library, which would make sense in the context of antique book production. Indeed, books were costly and rare in the ancient world. Eusebius must have been aware that a written work including many excerpts was a useful acquisition, especially at a time when compendia were most popular. Before him, ancient writers of universal histories, such as Polybius, had spoken in favour of this genre (to which the *Praeparatio* is, to some extent, fairly close), stressing their practical character.[12] The *Praeparatio* may have been conceived as a portable

---

more recently L. Casson, *Libraries in the Ancient World* (New Haven: Yale University Press, 2001).

    [6] *De uiris inlustribus* 75 (*vita Pamphili*): Pamphilus "was so inflamed with love of sacred literature, that he transcribed the greater part of the works of Origen with his own hand and these are still preserved in the library at Cæsarea." (*tanto bibliothecae divinae amore flagravit, ut maximam partem Origenis voluminum sua manu descripserit, quae usque hodie in Caesariensi bibliotheca habentur*).

    [7] *Praep. ev.*, II.1.55, (he is also a πᾶσαν τὴν παλαιὰν συναγαγὼν ἱστορίαν at *Praep. ev.*, II prol. 6); cf. *Praep. ev.*, XV.22.69 on Plutarch as *sunagagón* philosophical opinions on private collections of books see the interesting passage from Strabo, *Geogr.*, XIII.1.54 in which he deals with the books of Aristotle and Theophrastus.

    [8] *Deipn.*, XII.515ᵉ.

    [9] See Chr. Jacob, "Athenaeus the Librarian," in D. Braund and J. Wilkins (eds.), *Athenaeus and His World. Reading Greek Culture in the Roman Empire* (Exeter: University of Exeter Press, 2000) 85–111, p. 95.

    [10] *S.v. Philôn Byblios*.

    [11] On Eusebius' use of Philo of Byblos, see A.P. Johnson, *Ethnicity and Argument in Eusebius' Praeparatio Evangelica* (Oxford: Oxford University Press, 2006), 65–72.

    [12] Cf. Polybius, *Hist.* III.32: "Another mistake is to look upon my history as difficult to obtain or master, because of the number and size of the books. Compare it in these particulars with the various writings of the episodical historians. Is it not much easier to purchase and read my forty books, which are as it were all in one piece, and so to

library: as Barnes has suggested, it may have been used by Christians as a comprehensive handbook for use in polemical discussions.[13]

The way in which Eusebius introduces the excerpts he cites and the constant use of bibliographical methods initially created in Alexandria suggest that Eusebius chose to represent his apologetic masterpiece as a reflection of the bookish environment in which he worked. This environment included space, objects, and people: a library, books, quotations, scribes, and, last but not least, a librarian.[14] In the *Praeparatio*, Eusebius invites his readers to embark on a long reading journey throughout his own apologetic library, which includes the consultation of specific passages when needed.

His invitations to read an excerpt call up the idea of an actual reading session in a library, the books being taken up from a shelf and read one after the other. This is suggested, e.g., by the numerous occurrences of μεταβαίνω, μέτειμι to introduce new citations:[15] after reading the passage of a work, one goes to the next book. One also finds, e.g., μεταβὰς ἐπί 'title', ἀναγνῶθι...[16]

The fact that in most cases Eusebius stresses that he interrupted a passage to quote another one which comes further in the book is also

---

follow with a comprehensive glance the events in Italy, Sicily, and Libya from the time of Pyrrhus to the fall of Carthage, and those in the rest of the world from the flight of Cleomenes of Sparta, continuously, to the battle between the Achaeans and Romans at the Isthmus? To say nothing of the fact that the compositions of these historians are many times as numerous as mine, it is impossible for their readers to get any certain information from them" (transl. W.R. Paton); cf. Diodorus I.3.8.

[13] T.D. Barnes, *Constantine and Eusebius* (Cambridge, MA – London: Harvard University Press, 1981), 184.

[14] It is difficult to define precisely the task of the librarian in Caesarea. Regarding Eusebius, I use this word *lato sensu*, referring to his scholarly bookish activities in Caesarea, including purchasing books and enlarging the library. For more on this subject, see A. Carriker, *The Library of Eusebius of Caesarea* (SVigChr 67; Leiden – Boston: Brill, 2003). In general, the role of the librarian in the ancient world is ill defined, and so is the relationship between the bishops and the libraries. We know from the *Martyrdom of St. Felix*, which describes the impact of Diocletian's edict in Tibiuca (N. Africa), that in some congregations at least the books were in the possession of the bishop, but, as H. Gamble suggests (H.Y. Gamble, *Books and Readers in the Early Church. A History of Early Christian Texts* (New Haven – London: Yale University Press, 1995), 148), this may be due to the fact that this community was looking to avoid confiscation. Moreover, this parallel may be irrelevant since a 'congregational library' such as that of Tibiuca certainly did not function as a research library such as that of Caesarea.

[15] E.g. *Praep. ev.*, X.10.23; X.11.35.

[16] E.g., *Praep. ev.*, V.36.5.

relevant to this analysis: for instance, he uses καὶ ἐπιλέγει/ἐπιφέρει[17]/ προστίθησι,[18] with or without adverbs or adverbial formulas like καὶ μετὰ βραχέα, καὶ μεθ᾽ ἕτερα, καὶ αὖθις, or πάλιν, which are occasionally used alone.[19] He sometimes uses the term ὑπο(κατα)βαίνω.[20] These terms do not only reflect Eusebius' scholarly exactness in referencing passages, but it may also suggest that the reader is engaged in a real reading session staged in a well-stocked library.

The repeated use of (ἐπι)συνάπτω[21] to connect a citation to another is also indicative of an accumulation process which is reminiscent of the accumulation process at play in a library. Eusebius occasionally refers to the plenty of books and works he could have cited had he had enough space.[22] If this is certainly a sophistry aiming to support his case for Christianity, it also suggests the endless possibilities of Eusebius' bookish world: the *Praeparatio* is only one of the potential collections possibly gathered on the subject. The idea of an infinity of books is not only reminiscent of J.L. Borges' library, but also of the library of Alexandria.

In many cases, Eusebius emphasizes that he gives a literal quotation, using expressions such as πρὸς λέξιν,[23] κατὰ λέξιν,[24] πρὸς ῥῆμα,[25] ῥήμασιν αὐτοῖς.[26] In general, these formulas have been understood as indicating that the quotation given is exactly reproduced by Eusebius.[27] However, they may also have been used by the bishop to theatralize the reading of the *Praeparatio*: Eusebius presents the quotations to the reader as if he was directly reading from a book. Whether or not Eusebius really had the books from which he quotes at his disposal is not a relevant question here.[28] What matters is the impression he tries

---

[17] E.g., *Praep. ev.*, X.13.2.

[18] E.g., *Praep. ev.*, V.4.3.

[19] E.g., *Praep. ev.*, X.11. 6; IV.14.8; X.10.15; V.7.2 respectively.

[20] *Praep. ev.*, XI.10.9; XI.28.13. Cf. Eust. 1351, 43.2.

[21] E.g., *Praep. ev.*, X.6.15.

[22] E.g., *Praep. ev.*, VI.9.32; IX.42.4.

[23] E.g., *Praep. ev.*, I.9.20; III.7.2.

[24] E.g., *Praep. ev.*, I.10.49; II.2.52.

[25] E.g., *Praep. ev.*, IV.15.9; XI.18.26.

[26] E.g., *Praep. ev.*, V.1.11; X.6.15.

[27] On the literality of Eusebius' quotations, see, e.g., S. Inowlocki, *Eusebius and the Jewish Authors. His Citation Technique in an Apologetic Context* (AJEC 64; Leiden – Boston: Brill, 2006), ch. II, IV, and V, and the bibliography cited.

[28] Indeed, the fact that Eusebius quotes from a certain work does not necessarily mean that he had it in his library. He may have copied it from some place else, e.g., the Library of Jerusalem. See the methodological introduction by A. Carriker, *The*

to create: that his citations are the 'real' text excerpted as if taken up from a book and read to the reader.

On many occasions, Eusebius invites his reader to read a quotation by using an imperative form in the present or in the aorist, second person singular, of the verbs ἀκούω, ἐπακούω in order to introduce citations. Expressions such as ἄκουε…λέγοντος are also abundantly used.[29] For K. Mras,[30] these expressions reflect the concrete circumstances of the redaction of the *Praeparatio*, that is to say, the interaction between Eusebius, reading the text aloud, and the copyist. Yet as D. Schenkeveld has shown, this expression should be translated by 'read' rather than by 'listen'.[31] Eusebius also uses the terms ἀναγιγνώσκω,[32] or παραναγιγνώσκω:[33] the latter is a *terminus technicus* for the collation of texts, which calls to mind the idea of the library and *scriptorium*.[34]

Other terms or expressions point to the bookish context in which Eusebius seems to inscribe the *Praeparatio*. For instance, Eusebius uses the verb ἐπιτέμνω to describe his cutting off of excerpts.[35] This is also a *terminus technicus* for the epitomization of books,[36] which sends us back to Eusebius' activities as a book expert.

Along the same line, Eusebius frequently uses the words προκείσθω or κείσθω to close a citation.[37] The verb κεῖμαι is used in a typically bookish context. For example, Athenaeus of Naucratis, describing a relentlessly curious guest, says he was nicknamed *Keitoukeitos,* as a reference to his mania to ask every now and then "κεῖται ἢ οὐ κεῖται;"

Library of Eusebius of Caesarea, cit., 37–74. Likewise, D. Runia ("Caesarea maritima and the Survival of Hellenistic-Jewish Literature," in H. Raban and K.G. Holum (eds.), *Caesarea maritima. A Retrospective after two Millenia* (Leiden – Boston: Brill, 1996), 476–495) has pointed out that the works cited in Eusebius' bibliographical lists in the *HE* do not need to reflect the possession of Eusebius' *Library*: he may have inflated these lists for apologetic purposes.

[29] E.g. *Praep. ev.,* II.1.56; III.3.21; III.7.2; IV.2.14; V.1.2; VI.2.2; VI.6.74; XI.29.1.

[30] K. Mras (ed.), Eusebius Werke VIII. 1. *Die Praeparatio Evangelica* (GCS 47; Berlin: Akademie-Verlag, 1982²), lviii.

[31] D. Schenkeveld, "Prose usages of AKOUEIN 'to read'," *CQ* 42 (1992), 129–141 has shown that this verb, when associated with a participle in the genitive translates "to read that which someone has written." This verb is also repeatedly used by Simplicius to indicate that a citation is given (H. Baltussen, *Philology or Philosophy? Simplicius and the Use of Quotations* (Leiden – Boston: Brill, 2002) 185).

[32] E.g., *Praep. ev.,* V.36.5.

[33] E.g., *Praep. ev.,* VI.7.44.

[34] LSJ, *s.v.*

[35] *Praep. ev.,* VI.9.32; VIII.5.11; 6.10.

[36] LSJ, *s.v.*

[37] E.g. *Praep. ev.,* I.10.42; III.4.3.

("Is it attested or not?"), talking about the occurrences of certain words or their use in literature.[38] κεῖμαι indeed refers to an occurrence; τὸ κείμενον can designate a received text.[39]

The term χράομαι is also used in the *Praeparatio* to introduce testimonies (μαρτύρια).[40] This word or cognate terms are specifically used in bookish contexts: for instance, a bibliographical tool written by Artemon of Cassandreia was entitled the βιβλιῶν χρῆσις.[41] It is not impossible that Eusebius, like Athenaeus, resorted to pinacographical works such as that of Artemon in order to provide his readers with short biographical information on the authors he quoted (e.g. Diodorus, Polyhistor etc.).

The exactness with which Eusebius refers to the works he uses, whether directly or indirectly, the titles of the chapters he appended himself to the text, as well as the table at the beginning of each book, all reflect Eusebius' role as a librarian in Caesarea. His bibliographical references include the name of the author, that of the work, and even the number of the book cited.[42] In the short summary of the chapter placed at the beginning of each chapter, Eusebius occasionally provides a *lemma* of the works he cites. This, however, only starts from the end of book VI, and some books display such *lemmata* more systematically than others. For instance, book VII has none, while VIII–XV are almost exclusively constituted of references to author.

It is worth noting that throughout the *Praeparatio*, the authority of the excerpts does not stem from the text quoted itself, but from the authors quoted: despite his deep involvement in a bookish culture, he deems the book important only because it conveys the voice of its author. This is why the latin term *auctoritas* in its medieval signification is useful to define the sort of authority Eusebius is building through the citation process.[43] Indeed, this medieval term best defines the principle of authority as it is exploited in the *Praeparatio*. One may argue that this word designates a doctor of the Church in the Middle Ages whereas Eusebius cites almost only secular authors in the *Praeparatio*. However, the function of the *auctoritas* proves to be

---

[38] *Deipn.*, I.2e.
[39] LSJ, *s.v.*
[40] E.g., *Praep. ev.*, I.9.6; IV.7.2.
[41] *Deipn.*, XII.515ᵉ.
[42] See Inowlocki, *Eusebius and the Jewish Authors, cit.*, chapter V.
[43] *Ibid.*

identical in the *Praeparatio* as in medieval theological writings. Indeed, Compagnon defines this term as "une citation nécessairement référée à un auteur," and he adds that "sans cela sa valeur est nulle... Toute la puissance de l'*auctoritas* tient à son éponyme, et le mot renvoie à un sujet de l'énonciation plutôt qu'il ne désigne un énoncé."[44] This is the exact contrary of the death of the author as theorized by Roland Barthes.

In the books themselves, more precise references are offered: the number of the book (ordinal number) is placed before the title and the name of the author. At some point, Eusebius even omits sentences of introduction and closing of the citations: only the title of the next chapter, which constitutes some kind of *lemma*, indicates that the citation included in the previous chapter is over and that a new one is given. In other words, extensive citations are unfolding under the eyes of the reader and only the different *lemmata* announcing the next chapter interrupt the reading.

The *lemmata* provided in the *Praeparatio* are probably reminiscent of those which served to identify works in his library. Yet even though such *lemmata* certainly meant to help readers to find the passage or the work if they wish to go back to it,[45] they also contributed to provide Eusebius' work with the scholarly legitimacy which his apologetic project required.

In several passages, Eusebius carefully defines the identity of the author quoted. For instance, he stresses that he is speaking about Philo of Byblos, not Philo 'the Hebrew';[46] in a table of content, Diodorus is presented as 'the Diodorus of the βιβλιοθήκη',[47] Clement of Alexandria is 'our Clement';[48] Aristobulos is the one mentioned at the beginning

---

[44] See A. Compagnon, *La seconde main ou le travail de la citation* (Paris: Seuil, 1979), 218. On Eusebius' use of *auctoritas*, see Inowlocki, *Eusebius and the Jewish Authors, cit.*, 59.

[45] On the question of titles, tables of content, *lemmata* etc., see J.C. Fredouille, M.O. Goulet-Cazé, P. Hoffmann et al., avec la collab. de S. Deléani (eds.), *Titres et articulations du texte dans les oeuvres antiques: actes du colloque international de Chantilly, 13–15 décembre 1994*, (EAug, Série Antiquité 152; Paris: Études Augustiniennes, 1997) and more specifically on tables of content in the imperial times, see A.M. Riggsby, "Guides to the Wor(l)d," in J. König and T. Whitmarsh (eds.), *Ordering Knowledge in the Roman Empire, cit.*, 88–107.

[46] *Praep. ev.*, I.9.20.

[47] *Praep. ev.*, X.8 Table of contents.

[48] E.g., *Praep. ev.*, X.1.9.

of the second book of the Maccabees,[49] etc. As Jacob has pointed out, "homonymy was an immediate pitfall for ignorant book-collectors and a constant nightmare for advanced one."[50] Therefore, Eusebius, by giving precise references to the authors quoted, not only acts as a professional book collector and librarian,[51] but also presents himself as the master of his own very personal library, the *Praeparatio*.

Eusebius' scholarly work was certainly influenced by Alexandrian scholarship, and, in particular, by the philological tradition it developed. So were Origen and Pamphilus before him. Jerome himself said that Pamphilus wished to match Demetrius of Phalerum and Peisistrates "in his zeal for the sacred library."[52] But Eusebius is indebted more specifically to the bibliographical methods which seem to have developed in the Hellenistic Alexandria. Indeed, Eusebius' methodology in citing is similar to that, e.g., of Athenaeus of Naucratis, a well known citator who, as Christian Jacob has shown,[53] exemplifies the Alexandrian bibliographical tradition.[54] It may also be compared to that of Clement of Alexandria, his Christian predecessor to which it is closer than to that of Origen.

As Eusebius' *Praeparatio*, Athenaeus of Naucratis' *Deipnosophistai* (end 2nd century CE)[55] is built as a store house for citations, and, as Christian Jacob has pointed out, constitutes a library in its own right.[56] Athenaeus' methodology in quoting texts compares closely to that of Eusebius: for instance, the absence of anonymous quotations, the references to book numbers, and the pattern of bibliographical references[57] are very similar to Eusebius' method in the *Praeparatio*.[58] As Eusebius is the first Greek Christian author to use explicitly Diodorus Siculus' Library, Athenaeus is the first and only Greek pagan author of the Roman period we know of to cite Diodorus. Christian Jacob has beautifully described how, in his work, he playfully elaborates on

---

[49] *Praep. ev.*, VIII.9.38.
[50] Jacob, "Athenaeus the Librarian," *cit.*, 97.
[51] The difference between the two may have been unclear in Antiquity.
[52] Jerome, *Epist.* XXXIV.1.
[53] cf. Jacob, "Athenaeus the Librarian," *cit.*, 92.
[54] See *infra*.
[55] See the new volume by S. Douglas Olson (ed.), Athenaeus: *The Learned Banqueters* (LCL; Cambridge, Mass.: Harvard University Press, 2007).
[56] Jacob, "Athenaeus the Librarian," *cit.*, 85–111.
[57] *Ibid.*, 91–93.
[58] Cf. Inowlocki, *Eusebius and the Jewish authors*, *cit.*, chapters II, III, V.

the concepts of memory and the endlessness of Greek culture and its library.[59]

Clement of Alexandria, a heir to both Alexandrian erudition and Jewish Hellenistic culture, may also have influenced Eusebius.[60] Like him, he made a massive use of quotations in his *Stromateis*.[61] He quotes in the same proportions Christian and non-Christian authors,[62] which he occasionally claims to cite κατὰ λέξιν, as Eusebius does. Clement seems to enjoy and even to boast about the extent of his literary knowledge and pedantry is not absent from the *Stromateis*. He playfully exploits citations in a way that is occasionally reminiscent of Athenaeus of Naucratis, albeit in a Christian form. Both authors are close in many ways: in both, citations are organized in a labyrinthic manner, they are part of a game of erudition that is typical of a certain Alexandrian cultural sphere.

Eusebius' methodology, however, also differs from that of his predecessors. If his performance of erudition is inspired by the Alexandria bibliographical tradition, his methodology in using quotations has little in common with that of Clement or Athenaeus. Eusebius deals with citations in a far more orderly manner, organizing his material according to clear and definite purposes. He is not, like Longinus, "a living library and a walking museum",[63] a quotation which could be applied to, e.g., Athenaeus and his fellow deipnosophists. In Eusebius' *Praeparatio*, the reflection of the library, that which I called 'the performance of erudition', serves purposes other than mapping, preserving and playing with Greek culture.

The overarching principle that rules the library of the *Praeparatio* is the Logos-Christ and the message of the Gospel. The whole collection of the *Praeparatio* aims both to defend the Christian faith and to prepare the new converts to more elevated teachings. The performance of erudition is now at the service of Logos. Following Origen and Pamphilus, Eusebius devoted his work as a librarian and author to the spread of the Gospel and the defense of the Christian faith.

---

[59] Jacob, "Athenaeus the Librarian," *cit.*, 85–111.

[60] For an assessment of his influence on Eusebius in the *PE*, see Inowlocki, *Eusebius and the Jewish Authors*, *cit.*, 139–141.

[61] Cf. A. van den Hoek, "Techniques of quotation in Clement of Alexandria: A view of ancient literary working methods," *VigChr* 50 (1996), 223–243.

[62] *Ibid.*

[63] βιβλιοθήκη τις ἦν ἔμψυχος καὶ περιπατοῦν μουσεῖον in Eunapius, *Lives of the sophists* IV.1.3.

Therefore, if the Alexandrian influence on Eusebius is undeniable, his *Praeparatio* as well as other works such as the *Historia* rather reflect the new Caesarean reinterpretation of the bibliological work initiated by Origen. As a library and a performance of erudition, the *Praeparatio* is an *interpretatio Christiana* or even *Caesariana* of the Alexandrian erudition, in which erudite games have been replaced by a strong, well-structured apologetic strategy.

PORTRAITS OF THE HEBREW SAINTS IN THE LIBRARY?

Finally, I wish to make a suggestion regarding the role of the lives of the ancient Hebrew saints as described in book VII of the *Praeparatio*. These saints are presented as εἰκόνες.[64] As A. Johnson has shown,[65] by using the metaphor of the icon in order to depict the lives of the ancient Hebrews, Eusebius goes beyond the traditional descriptive relation between writing and painting: "the metaphor of the written life as a painted image held a crucial role in Eusebius' legitimation of Christian identity as rooted in Hebrew holiness."[66] I would add that, in the context of the *Praeparatio* as library, this reference to the icons could be a subversive alternative to the pictures of great figures displayed in ancient pagan libraries.

It is well known that representations of the great men of the past decorated ancient libraries. In late antiquity, as R. Cribiore has recently summarized in her work on Libanius' school,[67] late antique schools (διδασκαλεία in Libanius) and libraries also displayed sculptures and images of great cultural figures of the past. Archaeologists have identified a group of fourth-century houses on the Areopagus in Athens as 'teaching classes'. They contain a large room preceded by a peristyle court and ending in an apse with niches for statues.[68] A similar house

---

[64] *Praep. ev.*, VII.7.4; 8.15; 8. 18.
[65] See A.P. Johnson, "Ancestors as Icons: the Lives of the Hebrew Saints in Eusebius' *Praeparatio evangelica*," *JECS* 44 (2004), 245–264. Eusebius also uses this imagery in other instances: *Vita Const.*, I.3; 40; III.3; *Dem. ev.*, V.4 226d; *Hist. eccl.*, VII.18; *Praep. ev.*, VII.10.12.
[66] Johnson, "Ancestors as Icons," *cit.*, 264.
[67] R. Cribiore, *The School of Libanius in Late Antique Antioch* (Princeton – Oxford: Princeton University Press, 2007), esp. 43–47.
[68] Cribiore sends back to A. Frantz, *Late Antiquity: AD 267–700* (The Athenian Agora 24; Princeton, NJ: American School of Classical Studies at Athens 1988), 37–48.

210   SABRINA INOWLOCKI

has been identified as that of Plutarch, the head of the Neoplatonic school at Athens.[69] These buildings are identified as places for teaching and lecturing and could have housed libraries. A similar house was also found at Aphrodisias in Caria and marble portraits representing Pindar, Alcibiades, Alexander, Socrates, Aristotle, Pythagoras, and Apollonius of Tyana were found.[70] In Apamea, in Syria, a comparable arrangement was excavated beneath a Church, and its floor displayed mosaics representing scenes from the Odyssey as well as Socrates surrounded by the seven sages.[71]

In the 5th or the 6th century, in the Capella Sancta Sanctorum in Rome, the remains of a room of the earliest Lateran library was found; on one wall is the famous fresco of (presumably) Augustine reading a codex, under which a legend reads: *diversi diversa patres s[ed hic] omnia dixit / Romano eloquio mystica sensa tonans* ("different fathers say different things, but this one said everything / making mystical meaning resound in the Roman language").[72]

In the same period, Pope Agapetus (535–536) built a library in Rome, at the instance of Cassiodorus. The latter wished to establish a Christian academy of sorts, comparable to those of Alexandria and Nisibis.[73] The library was built in Agapetus' residence on the Caelian hill and eventually became part of the monastery established by Gregory the Great in his family residence on the same hill. Its remains were found as well as an inscription reading: *Sanctorum veneranda cohors sedet ordine longo / Divinae legis mystica dicta docens / Hos inter residens Agapetus jure sacerdos / Codicibus pulchrum condidit arte locum* ("A venerable company of saints sits in a long line / teaching the mystical precepts of the divine law / the priest Agapetus is appropriately seated among them / he has built with art this beautiful

[69] *Ibid.*, 45.
[70] Cribiore sends back to R.R.R. Smith, "Late Roman Philosopher Portraits from Aphrodisias," *JRS* 80 (1990), 127–155.
[71] See J.C. Balty, "Mosaïques païennes à Apamée de Syrie," *CRAI* (1972), 103–127.
[72] See Gamble, *Books and Readers in the Early Church, cit.*, 303, n. 58 referring to P. Lauer, "Les fouilles du Sancta Sanctorum au Lateran," *MAH* 20 (1900), 251–287 (plates 9–10) and G. Wilpert, *Die römischen Mosaiken und Materien der Kirchlichen Bauten vom 4.-13. Jahrhundert* (Freiburg: Herder, 1976 (*ibid.*, 1916)), 151–152.
[73] *Inst.*, 1, praef.

place for books").[74] According to Gamble,[75] this inscription refers to a fresco that must have run along the wall above the bookcases: "here we glimpse a Christian appropriation of the classical practice of decorating library rooms with busts, paintings, or mosaics of the revered authors."[76] Interestingly, Marrou has conjectured that this library also contained pagan books and was a center for their collection and critical reconstitution.[77] This is reminiscent of Eusebius' own library (as well as the *Praeparatio*), which undeniably contained pagan works. Gamble identifies 'the venerable company of saints' as 'Christian writers'[78] but this is rather vague. Are we to think of theologians such as Augustine or to evangelists or other Christian authors? It is also possible that that these 'saints' refer to biblical prophets or even, as in Eusebius, to patriarchal figures. Indeed, they could be seen as teaching the 'mystical precepts of the divine law' since, for some fathers, they were proto-Christians who knew and obeyed the natural law before the Mosaic law was given to Moses, and some of them were also perceived as teachers: this is especially the case with Moses.[79] It is also likely that the fresco included both Old Testament, New Testament and later figures, which formed 'a long line'.

In the light of this material, it may be suggested that Eusebius established book VII—which lies exactly at the centre of the *Praeparatio*—as the apse of his library with the portraits of the founders and ancestors. The question whether such Christian libraries already existed in Eusebius' time or whether the library at Caesarea displayed such figures cannot be answered; but it is very likely that he knew about the representations found in pagan libraries. Thus Eusebius' gallery of saints could be read as the Hebrew-Christian counterpart of the portraits of the Graeco-Roman schools/libraries. His presentation of the Hebrew saints as a Christian fresco of sorts could be interpreted as a fairly radical cultural statement: the Christians have abandoned the icons of

---

[74] J.B. de Rossi, *Inscriptiones Christianae Urbis Romanae* (Romae: Befani, 1822–1894), II, 28 (55).

[75] Gamble, *Books and Readers in the Early Church*, cit., 164–165.

[76] *Ibid.*, 165.

[77] H.-I. Marrou, "Autour de la bibliothèque du pape Agapit," *MEFR* 48 (1931), 124–169.

[78] Gamble, *Books and Readers in the Early Church*, cit., 165.

[79] E.g., Eusebius, *Praep. ev.*, VII.7.1–4.

the Graeco-Roman literary culture to the profit of the Hebrew icons of virtue and piety.

Interestingly, in his *Naturalis historia* XXXV.2–6, dealing with the portraits of family members, Pliny claims that:

> There is a new invention too, which we must not omit to notice. Not only do we consecrate (*dicantur*) in our libraries, in gold or silver, or at all events, in bronze, those whose immortal spirits hold converse with us in those places, but we even go so far as to reproduce the ideal of features, all remembrance of which has ceased to exist; and our regrets give existence to likenesses that have not been transmitted to us, as in the case of Homer, for example. And indeed, it is my opinion, that nothing can be a greater proof of having achieved success in life, than a lasting desire on the part of one's fellow-men, to know what one's features were. This practice of grouping portraits (*dicando ingenia hominum*) was first introduced at Rome by Asinius Pollio, who was also the first to establish a public library, and so make the works of genius the property of the public. Whether the kings of Alexandria and of Pergamus, who had so energetically rivalled each other in forming libraries, had previously introduced this practice, I cannot so easily say. That a strong passion for portraits (*imaginum amorem*) formerly existed, is attested both by Atticus, the friend of Cicero, who wrote a work on this subject, and by M. Varro, who conceived the very liberal idea of inserting, by some means or other, in his numerous volumes, the portraits (*imaginibus*) of seven hundred individuals; as he could not bear the idea that all traces of their features should be lost, or that the lapse of centuries should get the better of mankind. Thus was he the inventor of a benefit to his fellow-men, that might have been envied by the gods themselves; for not only did he confer upon them immortality, but he transmitted them, too, to all parts of the earth; so that everywhere it might be possible for them to be present, and for each to occupy his niche. This service, too, Varro conferred upon persons who were no members of his own family.
> (Trans. John Bostock and H.T. Riley)

This text is crucial to my argument because it ties together the connection between, on the one hand, portraits and libraries, and, on the other, portraits and books. The connection made by Asinius Pollio (and Pliny) between portraits and libraries is based on the idea that both contribute to publicize the geniuses' works. The importance of portraits as being part of the bookish culture is further exemplified by the fact that, according to Pliny, Varro inserted *aliquo modo* seven hundred portraits in his works. These 'proto-illustrated books' had a clear function: to immortalize the 'portraitee'—a benefit which may be envied by the gods themselves! As is well known, this function is also that of the mention of patrons, emperors and other important figures in texts: by inscribing the name of the individual in a text, the author confers immortality on the named individual. Eusebius also emphasized that by transmitting the Hebrews' lives in his writings, Moses conferred on them an "eternal memory".[80] But more importantly, Pliny explains that the portraits embody the individuals they represent and enable them to be actually present wherever their representation circulates. Collecting books of the great geniuses and setting up their portraits are seen as the same attempt to publicize their work and genius. The same effort towards publicizing the virtues of the Hebrew friends of God can also read in Eusebius' description of Moses' endeavour: the latter wished the remarkable piety to be known. Yet in the *Praeparatio*, this effort has a pedagogical dimension.[81] Indeed the εἰκόνες are permanent role models and their portraits have a clear pedagogical purpose: they fix forever the features of the saints who are to be imitated by the new/potential converts. From this point of view, both his actual library (that of Caesarea) and his virtual library (the *Praeparatio*) are associated to both an actual school (the school of Caesarea)[82] and a virtual school (the *Praeparatio* as a pedagogical work).

To conclude, as all the other marks of erudition and bookish culture in the *Praeparatio,* the presence of this gallery of Hebrew icons is not a gratuitous reflection of Eusebius' cultural environment. It is part and parcel of his performance of erudition. I will now attempt to define the purposes of this strategy.

What's in a Library?

In the previous paragraph, I hope to have shown that Eusebius' references to the 'libraryish' context of Caesarea are numerous enough to argue that he deliberately constructed the *Praeparatio* as a reflection of the library defined both as a space for books and as a place of bookish practices and teaching. The question is: why did he choose this paradigm? How does it contribute to his apologetic project and how does it affect his status as a Christian author?

---

[80] *Praep. ev.*, VII.7.2.

[81] *Praep. ev.*, VII. 7. 2–3. See S. Morlet's and A. Johnson's contributions in this volume: both have pointed out the pedagogical nature of the *Praeparatio* and the *Demonstratio evangelica.*

[82] On the concept of 'school' for Caesarea and all the difficulties it raises, see L. Penland's contribution to this volume.

It must be pointed out from the outset that in Eusebius' eyes, the library emblematizes cultural prestige. For instance, in the *Historia ecclesiastica*, he stresses that Josephus' and Philo's works were judged worthy of being placed in libraries at Rome.[83] This was worth mentioning because for him, it was a sign of the acknowledgement of the excellence of these works beyond the Jewish and Christian worlds.

The most important library on a symbolic level was definitely the library—or rather, according to Eusebius, the libraries—of Alexandria. For most of Jewish and Christian authors of the Graeco-Roman period, the royal library of Alexandria was "the locus of the textual authority of the Old Testament translated into Greek."[84] Before quoting the *Letter of Aristeas* in the *Praeparatio*, Eusebius tells us that the translation of the seventy translators was judged worthy of being placed in the libraries of Alexandria (τῶν κατὰ τὴν Ἀλεξάνδρειαν βιβλιοθηκῶν ἠξιώθη),[85] an expression reminiscent of those used about Josephus' and Philo's writings. In Eusebius' eyes, that which libraries in Alexandria materialized was the possibility for the translation to spread among the nations:

> As God himself…arranged that the predictions concerning Him who was to appear before long as the Saviour of all mankind, and to establish Himself as the teacher of the religion of the One Supreme God to all the nations under the sun, should be revealed to them all, and be brought into the light by being accurately translated, and set up in public libraries (δημοσίαις βιβλιοθήκαις). So God put it into the mind of King Ptolemy to accomplish this, in preparation (εἰς προπαρασκευήν), as it seems, for that participation in them by all the nations which was so soon to take place…[86]

Thus in Eusebius' *Praeparatio*, the libraries of Alexandria, especially the public ones (δημόσιαι), are strongly associated not only with the translation of the Hebrew scriptures, but also with the spread of the prophecies in the gentile world, as well as with its preparation to

---

[83] *Hist. eccl.*, III.9.2–3 (see also *ibid.*, II.18 8).
[84] See P. Nelles, "Juste Lipse et Alexandrie: les origines antiquaires de l'histoire des bibliothèques," in M. Baratin et Chr. Jacob (eds.), *Le pouvoir des bibliothèques. La mémoire des livres en Occident* (Histoires; Paris: Albin Michel, 1996), 224–242, p. 234. Justus Lipsius is described as questioning this status of the library for the first time.
[85] *Praep. ev.*, VIII.1.8.
[86] *Praep. ev.*, VIII.1.6.

the Gospel.[87] This, I would surmise, is also the case with the library constructed by Eusebius, that is, the *Praeparatio*: Eusebius has chosen to construct his apologetic work as a library of sorts because, in his world, a library embodies a potential *locus* for the preparation of the nations and the diffusion of the message of the gospel.

The performance of erudition staged by Eusebius has other purposes too: the readers intended by the *Praeparatio*, whether new converts or Greeks not yet converted, were certainly highly educated people. By reproducing the gestures and bibliographical practices of the librarian, Eusebius projected a sophisticated image of Christianity, capable of attracting cultural elites interested in Christianity, or already converted. But there is more to it.

By appealing to a wide range of Greek writings, by presenting himself as the educated librarian who excerpted quotations from them, and by showing his command of the Alexandrian bibliographical methods, Eusebius exhibited his ability to master a large corpus of Greek literature. He showed not only the extent of his knowledge, but also that he mastered it to the detriment of Greek paganism.

Needless to say, the decision to represent the *Praeparatio* as a performance of erudition and as a library is not innocent in the context of the 'battle of books' raging between Jews, Greeks, and Christians in the first centuries CE.[88] There has always been a strong connection between library and power.[89] Ancient libraries—at least the ones that have struck the western imagination—are not only sources of knowledge, but they also generate power.

The activities connected to the library also constitute manifestations of power and control over texts. In the *Praeparatio*, the theatralization of these bookish practices are intended to give a sense of the power which Eusebius—and Christianity as a whole—had not only on the scriptures and ecclesiastical writings, but also on pagan literature.

---

[87] This is remindful of Pliny's passage cited above: libraries are public places. The idea of a library reserved to the research led by a small intellectual elite patronized by the king, as it was in the Mouseion, has been replaced by that of a place in which books can be publicized.

[88] On which, see, e.g., F. Young, *Biblical Exegesis and the Formation of a Christian Culture* (Cambridge: Cambridge University Press, 1997); G. Veltri, *Libraries, Translations, and 'Canonic' Texts, The Septuagint, Aquila and Ben Sira in the Jewish and Christian Traditions* (JSJ, Supplements 109; Leiden – Boston: Brill 2006).

[89] See, e.g., the beautiful volume of Baratin et Jacob (eds.), *Le pouvoir des bibliothèques, cit.* (n. 84).

This remark could also be applied to the *Historia*, and perhaps even
to Eusebius' whole corpus. His performance of erudition as well as the
play of reflection between his works and a library (that of Caesarea
in particular) betray Eusebius' intention to turn the Christians, and
perhaps the Caesarean school in particular, as the new "guardian of
letters,"[90] both Greek and Christian.

In the *Praeparatio*, by excerpting, organizing, archiving, presenting, and citing Greek texts on pagan religion, philosophy, and history,[91]
Eusebius succeeds in domesticating both this literature and its contents. By including them in his apologetic library, he forces them into
his Christian salvation history. The quotation process, far from being
the objective method which Eusebius pretends it is, is a formidable
weapon and a tool of control. The Greek texts cited are conveniently
appropriated by Eusebius, who turns the Christians into the owners
of some of the most important writings of Hellenism, while subjecting
others to Christian control.

LIBRARY AND PIETY

In addition, the work on books performed at Caesarea certainly
appeared to Eusebius as a form of piety. While in Alexandria, bookish work (copying, editing, correcting, etc.) was seen as a practice of
erudition centred on Greek culture and knowledge (albeit also under
the auspices of the Muses or certain gods), for Eusebius (as for Pamphilus and Origen), collecting and listing books could become a mark
of Christian devotion, at least as far as biblical and ecclesiastical writings were concerned.

A passage from the *Historia* is revealing in this regard: Eusebius says
he will not provide the catalogue of Origen's work because he has no
space and already did so in his *Life of Pamphilus*. According to him,
"There I offered as evidence of how zealous Pamphilus was for holy
things the catalogues of the library he [Pamphilus] assembled of the
works of Origen and other Christian writers."[92] Thus collecting Christian works, and presumably also copying/preserving/spreading them

---

[90] Cf. K. Haines-Eitzen, *Guardians of Letters. Literacy, Power, and the Transmitters
of Early Christian Literature* (Oxford: Oxford University Press, 2000).
[91] See my *Eusebius and the Jewish Authors*, cit., Chapters II, III, V.
[92] *Hist. eccl.*, VI.32.3.

was a form of Christian piety. This is rightly emphasized by Grafton-Williams who conclude from a reading of the *Martyrs of Palestine* that Eusebius establishes "what seems almost a natural transition from biblical study to martyrdom."[93]

Along the same line, the image of Pamphilus giving away copies of the scriptures not only to men, but also to women, is perceived by Jerome as demonstrations of Pamphilus' piety;[94] so is the fact that, according to Jerome, his humility was so deep that he did not write anything himself but was content to read and meditate on others' writings (which we know was not true since he wrote the *Apology for Origen*).[95] To sum up, Pamphilus was the librarian *par excellence*, being exclusively devoted to the works of others.

To a certain extent, Eusebius certainly attempted to imitate his master in copying excerpts rather than throwing freely his own thoughts on the paper. It is no coincidence that in the *Praeparatio*, he borrows the methodology which Pamphilus applied in the *Apology for Origen*. Just as in the *Apology for Origen* 19, Pamphilus claimed to restrict himself to quotations from Origen in order to avoid his opponents' suspicion, in the *Praeparatio*, Eusebius asserts that he chose to cite others in order not to seem complacent towards his own doctrine.[96]

But what about the 'Pagan' collection of books at Caesarea? Very little is known about this collection and most hints are provided by the citations in the *Praeparatio*. Eusebius, like later authors such as Jerome, does not lay emphasis on this sort of works. In this paper, I will not delve into this issue. Suffice it to say that Kalligas recently suggested that books XI–XIII of the *Praeparatio* betrays Eusebius' acquisition of Longinus' library.[97] Whether that is correct or not, I surmise that Eusebius had these works at his disposal because he

---

[93] A. Grafton and M. Williams, *Christianity and the Transformation of the Book: Origen, Eusebius, and the Library of Caesarea* (Cambridge, Mass.: The Belknap Press of Harvard University Press, 2006), 192–193 on *Mart. Pal.*, IV.6 (long version).

[94] Jerome, *Contra Rufinum*, 1.9.

[95] Cf. Plotinus' reluctance to write according to Porphyry's *Life of Plotinus*.

[96] *Praep. ev.*, I.6.8.

[97] P. Kalligas, "Traces of Longinus' Library in Eusebius' *Praeparatio Evangelica*," *CQ* New Series, 51.2 (2001), 584–598. For an alternative explanation, see R.M. Grant, "Porphyry among the Early Christians," in W. den Boer et al. (eds.), *Romanitas et Christianitas. Studia J.H. Waszink oblata*, (Amsterdam: North Holland Publishing Company, 1973), 171–188, who suggests that Anatolius may have brought these works to Caesarea. Cf. J. Rist, *Platonism and Ancient Heritage* (London: Variorum, 1985), 163–164.

provides citations too long to come from a collection, and also because we have no knowledge of a work from which he could have excerpted them. The fact that Eusebius' *Praeparatio* also includes works which are later than Longinus (Porphyry's *Letter to Anebon, De abstinentia, Contra Christianos*, as well as his edition of the *Enneads*)[98] indicates that he did not rely only on one collection but may have acquired books himself. Anyhow, the sort of work required by the preservation and acquisition of such a literature was obviously not seen by Eusebius as a practice of piety, in the way work on Christian writings was. Yet his dedication to defend and promote Christianity in the *Praeparatio*, be it through citing pagan texts, certainly contributed to the construction of his self-perception and his self-presentation as a distinctively Christian author: assembling the *Praeparatio* was an act of piety who allowed him to situate himself amongst 'the defenders of the faith', i.e. the apologists he mentions in the *Historia* IV, and "those who in each generation proclaimed the Word of God by speech or pen."[99]

Indeed, although Eusebius tells us very little about his work with Greek books, in his different writings, he clearly stresses the Greek culture of many Christian authors. In the *Praeparatio*, citing Julius Africanus, Tatian and Clement, he announces their testimonies as those of 'erudite men' (λόγιοι ἄνδρες), 'in no way inferior to educated people' (καὶ τῶν ἀπὸ παιδείας οὐδενὸς δεύτεροι).[100] He also considers Origen one of 'the greatest' (τοῖς κρείττοσι),[101] ascribing his fame to his 'zeal towards the knowledge [of the Pagans]' (πρὸς τὰ τῶνδε μαθήματα φιλοτιμίαν).[102] In the *Historia*, he stresses that Dorotheos, a priest from Antioch, mastered both Hebrew and the liberal arts as well as Greek elementary education;[103] Anatolius is praised for his learning and knowledge on secular studies;[104] Stephen,[105] Pamphilus,[106] Pierius and Melitius[107] are other examples; Heraclas, his teaching assistant

---

[98] As R. Goulet has pointed out ("La conservation et la transmission des textes philosophiques grecs", in C. D'Ancona, *The Libraries of the Neoplatonists*, (PhAnt 107; Leiden – Boston: Brill, 2007), 29–62, p. 41).
[99] *Hist. eccl.*, I.1.
[100] *Praep. ev.*, X.9.26.
[101] *Praep. ev.*, VI.10.50.
[102] *Ibid.*
[103] *Hist. eccl.*, VII.32.2-4.
[104] *Hist. eccl.*, VII.32.6.
[105] *Hist. eccl.*, VII.32.22.
[106] Cf. *Mart. Pal.*, VII.4–5; XI.1; IV.5–6; V.2.
[107] *Hist. eccl.*, VII.32.25–28.

is described as 'a man of theological fervour skilled also in secular philosophy.'[108]

Therefore, the double culture of his fellow Christians seems to have been a mark of distinction in his eyes. Greek culture was important to Eusebius and the fact that the *Praeparatio* is mainly made of Greek pagan texts is important: Eusebius was showing not only that the Christians mastered a great deal of literature, but also—and this is often overlooked—that Eusebius himself was as knowledgeable as his predecessors in terms of Greek *paideia*. Indeed, even though in the *Praeparatio* Eusebius remains an elusive figure as an author, the accumulation of books and quotations somehow affected his own status both as an author and as a Christian. Thanks to the abundance of Greek quotations of the *Praeparatio*, Eusebius (re)presented himself as a bi-cultural Christian, well versed both in Greek *paideia* (in the *Praeparatio*) and in the knowledge of the scriptures (in the *Demonstratio*). To some extent, one may even wonder if his presentation of Christian predecessors as knowledgeable in Greek matters is not also meant to justify his own appreciation and use (and preservation?) of Greek literature.

Library and Memory

It has often been noted that Eusebius' intention in the *Praeparatio* was not to preserve the texts from which they excerpted citations. Yet Eusebius' works turned out to be goldmines for texts no longer extant. This phenomenon certainly played a role in the preservation of the *Praeparatio* itself: as Edward Gibbon noted, the works that were most preserved were the ones in which previous knowledge was collected.[109]

---

[108] *Hist. eccl.*, VI.15.

[109] E. Gibbon, *Decline and Fall of the Roman Empire* (London – New York: Penguin Press, 1994 (1776–1788)), t. II, chapter LI; cf. L. Canfora, "Les bibliothèques anciennes et l'histoire des textes," in Baratin et Jacob (eds.), *Le pouvoir des bibliothèques, cit.*, 261–272: L. Canfora pointed out that "l'exemple le plus évident est celui de Pline (*Histoire naturelle*), dont le premier livre est entièrement consacré, outre les sommaires de chaque ouvrage, à l'énumération de tous les auteurs (latins et étrangers) repris dans chacun des livres" (p. 265). It is certainly also the case of Diodorus Siculus' *Library* and some doxographical works (e.g., Pseudo-Plutarch), which also served as goldmines for Eusebius. Comparing the fate of Diodorus' work (a universal history of which approximately half is extant) and Theopompos' *Historiae Philippicae* (which dealt with Philip II and is no longer extant), Canfora notes that the "disparité [between the fate of these two works] s'explique probablement par le fait que la

Even though Eusebius is not likely to have been aware of this, it is significant that the format of the 'library' chosen for some of his works made it through the centuries. In other words, Eusebius proved to be acutely perceptive by choosing the genre of the *Praeparatio* in order to establish and empower a new Christian culture.

Yet the case of the *Historia* differs slightly from that of the *Praeparatio*. As we have seen, in this work, Eusebius claims to be "content if we *preserve the memory* of the successions of the apostles of our Saviour; if not indeed of all, yet of the most renowned of them in those churches which are the most noted, and which even to the present time are held in honor."[110] Thus memory is explicitly said to be part of Eusebius' concern, which is not the case in the *Praeparatio*. This may explain why the *pinakes* appear in the *Historia* and not in the *Praeparatio*: the library-like character of the *Historia*, which the presence of Christian bibliography considerably enhances, is related to Eusebius' historical and 'mnemonical' project. Library and memory are deeply interwoven in the *Historia*.

The fact that there is undeniably a play of reflection between this work and a library, must lead us to go back to the question of Eusebius' work as a project of book preservation. Since Caesarea seems to have been a centre of preservation, copy, and transmission for Christian writings,[111] a project to which Eusebius actively participated, it must be asked how this relates to his endeavour in the *Historia*. I would suggest that—to some extent—Eusebius deliberately attempted to turn his *Historia* into a depository for Christian writings, a library of sorts, aiming to preserve Christian works and names. He was definitely successful since, without him, numerous Christian writers would not even be known. Obviously, his whole endeavour must be understood in its apologetic and polemic framework: only those whom he thought were worth mentioning made it in his works. Therefore, Eusebius is definitely one of the most important Christian actors among those who prepared the ground for the Christian history of the victors.

Bibliothèque 'universelle' de Diodore donnait en 40 livres toute l'histoire gréco-romaine, du début jusqu'à l'époque d'Auguste, tandis que la matière traitée par Théompompe était incontestablement plus exigüe" (p. 269).

[110] *Praep. ev.*, I.1.5. My italics.

[111] The most famous examples are the case of Origen's and Philo's writings as well as, needless to say, scriptures. See, e.g., Runia, *Philo in Early Christian Literature* (Assen: Van Gorcum, 1993; Minneapolis: Fortress Press, 1993) and Grafton – Williams, *Christianity and the Transformation of the Book, cit.*

In the *Praeparatio*, as we have seen, Eusebius does not provide *pinakes*, and it would be hard to defend the thesis that he attempted to preserve pagan works. In the representation of the *Praeparatio* as a library, a rationale, different to that of the *Historia*, is at play. The absence of *pinakes* in the *Praeparatio* confirms that the use of texts in these two works is radically different.[112]

In the *Praeparatio*, Greek literature is appropriated and becomes part of Christian culture only as far as it supports Eusebius' apologetic purposes. While the *Historia* aims to construct and preserve Christian cultural memory by storing Christian texts in a single work, the collection of Greek texts of the *Praeparatio* aims to appropriate some Greek literature in order to subordinate it to the Christian cause and to situate the Greek culture in the Christian context. Eusebius' inclusion of numerous lengthy citations of Greek authors in the apologetic framework of the *Praeparatio* may be read as a means to regulate the Christian use of this literature. Greek literature may be read, but preferably in the *Praeparatio*…

For example, the citations of Plato in books XI–XIII are meant to demonstrate the agreement between scriptures and the best representative of Greek philosophy.[113] In this apologetic context, the comprehensive dossier of citations offered by Eusebius must be sufficient for the Christian reader, whose interest in Plato should be restricted to the *loci* agreeing with the Bible. Book XIII, which is devoted to the contradictions between the two, clearly demonstrates that the Hebrew scriptures are superior to the Greek philosopher's writings.

In order to explain the numerous similarities between Plato and the Hebrew scriptures, Eusebius does not only resort to the dependency theme,[114] he also fruitfully exploits the paradigm of the translation: on several instances, Plato is described as translating, as it were, the scriptures into Greek.[115] Yet this does not confer on his writings a

---

[112] It is worth noting that later historians of the Church did not follow Eusebius' practice: Jerome, for example, kept bibliographical items separated in his *De uiris inlustribus*. Interestingly, in his *Life of Plotinus*, Porphyry also presents the bibliographical list of his master's works. But this list was conceived as an introduction to his edition of the Enneads, which explains the presence of the bibliography.

[113] On the question of Eusebius' purpose in *Praep. ev.*, XI–XIII, see Johnson, *Ethnicity and Argumentation*, *cit.*, 126–152 and my response in my review of his work: (http://ccat.sas.upenn.edu/bmcr/2007/2007-07-03.html).

[114] On which see D. Ridings, *The Attic Moses: the Dependency Theme in Some Early Christian Writers* (SGLG 59; Göteborg: Acta Universitatis Gothoburgensis, 1995).

[115] *Praep. ev.*, XI.9.6; XI.26.8; XII.13.1; XII.21.6; XIII.Prol.

status comparable to the Septuagint: on the contrary, it emphasizes their subordination to the original source of wisdom: the scriptures. But there is more to it: their subordination to the Christian scriptures as well as the material space given to them in the *Praeparatio* enabled Eusebius to turn the Christians into the legitimate owners of the Platonic writings.

Diodorus Siculus, who himself authored a 'library', is also appropriated by Eusebius,[116] especially the parts of the *Bibliothèkè* which deal with euhemerism.[117] While Plato is obviously explicitly used by Clement and Origen, Diodorus is never mentioned by them. Eusebius, following Tertullian, Minucius Felix, and Lactantius, is the first Greek speaking Christian who explicitly used Diodorus. Although he emphasizes his widespread reputation as an erudite (*philologos*) among the Greeks,[118] by including the library in his own library, he makes Diodorus' work part and parcel of the Christian culture. This participation to Christian culture is not only a concept, but it is also practically and empirically implemented in the *Praeparatio* conceived as a material object: the fact that Diodorus' text in book II is inserted into the *Praeparatio* between Eusebius' introduction and a citation of Clement of Alexandria's *Protrepticus* (II.3.1–42) turns Diodorus into a witness of the truth of Christianity. Thanks to Eusebius, the *Bibliothèkè* is now part of the works preparing new Christian converts for the scriptures.

CONCLUDING REMARKS

"Manuscrits ou imprimés, (et maintenant électroniques), les livres, dans leur matérialité même, commandent la possible appropriation des discours. Ceux-ci sont toujours des réalités physiques, inscrits sur les pages d'un livre, transmis par une voix, donnés à entendre sur une scène. Il n'est donc pas 'd'ordre du discours' (pour reprendre

---

[116] P.F. Beatrice, "Diodore de Sicile chez les apologistes," in B. Pouderon et J. Doré (eds.), *Les apologistes chrétiens et la culture grecque* (Paris: Beauchesne, 1998), 219–235; G. Bounoure, "Eusèbe citateur de Diodore," *REG* 95 (1982), 433–439; G. Zecchini, "La conoscenza di Diodoro nel Tardoantico," *Aevum* 61 (1987), 43–52.

[117] *Praep. ev.*, II.2.52–62.

[118] *Praep. ev.*, II. prol. 6. From Domitian onwards, Diodorus seems to have been successful, in particular among Christian authors: Beatrice, "Diodore de Sicile chez les apologistes,", *cit.*, 219–221. See Pliny, *Nat. Hist.*, praef. XXV; Athenaeus, *Deipn.* XII.59.

l'expression de Foucault) qui puisse être dissocié de l'ordre des livres qui lui est contemporain."[119]

This citation, excerpted from Roger Chartier's acclaimed book *Culture écrite et société*, seems to be of special relevance to the study of Eusebius' works. As A. Grafton and M. Williams have recently shown,[120] Eusebius seems to have been especially aware of the crucial nexus between the practicalities of book production and the production of discourse pointed to by Chartier. It is especially in his *Chronicle* that he managed to draw the best from the possibilities offered by the codex to visibly show the victory of Christianity over Judaism and paganism.

However, the *Praeparatio evangelica* also attests to the inseparability of the material aspect of the book and the discourse it comprises. Eusebius' presentation of the *Praeparatio* as a performance of erudition and a library, on the one hand, and his apologetic discourse on the other, are deeply interrelated. By building this work as an accumulation of citations and by associating pagan, Jewish and Christian authors in the same material ensemble, Eusebius produces a specific picture of the Christian culture that ultimately aims to prove its superiority and triumph over the other alternatives. Both as a library and a performance of erudition; the *Praeparatio* can be read as a metaphor of Eusebius' control on Greek culture. The library and the practices attached to it are definitely practices of control.

Regarding his methodology, as I have pointed out, it is inherited from Alexandrian scholarship revisited by Origen and Pamphilus in Caesarea. In a way, the point Eusebius seems to make through his writing practice, his scholarly work, and his construction of the key figures of Caesarea is perhaps that just as the new covenant replaced the old one, and a Christian empire was replacing a pagan empire, Caesarea replaced Alexandria. With Eusebius, the rhetoric of supersession found its place in a new Christian cultural history.

---

[119] R. Chartier, *Culture écrite et société. L'ordre des livres (XIVe–XVIIIe siècle)* (Histoires; Paris: Albin Michel, 1996), 15.

[120] Grafton – Williams, *Christianity and the Transformation of the Book, cit.*

ALEXANDER POLYHISTOR'S *PERI IOUDAIŌN* AND LITERARY CULTURE IN REPUBLICAN ROME

William Adler

The scattered remains of the literary corpus of Lucius Cornelius Alexander Polyhistor (hereafter, Polyhistor) remind us of the risks associated with the study of documents from antiquity. Countless in number according to the Suda,[1] Polyhistor's writings stretched from works on philosophy, philology, poetry, and rhetoric to expositions on peoples and places of the known world. But while ancient authors recognized in Polyhistor a scholar of vast learning, not a single one of his treatises survives intact. For most of them, we have little more than a handful of notices, mainly topographical in character.[2]

Thanks mainly to Eusebius' *Praeparatio Evangelica*, we know more about Polyhistor's treatise on the Jews than any of his other collections. For that reason, modern judgments about Polyhistor's methods as a historian and ethnographer are largely extrapolations from that work. Eusebius' excerpts, amassed from an assortment of Jewish, Samaritan, and Greek authors, span the history of the Jews from Abraham down to the fall of Jerusalem to the Babylonians. We are in Polyhistor's debt for having preserved authors who might otherwise have perished for good.[3] But what survives of them is at least two steps removed from the original. To his credit, Polyhistor avoided doctoring his sources for partisan reasons. And Eusebius for his part conscientiously identified his citations from Polyhistor with his customary formulae: e.g. "this is what Alexander Polyhistor says verbatim." But Eusebius had a narrowly defined objective in assembling his material for the ninth

---

[1] Suda, s.v. <Ἀλέξανδρος ὁ Μιλήσιος>: οὗτος συνέγραψε βίβλους ἀριθμοῦ κρείττους, ed. A. Adler (Leipzig: Teubner, 1928–1935).

[2] For testimonia and fragments of Alexander Polyhistor's writings, see F. Jacoby, *Die Fragmente der Griechischen Historiker* (hereafter, *FGH*), IIIa (Leiden: Brill, 1993), n° 273, pp. 96–126 (T 1–8; F 1–145).

[3] For edition and translation of the fragments of the Hellenistic Jewish authors preserved by Polyhistor, see C.R. Holladay, *Fragments from Hellenistic Jewish Authors*, I. Historians (SBLTT 20; Chico, CA: Society of Biblical Literature, 1983) (hereafter, *Fragments 1*); Id., *Fragments from Hellenistic Jewish Authors*, Vol. II: Poets (SBLTT 30; Atlanta: Scholars Press, 1989) (hereafter, *Fragments 2*).

book of the *Praeparatio*: namely, to demonstrate that Greek authors attested the antiquity, traditions, and accomplishments of the Jews.[4] Source material from Polyhistor's collection not amenable to this end would presumably have been omitted. And Eusebius could be a slippery, even deceptive, excerptor, especially in a work as tendentious as the *Praeparatio*. When he tells his readers: "After some other passages, Alexander Polyhistor says," we can only speculate as to what might have been excised along the way.

ALEXANDER POLYHISTOR: HISTORIAN OR COMPILER?

When Eusebius introduces Polyhistor as a "man of great intellect and much learning" (πολύνους ὢν καὶ πολυμαθὴς), he could make that claim without much fear of contradiction.[5] In recognition of his knowledge of the past, writes Suetonius, many people conferred upon him the title 'Polyhistor'; but there were some who called him simply 'History' (*quidam Historiam vocabant*).[6] In learned Roman circles, Polyhistor was more than a historian; he personified the very discipline.

Modern critics continue to praise Polyhistor for his impartiality, industry, and his advocacy of otherwise marginal writers of the Greek-speaking Near East. But the overall verdict on him is rather more mixed. 'Antiquarian' and 'compiler' are the usually preferred epithets today.[7] Polyhistor's reputation, it seems, never fully recovered from

---

[4] Eusebius, *Praep. ev.*, 9.1.1, ed. K. Mras (GCS 43; Berlin, 1956).

[5] Eusebius, *Praep. ev.*, 9.17.1.

[6] Suetonius, *De grammaticis et rhetoribus*, 20.1, ed. and trans. R.A. Kaster (Oxford: Clarendon Press, 1995).

[7] For a sampling of negative assessments, see, for example E. Renan's judgment of Polyhistor's *Peri Ioudaiōn* (*History of the People of Israel* (Boston: Roberts Brothers, 1896), 4.213): "a mere uncritical collection of extracts. Alexander had not a fortunate hand; he stumbled on the weak literature we have described; it is through him [...] that they were saved from the oblivion they well deserved"; see further F. Susemihl, *Geschichte der griechischen Litteratur* (Leipzig: Teubner: 1892), 2.358–359: "as uncritical as he is industrious, ... a mere compiler and collector of excerpts and notices lacking taste and judgment, without any attempt at an artistic arrangement of his texts, and without independence, indeed almost devoid of his own opinions"; J.E. Sandys, *A History of Classical Scholarship* (2nd ed. Cambridge: Cambridge University Press, 1906), 161: "remarkable for their quantity rather than quality"; F.W. Walbank, "Alexander (11) Polyhistor," *OCD* (Oxford: Clarendon Press, 1970), 35: "industrious and honest, he lacked taste and originality"; M. Hengel *Judaism and Hellenism* (Philadelphia: Fortress Press, 1974), 1.70: "collector of curiosities"; *Id.*, "The Interpenetration of Judaism and Hellenism in the pre-Maccabean Period," in W. Horbury, W. Davies and W. Sturdy (eds.), *The Cambridge History of Judaism* (Cambridge: Cambridge Uni-

the battering it sustained from German philology of the early decades of the last century. The undifferentiated miscellany of source material and subject matter that made up the content of his ethnographic treatises, wrote Eduard Schwartz, qualified as history only in the archaic sense of the Greek word 'historia,' that is a collection of unrefined data. But if Polyhistor's collections lacked "even a shred of critical sense," it was only because his Roman readers expected nothing more of him.[8] In his still unsurpassed study of Polyhistor's collection on the Jews, Jacob Freudenthal wrote him off as a hack, albeit an industrious one.[9] Freudenthal gave Polyhistor credit for having rescued little-known material from the darkest recesses of libraries and archives; but this hardly compensated for his deficiencies as an original or analytical thinker.

Above all, Polyhistor lacked the one non-negotiable requirement of history: critical judgment. For the most part, Polyhistor was satisfied to let his authorities have the final word, even when they contradicted one another. From Eupolemus and Cleodemus, Polyhistor knew that Moses had given written laws to the Jews.[10] How, then, Freudenthal asked, could he have allowed to go unchallenged another report ascribing the Jewish law to a woman named Moso?[11] For Freudenthal, Polyhistor exemplified the intellectual ossification of his day, an age in which antiquarians, encyclopedists, and collectors would soon eclipse historians, artists, and original thinkers.[12] In Polyhistor, the quest for universal knowledge that was the hallmark of Alexandrian scholarship had devolved into the accumulation of useless and superficial knowledge. What we have in Polyhistor, wrote Freudenthal, was uncontrolled pedantry, a jumble of history and myth, marvellous tales, and absurd

---

versity Press, 1984), 3.199: "magpie-like Roman collector"; J. Dillery, "Quintus Fabius Pictor," in J. Miller et al. (eds.), *Vertis in usum: Studies in honor of Edward Courtney* (Munich: Saur, 2002), 17: "eccentric."

   [8] E. Schwartz, *s.v.* "Alexandros Polyhistor," *RE*, I, 1452, reprinted in *Id., Griechische Geschichtschreiber* (Leipzig: Koehler and Amelang, 1959), 244.

   [9] J. Freudenthal, *Alexander Polyhistor und die von ihm erhaltenen Reste jüdischer und samaritanischer Geschichtswerke* (Hellenistische Studien 1; Breslau 1874), 21–23.

   [10] Cleodemus Malchus, Frg. 1.b (Holladay, *Fragments* 1, 254.10–12) = Eusebius, *Praep. ev.*, 9.20.3; Eupolemus, Frg 1.b (Holladay, *Fragments* 1, 112.13–14) = Eusebius, *Praep. ev.*, 9.26.1.

   [11] Suda, *s.v.* <Μωσω> γυνὴ Ἑβραία, ἧς ἐστι σύγγραμμα ὁ παρ' Ἑβραίοις νόμος· ὥς φησιν Ἀλέξανδρος ὁ Μιλήσιος, ὁ Πολυΐστωρ (= *FGH* 273 F 70). Cf. Freudenthal, *Alexander Polyhistor, cit.*, 30: "Alexander took up this genealogical frivolity, as well as the stories of Moso and untold other fictions, as an uncritical trafficker in notices."

   [12] Freudenthal, *ibid.*, 22.

etymologies. Polyhistor was a scavenger and drudge, a gofer for more accomplished artisans. Whatever useful stones he had found for them to build with lay buried beneath a pile of unsifted rubbish.[13]

Freudenthal's scorn was not entirely earned. Ancient descriptions of Polyhistor's historical and ethnographic treatises as συντάξεις or συναγωγαί mask a much greater complexity than is implied by the words 'compilation' or 'collection.'[14] In the *Peri Ioudaiōn*, Polyhistor's compilation and arrangement of texts were not a purely mechanical process. The ordering of his sources as it is preserved by Eusebius is not according to author, but rather according to chronological sequence.[15] To achieve this goal, Polyhistor had to do his own paste and scissors work. Artapanus, for example, is dissected into three parts, one part for Abraham, another for Joseph, and one more for Moses. Doing all of this would have required some editorial discretion, prior familiarity with the narrative history of the Jews, and an ability to contour his sources accordingly. Nor was Polyhistor purely an uncritical compiler of everything and anything. Polyhistor understood the intellectual appetites of his age. For universal historians and ethnographers of the Hellenistic age, regional topography, narratives of origins, and the genealogies of cultures and peoples of the world were matters of on-going interest. For his work on the Jews, Polyhistor chose his material accordingly. Timochares, Philo the poet, and an anonymous work on Syria surveyed the topography of Jerusalem. Eupolemus and Artapanus treated the contributions of Abraham, Joseph, and Moses to astronomy, writing, and other vital ingredients of world civilization. In his introduction to Theodotus, the one detail from his epic poem to which Polyhistor calls his readers' attention is the story of the founding of Shechem by Sikimius, "son of Hermes."[16] In the text of Cleodemus Malchus, Polyhistor found a genealogy deriving the names of Assyria and Africa from two of the sons of Abraham and Keturah, and

---

[13] Freudenthal, *ibid.*, 22.

[14] For descriptions of Polyhistor's treatises as συναγωγαί, see *FGH* 273 F 77 (his treatise on Phrygia), F 82 (his treatise on marvels). Eusebius calls his work on the Jews a 'syntaxis' (*Praep. ev.*, 9.17.1).

[15] Because Eusebius retained the words that Polyhistor used to string the fragments together, this arrangement must have come from Polyhistor himself, and not the hand of a later editor. See E. Schürer, *A History of the Jewish People in the Time of Jesus Christ*, S. Taylor and P. Christie (Edinburgh: T&T Clark, 1890), 2.3, 198. Independent attestation of this ordering in the *Stromata* of Clement of Alexandria (1.23.154–155) is further evidence for the originality of this ordering.

[16] In Eusebius, *Praep. ev.*, 9.22.1 (= Holladay, *Fragments* 2, 107.1–5, frg.1).

even connecting Heracles with the line of Abraham through marriage.[17] More contemporary history, on the other hand, was overshadowed by Polyhistor's attention to foundation myths, genealogies of nations, and culture heroes of the remote past.[18]

One feature of Polyhistor's treatises that often gets lost behind the description of them as 'collections' is his attentiveness to literary genre. Three of the Hellenistic Jewish authors whom Polyhistor cites in his treatise on the Jews were poets. Two of their works, *On Jerusalem* by Philo the epic poet, and Theodotus' *On the Jews*, were written in hexameter verse. The third author, Ezekiel the 'poet of tragedies,' wrote his *Exagoge* in iambic trimeters. The existence of works on biblical history composed according to the conventions of Greek verse is a striking illustration of the depth of Jewish Hellenism. But there is another less explored dimension to this question, and that is the way in which Polyhistor cites them. Both here and in his other treatises, Polyhistor's customary mode of citation was *oratio obliqua*.[19] But for his poets, Polyhistor observed a different practice. He quotes all three in direct speech, occasionally glossing his citations with his own summaries and explanations. Why did Polyhistor make this exception for poetry? More broadly, why did he cite poets in what is purportedly a work of ethnography?

Polyhistor, the *grammaticus*, was himself a student of poetry. Both Greek and Roman authors later consulted him for explications of Greek and Latin poets.[20] In teaching poetry and meter, standard parts of their curriculum, *grammatici* often liked to use recherché names as specimens for study. Polyhistor was no different. His taste for less familiar poets is evidenced by his commentary on the lyric poetry (written in the Boeotian dialect) of the poet Corinna (sixth (?) century BCE); he also is credited with a commentary on Alcman's choral lyric poetry, written in the Doric dialect (seventh century BCE).[21]

---

[17] Stephanus Byz. (= *FGH* 273 F 121): Ἀλέξανδρος ὁ Πολυΐστωρ ἀπὸ τῶν παίδων Σεμιράμιδος Ἰούδα καὶ Ἰδουμαία, ὡς δὲ Κλαύδιος Ἰόλαος ἀπὸ Ἰουδαίου Σπάρτωνος ἐκ Θήβης μετὰ Διονύσου ἐστρατευκότος.

[18] See further below p. 237.

[19] For *oratio obliqua* in Polyhistor's other writings, see *FGH* 273 F 14, 29, 46, 60, 68.

[20] See *infra* p. 239.

[21] For Polyhistor's commentaries on Alcman and Corinna, see *FGH* 273 F 95–97. For the study of Corinna and Alcman by Greek grammarians in Rome, see C. McNelis, "Greek Grammarians and Roman Society during the Early Empire," *ClA* 21 (2002), 80, 82, 84–86.

Polyhistor's Jewish poets, hardly familiar names to Roman readers of the first century BCE, would have satisfied the same requirements. While modern critics have widely different assessments of their literary and stylistic merits, all three had a sound grasp of Greek meter.[22] Polyhistor's decision to quote their works in direct speech (and his insertion of explanatory glosses) thus suggest that he intended his work on the Jews to be more than an ethnographic treatise. There were aesthetic and pedagogical considerations as well.

Polyhistor and Hellenistic Book Culture

The same quality that has won for Polyhistor our lasting gratitude is also the one thing that bothered Polyhistor's detractors most about him: namely, his seemingly slavish attachment to written documents. All this bookishness was after all a marked departure from the established norms of Greek historiography. A scarcity of reliably preserved archival documents had taught previous generations of Greek historians to distrust them. Oral eyewitness testimony and autopsy were always preferable. Aesthetic reasons alone precluded the transcription of long excerpts from older authorities. But Greek authors of the Hellenistic age did not share the same misgivings about documents. Many of the defining genres of Hellenistic culture—universal chronicles and histories, anthologies, compilations, and other forms of antiquarian and encyclopedic learning—owe their existence to the improved availability and credibility of written sources made possible by the requirements of Hellenistic bureaucracies for accurate records and with them the foundation of libraries and city archives.

To this extent, Polyhistor was a creature of his age. To be sure, Polyhistor's treatises did not rely exclusively on written documents. Photius' description of a paradoxography of Polyhistor, entitled Θαυμασίων

---

[22] Of the three, Philo's *On Jerusalem* has been judged most harshly for its bombast and obscurity. For analysis of the style and literary character of these poets, see, among other studies, R.G. Robertson, "Ezekiel the Tragedian," in J.H. Charlesworth (ed.), *The Old Testament Pseudepigrapha* (New York: Doubleday, 1985), 2.803–807; H. Attridge, "Philo the Epic Poet," *ibid.*, 2.781–782; "Theodotus," *ibid.*, 2.785–789; Holladay, *Fragments* 2, 72–73 (Theodotus); 207–208 (Philo epicus); 313–316 (Ezekiel); G. Nickelsburg, "The Bible Rewritten and Expanded," in M. Stone (ed.), *Jewish Writings of the Second Period* (CRINT 2; Assen: Van Gorcum, 1984), 118–130; J. Strugnell, "Notes on the Text and Metre of Ezekiel the Tragedian's 'Exagoge,'" *HThR* 60 (1967), 453.

συναγωγή, reveals that it was more than a collection of excerpts compiled from earlier authorities. Photius, who praises the "charm" and "clarity" of the work, states that the sixth book of this treatise wove together reports from older written authorities with eye-witness testimony (πολλὰ δὲ καὶ εἰς αὐτοψίαν ἕλκει).[23] But in a treatise on marvels, readers would have expected at least some eyewitness testimony. In general, Polyhistor seems more comfortable citing documents. We are dealing here with a confirmed bibliophile. In his *Succession of the Philosophers*, he recalls having found the written memoirs of the Pythagoreans.[24] The same reverence for documents defines his treatises about the various peoples and places of the world. Polyhistor, said by the Suda to be a native of the city of Miletus,[25] presumably knew Asia Minor well. If Freudenthal is correct, he also visited Egypt. Even so, he betrays no personal knowledge of these places.[26] The same is true of his treatise on the Jews. We have no indication that Polyhistor ever spoke to an oral informant, or gathered information from unnamed authorities or oral traditions. Everything he knows about the subject originated in documents, with named authors.

The few occasions on which Polyhistor renders a judgment on the accuracy of his authorities reveal the same mindset. The one virtue that seems to matter most to him is their adherence to what he calls "sacred books." That standard of truth again reminds us of the increasing reverence towards documents introduced by Greek interactions with the cultures of Egypt, Persia, and the Near East.[27] Going back to the time of Hecateus and Herodotus, native spokesmen for these civilizations made a point of contrasting the accuracy of their temple records with the slipshod records of the Greeks. For Eastern historians of the Hellenistic age, this was their trump card. In the prologue to *Against Apion*, Josephus hammered the point home ceaselessly. Because Greek historians had to depend on unsubstantiated oral

---

[23] Photius, *Biblioth.*, 188.145b, ed. R. Henry (CUF; Paris: Les Belles Lettres, 1959–1977) (= *FGH* 273 T 4).

[24] In Diogenes Laertius, *Lives of the Philosophers*, 8.24.8; 8.36. For fragments, see *FGH* 273 F 85–93.

[25] Suda, *s.v.* (= *FGH* 273 T 1).

[26] See Freudenthal, *Alexander Polyhistor, cit.*, 21.

[27] On Eastern influences on the use of archival documents by Greek historians, see A. Momigliano, "Eastern Elements in Post-Exilic Jewish, and Greek, Historiography," in *Id., Essays in Ancient and Modern Historiography* (Oxford: Blackwell, 1977), 32–33.

tradition with no sure documentary foundation, their Eastern counterparts, with access to carefully preserved written records extending
thousands of years, were far superior. To be successful, all the latter
had to do was to represent their native records accurately.[28] Polyhistor was apparently sympathetic to the argument. Philo the epic poet,
he writes, "bears witness to the sacred books" (μαρτυρεῖ ταῖς ἱεραῖς
βίβλοις).[29] What Demetrius the chronographer records about Moses'
slaying of the Egyptian man is "in agreement with the writer of the
sacred book" (ὁμοίως τῷ τὴν ἱερὰν βίβλον γράψαντι).[30] He brings the
same standard to his other authorities on the peoples of the East. His
introduction to his excerpts from Berossus' *Babyloniaca* commends
the work as a careful transcription of temple records preserved "with
great care" (μετὰ πολλῆς ἐπιμελείας) and extending over hundreds of
thousands of years.[31] Books beget books beget books.

POLYHISTOR, THE NEUTRAL OBSERVER

One thing for which Polyhistor has earned almost universal approbation was as an honest broker. It is hard to know where to lay the
blame for the numerous errors in transcription that disfigure the text
of his work on the Jews: with Polyhistor, Eusebius, or some unknown
copyist. But there is no trace of an ulterior or underhanded motive
underlying any of them.[32] The same neutrality governs his choice of
authorities. If Polyhistor privately entertained his own opinions on
the subject of Judaism and the Jews, they are hardly transparent either
from his own sparse comments or from his choice of source material.
While the inclusion of so many favorable witnesses may reveal something about his own stance, Polyhistor was hardly one-sided in his
selection. Alongside Artapanus' effusions about Moses, he reproduces
without comment a passage from Apollonius Molon's tract *Against the*

---

[28] Josephus, *Ag. Ap.*, 1.6–29.

[29] In Eusebius, *Praep. ev.*, 9.24.1.

[30] In Eusebius, *Praep. ev.*, 9.29.1; see also 9.29.15: ὡς αὐτός τε ὁ Δημήτριος λέγει
καὶ συμφώνως τούτῳ ἡ ἱερὰ βίβλος. Cf. also Polyhistor on Cleodemus Malchus in Jos.
Ant. 1.240: Κλεόδημος δέ φησιν ὁ προφήτης ὁ καὶ Μάλχος ἱστορῶν τὰ περὶ Ἰουδαίων,
καθὼς καὶ Μωυσῆς ἱστόρησεν ὁ νομοθέτης αὐτῶν.

[31] *FGH* 273 F 79 (= Berossus, *FGH* 680 F 1). The Greek text of the passage is preserved in George Syncellus, *Ecloga Chronographica* 28.21–32.3, ed. A.A. Mosshammer
(Leipzig: Teubner, 1983).

[32] See Freudenthal, *Alexander Polyhistor*, 28.

Jews, the latter a work which according to Josephus helped to propagate some of the more rabid calumnies against the Jews.[33]

What we can say in any case is that Polyhistor cast a wide net. This degree of inclusiveness was far from standard operating procedure among historians of his day. Greek writers on Egypt and the Near East generally ignored native Eastern informants, for the most part preferring histories written by their fellow countrymen. Historians had misgivings about Herodotus and the mendacious Ctesias, but they continued using them anyway. Greek parochialism griped their Eastern counterparts. In *Against Apion*, Josephus, speaking on behalf of all Eastern historians, complained bitterly about the deafness of the Greeks to the testimony of native historians.[34] The one notable exception was Polyhistor. Without his lengthy excerpts from the *Babyloniaca*, Berossus would now be little more than an obscure curiosity from the past. Polyhistor rescued his Hellenistic Jewish and Samaritan sources from the same fate. For a self-standing treatise on the Jews, Polyhistor had chased down little-known informants and let them speak directly and unfiltered, without an apparent agenda of his own.

The idea that Polyhistor's native curiosity and love of learning allowed him to transcend the parochialism of his fellow countryman is an appealing notion. It makes of the *grammaticus* of Miletus and manumitted Roman slave a sympathetic, even heroic, figure, a champion of multi-culturalism open to the voices of the other. But we should not push the image too hard. There were limits to Polyhistor's embrace of Eastern wisdom. Consider, for example, his use or, in this case, non-use of Jewish scriptures. Either out of ignorance or because they found the work too foreign, few, if any, Greek authors of Polyhistor's age ever quoted the Septuagint. Polyhistor was no different. Scholarly opinions on his acquaintance with the Septuagint are

---

[33] We cannot rule out the possibility that Polyhistor's original work contained more works negative to the Jews, but that Eusebius, for his own reasons, chose to exclude them. On Polyhistor's choice of sources as a measure of his attitude towards Judaism, see E. Gabba, "The Growth of Anti-Judaism, or the Greek Attitude toward the Jews," *CHJud*, II. The Hellenistic Age (Cambridge: Cambridge University Press, 1989), 3.651; B.Z. Wacholder, *Eupolemus: A Study of Judaeo-Greek Literature* (HUCM 3; Cincinnati, 1974), 49. On Polyhistor's neutrality, see also Jacoby: "For him it is more important that he has collected the material in a completely neutral way (this term is probably better than 'objective'), just as he does for the Egyptians, Lycians and Carians; he is neither a philo-Semite nor an anti-Semite, but here too simply a collector" (*FGH* Kommentar zu nr. 273 (Leiden: Brill, 1943), 249).

[34] Josephus, *Ag. Ap.*, 1.6–14.

widely at odds, ranging from deep familiarity at one extreme to little
or no knowledge whatsoever at the other.[35] But while Polyhistor was
aware that the Jews had "sacred books," the fact remains that, at least
at far as we can tell, he avoided quoting the Septuagint in his work on
the Jews. It was enough for him simply to reassure his readers that his
authorities represented these books accurately. Polyhistor for his part
preferred more sanitized works, composed by named authors, written
in a genre, language, and idiom that he could appreciate and dealing
with subject matter that better served his needs and interests.

If we are to see in Polyhistor an agent of Eastern wisdom, we
would at least need some assurance that when he began compiling
his sources, he took account of their 'ethnic identity.' But where is
the evidence that he did? Modern scholarship exerts itself mightily
foraging through Polyhistor's sources for clues to the ethnicity of their
authors. Everyone is more or less agreed that Eupolemus, Artapanus,
Demetrius, Philo the poet, and Ezekiel the tragedian were Jews, and
that the rhetor Apollonius Molon, the teacher of Cicero and author
of a treatise entitled "Against the Jews," was a Greek. An account
of how Abraham was received with hospitality on Mt. Gerizim has
convinced most, but not all, critics that a passage attributed by Polyhistor to Eupolemus actually originated in the work of an unknown
Samaritan writer.[36] After that the consensus unravels. Theodotus, the
author of the epic poem on the Jews, has been called a Samaritan and a
violently nationalistic Jew.[37] On Ezekiel the tragedian, opinions waver
between Jew and Samaritan.[38] Theophilus may have been a Samaritan,
a Jew, or a pagan. Cleodemus Malchus is the real chameleon, variously
described as a Jew, a Samaritan, a Syrian, and a Phoenician.[39] While all

---

[35] For arguments in support of Polyhistor's knowledge of the Septuagint, see
Wacholder, *Eupolemus, cit.*, 49–50; J.G. Gager, *Moses in Greco-Roman Paganism*
(SBLMS 16; New York: Abingdon, 1982), 20.23. For the opposing view, see Freudenthal, *Alexander Polyhistor, cit.*, 31, who doubted that Polyhistor had any real familiarity with the Septuagint; Schwartz, "Alexandros," 243–244; G. Sterling, *Historiography
and Self-Definition* (NovTSup 64; Leiden: Brill, 1992), 148. For a more recent assessment of the evidence, see J.G. Cook, *The Interpretation of the Old Testament in Greco-
Roman Paganism* (Tübingen: Mohr Siebeck, 2004), 13–15.

[36] Eupolemus, Frg. 1 (Holladay, *Fragments* 1, 172.15) = Eusebius, *Praep. ev.*, 9.17.5–6.

[37] Freudenthal, 99–100. Cf. J.J. Collins, "The Epic of Theodotus and the Hellenism
of the Hasmoneans," *HThR* 73 (1980), 93–104.

[38] For review of the question, see Holladay, *Fragments* 2, 303; 317–318; 324, n. 31;
H. Jacobson, *The Exagoge of Ezekiel* (Cambridge: University Press, 1983), 14–15.

[39] For the arguments, see Holladay, *Fragments* 1, 245–246.

the uncertainty highlights the difficulty of ethnic definition in the Hellenistic age, it is surely noteworthy that none of the ancient witnesses to these writers provide much help. Josephus treats Philo, Eupolemus, Demetrius, and Theodotus as if they were Greek historians.[40] And there is nothing in the extracts preserved in the *Praeparatio* to suggest that either Eusebius himself or his authority Polyhistor ever cared to sort out any of his informants according to our categories of Jew, Samaritan, Greek, Phoenician, and Syrian. Artapanus, the Hellenistic Jewish propagandist for Moses, Apollonius Molon, the Greek propagandist against the Jews, and ps.-Eupolemus the Samaritan, are, along with all the rest, simply authorities on the subject. Their ethnicity and their divergent opinions about the Jews may matter to us, but evidently not so much to him.

POLYHISTOR'S READERS

Polyhistor was one of a number of well-known *grammatici* employed as tutors of the children of noblemen in Rome of the first century BCE. Like him, some came to Rome as captives, achieved prominence as scholars and teachers, and, in exchange for their services, received their freedom.[41] Because of the conditions under which they arrived in Rome and the services they were asked to perform, they were for the most part more dependent on Roman patronage than Greek rhetors and philosophers. Some of the subjects on which they wrote did reflect their changed status and location. In his own ethnographic corpus, Polyhistor widened his geographic horizons to include treatises on Italy and Rome.[42] Examination of certain Roman customs

---

[40] Josephus, *Ag. Ap.*, 1.216, 218. For recent discussion of the problem, see S. Inowlocki, *Eusebius and the Jewish Authors* (AJEC 4; Leiden: Brill, 2006), 274–275; see further F. Siegert, "Early Jewish Interpretation in a Hellenistic Style," in M. Saebø (ed.), *Hebrew Bible, Old Testament: The History of its Interpretation. I,1: Antiquity* (Göttingen: Vandenhoeck and Ruprecht, 1996), 190, n. 309, who theorizes that Josephus' representation of these writers as Greeks casts his direct knowledge of them into doubt; also, G. Sterling, *Historiography and Self-Definition, cit.*, 282–284.

[41] In addition to Polyhistor, the more notable manumitted Greek *grammatici* included the elder Tyrannio from Amisus in Bithynia, and Parthenius, said to have been a tutor of Virgil. For Polyhistor and other Greek *grammatici* in Rome, see E. Rawson, *Intellectual Life in the Late Roman Republic* (Baltimore, Md.: Johns Hopkins University Press, 1985), 55–56; 66–76; McNelis, "Greek Grammarians and Roman Society," *cit.*, 77–86.

[42] *FGH* 273 7 F 20; 16 F 70.

(their board-games and social etiquette) led Aristodemus of Nysa, the tutor of Pompey's sons, to the ingratiating conclusion that Homer was a Roman.[43] Other Greek *grammatici* studied the dialects and the origin of the Latin language. But whether it was a matter of genuine interest or conceding to reality, these topics were well within the ambit of the discipline. *Grammatici* continued to write on traditional, and often recondite, subjects associated with the Greek language and literature, including studies of mythic references in obscure Greek poets, and learned treatises on Greek dialects, rare words, meters, etymologies, and Greek accents.

The continued publication of such works suggests that Greek *grammatici* in Rome did not substantially reorient their scholastic pursuits to suit changed circumstances.[44] Nor apparently did their Roman sponsors expect them to do so. In her fine study of Greek intellectuals in the Roman republic, Elizabeth Rawson likened the situation of Greek scholars in Rome to that of modern academics. Although the research that they pursued was often inaccessible, their Roman patrons were willing to support them, provided they continued teaching and performing other services. They were "grateful," in Rawson's words, "just to be allowed to overhear the Greeks arguing among themselves."[45] While Roman literary elites and gentlemen scholars prized their erudite explanations of arcane mythological references and little-known Greek poets, their broader impact on Roman society was limited.[46]

Was the reception of Polyhistor's literary output much different? Because his ethnographies mainly treated nations and regions of the East, Jacoby once theorized that Polyhistor composed these treatises to answer a demand for reliable and neutral information about recently conquered peoples with whom the Romans had limited previous interactions.[47] Momigliano saw Polyhistor's compilations as part of a

---

[43] See M. Heath, "Was Homer a Roman?" in *Papers of the Leeds International Latin Seminar,* 10 (1998), 23–56.

[44] See Rawson, *Intellectual Life, cit.,* 54–56.

[45] Rawson, *ibid.,* 56.

[46] On the prestige of erudite learning in the early Roman empire, see McNelis, "Greek Grammarians," *cit.,* 87–90; A. Wallace-Hadrill, *Suetonius: The Scholar and his Caesars* (New Haven and London: Yale University Press, 1983), 26–29; A. Cameron, *Greek Mythography in the Roman World* (Oxford: University Press, 2004), 121: "Learned citations were a highly visible indication of literary culture. It would be hard to overestimate the prestige of erudition for its own sake in the early Roman empire."

[47] Jacoby, *FGH*, Komm. zu Nr. 273, 251.

broader Roman initiative to recruit Greek intellectuals to gather information about new countries "opened up to Roman conquest by Sulla
and his successors."[48] But if Roman provincial officials had consulted
Polyhistor's ethnographic and historical writings for actionable intel-
ligence about subject Eastern peoples, they would have come away
disappointed. For the most part, they are what we would expect from
a Hellenistic *grammaticus* with a penchant for antiquarian study and
exotic sources. The geographical notices, while plentiful, lack practical
information about relative distances, local commerce, or agriculture;
they consist mainly of etymological explanations of cities and other
place names, and stories about their eponymous founders.[49] Beyond a
few scattered notices, little in the material surviving from Polyhistor's
ethnographic treatises deals with contemporary events. One looks in
vain in his corpus for a work on Parthia or Persia to assist Rome in
its difficult and inconclusive struggle with the Parthians.[50] What we
find instead is a work entitled the *Babyloniaca*, and comprised largely
from excerpts about the remotest period of Babylonian history from
the work of a Babylonian priest of the third century BCE.[51]

Polyhistor's compilation on the Jews—the work about which we are
best informed—illustrates the point most clearly. It is by no means
certain that the work was timed to coincide with Pompey's campaigns
in the East. A chronological note added to a fragment from Eupolemus
preserved by Clement would require a later dating than that, around
the year 40 BCE.[52] Nor does it appear to have been written as a guide
to ruling the Jews. Because the surviving witnesses to that work extend
only to the Babylonian exile, we have no way of knowing how, if at all,

---

[48] A. Momigliano, *Alien Wisdom* (Cambridge: Cambridge University Press, 1975),
121–122; on Greek ethnography and geography in the service of Roman hegemony, see
ibid., 72–73, 149–150. For the idea that Polyhistor's treatise on the Jews was meant to
aid and justify Pompey's conquest of Judea, see also Gabba, "Growth of anti-Judaism,"
650–652; B.Z. Wacholder, *Eupolemus, cit.*, 51, who describes Polyhistor's treatises as
"handbooks that served as a background for the Roman occupation forces."

[49] See Rawson, *Intellectual Life, cit.*, 62.256.

[50] For Polyhistor's treatment of Parthian history, see the small notice preserved in
Agathias and Syncellus (in *FGH* 273 F 81). See further Rawson, *Intellectual Life, cit.*,
62.256.

[51] *FGH* 273 F 79.

[52] The note appears to reckon 120 years from the fifth year of Demetrius Soter I
(= 158/157 BCE) down to the consuls Gnaeus Domitius and Gnaeus Asinius Pollio.
See J. Strugnell, "General Introduction, with a Note on Alexander Polyhistor," in J.H.
Charlesworth (ed.), *The Old Testament Pseudepigrapha*, 2.778; Sterling, *Historiography
and Self-Definition, cit.*, 148–150.

Polyhistor treated more contemporary Jewish affairs.[53] But given Polyhistor's partiality for the remote past, it is unlikely that he had much
to contribute on that front. The excerpts that do survive have much
to say about Jewish contributions to world civilization, their genealogical and cultural connections with other peoples, and Hellenistic
Jewish poetry. But what they have to offer about the peculiar Jewish
practices that both fascinated and confounded outside observers (e.g.
Jewish dietary laws, the Sabbath, and circumcision) is both minimal
and incidental.[54] If, as Momigliano suggests, Pompey was able to turn
his knowledge of Jewish "factions, customs and taboos" to his own
advantage, he would not have found much of use for that purpose in
Polyhistor's work on the Jews.[55]

By all accounts, Polyhistor was a success story in Rome. Undertaking a literary enterprise on the scale he envisioned would have
required substantial financial backing from his sponsors. At a time
when public libraries and archives in Rome were still rare, his encyclopedic collections helped to enrich literary culture in Rome.[56] According
to Suetonius, Julius Hyginus, for whom Polyhistor was both teacher
and model, went on to become director of the library of the Palatine.[57]
On their own, the works of his teacher, a walking library, could have
filled up much of it. If we can accept the testimonies of Eusebius and
Suetonius, Polyhistor's erudition was legendary among both Greeks
and Romans. But admiration of his scholarship and industry did not
necessarily translate into wide use of the material that he had so labo-
riously collected. Polyhistor's ethnographic treatises seem to have been
largely ignored by Roman governors in the East of the first century
BCE. This was not only because the works were lacking as practical
guides. Roman officials left the management of local populations to
native authorities, confining their own sphere of activity to policing
the borders, maintaining order, and administering justice to Roman

---

[53] But cf. Gabba, "The Growth of anti-Judaism," *cit.*, 651, who maintains that Polyhistor "certainly brought the narrative up to 63 BC."

[54] For circumcision, see Artapanus, where it appears, predictably, in an inventory of
the various things that Moses taught the Ethiopians (in Eusebius, *Praep. ev.*, 9.27.10–
11 = Holladay, *Fragments* 1, 212.5 [frg. 3]). There is also a reference to circumcision
in Theodotus' recounting of the story of Dinah (in Eusebius, *Praep. ev.*, 9.22.5 = Holladay, *Fragments* 2, 117.14–15 [frg. 4]).

[55] A. Momigliano, *Alien Wisdom*, *cit.*, 120–121.

[56] Schwartz, "Alexandros Polyhistor," *cit.*, 244.

[57] Suetonius, *De grammaticis*, 20.1–2.

citizens in the province. For these purposes, they found general works on governing more desirable than the specialized works of professional ethnographers and geographers.[58]

Later Roman authors made but sparse use of his treatises. Of the 145 fragments that Jacoby collected from his entire literary corpus, the Latin material, ten in all, originates in a smattering of authors: five from Pliny's *Natural History* (F 104–8), three from a commentary on Virgil by Servius Danielis (F 110–11; 145), one from Valerius Maximus (F 17), and one from Macrobius (F 103). None of these references is attributed to a specific work by Polyhistor, and Jacoby lists one of them as doubtful (F 145). Nor do Latin authors refer to Polyhistor's treatises on the East. Instead, they mined his studies for stories about natural oddities, explanations of figures of Greek and Roman mythology, and the origins of persons and places mentioned in Virgil.[59]

While more extensive, the use of Polyhistor's ethnographic and geographic works by Greek authors was hardly prolific. It consists chiefly of topographic notices from the *Ethnica* of the sixth century geographer Stephanus of Byzantium. Other Greek authors and scholiasts consulted him for the reasons we might expect: etymologies of proper names (F 76, 100, 109), theories on the origins of peoples and culture (F 20, 70), and explications of references in the poetry of Homer (F 143), Lycophron (F 144), and Apollonius of Rhodes (F 30, 97, 142). Here too Polyhistor's treatises on Near Eastern peoples were not widely received; most of what we know of them comes from Christian sources. In his *Stromata*, Clement of Alexandria attributes a report about the Brahmans to Polyhistor's *Indica*.[60] Were it not for Eusebius' salvage operation, Polyhistor's lengthy transcriptions of passages from Berossus' *Babyloniaca* would now be lost. Polyhistor's work on the Jews did not fare much better. Curiously, Polyhistor's treatise managed to escape the attention even of Josephus. Josephus knows some of the same sources that Polyhistor cited in his work on the Jews; but his one reference to Polyhistor's treatment of Judaism probably originated in his work on Libya.[61] When Eusebius would later set out his extensive

---

[58] Rawson, *Intellectual Life, cit.*, 62.

[59] On the use of Polyhistor in the explication of Virgil, see now Cameron, *Greek Mythography, cit.*, 213–214.

[60] Clement, *Stromata*, 3.60.2 (= *FGH* 273 F 18).

[61] Josephus, *Ant.*, 1.15.1, quoting Polyhistor on the three children of Abraham by Keturah. For discussion of the source of Josephus' reference, see Holladay, *Fragments* 1, 256, n. 7.

citations from the *Peri Ioudaiōn* in the *Praeparatio*, he too must have assumed that, for his readers, they were remote and untested witnesses. This would explain why he chose such an oblique, even confusing, way of citing them.[62] Unlike modern critics, who mostly value Polyhistor as a conduit of older primary source material, Eusebius treats him, not his sources, as the real authority. The latter had standing only to the degree that the highly-regarded Polyhistor, a man "very well-known to those Greeks who have gathered the fruits of education in no perfunctory manner," thought them worthy of our attention.

---

[62] E.g. "Alexander Polyhistor reports the following word for word: 'Eupolemus says that…'" (*Praep. ev.*, 9.17.1–2); "let us add the following from the same work of Polyhistor: 'Artapananus says that…'" (9.23.1). For discussion, see S. Inowlocki, *Eusebius and the Jewish Authors, cit.*, 276–278.

INDEX LOCORUM

CHRISTIAN AUTHORS

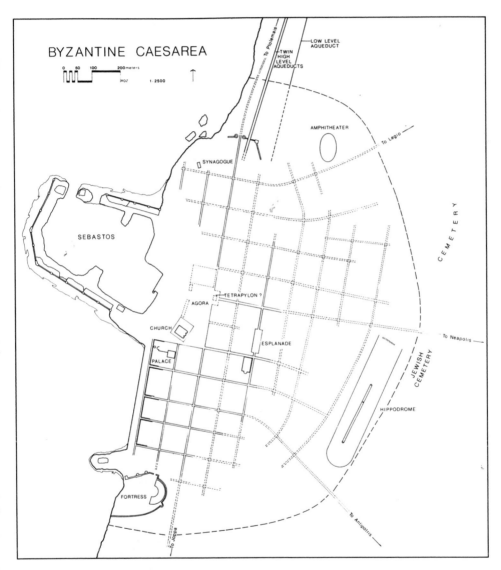

Figure 1. Map of Caesarea in the 4th c. (K.G. Holum et al., *King Herod's Dream: Caesarea on the Sea* (New York – London: Norton 1988, p. 163).

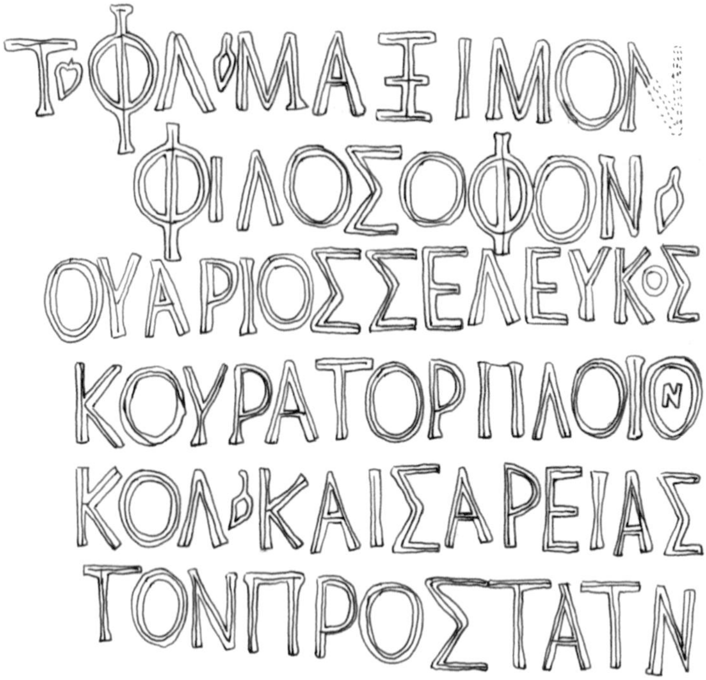

ΤῸΦΛΌΜΑΞΙΜΟΝ
ΦΙΛΟΣΟΦΟΝΟ
ΟΥΑΡΙΟΣΣΕΛΕΥΚΟΣ
ΚΟΥΡΑΤΟΡΠΛΟΙΩ
ΚΟΛΟΚΑΙΣΑΡΕΙΑΣ
ΤΟΝΠΡΟΣΤΑΤΝ

Figure 2. Greek inscription honoring the philosopher Titus Flavius Maximus, reading: "Varios Seleukos, curator of ships of the colony Caesarea, honors his patron the philosopher Titos Flavios Maximos" (English translation: Lehman – Holum, *The Greek and Latin Inscriptions of Caesarea Maritima, cit.*, inscr. no. 12 and Pl. XVb, drawn by Y. and Sh. Patrich).

Figure 3. Decumanus S2, looking west.

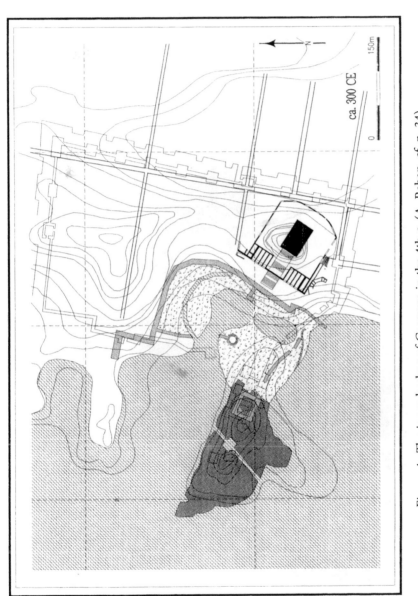

Figure 4. The inner harbor of Caesarea in the 4th c. (A. Raban, cf. n. 34).

Figure 5. The sacellum below the pulvinar of the truncated arena of the hippo-stadium, converted to a Martyrs' chapel.

Figure 6. The Louvre Cup. The scene depicts a libation rite by the governor in front of the city goddess (drawing: Sh. Patrich).

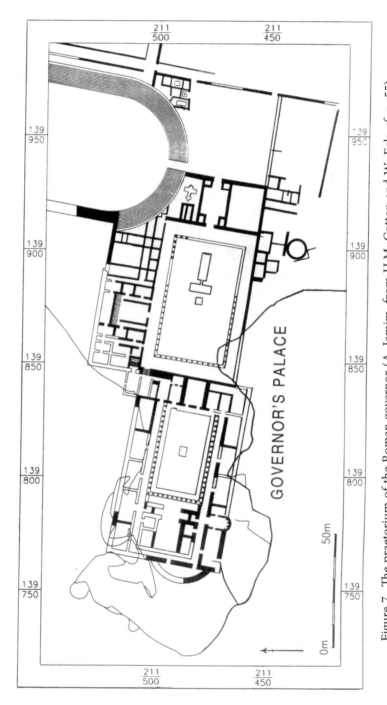

Figure 7. The praetorium of the Roman governor (A. Iamim, from H.M. Cotton and W. Eck, cf. n. 55).

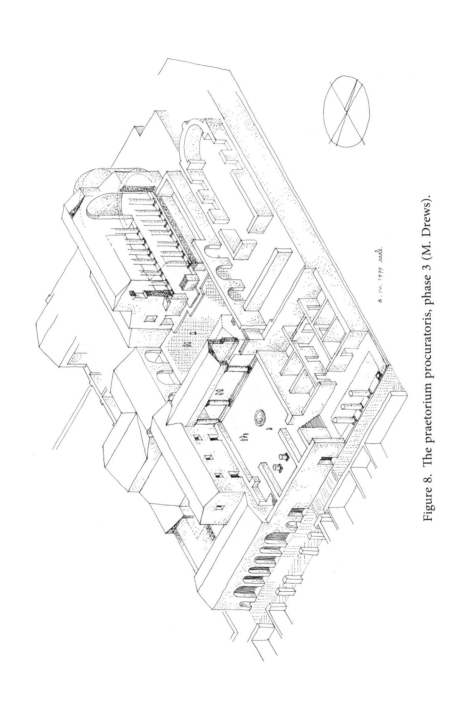

Figure 8. The praetorium procuratoris, phase 3 (M. Drews).

a

b

Figure 9 The archive(?) of the praetorium procuratoris: a. one of the cupboards (armaria) in the wall; b. the mosaic floor.

Figure 10. The courtyard of a palatial mansion with a bath-house and a complex of warehouses on the south-western zone.

Figure 11. A 4th c. hoard of gold coins (solidi) (photo: A.M. Levin, courtesy the Combined Caesarea Expedition).

Figure 12. The Roman theater adjacent to the praetorium of the Roman governor (Raqia Aerial Photography).

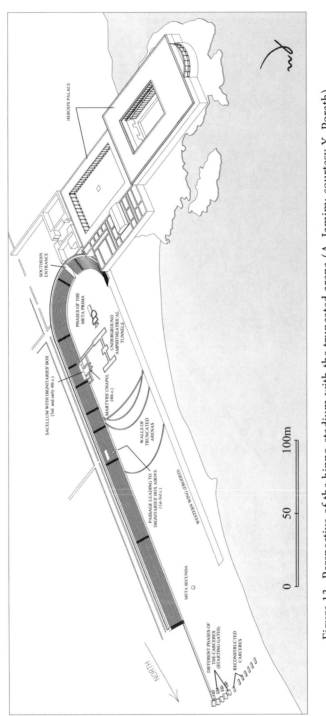

Figure 13. Perspective of the hippo-stadium with the truncated arena (A. Iamim; courtesy Y. Porath).

Figure 14. The two aqueducts leading to Caesarea (A. Baltinester).